| AUTHOR | CLASS No. |
| MCILROY, J. | 378 MCI |

TITLE	BOOK No.
Going to University : The	
Student Guide	1'94

Going to university

The student guide

John McIlroy and Bill Jones

If you want to go to university or have just started there, you need this book. This is the first integrated and comprehensive guide to the new higher education. Unlike other studies skills books, it explains the system, how you survive in it and how you can study successfully. Completely up-to-date and packed with information on recent changes, it is at once an essential manual on how to study and a book which puts studying at university in context.

The authors, with long experience of working with sixth formers, undergraduates and mature students, explain how higher education is organised, how the system developed, and how it is changing. They offer authoritative advice on how to apply, and detailed guidance on the crucial practical issues – grants and loans, accommodation, and time management. They analyse recent research on how students learn, and review the practicalities of studying – libraries and reading, lectures and classes, writing essays and reports, handling a research project, and passing exams. They conclude with advice on further study, developing life skills and deciding on a career.

Going to university will be indispensable reading for sixth formers applying for places at university, first year undergraduates, admissions officers, teachers and parents.

John McIlroy comes from Liverpool. After teaching in comprehensive schools in Liverpool and London he worked in the University of Oxford Department of External Studies before taking up his present appointment as Reader in Adult and Continuing Education at the University of Manchester. He has appeared regularly on radio and television and has been for 15 years a member of the Executive of the Society of Industrial Tutors. He has written extensively on education, industrial relations and politics. His books include *Going to Law* (1980), *Getting Organized* (1981), *Industrial Tribunals* (1983), *Strike!* (1984), *Trade Unions in Britain Today* (1988), *University Adult Education in Crisis* (1988), and *The Permanent Revolution? Conservative Law and the Trade Unions* (1991).

Bill Jones comes from mid-Wales where his parents were both teachers. After attending the grammar school in Shrewsbury he went to Aberystwyth University to study international politics, submitting his doctorate on Labour Party attitudes towards the Soviet Union. After two years as an Assistant Principal in Whitehall he joined Manchester University's Extra-Mural Department in 1973 where he was successively Staff and Senior Staff Tutor in Government and Politics before becoming Director in 1987. He was Chair of the Politics Association from 1983 to 1985 and has written several textbooks and articles on British politics. As well as specialising in return-to-study courses he has a longstanding interest in Swedish adult and higher education. Together with Roy Johnson he is the author of *Making the Grade*, a two-volume study programme for adult students.

Going to university

The student guide

John McIlroy and Bill Jones

Manchester University Press
Manchester and New York
Distributed exclusively in the USA and Canada by St. Martin's Press

Published by Manchester University Press
Oxford Road, Manchester M13 9PL, UK
and Room 400, 175 Fifth Avenue, New York, NY 10010, USA

Distributed exclusively in the USA and Canada
by St. Martin's Press, Inc., 175 Fifth Avenue, New York, NY 10010, USA

British Library Cataloguing-in-Publication Data
A catalogue record for this book is available from the British Library

Library of Congress Cataloging-in-Publication Data
McIlroy, John.
    Going to university : the student guide / John McIlroy and Bill Jones.
      p.   cm.
    ISBN 0–7190–3182–6
    1. College student orientation—Great Britain—Handbooks, manuals, etc. 2. Study, Method of—Handbooks, manuals, etc. I. Jones, Bill, 1946– . II. Title.
    LB2343.34.G7M37   1993
    378.1'98—dc20   93–11003

ISBN 0 7190 3182 6 *paperback*

Photoset in Linotron Sabon with News Gothic
by Northern Phototypesetting Co Ltd, Bolton

Printed in Great Britain
by Bell & Bain Limited, Glasgow

Contents

Foreword

Higher education in Britain has been changing rapidly in recent years. The proportion of young men and women passing, directly or indirectly, from school or college into higher education has risen sharply, and will certainly reach one third of the relevant cohort within a few years. Equally important, many people are entering university at other points in their lives, on both a full-time and a part-time basis, further increasing the diversity of the student body. The university system itself, now including all the former polytechnics, has expanded rapidly and seeks to meet the increasingly varied demands of its students by providing a range of courses, combining high quality with flexibility and offering, where appropriate, both academic excellence and vocational relevance.

This book offers advice and guidance of a highly practical kind to all those people, whatever their age and whatever their provenance, who have just entered, or who are about to enter, a university. Academic advice, rightly, makes up the bulk of such a work, since study must always remain the principal responsibility and challenge of everyone within an institution of higher education. This advice is, however, supplemented by suggestions on how to choose a course appropriate to yourself and how to maximise the chances of gaining a place in the department which you most wish to enter. Of ever greater importance too is the range of financial information designed to help students to make the most of the increasingly constrained resources made available to them, and the introduction to the many and varied forms of support and counselling services which contemporary universities provide.

I am happy to recommend *Going to university* in the warmest of terms. Life at university is full of challenges and opportunities: this book will help you to make the most of them.

Martin Harris
Vice-Chancellor
University of Manchester

Acknowledgements

Both authors would like to thank the late Pat Barnett, Roy Johnson, and in particular John Hostler for their guidance, support and encouragement as fellow tutors on access and induction courses at the University of Manchester. The book was put on disk with speed and efficiency by Stephanie Jackson without whose heroic efforts it would not have been possible.

Bill Jones would like to thank Liz Brody, Colin Jakeway, Edith Newman, Professor Keith Gull, Dianne Gull, Norman Lloyd and Malcolm Carter for help with his chapters.

p. 16: Extract from John Henry Newman, *The Idea of a University* [1851], 1976, quoted by permission of Oxford University Press.

p. 18: Extract from Karl Jaspers, *The Idea of the University* [1923], 1965, quoted by permission of Peter Owen Publishers, London.

p. 141: Extract from Mick Jagger and Keith Richards, 'Time waits for no one' © 1975. Reproduced by permission of EMI Music Publishing Ltd, London WC2H 0EA.

p. 163: Adaptation of 'Deep Relaxation Technique' (pp. 209–210) from *Living With Stress* by Cary L. Cooper, Rachel D. Cooper, Lynn H. Eaher (Penguin Books, 1988), copyright © Cary Cooper, Rachel Cooper, Lynn Eaher, 1988.

pp. 224–5: Extract from Georgina Bathscombe, *Christina Rossetti*, quoted by permission of Constable & Company Ltd.

p. 353: Extract from A. S. Byatt, *Possession*, quoted by permission of the publisher, Chatto and Windus.

p. 395: Extract from Willy Russell, *Educating Rita*, Methuen, London.

Introduction

Recent years have seen the biggest expansion in higher education since the 1960s. There were then 32 universities in Britain educating 220,000 full-time students. By the end of the century there will be more than 100 universities educating over one million students. We are also witnessing major changes in organisation and structure. The binary divide – the division between universities and polytechnics – has disappeared. Polytechnics and some colleges have become universities. Controversies continue about the resources devoted to higher education and the kind of role it should fulfil in society. But the blend between the traditional academic approach of the old universities and the more vocationally rooted curriculum of the new will be an exciting one. Taken together with the growth of modularisation and credit transfer – hopefully attracting a wider range of mature students – it promises a fertile marriage. The promise is of a bigger, better, rigorous but more relevant higher education for the 21st century.

This book is intended for all those thinking about entering higher education in these challenging times. It aims to cover most aspects of student life. It can be used as a reader by students, their parents or friends; the basis for a course pursued through the sixth form or college; or as part of access provision for those intending to enter higher education outside the conventional route. It reflects our experience in the social sciences and humanities and it will be most useful to students in those areas. But we hope much of it will help those in other disciplines too.

Going to University is based upon materials developed by the authors for courses at the University of Manchester for university entrants and applicants in recent years. Sixth-form teachers have also told us they find the approach useful, particularly if used over the two years of an A-level course. But we hope that students intending to go to university will find the book useful as an individual guide.

Books such as *Going to University* often consist almost wholly of advice to students on study skills. This is an area of obvious importance, but in our experience new entrants are not only interested in learning strategies. They wish to know more about the organisation and history of the institutions they hope to become part of. They welcome some discussion of the nature of the experiences they will have in the coming years and of the practical problems they will encounter.

So they should. At least a little reflection on the idea of the university, its evolution and its relationship to contemporary society is important for students, their teachers and their families. Learning cannot be divorced from the total experience of which it forms part. Student learning has to be related to its context and to a wider canvas so that those who go to university may be helped to become, in the full sense, citizens of their new community. We think that access and induction courses require three interwoven elements addressing *what*, *how* and *where*: an introduction to the subject or subjects students are interested in studying, a discussion of how to learn and an exploration of the educational system within which learning takes place. Whilst it does not neglect learning strategies, *Going to University* attempts to constitute a broader induction for new students.

In recent years there has been some debate about the best way to provide students with help with learning skills – although the ghost at the discussion has been the *overall lack of such provision*, both in higher education and the schools. If discussion of learning strategies is part of students' subject course, it will be effective. Ideally, in higher education itself, every department, or at least every faculty, would organise custom-made provision, organic to subject work, *through* the three or four years of the degree programme. Reality, often through lack of resources, falls far short of this ideal; present conditions in higher education promise only slow progress towards it.

The second relevant point is that the earlier students start thinking in an organised way about how they learn, the better. A general review of the literature and the 'state of the art' at sixth-form or pre-college level can lay a good basis for later development.

Given this situation, we feel that students – and their teachers – can usefully utilise the approach taken in the second half of this book to reflect on their learning approach and strategies and relate them to the contexts they will encounter in higher education. Where possible we have outlined the results of recent research. But we have not hesitated to make suggestions to be thought about, implemented or rejected, deriving from 'ordinary knowledge' generated by the practical experience of teacher and students. We hope that this approach will be supplemented later by more integral work on learning in the students' own department. The whole area of access is still in its infancy and a number of different approaches are emerging. If you would like to let us know what you think about *Going to University* and how it could be improved, please write to

John McIlroy and Bill Jones
Department of Extra-Mural Studies
Humanities Building
University of Manchester
Oxford Road
Manchester M13 9PL

How to use this book

Going to University assumes that you start your university life by thinking about becoming a student. You find out about higher education. And then you think about which course and college is right for you. You then set about applying by filling in your application form. Hopefully, you are accepted; you then need to think about accommodation and grants. With these problems negotiated you get down to some hard studying.

That is the pattern the book follows and the way it is organised. But you may come across the book when you are already on your way to university. You may therefore want to miss Chapter 3: 'Getting in' or even go straight on to Chapter 4: 'Getting on'. Or if you already have problems of finance and accommodation sorted out you may want to move from Chapter 2: 'Higher education today' to Chapter 5: 'Getting organised'. One of the points we make later on is that books have to be taken away from the structure their authors intended and used by you in a way which helps you to get what you want. If you are a teacher using this book for course work you may want to follow the chapters through sequentially. Or you may wish to leaven the first two chapters with some exercises based on the learning skills part of the book.

By the time you read this book you will already have developed some methods for organising your learning and some strategies for facilitating successful study. Whatever you do, do not simply disregard these in favour of some of the suggestions offered here. Consider the points made in this book, relate them to your own mind and personality and then decide which are transferable to you, which you will adopt or adapt, which of them you will reject. You also need to consider how you will go about assimilating new practices to old habits. Always remember that *there is no* one best way to learn. There are only best ways for you in a particular situation. Before they work through the sections on learning some students find it useful to do an audit of the tools they use now, and then critically scrutinise their present practice in the light of the discussion in the text.

So use the book to meet your own needs. To help you with this, we planned the book in the following ways.

- Each chapter deals with one topic or a series of related topics and is divided into separate sections.
- Each chapter begins by telling you what it is about and how it is laid out. At the end of each chapter we briefly sum up the main points we have made.
- Each chapter ends with a list of further reading. We have tried to avoid too many references in the text but at times this is unavoidable; you will find the full details of the references in the bibliography at the back of the book under the name of the author and the date of the work.
- Each chapter has brief suggestions at the end for things to do. But you may wish to supplement these by examples taken from your course work.
- We have tried to write in a readable style but there may be phrases and ideas you may not have come across before. Be prepared to think and use your dictionaries.

Both authors have read and commented on each other's contributions but are responsible for their own chapters. We hope you find the result useful. Good luck with it – and with your studying.

1

Higher education: what's it all about?

When an institution – a university, say – is the bearer of a
tradition of practice, its common life will be partly, but in a
centrally important way, constituted by a continuous argument
as to what a university is or ought to be ... Traditions where
vital, embody continuities of conflict.

Alasdair McIntyre, *Beyond Virtue*

1.1 Introduction

This chapter will give you some information about the sort
of institution where you could be spending the next three or
four years. The aim is to answer the questions: How did
universities get here? What are they *for*? How did the system of
higher education develop in the United Kingdom?

- Section 1.2 begins by asking, 'What is higher education?'
  and goes on to talk about the purposes and development of
  higher education.
- Section 1.3 provides an outline of the history of higher
  education.
- Section 1.4 looks at the different conceptions that different
  people – from Cardinal Newman to Mrs Thatcher – have
  had about the purpose of the university, and discusses some
  of the arguments about the goals of higher education today.
- Finally, Section 1.5 briefly examines the kind of learning
  universities are trying to develop, how the processes in
  higher education differ from those in school, and how they
  will inform your learning over the coming years.

1.2   **What is higher education?**

If you are asked this question, the word 'universities' probably comes quickly to mind, accompanied by images of
dreaming spires . . . or crowded lecture rooms. But what *happens* in higher education? What do universities do? What kind
of education do they offer? How does it differ from what goes
on in a school? Where does the 'higher' in *higher education*
come in?

What does 'education' mean?

What does the word *education* itself mean to you? A good
dictionary will show you that our word comes from the Latin
educare. This meant 'to bring up' and was related to *educere*
which meant 'to lead forth'. In a broad sense then, to educate
means to develop a young person – 'to *help* him or her to *learn*'.

For most people hundreds of years ago, learning would be
picked up in the family and taught on the job. More systematic
education was for the ruling classes. Our word *school*, for
example, comes from a Greek word meaning 'leisure'. Only the
rich with time on their hands went to school and received
formal education.

How is education organised?

Modern education is a function of a society with a science
base and high level of technology, where people have to be able
to communicate in a sophisticated fashion. In our daily work
most of us need to be able to think for ourselves and learn
autonomously. But young people have been educated for
different purposes and to different degrees: some finish their
education at sixteen, some in their mid-twenties. Education
today is organised into *primary*, *secondary*, *further* and *higher*

education; it is organised on a scale unknown even a century ago; it is organised by the state, whereas a century ago it was largely left to private provision.

What is education for?

It is unlikely that the young British woman of, say, 800 years ago would ever attend a school. Yet she would be educated, in the home and on the land, in the techniques of domestic and agricultural labour – the knowledge required by a wife and mother in a subsistence economy. She would acquire a basic stock of local custom, folklore, and pagan and Christian knowledge. She would learn, through word of mouth and rough experience, what the roles of the feudal lord and peasant were, and about the organisation of the manor that she would probably stay within for her whole life. In a primitive way, she would have been prepared for the life she was to lead through being socialised into its culture and its techniques.

In today's very different United Kingdom, where all young people attend school until they are 16, some of the purposes of education are similar to those applying to the young peasant of the 12th century. The content, of course, is very different, but like the informal, custom-based education of the past, the organised education system of the 20th century seeks to

- transmit the culture of the past;
- socialise pupils and students to conform with the norms of existing society;
- train pupils and students in skills useful to the jobs they will do;
- develop personal attitudes and values to facilitate the pupil's or student's future job performance and social role.

The medieval peasant had little chance of advancement or personal development; she was regarded as a chattel, her lord's property. Today's education aims not only to train the individual for his or her social role but to develop the individual as a human being. In feudal times such a purpose would have been subversive of the social and economic status quo.

Another big difference is the *dynamism* of modern technology and social change. Our young peasant's life would be very similar to those of her grandmother and grandson. Today's young people will see more important changes in work and society during one lifetime than have taken place in our society since 1900. Their education, therefore, needs to develop a greater degree of creativity and adaptability.

If we now turn back to higher education we can see that it *selects those young people who have done sufficiently well at earlier stages of the system to qualify to be trained to keep up with change and perform key jobs in the future.* These key jobs often involve

- decision making,
- specialist knowledge,
- autonomous thinking,
- managing resources, and
- managing and teaching other people

– as well, of course, as including the academic jobs which are part of the system of higher education itself. Higher education has thus traditionally included only a minority of the 18–21 age group – although the number has increased in recent decades.

Research

Higher education deals in a significant and organised way with research; it is the part of the education system which seeks to develop *new* knowledge and to teach the advanced knowledge and techniques which are required by a dynamic, constantly changing economy and society. It is that part of the education system which, building upon earlier stages, seeks to produce the self-learning personality. Its expansion this century is ultimately rooted in the development of science and technology; its research has helped to cure disease, put men and women into space, develop the revolution in information technology.

But higher education has also opened the road to individual growth and developed our culture. It has taught millions about the secrets of ancient civilisation, cultivated their appreciation of art, music and literature, and equipped them with the skills and knowledge to participate in the democratic government of society.

We have mentioned some of the purposes of higher education, but there is no agreement as to which of these should take priority. We will look at some of the competing conceptions later in this chapter. Higher education is a contested concept. In higher education, one question seldom leads to a simple answer; often it produces more questions!

1.3   How it all started

So how did we get to the present complicated position? The story goes back a long way.

Our first universities

Universities originated in medieval times. Oxford received full recognition by the church in 1214 and Cambridge in 1318. However, English universities were soon outnumbered by Scottish ones. In the 1400s universities were established at St Andrews, Glasgow and Aberdeen – followed in the next century by Edinburgh. The medieval university lay firmly under the control of the church and the feudal lords. Its objective was to train priests, doctors, lawyers and teachers – those who would get the top jobs in church and state.

But the roots of Oxford and Cambridge go back earlier still – to Ancient Greece, in the schools founded by Aristotle, Plato, Socrates and other great classical thinkers. Plato, for example, founded his school in a grove called Academy, from which we derive the word *academic*. The medieval scholars followed the tradition of Greece through Rome. The main teaching method was by the transmission and interpretation of texts. Books were scarce; therefore lectures (our word comes from the Latin *legere*, 'to read out') were read from the *lectern* – although scholars also practised debating in their struggle to further their understanding.

The *universitas* was a self-governing community which was very similar to the guilds of craftsmen, and it was organised into similar collectives – faculties and colleges. The certificate of proficiency you received, if you successfully completed your academic apprenticeship, was called a *degree*. At first all degrees were *Master's* degrees, denoting that a person was skilled in the academic craft and able to pass on his knowledge by teaching others. Those well on their way to such a work permit were allowed to teach new students and were termed *Bachelors*, or novices. (Students were, of course, all men. It was many centuries before women were able to take their rightful place in universities).

The medieval university did not play a major role in the Renaissance – the great flowering of scientific and cultural ideas in the 1500s – in the Enlightenment, nor in the scientific revolutions of the 1700s and 1800s. The basic university education was an education in the classics, philosophy, theology and law. Educational thinkers from Aristotle on had seen these disciplines as suitable for the 'free man'. It was contrasted with more practical training. By 1800, the free man was all too often an English gentleman of leisure, and Oxford and Cambridge went into decline. London University (1836) was established as an alternative to 'Oxbridge' to counter the existing bars to Catholics, Nonconformists and Jews.

Capitalism and the universities

The entrepreneurs who built the capitalist society we live in today had little idea of what the inside of a university looked like; we owe the pioneering of economics and social science to the Scottish universities. There were no laboratory-based physics classes at Oxford until the 1870s.

The most important development in the university system came in the great industrial cities, as Britain's international economic supremacy came under challenge from the new industrial nations, Germany and the USA. A new university system took shape. The colleges of the Victoria University established in the 1880s were gradually launched as the independent Universities of Manchester, Liverpool and Leeds in 1903–4. The early years of this century also saw the chartering of the Universities of Birmingham (1900), Sheffield (1905) and Bristol (1909). Royal charters established universities as independent, self-governing bodies with responsibility to teach and research.

The emphasis now was on the university as a training and *research* centre whose efforts could serve the needs of local industrialists. They, in return, might be expected to give financial support. The new ambition and pursuit of excellence were clear in the establishment of institutions such as Imperial College in 1907 to provide 'the most advanced training and research in various branches of science especially in its application to industry'.

The provincial universities did not completely throw off the influence of Oxford and Cambridge. They remained dedicated to the ideal of producing the cultured personality *and* training the mind. The civic universities, founded by local magnates in the great urban centres of Victorian England, also began to cater for a national rather than a local clientele. Local capital showed few signs of bearing the cost. From the 1880s the state was increasingly drawn into university finance. In 1919 the University Grants Committee was established. Its founding documents pledged it 'to enquire into the financial needs of university education in Great Britain; and to advise the Government as to the application of any grants that may be made by Parliament towards meeting them'.

A national system of higher education

By the 1920s, a national system had taken shape but its development was limited:

- In the years leading up to World War I, Germany had twenty-three universities; the UK, nine.
- By 1914 there were only 26,711 university students in Britain – about one per cent of the age group. On the eve of World War II there were around 50,000 university students – still only 1.7 per cent of the age group.
- Not only Oxbridge but the universities in general served the upper classes. Children born in the 1920s into the semi-skilled and unskilled manual groups had less than a 0.5% chance of going to any university.
- In the 1930s 1:215 of the population of the USA attended university, 1:480 in France, 1:604 in Hitler's Germany – and only 1:885 in the UK.

A university education in Britain was good but expensive and available only to a small elite.

Box 1.1   Universities were elite institutions ...

The communication was brief and not exactly what he had expected; though it really was from the Master in person ...

Biblioll College

Sir – I have read with interest; and judging from your description of yourself as a working man, I venture to think that you will have a much better chance of success in life by remaining in your own sphere and sticking to your trade than by adopting any other course. That therefore is what I advise you to do. Yours faithfully,

T. Tetupnenay

To Mr J Fawley, Stone Mason

....

The gates were shut and, by an impulse, he took from his pocket the lump of chalk which as a workman he usually carried there, and wrote along the wall.
I have understanding as well as you; I am not inferior to you: yea who knoweth not such things as these? JOB XII 3

Thomas Hardy, *Jude the Obscure*

The post-war period

There was some expansion during the post-war period. Charters were granted to Nottingham (1948), Southampton (1952), Hull (1954), Exeter (1955) and Leicester (1957). The 1944 Education Act produced more qualified school leavers. There was a belief that if Britain were to compete effectively in world markets it would need to expand higher education. The nation needed universities that would educate the modern scientist, technologist and social engineer. The universities should open their doors to more working-class adolescents: a large pool of potential talent was going untapped. But majority public opinion still felt that essentially universities were doing a good job.

By 1955 the Scientific Manpower Committee was advising that the number of trained scientists and technologists leaving the universities must be doubled. In the era of Sputnik and the space race there was concern over competition from the USSR, Germany and Japan, who were recovering from the devastation of World War II. Prime Minister Sir Antony Eden summed up the mood in 1957 when he argued: 'The prizes will not go to the countries with the largest population. Those with the best systems of education will win.'

Robbins and expansion

The 1959 Crowther Report described how expansion was needed, on the grounds that around a quarter of those qualified to enter were being turned away each year, and the situation was likely to worsen, given the post-war 'baby boom'. Student numbers had already increased from 85,000 in 1955 to 130,000 by 1963 and several new universities were coming on stream. The Robbins Report of 1963 attempted to address the problems of higher education.

- Expansion should be speeded up.
- There was no genetic reason to restrict higher education to those with a 'high' IQ: *good education could raise IQ*.
- Student numbers needed to be tripled by the mid-1980s.
- Intellectual development should be promoted in tandem with the needs of the economy.
- Greater access was essential: 'the good society desires equality of opportunity for its citizens to become not merely good producers but also good men and women' and 'courses of higher education should be available to all those who are qualified by ability and attainment to pursue them'.
- Greater state control of higher education should be discouraged.
- Universities which would deal specifically with technological subjects should be established.

Governments accepted expansion without stricter government control. During this time, a new wave of universities was established, at Sussex (1961), York and East Anglia (1963), Essex, Kent, Lancaster and Warwick (1964–5), followed by Stirling (1967) and Ulster (1968). Between 1964 and 1967 Colleges of Advanced Technology at Strathclyde, Aston, Bath, Bangor, City (in London), Loughborough, Surrey, Herriot Watt (in Edinburgh) and Salford joined the swelling ranks of the universities.

A change of heart

The incoming Labour government in 1964 accepted the Robbins Report. But it was concerned that a doubling of the number of undergraduates between 1939 and 1960 had not halted economic decline. Nor had it helped class, sex and regional imbalances. Children from the semi-skilled and unskilled manual groups still had only a one per cent chance of going to university compared with a 30% chance in the professional and managerial groups.

In 1965 Labour announced the creation of the polytechnics. The decision was itself criticised (for example, by Lord Robbins) as introducing a binary line across higher education. The government argued that technical degree courses and vocationally related higher education should be concentrated in centres of excellence. From 1969 these centres of excellence – the polytechnics – came into being, their curriculum centred more on science, technology and business studies.

The 'Student Revolt' of the late 1960s and early 1970s involved serious questioning of the purposes of higher education. The Revolt swept the world in a wave of occupations, culminating in social disorder in France in 1968. In the UK, students occupied the London School of Economics in 1967 over the appointment of a new director. Students were expressing the desire for a greater say in what was taught and how colleges were organised. To some extent the Revolt was related to the failure of universities to fulfil expectations engendered by post-war prosperity and the expansion of higher education.

The Student Revolt produced a backlash. Some had already claimed: 'more means worse'. The negative images of long-haired, under-occupied, drug-addicted students misusing opportunities provided by hard-pressed taxpayers, and left-wing staff misusing their privileged 'jobs for life' position in the manner of Malcolm Bradbury's *History Man*, came to occupy a permanent niche in Conservative ideology and in popular stereotype. The era of expansion was coming to an end. Apart from the private University of Buckingham there would be no new universities in the next two decades.

The backlash

From 1969 a group of university teachers and politicians of the right published a series of 'Black Papers', in which pertinent criticism of some of the excesses of the progressive movement in education was melded in a wholesale attack on teaching methods and teachers. There was a retreat to traditionalism.

The economy was in decline in the UK and there were calls for cuts in public spending. Many felt higher education had failed to deliver a revived economy and a better society. It had expanded but was still very much a middle-class affair which excluded the majority.

The 1974–9 Labour government began to retrench. In October 1976 Prime Minister James Callaghan made a speech at Ruskin College, Oxford arguing that

- the education system over-emphasised preparation for social roles rather than employment;
- expansion had produced declining standards;
- methods of teaching had been too easy-going;
- a new 'core curriculum' with greater emphasis on vocational subjects was needed.

Although all this related to schools, the critical backlash also hit higher education. Some felt that

- higher education was essentially about personal development;
- students should choose what they wanted to study;
- the binary divide represented a useful division: higher education made an acceptable contribution to society's cultural *and* economic well-being.

Others were more critical. They felt that higher education

had failed to broaden entry and had created first- and second-class tiers of higher education. But these commentators defended autonomy and were far from harsh on the overall track record.

Other critics, on the right, felt universities were over-privileged. Higher education, they argued, had been too much about personal development, too little about helping to arrest our economic decline, and teaching the facts of life:

- The mismatch between economic needs and student choice needed correction: too many students were studying literature; too few were studying science.
- Higher education needed a more entrepreneurial culture: it should give better value for money; students should pay more towards the cost of their education, and staff should earn more of their upkeep working with industry.

One thing was certainly clear: higher education no longer held the pole position in public esteem it had held 20 years earlier.

Higher education challenged

The 1979 Thatcher government, determined to halt economic decline by a greater resort to market forces, said that the country could no longer afford the higher education that had developed since the sixties and that universities should be more responsive to national needs. The government cut back expenditure to save money and shake up institutions. Grants were now awarded for specific purposes.

Relations between government and universities deteriorated. The 1987 White Paper *Meeting the Challenge* asserted that higher education could no longer be governed by student choice: 'a major determinant must also be the demands of highly qualified manpower . . .'. Government cut-backs in local authority expenditure capped the pool of money available.

The polytechnics were not immune. Twenty years after they were established, many felt that the polytechnics too had 'gone academic'.

- The panels which validated degrees had strong representation from the universities.
- University graduates increasingly taught in polytechnics.
- Degree studies often possessed a greater cachet and pull.
- Polytechnic teachers were increasingly involved in research.
- Well-qualified senior staff began to emerge as 'professors'.

There was convergence between universities and polytechnics. However, a decision was made that from 1988 polytechnics could validate degrees; this was seen as an acceptance that they had come of age, and they continued to expand.

There was intense pressure on universities from the government to take in more students at no additional cost. The challenge was taken up: student numbers grew faster than at any time since the 1960s. But many questioned the desirability of expansion on the cheap. The decline in academic salaries did not help morale. It was argued that universities would become more efficient if the system of tenure (which protected staff against redundancy) was abolished and only certain universities and staff were involved in research. The government continued to accuse the universities of being inefficient and to emphasise the need for greater accountability. The universities protested that the government's emphasis on the economy was threatening to deprive higher education of its autonomy and breadth.

In 1988, legislation replaced the Universities Grants Committee with the Universities Funding Council, which was more interventionist. The government attempted to replace block grants with a system of contracts between the Universities Funding Council and universities for the 'delivery' of students and research. These would be awarded after competitive bidding between institutions; there would be monitoring and financial penalties for non-compliance. The 1988 Education

Reform Act removed the polytechnics from local authority control and included, in the new polytechnics and colleges, sector colleges which carried out a certain proportion of degree work.

And then came the great shake-up. The 1992 Further and Higher Education Act laid the basis for the polytechnics to become universities. The Polytechnics and Colleges Funding Council and the Universities Funding Council were abolished and replaced by a new Higher Education Funding Council, which had enhanced powers.

1.4   The individual *vs* the economy?

Throughout history people have debated about the different conceptions of the role of the university.

- Should higher education emphasise the needs of the economy and prepare students largely for their future work roles (the *vocational* rationale)?
- Should it be more about developing the individual personality and the disinterested pursuit of knowledge (the *liberal* perspective)?
- Should the university transmit rather than criticise existing values, should it maintain rather than change society?

A knowledge of different approaches can help in understanding contemporary arguments.

1   The liberal approach

The ideas of J. H. Newman (1801–90) are still referred to today. Newman was a Catholic churchman, later a Cardinal, whose work was originally published in the 1850s.

Box 1.2   The liberal approach

The process by which the intellect, instead of being formed or sacrificed to some particular accidental purpose, some specific trade or profession, or study or science, is disciplined for its own sake, and for its own highest culture, is called Liberal Education. The direct end of a university is knowledge, in the same way that the direct end of Trade is wealth ... it is well to have a cultivated intellect, a delicate taste, a candid, equitable, dispassionate mind, a noble and courteous bearing in the conduct of life; these are the connatural qualities of a large knowledge; they are the objects of a university.

J. H. Newman, 1851

Knowledge as an end in itself, the cultivated intellect – these were the keys to Newman's conception of the university. Central to the concept of liberal education was the idea that it should be suitable to develop the free *individual*, the good person. This meant providing a broad education; Newman was firmly opposed to narrow specialisation. He believed that 'All knowledge forms one whole'. The Professor of Law, Medicine or Economics, he asserted, had to be something more than a lawyer, physician or economist. The cultivated intellect was its own justification. But the thinking, civilised, whole person would be able to exercise discrimination and judgement in all areas of their lives, including their occupation.

Newman's ideas were used to justify education which produced the classically trained mind capable of doing the work of judge, politician or civil servant with minimal direct training. His ideas justified the university that was autonomous, elitist and devoted to teaching, not research. But liberalism was eroded by economic change. Some would go further and argue that traditional liberal education was part of a wider cultural approach which, together with antiquated social and economic institutions, would produce the UK's gradual economic decline. None the less, we can still learn much from Newman, particularly from his emphasis on

- personal development,
- the interconnectedness of the different branches of knowledge, and – at a time of intense specialisation –
- its ultimate wholeness.

2 The modernised liberal approach

Newman wrote at the high tide of Victorian certainty in a country which dominated the world. Karl Jaspers (1883–1969) was a German Professor of Philosophy who wrote after World War I. He appealed to many at a time when the traditional university was under threat from jackboots and book burning on the one hand and mass technology and economic renovation on the other. Jaspers' ideas were influential during the Robbins period.

Box 1.3 The research university

The university is a community of scholars engaged in the task of seeking truth. It is a body which administers its own affairs regardless of whether it derives its means from endowment, ancient property rights, or the state.

... It derives its autonomy from the idea of academic freedom, a privilege granted to it by state and society which entails the obligation to teach truth in defiance of all internal and external attempts to curtail it ...

It is intended not merely as a place of instruction; rather the student is to participate actively in research and from this experience he is to acquire the intellectual discipline and education which will remain with him throughout his life. Ideally

the student thinks independently, listens critically and is responsible for himself.

Karl Jaspers, 1923

Jaspers emphasised the importance of research. This was
related to the technological requirements of 20th-century
society. He also emphasised autonomy: teaching was essential
to disseminate knowledge, but it was also important for
teachers to be involved in the *creation* of knowledge. Successful
students of these processes would emerge trained as thinkers,
critics and self-critics. This demanded independence and self-
government. Universities could also apply this approach to
vocational studies. For Jaspers, a university was at one and the
same time 'a professional school, a cultural centre and a
research institute'.

3 The plural multiversity

Clark Kerr (b. 1911) – a leader of American academic
thinking – wrote a well-known book in the 1960s, *The Uses of
the University*. He argued that a university did a number of
different things – he used the term *multiversity* – and made a
variety of contributions to society. The age of Newman and
Jaspers was long past.

- Instead of the good of the individual student, the 'needs of
  society' were increasingly urged.
- New social groups wanted a more relevant, career-oriented
  education.
- The government made demands for more 'breakthrough'
  research.
- The 'gentleman scholar' had been replaced by professional
  administrators and academic specialists.

The Robbins Report (see p. 10) had similar emphases. In

addition to the points we made earlier, it argued that higher education had four main purposes:

- Instruction in skills to play a part in the social division of labour and an efficient economy.
- Promotion of the general powers of the mind. The aim should be to produce not simply specialists but cultivated men and women.
- The advancement of knowledge: 'The search for truth is an essential function of institutions of higher education.'
- The transmission of a common culture and common standards of citizenship. Universities should enrich the cultural life of their students and the national community and enhance democracy.

Robbins sought to consider economic demands whilst bearing in mind individual development, cultural renewal and responsible citizenship.

Box 1.4 Sixties liberalism: pluralism

As university teachers we are naturally expected to provide acquaintance with particular branches of knowledge and training in the exercise of various intellectual skills. But we are expected to do more than that: we are expected to inculcate general capacities for thought and contemplation and to cultivate intellectual and moral habits suitable for adult membership of a civilised society.

... I should in no way accept the maximisation of a growth of Gross National Product as necessarily the final criterion of policy ... for myself if it were a choice between more education and less wealth or less education and more wealth, I should not always regard the latter as the more desirable.

Lord Robbins, 1966

Robbins – a Professor of Economics who had taught at Oxford and the London School of Economics – attempted to blend liberalism with the new economic and technological ideologies. It was a compromise which many would defend today.

4 Student power

The philosophy of student radicals in the 1960s was summed up in the famous dictum of Karl Marx: the class that controls the means of production controls the means of mental production. Some of the following statements expressed the student radicals' convictions.

- Universities were elitist institutions serving the children of the ruling class.
- The 'freedom and autonomy' of universities was a myth which served to legitimise their role as knowledge factories for capitalism.
- Courses were constructed on the basis of the needs of capital, to provide the system with a stream of well-trained, well-conditioned manpower and to legitimise the status quo.
- Knowledge was not objective knowledge but capitalist ideology.

Box 1.5 Sixties radicalism: capitalist reproduction

The primary role of higher education is now to train the flood of technicians and manipulators which neo-capitalism demands. Any student who has gone through the mangle of repeated examinations, set text books, accepted authorities and styles of work (classes, lectures, weekly essays, tutorials) has undergone a most formidable conditioning process. The burgeoning departments of social science, the colleges of art and design, the new universities all help to provide the specific skills which neo-capitalism requires.

Alexander Cockburn, 1969

The Student Revolt was part of a reaction to the idea that higher education should serve the economy. Its theorists correctly argued that higher education was elitist and socially restricted. It did reflect the goals of the state and capital more directly than in the past. But the radicals ignored the fact that higher education still enjoyed a high degree of autonomy. Instead of defending and extending that autonomy, the only strategies they had for changing higher education were in the form of demands that universities be turned into 'Red Bases' for a speedy revolution or that students should go and work in factories to facilitate social change.

5 The economic approach

In the 1970s, the state supported the call for higher education to serve the economy. Proposals for the 'economic approach' became clearer, although they were still usually argued in terms which paid lip service to the ideas of liberal education. A 1972 White Paper stated that although 'the government consider higher education valuable for its contribution to the personal development of those who pursue it', they hoped that 'those who contemplate entering higher education – and those advising them – will the more carefully examine their motives and requirements and be sure that they form their judgement on a realistic assessment of its usefulness to their interests and career intentions'.

The economic approach was at the centre of government policy in the 1980s; it places greater emphasis on the market and competition than planning and co-operation in allocating resources to higher education. It asserts that higher education has to relate to the society in which it lives.

Box 1.6   The economic approach

Above all there is an urgent need in the interests of the nation
as a whole, and therefore of the universities, polytechnics and
colleges themselves, for higher education to take increasing
account of the economic requirements of the country. This aim
must be vigorously pursued. . . . The government and its central
funding agencies will do all they can to encourage and reward
approaches by higher education institutions which bring them
closer to the world of business.

Conservative Government White Paper, 1987

Current debates

The story does not end there.

- Today some question the idea that knowledge can help us
  understand ourselves and the world, master reality and stimulate social progress.
- Post-modernist writers claim that without independent
  thought and language, there is no reality.
- Others assert that no approach to understanding is
  superior to another, for it is not clear we *can* understand.

Higher education remains a contested concept. However,
most thinking people today would probably take a pluralistic
approach: they would argue that universities should teach *and*
research, develop life skills *and* culture, technology *and* the
individual personality. They would probably take the Robbins
Report as a starting point. However, the problem remains of
deciding which purposes are most important.

The shake-up which the present version of the economic
ideology has created has been welcome in the sense that it has
raised basic questions of purpose and organisation. The higher
education of the past was far from perfect; undoubtedly, there

was complacency and inefficiency. Standards were high, but the price of this was that universities remained elite institutions reproducing social inequality. There was a need for increased access.

But there are problems with present policies.

- If you wish to expand higher education and maintain standards you initially need to expand funding.
- If you want universities to serve society then you have to make their expertise available to all sections of society.
- It is not helpful to model a university on a company. To regard education simply in economic terms and impose a competition model confuses the complex process of education with selling nuts or bolts or cabbages.

Countries such as Germany and Japan benefit from the stream of trained graduates produced by state investment. However, there is vigorous debate about the wisdom of linking educational policy and economic performance. Many of the issues involved in the decline of the UK economy have little to do with higher education. It is not the fault of new graduates that they cannot get jobs during economic downturns. A more significant factor is the poor economic management of governments. Too great a degree of dependence on industry can compromise higher education and its creativity.

The creation of a science-based culture cannot be left to higher education. It costs more to educate a science graduate. (However, even though there *has* been a swing away from science, around 50% of students are in science-based disciplines. Many more study vocationally related subjects such as accountancy and business studies.) *The roots of present student choice lie further down in the schools and in our wider social culture.* And our young people have to be convinced as to the desirability of studying science subjects. Coercion is not available!

Where we *have* fallen down is in having such a small percentage of the age group involved in higher education. The figures are disputed. But it is clear that the UK is some way down the European league and lags behind America and Japan. We fail to use the pool of talent that does exist: in the 1980s the parents of 9% of accepted university candidates were in social classes IV or V compared with 70% from classes I and II (UCCA, 1989). Although the recent expansion of higher education has increased access, much remains to be done. We need to:

- *have wider access and more government investment*;
- reconsider A levels and their impact on subject choice;
- look at our education system as a whole if we are to produce a bigger and better system of lifelong learning.

Over the past century, the western education system has attempted to combine personal development and social responsibility with economic benefits, and the transmission of existing social values with space to challenge orthodoxy. Past compromises are now up for renegotiation. How *do* we

- blend vocationalism with personal development?
- increase access without sacrificing excellence?
- draw the line between social needs and state domination?
- make higher education more socially relevant without limiting independence?

These are not easy questions and they have no simple answers. They will constitute key issues in the coming years; the inheritance, from Newman to Robbins, can help us in pondering them.

1.5　What kind of education?

What do you see as the goals of higher education? Some institutions are now starting to formally lay out their goals in fairly general terms.

Box 1.7 Mission statement

Mission
- To be an accessible and responsive institution of higher education of the highest quality
- To be a centre of excellence in its teaching, scholarship and research
- To serve the aspirations of all with the ability and motivation to benefit
- To meet the needs of industry, business, the professions and the wider community

Strategic aims
- To offer opportunities for study in an educational environment which enables students to realise their aspirations and enhance their lives and careers
- To increase the participation of students from a variety of backgrounds, at various stages of their lives and careers, and with a wide range of qualifications and experience
- To provide a network of courses of high quality, with different modes of attendance and opportunities for progression, which lead to qualifications at all levels of higher education
- To promote studies of particular relevance to the needs of industry, business and the professions, which contribute to the country's economic and social well-being
- To develop strong links with business, industry, the professions and the wider community, and make available its expertise and resources through applied research, scholarship and consultancy
- To contribute to the economic, social and cultural life of the region, whilst seeking to enhance its national and international role and reputation
- To secure its activities and further development within a

sound financial framework and by the effective and efficient use of its resources

Manchester Metropolitan University

Having thought about some of the ideas we have just reviewed perhaps you would like to look at some more specific questions.

Box 1.8   Key questions in the debate

- Should more funds come from industry and less from government?
- Should students pay more for their education through loans or a graduate tax?
- Should there be greater competition between university bodies for students and funding?
- Should courses be more vocational?
- Should higher education produce more scientists?
- Should courses be less specialised and more broadly based?
- Should all teachers in higher education teach and research?
- Should academics receive more training as teachers?
- Should students receive more courses in the skills of studying?

Now let's consider the individual student. What kind of learning do you think your teachers will expect from you? They will want to guide you into your subject discipline, its key concepts, theories and language; and they will expect you to gradually take personal responsibility for your own induction. At the heart of this process are a number of abilities that students should try to develop. Sometimes you will have made a start on these at school. In other cases *higher* education represents a break with the way you learned at school. Your teachers will want you

- **To understand different concepts and theories,** to grasp alternative ways of analysing problems and to understand how different approaches can be used in different contexts
- **To think logically and understand how the core concepts and theories of your discipline are put together and interact**
- **To be able to analyse critically the validity of concepts and theories,** to weigh evidence and form your own judgements
- **To cultivate a questioning approach to authority and orthodoxy,** taking little for granted and assuming that existing approaches which seem to satisfactorily explain phenomena are themselves tentative and open to challenge
- **To be self-motivating and self-critical.** They will want you to become more and more autonomous as a learner.
- **To refuse to accept secondhand statements** and move gradually from your textbooks to primary sources
- **To be able to communicate with others through dialogue and argument,** in the understanding that knowledge develops through collective enterprise, conflicting views and criticism, and that the ability to frame questions is important in developing answers.
- **To accept that education is exploration, and that there are no final answers or theories which explain everything.** But they will hope that you will develop the ability to give your reasons for adopting certain ways of viewing and using your discipline as against others.
- **To be able to stand back and see the shape of your discipline,** and to strive for understanding of how it relates to other disciplines.

Finally, your teachers will hope that your experience of higher education will **contribute to making you a lifelong** *thinker*, a more cultured, understanding and imaginative person with the resources to act creatively in a number of social roles.

For some of you, this statement may seem a little pious. For others, it may strike a chord with your best experiences as a student. It would not represent the views of all academics. It is perhaps an ideal that is fulfilled in only the best teachers and the best students. (But see Box 1.9.) The pursuit of the ideal may not make us all good scholars. But it may make us all better students. At times you will certainly glimpse and, hopefully, grasp, the ideal.

Box 1.9   Ideals that can be attained

Research shows that students can develop in the way we have just outlined during their higher education years. Graduates interviewed state:

- 'I didn't gain so much a body of knowledge as an approach. I became a problem solver . . .'
- 'I think I learnt to organise my work and myself, to think theoretically and evaluate concepts, to look up things before I made statements . . .'
- 'What I believe I learnt was a capacity to apply logical principles . . .'
- 'I learned how to write and to argue cogently and logic-ally . . .'
- 'I respected her scholarship immensely and she became a model for me to emulate . . .'

From J. Powell (1985)

Key points

1 Higher education is the product of a science-based, hi-tech society. It selects students to do skilled jobs which require independent thinking and contributes through its research to scientific development, cultural enrichment and social progress.
2 Although it still serves a minority it has expanded throughout the century, particularly in recent decades.
3 There have been different conceptions of the role and purpose of universities. The idea of the university remains contested today.
4 Thinkers such as Newman and Jaspers – with different emphases –

saw the university as a community of scholars centred on development of the individual. Jaspers emphasised research, autonomy and academic freedom.

5 In the middle of this century Clark Kerr and the Robbins Committee attempted to reconcile different conceptions of higher education. They insisted it should serve the individual and the economy and society. It should instruct students in vocational skills, promote the intellect, advance knowledge and transmit a common culture.

6 There has been increasing pressure to move higher education from an individual-liberal to an economic-vocational axis. The economic approach has moved to the centre of policy.

7 In the 1990s universities have thought more about goals and have begun to develop mission statements. Debates continue about liberalism and vocationalism, the subject mix, accountability and academic freedom, and the relationship of teaching and research.

8 Learning in university may be different from learning in school. You will gradually have to take more responsibility; view knowledge as contested, fluid and constantly developing; grasp the structure and geography of your discipline; give qualified support to certain theories rather than others.

Things to do

1 Discuss the differences between education in the 1290s and the 1990s.

2 Make a chronological chart showing the major landmarks in the growth of higher education.

3 Explain why the Robbins Report was important.

4 Compare and contrast the liberal and the economic approach to the university.

5 Find out if the university nearest to you has a mission statement.

6 Make a list of the main goals of universities.

7 Draw up a report on your answers to the questions on p. 26.

8 A quotation from the famous philosopher Alasdair McIntyre heads this chapter. Discuss how the statement, 'Traditions where vital, embody continuities of conflict', applies to universities.

Further reading

Michael Sanderson's *Educational Opportunity and Social Change in England* (Faber, 1987) is a general survey with useful sections on the historical development of higher education. A small gem which strives to set arguments about the purposes of the university in their historic context and start you off thinking what it's all about is Peter Scott's *The Crisis of the University* (Croom Helm, 1984).

Why not try one of the classic texts themselves? Recent editions of key works are: John Henry Newman, *The Idea of a University* (Oxford University Press, 1976); Karl Jaspers, *The Idea of the University* (Peter Owen, 1965); Clark Kerr, *The Uses of the University* (Harvard University Press, 1973). A good commentary is John Wyatt's *Commitment to Higher Education: Seven Western European Thinkers on the Essence of the University* (Society for Research into Higher Education/Oxford University Press, 1990) – a book worth the effort it demands. Stimulating, controversial and easily accessible is *English Culture and the Decline of the Industrial Spirit, 1850–1980* by Martin Wiener (Penguin, 1985).

2

Higher education today

The University is the key knowledge institution of modern society.

Peter Scott, *The Crisis of the University*

2.1 Introduction

In the mid-1980s one out of eight 18-year-olds went into higher education. By the early 1990s the figure was 1:4 and accelerating towards 1:3. A quarter of a century after they were established, polytechnics – the alternatives to the universities – ceased to exist. The binary divide crumbled almost as suddenly as the Berlin Wall and a new system was in the making. In this chapter I set out the bones of that system although it will undoubtedly change dramatically in the run-up to the 21st century.

- Section 2.2 provides some basic facts and figures about Britain's old and new universities, which may help you find out how the system works overall.
- Section 2.3 tells you about the system of degrees and the different kinds of staff who work in higher education.
- In Section 2.4 there is a brief description of how your university is governed, and then
- Section 2.5 mentions some of the external bodies whose activities influence how universities operate.

ABERDEEN
1 21

15 4 DUNDEE

38 ST. ANDREW'S

STIRLING
42

GLASGOW
21 43 6 18

EDINBURGH
18 22 14

COLERAINE
47

BELFAST
6

NEWCASTLE *34 15*
SUNDERLAND *24*
DURHAM *16*

MIDDLESBOROUGH
25

LANCASTER
27

PRESTON
10   BRADFORD *8*   YORK *50*

BOLTON *2*   LEEDS *28 11*
SALFORD   HULL *23 9*
39   HUDDERSFIELD *8*
             MANCHESTER
BANGOR *4*   LIVERPOOL   *32 33* SHEFFIELD
             30 13   *40 22*

             KEELE   STOKE-ON-TRENT *23*
             24   NOTTINGHAM
                    DERBY *35 16*
                    4   LOUGHBOROUGH *31*
ABERYSTWYTH *2* WOLVERHAMPTON *30*
                              LEICESTER
LAMPETER   BIRMINGHAM   *29 12*   NORWICH
26   *3 7 28*   WARWICK *48*   *17*
                      COVENTRY *29*

                              CRANFIELD
SWANSEA *46* BUCKINGHAM   *51*   CAMBRIDGE
              10   MILTON   LUTON *5* *12*
PONTYPRIDD *5* CHELTENHAM KEYNES *52*
CARDIFF   *3*   COLCHESTER
13 49   OXFORD   *19*
          BRISTOL *9 26* *36 17*
          BATH *5 1*   HATFIELD *7*   CHELMSFORD
                    READING *37*   LONDON   *51*
                  FARNHAM *6*   CANTERBURY *25*
                            GUILDFORD *44* WYE
          SOUTHAMPTON   F
          41   PORTSMOUTH
EXETER *20* BOURNEMOUTH *19*
PLYMOUTH *20*   *2*   BRIGHTON *3 45*

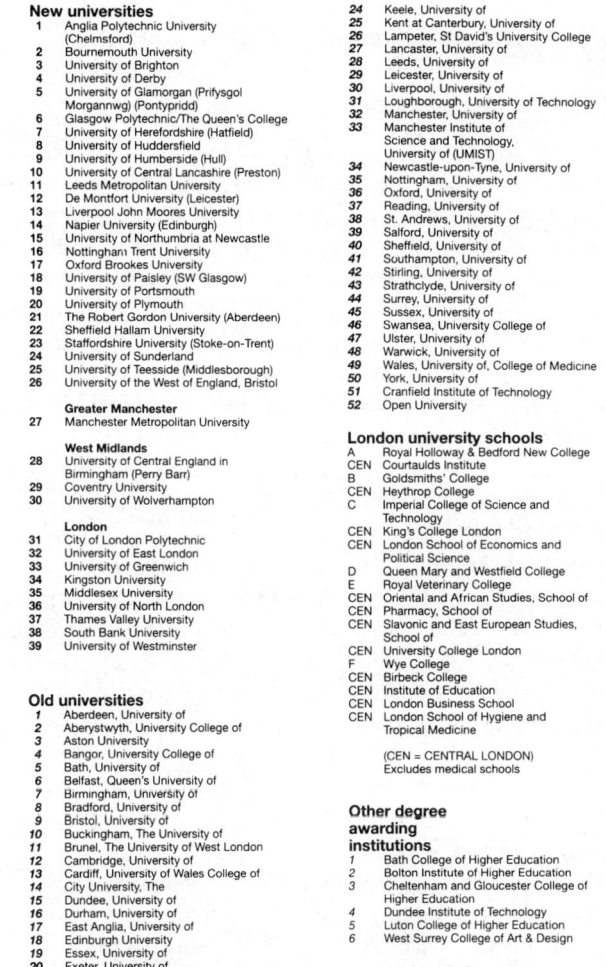

New universities
1   Anglia Polytechnic University (Chelmsford)
2   Bournemouth University
3   University of Brighton
4   University of Derby
5   University of Glamorgan (Prifysgol Morgannwg) (Pontypridd)
6   Glasgow Polytechnic/The Queen's College
7   University of Herefordshire (Hatfield)
8   University of Huddersfield
9   University of Humberside (Hull)
10 University of Central Lancashire (Preston)
11 Leeds Metropolitan University
12 De Montfort University (Leicester)
13 Liverpool John Moores University
14 Napier University (Edinburgh)
15 University of Northumbria at Newcastle
16 Nottingham Trent University
17 Oxford Brookes University
18 University of Paisley (SW Glasgow)
19 University of Portsmouth
20 University of Plymouth
21 The Robert Gordon University (Aberdeen)
22 Sheffield Hallam University
23 Staffordshire University (Stoke-on-Trent)
24 University of Sunderland
25 University of Teesside (Middlesborough)
26 University of the West of England, Bristol

Greater Manchester
27 Manchester Metropolitan University

West Midlands
28 University of Central England in Birmingham (Perry Barr)
29 Coventry University
30 University of Wolverhampton

London
31 City of London Polytechnic
32 University of East London
33 University of Greenwich
34 Kingston University
35 Middlesex University
36 University of North London
37 Thames Valley University
38 South Bank University
39 University of Westminster

Old universities
1   Aberdeen, University of
2   Aberystwyth, University College of
3   Aston University
4   Bangor, University College of
5   Bath, University of
6   Belfast, Queen's University of
7   Birmingham, University of
8   Bradford, University of
9   Bristol, University of
10 Buckingham, The University of
11 Brunel, The University of West London
12 Cambridge, University of
13 Cardiff, University of Wales College of
14 City University, The
15 Dundee, University of
16 Durham, University of
17 East Anglia, University of
18 Edinburgh University
19 Essex, University of
20 Exeter, University of
21 Glasgow, University of
22 Heriot-Watt University
23 Hull, University of

24 Keele, University of
25 Kent at Canterbury, University of
26 Lampeter, St David's University College
27 Lancaster, University of
28 Leeds, University of
29 Leicester, University of
30 Liverpool, University of
31 Loughborough, University of Technology
32 Manchester, University of
33 Manchester Institute of Science and Technology, University of (UMIST)
34 Newcastle-upon-Tyne, University of
35 Nottingham, University of
36 Oxford, University of
37 Reading, University of
38 St. Andrews, University of
39 Salford, University of
40 Sheffield, University of
41 Southampton, University of
42 Stirling, University of
43 Strathclyde, University of
44 Surrey, University of
45 Sussex, University of
46 Swansea, University College of
47 Ulster, University of
48 Warwick, University of
49 Wales, University of, College of Medicine
50 York, University of
51 Cranfield Institute of Technology
52 Open University

London university schools
A   Royal Holloway & Bedford New College
CEN Courtaulds Institute
B   Goldsmiths' College
CEN Heythrop College
C   Imperial College of Science and Technology
CEN King's College London
CEN London School of Economics and Political Science
D   Queen Mary and Westfield College
E   Royal Veterinary College
CEN Oriental and African Studies, School of
CEN Pharmacy, School of
CEN Slavonic and East European Studies, School of
CEN University College London
F   Wye College
CEN Birbeck College
CEN Institute of Education
CEN London Business School
CEN London School of Hygiene and Tropical Medicine

(CEN = CENTRAL LONDON)
Excludes medical schools

Other degree awarding institutions
1   Bath College of Higher Education
2   Bolton Institute of Higher Education
3   Cheltenham and Gloucester College of Higher Education
4   Dundee Institute of Technology
5   Luton College of Higher Education
6   West Surrey College of Art & Design

Figure 2.1   Universities 1992: the new map of higher education. This map locates and identifies all the universities in the United Kingdom, new and old, together with other degree-awarding institutions recognised in September 1992
(Source: *The Times Higher Education Supplement*, 2 October 1992)

2.2 The new system of higher education

The traditional universities

Figure 2.1 shows the location of the universities in the UK before abolition of the binary divide. In 1991 the traditional universities received £2,139 million in recurrent grants and fees and £207 million in capital grants. Recurrent grants largely finance teaching and research – two thirds to teaching, one third to research. Nearly £700 million in tuition fees was paid by local education authorities. Funds for teaching have increasingly been related to student numbers. Research funds are now related to how departments perform in detailed research assessment exercises.

In the 1990s it is very clear that higher education is dependent upon the state. Despite investments, private endowments and an increased amount of funding from industry, universities could not exist without funding from the government. More than 60% of their funds come from government grants. This raises questions about how independent they can be. Most of these funds are channelled from government through the Higher Education Funding Council. This body consists not only of academics but members with experience of business and industry, and it was established to be directive and ensure compliance with government objectives. Grants now tend to be made for more specific purposes, with strings attached. The Higher Education Funding Council can also make specific recommendations to the universities.

The funding system has increasingly separated the funding of teaching and research. Universities can also bid for funding from the five research councils:

- the Agriculture and Fisheries Research Council;
- the Economic and Social Research Council;
- the Medical Research Council;
- the National Environment Research Council; and
- the Science and Engineering Research Council.

The 'old' universities in Figure 2.1 fall into a number of different categories. Oxford and Cambridge are traditionally thought to be at the apex of the university system – they are its oldest, most prestigious, best endowed institutions. They creamed off the best students and continued the public school tradition of providing training for elite occupations. Oxford and Cambridge ('Oxbridge') have differed from most other universities in their longstanding college system, control of entry through special examinations and their rich endowments. The structure of both universities is now complex: in many subjects a system of departments is superimposed upon the colleges. Durham operates on a similar collegiate model. But within London University the constituent colleges tend to operate more like independent universities.

Different again are the 19th-century 'redbrick' universities such as Birmingham, Liverpool, Leeds and Manchester, constructed as alternatives to Oxbridge with a broader curriculum and closer links with local industry and the wider community. In somewhat similar mould are the second wave of civic universities – Exeter, Nottingham, Reading, Southampton – institutions which evolved from local colleges and awarded external London degrees before being fully recognised in the 1950s.

Strathclyde, Bradford and Aston are examples of *technological universities*, chartered in the 1960s to increase the flow of skilled manpower to industry. Similar concerns prompted the establishment of business schools at Manchester and London. In contrast, the wave of universities established in the 1960s – Essex, Sussex, Kent and Warwick – were built on greenfield sites outside smaller cities such as Colchester, Brighton and Canterbury. They sought to avoid narrow specialisation by requiring that all students study a range of subjects in foundation courses and by pioneering degrees in interdisciplinary studies.

Students, subjects and organisation

Britain's traditional universities differ a great deal in size. London has in total well over 40,000 full-time students, whilst Oxford, Cambridge, Leeds and Manchester each have between 13,000 and 15,000, with numbers increasing at around 3,000 a year. At the other end of the scale, universities such as Essex, Keele and York have 4,000–5,000 students, with numbers increasing at around 1,000 a year. All the conventional universities are of course dwarfed by the Open University (see pp. 88, 99).

In 1991 there were more than 404,000 students studying for degrees in the traditional universities. Of these, more than 106,000 were studying for higher degrees, 289,000 were studying full time for first degrees and 8,600 were studying part time for first degrees (see Table 2.1). You can also see from Table 2.1 that studying for a first degree still remains the preserve of the full-time student; only a relative handful were studying on a part-time basis. The majority of full-time first-degree students in the old universities still come from the 18–21 age group. In the face of increased fees, overseas students continue to constitute a healthy ingredient.

Women have always been in a minority amongst full-time undergraduates, but recently there has been progress. The proportion of women undergraduates has increased from 39% in 1979 to 45% in 1991 (see Table 2.2).

The statistics demonstrate how universities have expanded recently. The 1992 intake was 7% up on the previous year and the number of first-year students was up more than 40% on the 1980 figure. Staff-student ratios, however, are worsening. In recent years, there has been barely a 3% increase in full-time lecturers.

Table 2.3 shows the subjects studied at universities. In recent years, increases in student numbers in arts and social sciences are higher than those in science subjects, and indeed there has been a decline in some areas of science, despite government encouragement.

Table 2.1 Student numbers in traditional universities, 1985–86 to 1990–91

	1985–6 (000s)	1986–7 (000s)	1987–8 (000s)	1988–9 (000s)	1989–90 (000s)	1990–1 (000s)	Percentage change since 1985–6	Percentage change since 1989–90
Undergraduates								
Full-time	242.9	246.4	250.7	260.7	275.3	289.1	+19.02	+ 5.01
Part-time	6.5	6.8	7.2	7.3	7.7	8.6	+32.31	+11.69
Total	249.4	253.2	257.9	268.0	283.1	297.7	+19.37	+ 5.16
Postgraduate								
Full-time	52.6	54.9	54.7	56.9	59.2	63.5	+20.72	+ 7.26
Part-time	30.6	32.6	33.5	37.2	40.2	43.4	+41.83	+ 7.96
Total	83.2	87.5	88.2	94.1	99.4	106.9	+28.49	+ 7.55
Total								
Full-time	295.5	301.3	305.4	317.6	334.5	352.6	+19.32	+ 5.41
Part-time	37.1	39.4	40.7	44.5	47.9	52.0	+40.16	+ 8.56
Total	332.6	340.7	346.1	362.1	382.4	404.6	+21.65	+ 5.81
Continuing education	492.3	545.6	555.3	648.2	699.3		+42.05 to 1988–90	

Source: Universities Statistical Record

Table 2.2   Sex of UK-domiciled full-time students, 1985–86 to 1990–91

	1985–6 (000s)	1986–7 (000s)	1987–8 (000s)	1988–9 (000s)	1989–90 (000s)	1990–1 (000s)	Percentage change since 1985–6	Percentage change since 1989–90
Undergraduates								
Men	128.9	129.4	130.0	133.0	137.8	142.4	+10.47	+ 3.34
Women	95.1	96.5	98.6	103.4	110.2	116.7	+22.71	+ 5.90
Total	224.0	225.9	228.5	236.4	248.1	259.1	+15.67	+ 4.43
Women as a % of the total	42.4	42.7	43.1	43.7	44.4	45.0	+ 2.00	+ 1.35
Postgraduates								
Men	20.4	20.8	20.0	20.4	20.5	21.6	+ 5.88	+ 5.37
Women	12.1	12.7	12.8	13.4	14.4	15.5	+28.10	+ 7.64
Total	32.5	33.5	32.8	33.8	34.9	37.1	+14.15	+ 6.30
Women as a % of the total	37.3	37.9	38.9	39.7	41.3	41.8	+ 4.00	+ 1.28

Source: Universities Statistical Record

Table 2.3 Subjects studied at universities

	Total	Men	Women
Undergraduate			
Medicine and dentistry	22,834	12,184	10,650
Allied medicine	8,256	2,668	5,588
Biological sciences	19,836	8,562	11,274
Veterinary/agricultural	4,547	2,322	2,225
Physical sciences	22,762	16,179	6,583
Mathematics	18,711	13,911	4,800
Engineering technology	35,322	30,671	4,651
Architecture/building/planning	4,460	3,203	1,257
Social studies	41,291	21,377	19,914
Business and administration	12,520	7,433	5,087
Communications and documentation	377	125	252
Languages	32,310	9,531	22,779
Humanities	17,873	9,262	8,611
Creative arts	4,204	1,633	2,571
Education	4,299	903	3,396
Multidisciplinary combinations	39,467	19,620	19,847
Total	289,069	159,584	129,485
Postgraduate			
Medicine and dentistry	2,587	1,477	1,110
Allied medicine	1,987	921	1,066
Biological sciences	4,910	2,725	2,185
Veterinary/agricultural	1,549	1,082	467
Physical sciences	7,113	5,568	1,545
Mathematics	3,931	3,105	826
Engineering technology	7,769	6,833	936
Architecture/planning	1,168	779	389
Social studies	9,984	5,751	4,233
Business and administration	5,263	3,671	1,592
Communications and documentation	999	463	536
Languages	3,376	1,562	1,814
Humanities	3,017	1,844	1,173
Creative arts	718	354	364
Education	8,387	3,341	5,046
Multidisciplinary combinations	747	494	253
Total	63,505	39,970	23,535

Britain's traditional universities have in the past been helped by the state but not controlled by it. They operate under a Royal Charter granted by the Privy Council and their own statutes and ordinances. The universities appoint their own staff and their academics administer their own institutions.

Academics have always argued that their intellectual freedom requires protection.

- In the pursuit of truth they should be subservient to no special interest – the government or captains of industry.
- They need *institutional autonomy* and *academic freedom* to govern themselves and choose what they teach and research.
- University teaching should be balanced; it should examine a wide range of different and conflicting theories and positions.

This and their research findings may make academics unpopular: for they may be critical of established opinion or subversive of established authority. Support for academic freedom, they claim, is therefore essential, and special job protection for lecturers is justified by the contribution they make to the development of socially valuable knowledge and cultural progress.

Institutional autonomy was thus protected by 'buffers' – such as the Universities Grants Committee – between universities and the state. Academic freedom has been traditionally underpinned by the system of tenure: under university statutes, academics could be dismissed only for 'gross moral turpitude' or serious neglect of their duties. The 1988 Education Reform Act has changed this. This Act abolished tenure, although it stated academics should be able to question received wisdom and put forward controversial views without endangering their jobs. The Act also gave the Higher Education Funding Council more powers to intervene in university activities. Some feel that, as a consequence of the Act, autonomy and freedom are diminished. Others believe universities should become more accountable to those who fund them.

In 1991 there were 49,377 academic staff employed by the old universities, of whom around 30,000 were lecturers, 9,500 senior lecturers and 5,000 professors. Women still comprise only 20% of full-time academic staff. There are around 15,000 staff employed in research posts in universities, often on short-term contracts. Most university academics are members of the Association of University Teachers, which is affiliated to the Trades Union Congress.

The new universities

The 36 new universities created in 1992 (Figure 2.1, Appendix 2.1) had a previous history as polytechnics and colleges of higher education.

The polytechnics

In David Lodge's novel *Nice Work*, a conversation takes place between Vic, an industrialist being shown around the university, and Robyn, a lecturer:

'You could build a whole polytechnic for the price of this little lot.'

'Oh, but polytechnics are such ghastly places', said Robyn. 'I was interviewed for a job at one once. It seemed more like an overgrown comprehensive school than a university.'

'Cheap, though.'

'Cheap and nasty.'

Robyn's views were common but unfair:

- The polytechnics did a good job with less resources than the traditional universities possessed.
- They were successful in developing new subjects at degree level.
- They pioneered the systems of modularisation and credit transfer.
- They catered for students who in the past never got near a university.
  - a. The proportion of ethnic minorities on courses, for example, was higher than in the universities and three

       times higher than the proportion in the general popu-
       lation.
b. Older students accounted for well over half the
      admissions.
c. The polytechnics recruited higher proportions of part-
      time students, and were more flexible and responsive
      than the established universities.

The polytechnics pioneered and bore the brunt of the recent expansion in higher education. Spending in universities fell less in real terms between 1979 and 1990 than in polytechnics, whilst student numbers rose more slowly, at around 15% compared with 21%. In their short existence they won their spurs.

By 1992 there were 33 polytechnics and their numbers were growing. Similar colleges in Scotland – Napier College and Robert Gordon's Institute of Technology were amongst the best known – were termed *central institutions*. Some polytechnics had become sizeable institutions. The City of Birmingham Polytechnic, formed in 1970 out of an amalgamation of nine local colleges, concentrated on art and design, education and music, as well as business studies and engineering. It had over 12,000 students. Liverpool and Nottingham had even larger numbers and Manchester Polytechnic around 20,000 students. The seven London polytechnics were also sizeable as were several of the Scottish colleges.

The polytechnics offered not only degrees but other qualifications – such as the Diploma in Higher Education, the Diploma of the Business and Technician Education Council – and short continuing education courses. The curriculum had developed to include degrees in the arts, humanities and social sciences. Although they still possessed a stronger vocational orientation, the bigger polytechnics were beginning to replicate comparable universities. Unlike at universities, there was no obligation to do research, there was less talk of academic freedom, and lecturers taught longer hours with less autonomy. But there was a growth in research, national recruitment and a thrust to independence.

The differences between the universities and polytechnics were usually defined along a vocationalism–research line. In practice, given the differences *within* both sectors, the differences *between* them were less than was often imagined, and they were diminishing.

The polytechnics were finally granted permission in 1992 to approach the Privy Council to turn themselves into universities. Henceforth, higher education would be unified and all universities would compete for funds from the Higher Education Funding Council. However, the new universities (Appendix 2.1, Figure 2.1) were not granted charters, tokens of independence in the past; the position on research remained unclear.

By the time the polytechnics became universities, more than 200,000 students were studying for first degrees (Figure 2.2). In 1992 there was an increase of 23% in the number of students admitted to degree courses, making an increase of 30% since 1990. However, there are a large number of the students in Britain's new universities who are not studying for degrees. Many of the 16,000 academic staff are members of the TUC affiliated National Association of Teachers in Further and Higher Education. Others belong to the Association of Polytechnic Lecturers.

The colleges and institutes of higher education

When they became universities, the polytechnics left behind some 50 smaller colleges which did significant work in higher education – some degree work as well as courses for the Graduate Certificate in Education (for aspiring teachers), the Higher National Diploma or the Higher National Certificate of the Business and Technician Education Council. Some, such as Cheltenham College of Arts and Technology and Bolton Institute of Higher Education, which were degree-awarding institutions, felt they should have been granted university status –

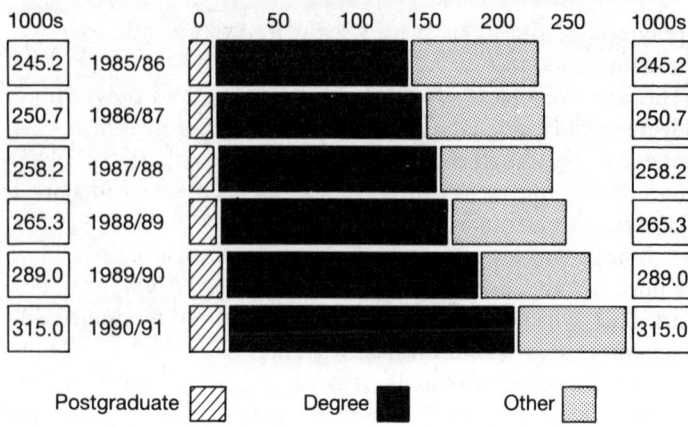

Figure 2.2 Numbers of students taking degrees in the former polytechnics, and level of study, 1985–91
(Source: Polytechnics Funding Council)

they lacked the required power to grant their own research degrees – and this may come in future years. Links between higher education and further education are likely to grow as more universities increasingly franchise their degrees in further education colleges: i.e., courses are taught in the college but validated by the university for the award of *their* degrees.

The unified system

Many recent changes have been as dramatic as those of the sixties: the Robbins agenda has moved forward. With the expansion in numbers during 1987–92, the system is on target for a third of 18-year-olds to be in higher education by 2000. But in the past, advances were supported by a level of resourcing that is unavailable now. By 1992 universities were receiving 15% less in state aid per undergraduate than in 1988 and the decline was accelerating. The policy of 'packing them' in *is* a threat to quality. Staff–student ratios are rising – from 9:1 in 1980 to 12:1 in the old universities, 15:1 in the old polytechnics – and this decline is also speeding up. Excellence is in danger and there is a fierce debate about two-year degrees. The government has been worried by the very success it demanded. It is now attempting to put the brakes on the speed of expansion by cutting the amount of money it pays in tuition fees to universities. Many feel that there will be more discussion about students paying more of their own fees.

But the abolition of the binary line does hold the promise of a new, bigger, comprehensive system of higher education. We are finally moving towards the *mass university*. A comprehensive system blending the traditions of academicism and vocationalism, autonomy and accountability could recapture public esteem and create a new diversity *within* a more integrated system. It is clear, to take one example, that the new universities will not have prerogatives to do research on the old model. 'Traditional' universities with prestigious records will be able to resist pressures to expand and do more teaching: a healthy slice of their income will come from research grants. Other universities will specialise in teaching. There will also be differences within institutions. Our system may look more American in future.

But there will also be major advantages:

- There will be increased access, with higher education shortly reaching a third of the 18–21 age group. There will be more part-time students, more lifelong education, more vocational courses and more women students. Fewer students will have followed the traditional, A-level route.
- As more students are more interested in career prospects and life skills, and as government demands and rewards more vocationalism and more life skills, courses are likely to have a more practical dimension.
- The two-semester year will replace the three-term year.
- There will be more modular courses, with credits transferrable between institutions – you won't have to study at one university in a three-year block.

- Higher education institutions will work more with external agencies, and research will be less motivated by free-range inquiry, more by a problem-solving approach.
- Social pressures will lead to greater emphasis on the application of knowledge as well as its creation. A greater concentration on learning method rather than subject content is probable – developing the skills of gaining knowledge rather than having it all 'presented on a plate'.
- The information technology explosion and the growth of distance learning motored by computers and videos will eventually transform the delivery of higher education.

But if all this is to be done well, as distinct from simply *done* – if British higher education is to maintain its reputation for excellence – then *more resources will be necessary*.

2.3   Degrees – and who helps you get them

This section gives you information about the system of degrees, and provides an outline as to who is who and who does what in higher education.

Students' degrees

The degree course is at the centre of the activity in higher education. Those studying for a first degree are normally called *undergraduates* and those for a second degree, *postgraduates*.

First degrees

- A first degree usually requires three or four years' *full-time study*.
- As well as the traditional *part-time study* for degrees catering largely for the full-time student, there are now many specifically designed *part-time degrees*, with study in the evenings for five or six years.
- There are many *sandwich courses* – 90,000 students are now involved – which usually last four or five years and include

work experience as part of the programme. In a 'thick sandwich', a complete year is spent in practical experience with an employer; in a 'thin sandwich', two or more shorter periods of six months are woven into the course.

- Modularisation and credit transfer are gradually being adopted, so that you can build credits towards a degree via a variety of courses, sometimes at different institutions.

First degrees are normally Bachelor's degrees:

- Bachelor of Arts (B.A.)
- Bachelor of Science (B.Sc.)
- Bachelor of Engineering (B.Eng.)
- Bachelor of Education (B.Ed.)
- Bachelor of Laws (LL.B.).

A B.A. or B.Sc. can cover a wide range of subjects. At many institutions you read subjects such as economics or social sciences for a B.Sc. At others, nearly all courses, including science courses, lead to a B.A. At Oxford and Cambridge all first degrees are B.A. degrees but the title of M.A. can be acquired through payment of a fee. At the older Scottish universities what in England and Wales are B.A. degrees are Master of Arts degrees.

First degrees are awarded as *honours* degrees. The normal grading for an honours degree is first class, upper second, lower second, third class. However, degrees which do not reach the honours standards are known as *pass* (or sometimes *ordinary* or *unclassified*) degrees. Degrees for which you specialise in two major subjects (more rarely, three) are sometimes termed *combined* or *joint* degrees.

Higher degrees

You usually need a first degree to study for a further degree, but you may be exempt from this requirement if you have practical experience in your chosen subject.

Master's degrees   This degree, which is the next stage up from a Bachelor's degree, can take one or two years of study. This may be an M.A. or M.Sc., regardless of the subject studied, or an M.Ed., LL.M and so on. A big difference is that a Master's degree may involve course work, perhaps with a dissertation – or it may be awarded on the basis of a research thesis. Some universities award special postgraduate degrees on the basis of a research thesis; the term for this degree is *Master of Philosophy* (M.Phil.). Graduates of Oxford and Cambridge who hold a B.A. may after a number of years apply for an M.A. without further examination.

Doctorates   A Ph.D. (or D.Phil., as it is sometimes known) is awarded for a higher thesis embodying original research in any subject. It may also involve some course work. A Ph.D. is assumed to take three years of study but often takes longer. Sometimes higher doctorates such as D.Sc. and D.Litt. are awarded to senior academics on the basis of a distinguished list of publications. Some universities are now introducing awards of Ph.D. by publication, so that staff can apply for a doctorate on the basis of books they have written.

Honorary degrees   These are awarded by institutions to respected local or national figures for their contribution to the arts, the sciences, the community, or the university or college.

Other qualifications in higher education

Diploma of Higher Education: Many new universities offer a two-year course leading to a Dip.H.E. It is usually non-vocational and intended for those who are unsure whether they wish to undertake degree study. Dip.H.E. courses are regarded as equivalent to the first two years of a degree course. They include a number of subjects, often on a modular basis, and students can usually be transferred to a degree course.

Diploma and certificate courses: Universities often mount a variety of such courses in a range of vocational and non-vocational subjects. The most well known is the two-year Diploma Course in Social Work.

Business and Technician Education Council, Higher National Diploma: These are vocational courses taught from a practical applied stance in business studies.

The academic staff

With so many different institutions with different traditions, terminology varies. For example, Oxford and Cambridge, as well as the older Scottish universities, tend to use distinctive terminology. What follows is a general guide to practice in most universities.

Lecturers Lecturers are the people you will meet most often in your lectures and classes and academic life generally. Lecturers are required to teach, research and publish. They usually have a higher degree, although there are no formal qualifications for the job.

Senior lecturers Senior lecturers are staff who usually have ten to fifteen years' experience. They are promoted from the ranks of lecturers, having demonstrated proficiency in teaching and a good research record. They are in no sense the boss of your ordinary lecturers, although they may take on more responsibilities in the department.

Principal lecturer In the new universities this was traditionally the top academic grade before there were professors.

Tutor The person responsible for admissions to a department is often termed the admissions tutor. Lecturers who take you in classes may be referred to informally as your tutors, although in Oxford and Cambridge with the tutorial system the term is more formal. In many institutions students are assigned to one of the lecturing staff who acts as their *personal tutor* dealing with any problems they may have.

Fellow This term, which is more often used at Oxbridge, denotes a senior member of a college who is paid to take tutorials at that college, and sometimes other colleges, and also to research.

Reader A reader stands in seniority between a senior lecturer and a professor. The title is usually awarded to senior lecturers who have demonstrated particular excellence in their research and publications.

Professor These are the senior academics usually appointed to 'a chair' (a professional post), partly on their teaching record but primarily because of their eminence in research.

- In the past, a professor was usually the head of an academic department and the chair was an *established* chair. When the professor retired as, say, Head of the History Department, a new professor would be appointed to take his or her place – although the person retiring could style his or herself *Emeritus* Professor of History (from the Latin *merere* 'to merit').
- Individuals whose record was excellent but who for one reason or another did not wish to take on the administration of a department were often granted *personal* chairs in the subject.
- Some universities have also introduced *promotional* chairs. Here the appointed person is expected to develop courses and research in a new or neglected subject area.

Head of department Traditionally, all heads of department held established chairs. Today a department can agree to rotate the role amongst staff who are senior lecturers and above. So, a person who does not hold an established, a personal or a promotional chair may be the head of your department at a particular time.

Research fellow, Research officer   These titles – the terms are often interchangeable – denote the more senior research staff, sometimes on permanent contracts, who are expected to work independently and supervise other research workers. Often they are financed by a body outside the university. They may take classes and seminars on your course or you may be referred to them for help with your project.

Research associate, Research assistant   These are usually junior research staff, often on short-term contracts, assigned to a senior academic or working as part of a larger research team. They will often be studying for a higher degree.

The academic and administrative staff

Director, Principal   In England and Wales, this is the the chief academic and administrative executive in the new universities – sometimes assisted by an *Academic Director*.

Vice-Chancellor   This is the chief executive responsible for all the work of the 'old' university. In Scotland the term *Principal* is sometimes used.

Chancellor   This is the titular head of a university, often a public figure, retired politician or member of the Royal Family. The post is often open to election; whilst it is largely ceremonial, an active chancellor can exercise a good deal of influence.

Pro vice-chancellors   These are appointed from the senior staff to aid the vice-chancellor. Given responsibility for particular areas of work they constitute a small cabinet around the vice-chancellor.

Pro-chancellor   A pro-chancellor may be appointed as a deputy for the chancellor.

Rector   A rector is elected as chair of the court in some Scottish universities and is usually is a public figure from the world of affairs or show business.

Dean   There may be a Dean of Undergraduates responsible for looking after policy issues affecting first-degree students. More usually, the dean will be charged with the administration of a faculty.

Registrar   If the director or vice-chancellor is the chief executive, the registrar is the chief administrator in relation to academic matters. He or she advises on and implements policy through his or her department on issues ranging from admissions and appointments to changes in the statutes and relations with government and the funding councils.

Clerk to the board of governors   The clerk has an increasingly important administrative job in the new universities; advising and administrating for the governing body. The clerk is usually secretary to the higher representative bodies of the institution.

Director of finance   In many institutions he or she is a chief administrative officer who reports to the chief executive on all financial matters, from grants to investment policy.

Bursar   In some institutions, the chief financial officer is called the bursar.

Director of Estates and Services   Somebody with this or a similar title reports to the chief executive and has responsibility for buildings and the campus environment.

Librarian   Always vital to the life of the institution, the librarian, like his or her fellow administrators, is even more important in these days of cutbacks and straitened financial circumstances.

And, of course, we should not forget the thousands of clerical, secretarial and administrative staff, porters, catering staff, maintenance workers, and technicians who all make a vital contribution to the operation.

2.4   Running the organisation

Decisions which will affect you as well as the staff are taken through the democratic machinery of your college. These include decisions on

- how many students will be admitted;
- what qualifications you need to get in;
- how long your course lasts;
- how many staff there will be to teach you;
- whether new departments are to open or old ones to close;
- how much money will be available for the library or halls of residence.

Although the processes for reaching these decisions may appear distant and difficult to understand, it is worthwhile to attempt to get a broad view of how your university operates. Once again, terms and practice may differ from institution to institution.

The department academic board   Academic staff are usually grouped in departments responsible for teaching certain courses and undertaking certain areas of research. (We are also seeing the development of smaller *centres* where staff

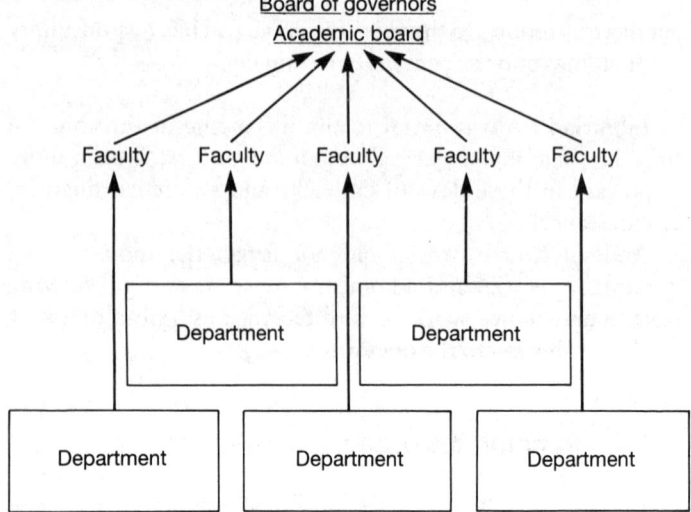

Figure 2.3   Governing a new university

do research and a certain amount of teaching. But the department remains the primary academic and representative unit.) All full-time academic staff will be members of the departmental academic board. The board will elect its own chair and secretary and advise the head of department on

- the academic programme;
- course regulations;
- student welfare and progress;
- the allocation of duties between staff; and
- financial arrangements.

In most departments there will be course committees or teams established to develop and supervise particular courses. Student representatives should be involved at both board and committee level.

The faculty board   The next step up from the department is the faculty. If a departmental board wishes to take up some aspect of wider university policy, or even pass a resolution on

Course representatives- What are they?

How often have you felt that you had no real say in the running of your course,Department,or Faculty?There is an effective way of making your voice heard through the **course representation** system. Elections to these will be held in October.

Course representatives put student demands at all levels of the University-whether it is queries about the way a course is being taught or perhaps about the facilities in the Department.

Aims for Course representative this year

To ensure courses meet a basic Charter of Quality
1.Good teaching
2.Sufficent access to Library books
3.A proper complaints procedure
4.Effective ways of assessing teaching quality
5.making sure tutors respond to student demand

The Union will provide training, advice, backup and a policy pack for student representatives.

If you don't want to be a course representative, but feel your courses are not reaching the charter of quality's criteria contact Bill Eyres the Academic Affairs Officer.

Figure 2.4 A course representatives election leaflet.

The government is committed to introducing a Students Charter to give students rights in relation to the quality of teaching and facilities at their college. The NUS, too, has published a series of guidelines on what students should be looking for – improved teaching, adequate study and reasonable accommodation, and delivery of finance. Many student unions are taking up these demands.

(Source: Manchester University Student Union)

it, it can pass this up to the faculty board. Faculties group together a number of academic departments according to broad subject areas, so a department may be in the Faculty of Arts, Science and Engineering, Law or Management and Business Studies. All full-time academic staff are entitled to attend the board and provision is made for representation of students.

The head of the faculty, responsible for supervising and co-ordinating its work, is a senior academic, the dean. It is the faculty which takes up proposals from departments on such matters as the establishment of new degrees and courses, new regulations and the appointment of internal and external examiners to supervise the course. Your faculty may well have a staff–student consultative committee. This will have elected student representatives and deal with teaching, course organisation, facilities and almost anything else you want to bring up.

Academic board   In the new universities this has been the next step up from the faculty. This board usually consists of

- the director or principal,
- the academic director (if applicable),
- the deans of faculty, and
- one head of department from each faculty.

The full-time teaching staff elect a number of representatives and there is provision for at least two representatives from the student union. A typical academic board has between 20 and 30 members – so it can be an active working body. It deals with all academic matters and advises the principal and the board of governors on them. It works through a small number of committees, but its size means all of its members are in a position to keep sight of important issues.

Senate   In the traditional universities, the next step up from faculty is senate. All major issues which are not resolved in the lower level machinery can be raised here. Senate gives final

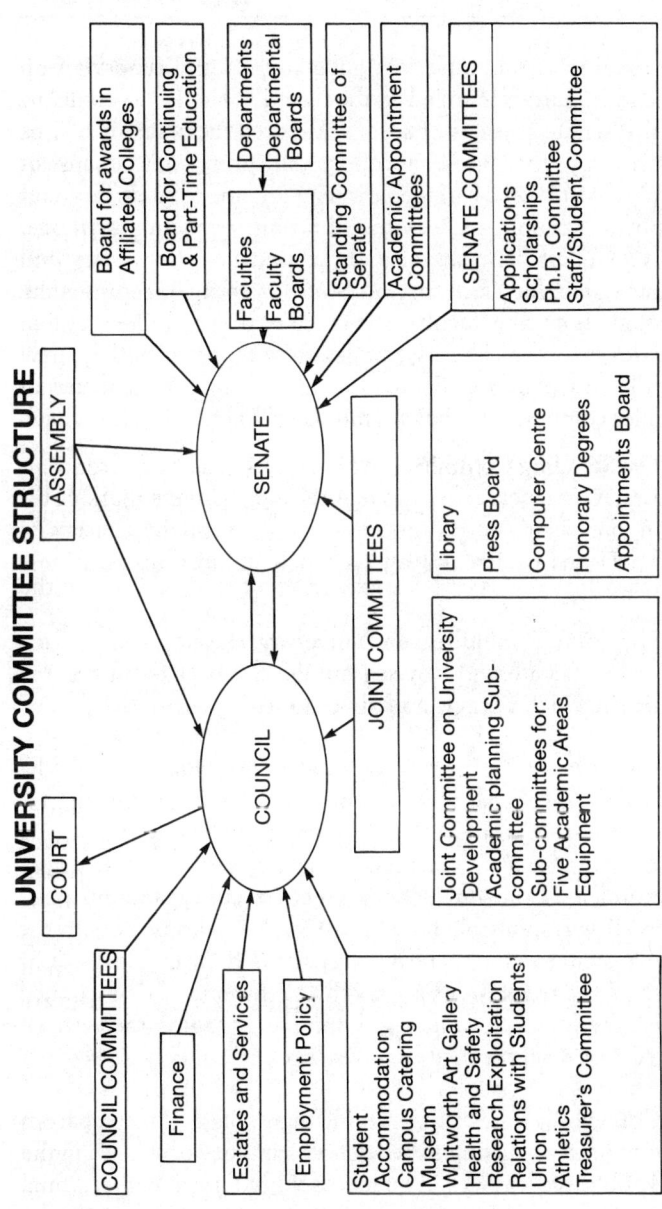

Figure 2.5 University committee structure

approval to regulations governing courses and supervises all academic matters handled by the faculties. Unlike an academic board, senate consists of several hundred members. It will be chaired by the vice-chancellor. All professors, deans of faculties and heads of department attend, as well as other important people such as the librarian. Academic staff also elect members of Senate, usually around a quarter of the total membership, for a fixed period. Students are again represented, through both the faculty structure and the student union. Senates are more like assemblies than working bodies; they handle much of the detailed work through a structure of smaller committees. The two most important committees are:

- **The Standing Committee,** which looks in detail at proposals for new courses, examines reports and recommendations for appointment and promotion of staff. It usually consists of the Deans of Faculty and a small number of additional members.

- **The Joint Committee on University Development**, which advises Senate and Council on allocation of resources, the distribution of grants and appointments policy.

Council   In the traditional universities, this body has the final word on academic matters, but if it feels an issue requires the exercise of academic judgement, it will only act after a report from Senate and usually on its advice.

Council is the university's chief executive and financial body. It is responsible for a university's relationship with the ever growing web of external agencies and the employer of its staff. So many decisions are taken at a lower level that Council often operates as a rubber-stamping body. But in the event of conflict or disagreement at lower levels it can play a decision-making role.

Council is a much smaller body than Senate. It usually has a 'lay' majority – distinguished people from the local community and public life – as well as members elected from Senate. Again, it will work through a number of committees dealing with such issues as finance, services, employment policy and student welfare.

Board of governors In the new universities, this is the supreme governing body. It has ultimate responsibility for determining the objectives and educational approach of the institution, resources and financial management, and all issues to do with the employment of staff. It appoints and can dismiss the principal.

The board of governors meets at least once a term. It consists of around 20 members, about a dozen of whom are chosen from distinguished leaders in industry and the local community – the *independent members*. There are also nominees from the academic board, the academic staff, the non-teaching staff and the student union – although recent changes mean students and staff have lost their right to *guaranteed* seats. The local authority nominates a member and the director sits *ex officio*. The board normally conducts much of its business through a small number of committees. These usually take the form of an audit committee, an estates and services committee, and a finance and employment committee.

Court This is the top body in the traditional universities; it is chaired by the chancellor and usually has several hundred members. These include representatives of the student body, Senate, Council, the assembly and Convocation. From outside the universities come representatives from

- the relevant local authorities,
- the Confederation of British Industry and the Trades Union Congress,
- learned societies in the area, and – because of the university status as a body incorporated under Royal Charter –
- nominees of the Lord President of the Council.

The court receives and discusses the university's annual

report and statement of accounts. It appoints the vice-chancellor and lay members of Council as well as approving changes in university ordinances and the conferment of honorary degrees. It normally meets twice a year.

Assembly This is a general meeting of all academic, research and academic-related staff which convenes once a year to receive a report from the vice-chancellor on the university's situation. It also elects members to court.

Convocation All graduates of the university are members of Convocation, and so are the members of the assembly. Membership can thus involve scores of thousands and it is often difficult for universities which use this mechanism to keep up-to-date lists. Convocation elects the chancellor and some of the members of the court.

2.5   National organisations for higher education

Association of University Teachers This is the lecturers' union in the old universities.

Committee of Vice-Chancellors and Principals The old CVCP, which linked the old universities, merged with the Committee of Directors of Polytechnics to form this co-ordinating body linking university leaders. The CVCP is able to co-ordinate internal initiatives and act as a pressure group in relation to government and other external bodies.

Department for Education This department has ultimate responsibility for higher education.

Higher Education Funding Councils The HEFCs in England, Scotland and Wales pass on government funds to institutions, attaching guidance and conditions, and convey the views of higher education to government.

Higher Education Quality Council   This council will oversee quality in higher education institutions and recommend whether aspiring colleges are qualified to join the ranks of universities.

National Association of Teachers in Higher and Further Education   This is the main trade union for academic staff in the former polytechnics and further education colleges.

National Union of Students   This is *your* trade union.

Association for Colleges   This body seeks to represent all further education colleges and develop closer links with higher education.

Standing Conference of Principals   This is the co-ordinating body for the heads of colleges of higher education.

Universities and Colleges Admissions Service   This body handles admissions to all universities, old and new, and colleges and Institutes of Higher Education covered by the former Polytechnics and Colleges Admissions System.

Key points

1 The abolition of the binary divide unites institutions with different traditions and approaches to higher education.
2 The traditional university sector represented a mix of institutions, but there was generally an emphasis on the unity of teaching and research, institutional autonomy, academic freedom and a liberal approach – all underpinned by generous funding. This inheritance was eroded in the 1980s.

3 The polytechnics were more open and accessible and less generously financed. Degree students were in a minority in polytechnics. There was a drift away from the polytechnics' original vocational emphasis towards more academic studies.

4 From 1987 there was dramatic expansion in student numbers in both sectors. Britain is on target to have one third of 18-year-olds in higher education by the year 2000.

5 The abolition of the binary divide implies continuing, if different diversity. It is likely that the research–teaching link will be broken, that different universities will develop different specialisms. A tiered system of universities on US lines may emerge.

6 State intervention, targetted funding, and moves to greater accountability are likely to continue.

7 There will be important changes in the nature of teaching and research.

8 It is useful to understand the qualification structure, the nomenclature of staff, and how teaching and research are organised.

9 Universities remain self-governing bodies with intricate decision-making machinery. It is useful to be aware of this and of how decisions pass from departments to faculties and governing bodies.

10 External organisations increasingly influence how universities operate.

Things to do

1 Outline the main differences between universities and polytechnics.

2 Consider which is more important, teaching or research.

3 Think about whether the abolition of the binary divide was a good idea.

4 Discuss your views on whether, as higher education expands, more will mean worse.

5 Find out all you can about the Higher Education Funding Council and what it does.

6 Describe what a vice-chancellor and a professor do.

7 See if you can get some material from the university nearest you on how it is governed; compare it with the description in this chapter.

Further reading

Recent change in higher education has not produced a great deal of accessible literature. Mary Warnock's *A Common Policy for Education* (Oxford University Press, 1989), however, has a powerful, thought-provoking Chapter 5 which is well worth reading. More difficult but excellent and well worth trying is Michael Allen's *The Goals of Universities* (Open University Press/Society for Research into Higher Education, 1988). Written by an educational practitioner, its focus is wider than its title might suggest. A substantial book you might want to use for reference on the background to recent developments is *Education and the Social Order, 1940–1990*, by Brian Simon (Lawrence and Wishart, 1991).

Appendix 2.1 **Britain's new universities**

Anglia Polytechnic   **Anglia Polytechnic University**
Birmingham Polytechnic   **University of Central England in Birmingham**
Bournemouth Polytechnic   **Bournemouth University**
Brighton Polytechnic   **The University of Brighton**
Bristol Polytechnic   **University of the West of England, Bristol**
Polytechnic of Central London   **The University of Westminster**
City of London Polytechnic   **London Guildhall University**
Coventry Polytechnic   **Coventry University**
Derbyshire College of Higher Education   **University of Derby**
Polytechnic of East London   **University of East London**
Glasgow Polytechnic/Queens College   **Caledonian University**
Hatfield Polytechnic   **University of Hertfordshire**
Polytechnic of Huddersfield   **University of Huddersfield**
Humberside Polytechnic   **University of Humberside**
Kingston Polytechnic   **Kingston University**
Lancashire Polytechnic   **University of Central Lancashire**
Leeds Polytechnic   **Leeds Metropolitan University**
Leicester Polytechnic   **De Montfort University**
Liverpool Polytechnic   **Liverpool John Moores University**
Manchester Polytechnic   **Manchester Metropolitan University**
Middlesex Polytechnic   **Middlesex University**
Napier Polytechnic   **Napier University**
Newcastle Polytechnic   **University of Northumbria at Newcastle**
Nottingham Polytechnic   **Nottingham Trent University**
Polytechnic of North London   **University of North London**
Oxford Polytechnic   **Oxford Brookes University**
Paisley College of Technology   **University of Paisley**
Polytechnic South West   **University of Plymouth**
Portsmouth Polytechnic   **University of Portsmouth**
The Robert Gordon Institute of Technology   **Robert Gordon**

University

Sheffield Polytechnic   **Sheffield Hallam University**
South Bank Polytechnic   **South Bank University**
Staffordshire Polytechnic   **Staffordshire University**
Sunderland Polytechnic   **University of Sunderland**
Teesside Polytechnic   **University of Teesside**
Thames Polytechnic   **University of Greenwich**
Polytechnic of Wales   **University of Glamorgan**
Polytechnic of West London   **Thames Valley University**
Wolverhampton Polytechnic   **University of Wolverhampton**

3

Getting in

'You've j'ined a College by this time I suppose?'
'Ah, no!' said Jude. 'I am almost as far off that as ever.'

Thomas Hardy, *Jude the Obscure*

3.1 Introduction

Now that you know something about higher education, do you think it is for you? University can provide a marvellous opportunity to educate yourself and lay the basis for personal development through life. Your years of study can be an incomparably rich experience in which you transform yourself, acquire new ideas and meet people who will be friends for life. They can lay the basis for a rewarding, satisfying career. This chapter outlines the points you'll need to consider to help you decide whether to apply.

- Section 3.2 discusses applying for a place in higher education and how self-analysis is required to approach your decision. Whilst you need to listen carefully to the information and views of parents, teachers, partners and friends, the decision has to be finally yours.
- Section 3.3 goes on to look at the courses available, the qualifications required for acceptance, and some of the factors to take into account in deciding where to study.
- Section 3.4 takes you through the basics of applying to universities. It looks at the admission process, from filling in your application form, through interviews, to the final clearing-house procedure.

- Section 3.5 examines the position from the point of view of mature students, those who may wish to study part time, those from overseas, and those with disabilities.

3.2 Decisions, decisions

You will normally start thinking seriously about this before your A-level studies or other pre-higher education course. The key question is: do you want to spend the next three or four years pursuing a course in higher education? It's a big chunk out of your life. For most people it comes when they are young and it may be the first big decision they have to take. A wrong choice can knock you out of your life stride. There is the opportunity cost: what you could have been doing instead. The decision needs careful consideration on the basis of full information and discussion with experienced people.

Here are some of the points you might like to consider.

Career Do you have a future career in mind? Will a course constitute a useful preparation for this? During your last years at school you will be spending some time hearing about and discussing the potential involved in a range of career opportunities.

A useful series of some 70 booklets linking degree studies to particular occupations and suggesting how you can use your degree in practical ways is the **Signpost** series published by the

Association of Graduate Careers Advisory Services
Central Services Unit
Crawford House
Precinct Centre
Manchester M13 9PL

The relationship of a degree to an occupation is one factor to consider. (See also Chapter 13.) But don't feel that whilst still at school you have to come to a firm, let alone irrevocable, decision as to the pattern of your future life. Around one third of jobs offered to graduates have the requirement of *any* degree. What is important now is thought and exploration, perhaps a tentative attachment to a future path. If you are sure – well and good. But remember you may change your mind.

You love the subject   Do you wish to spend the coming years studying physics or art history because you *like* them? Did you study them or read about them and feel sure you would find further study fulfilling? Or do you think it would be useful to study a particular subject? Think carefully: in higher education you will be expected to apply a searching, systematic and deep approach to your subject. Remember, you can study some subjects at university without having done them at A level. But you have to ask yourself whether you want to deal with your subject *in depth, full time, for three or four years, in an organised way, probably away from home.*

Independence and stamina   Do you have the commitment and the stamina to cope with the demands of a higher education course? How will you manage the abrupt break with family and friends? This can produce at least some emotional problems. How will you react to taking responsibility for your own learning, and your own life? Dealing with a new working environment and a new social life, with the problems of freedom, time organisation, accommodation and looking after yourself can be difficult at the best of times. For some, these new challenges do not mesh easily with the demands of independent study.

Proficiency and qualifications   If you have a strong interest in a subject, are you sufficiently proficient in it? Do you have the academic potential to pursue it more rigorously? Liking a subject is often necessary, but hardly sufficient, for achieving success in it. What standards have you set in your classwork? What is your feedback from your teachers? How have you performed in examinations? What qualifications are you likely to gain? Are you likely to meet the course requirements for entry (see p. 77).

Finance How will you cope with your problems in a tough financial situation? For that is what you will find yourself in. Over the last decade grants failed to keep pace with inflation. You will probably need to borrow money through the student loans system (see p. 77). Meanwhile, your former school-friends will be coining it in whilst you are studying. On the brighter side, whilst some graduates don't find work imme-diately, their overall unemployment rates are less than the national average. The lifetime earnings of graduates overtake those with only A levels. Those with arts degrees end up with 9% better lifetime earnings and those with science degrees end up 20% better off – even when allowance is made for lost earnings. So most students do not ultimately lose out financially – if they get a degree (and of course the large majority do).

Work and study More than one in five students has to take a job *during term* because of the inadequate level of grants. Students have traditionally worked in vacations but working whilst studying full time may create numerous study difficulties. Are you prepared for financial and work problems on top of studying?

For me . . . now? Some school students decide that they would like to do a degree . . . but not just yet! You may need a breather after your school studies are complete. You may wish to come to terms with a more independent way of life or induct yourself more gradually into a subject by taking a year off. You may feel work experience will help your personal development and/or give you a better understanding of where you want to go. Or you may want to travel. There is, after all, little reason to pack higher education into the years between 18 and 21. On the other hand, a break now could check the momentum you have built up while working intensively for A levels or at college.

A great opportunity But going into higher education doesn't mean confronting insurmountable problems. Research demonstrates that students acquire a wide range of competencies, from skill in organisation, critical thinking and communication to the ability to manage their emotions, develop personal autonomy and generate self-esteem and confidence (Brennan and McGeevor, 1988). Research also confirms that these competencies are *transferable*: higher education is a good preparation for living and working (Cormier and Hagman, 1987).

Higher education represents a great opportunity. You will have the time and space free from employment and its pressures to consider yourself, the society in which you live and what you want to do in it. You will have the opportunity to prepare yourself for a role in that society but also to make yourself a more skilled, cultured, interesting, *better developed person*. As Alan Bloom puts it in his controversial book *The Closing of the American Mind*, 'These are the charmed years when he can, if he so chooses, become anything he wishes and when he has the opportunity to survey his alternatives, not merely those current in his time or provided by careers, but those available to him as a human being.' (Professor Bloom needs reminding that half the human race consists of *women*!)

Higher education is a voyage of adventure that may never come again. What struck the novelist Martin Amis about his course was 'the unique freedom . . . Conventional ways of filling the time are gone; it is all yours now. It doesn't happen to you before and it never happens to you again. Perhaps once is enough – but not more than enough.'

What we have said is not aimed at discouraging you from entering higher education. It *is* intended to get you thinking about what is involved so that you can come to the right decision for you. This brings us to the Big M – *Motivation*. The most successful students possess a mix of personal, academic and vocational reasons for going to university. Such students have a powerful intrinsic interest in their subject which draws them into working hard at it. But they also possess *extrinsic* motivation. They like the idea of having a degree. In setting forth on their degree studies they will probably have the support and approbation of their parents. This helps. They are also aware that a degree opens career doors; hard work today means better pay and greater autonomy tomorrow.

There are no absolute rules. Some students whose prime aim is to get away from home and develop an independent life are successful academically. Others whose objectives are primarily vocational are often able to complete a course successfully because of their strong belief it will equip them for their future career. You are more likely to come to an informed, conscious decision if you think about where you want to go after school, discuss it with others, and weigh the possibilities.

- Make sure you have access to the information materials we will refer to.
- Talk to your parents and friends about the decision.
- Seek the opinions of your teachers and career advisers.
- Review your academic record. Does it do you justice? Can you do better? *How* can you do better?
- Remember that others who often have your welfare at heart find it difficult to stand outside their own experience. If your father wants you to go to a particular college because he did, he may be forgetting that you are a very different person with different objectives.

Listen to others, weigh their advice carefully, but finally ask yourself, is it for *you*? In the end it's your education, your life, your future.

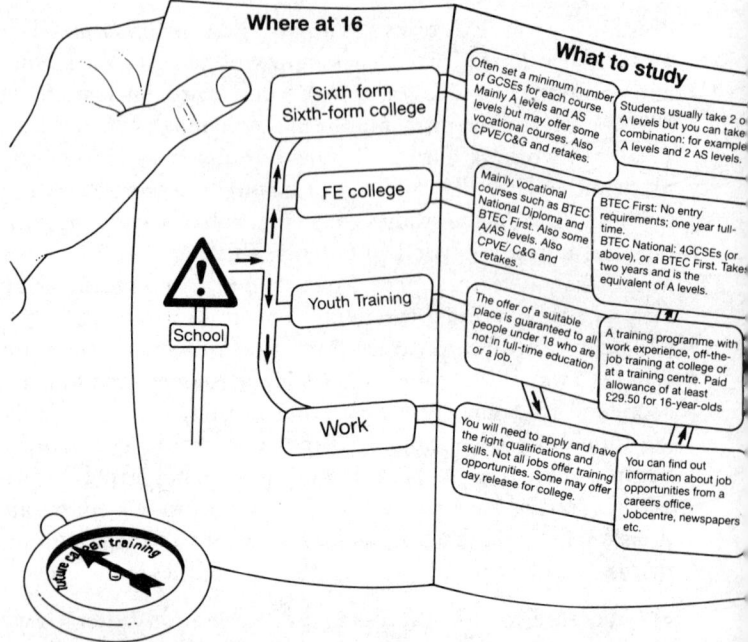

Figure 3.1   Higher education road map
(Source: *Guardian*, 15 September 1992)

3.3 Choosing a course

As you focus on a particular subject area, you need to assess:

● the depth of your interest, commitment and proficiency;
● your study record and estimation of your abilities in this subject; and
● future vocational possibilities.

Early consideration of these aspects will influence your choice of A-level subjects. If you take all your A levels in arts subjects, you will have problems in qualifying for a science degree later because you will normally need A levels in some science subjects to gain entry (see p. 77). You do not need to

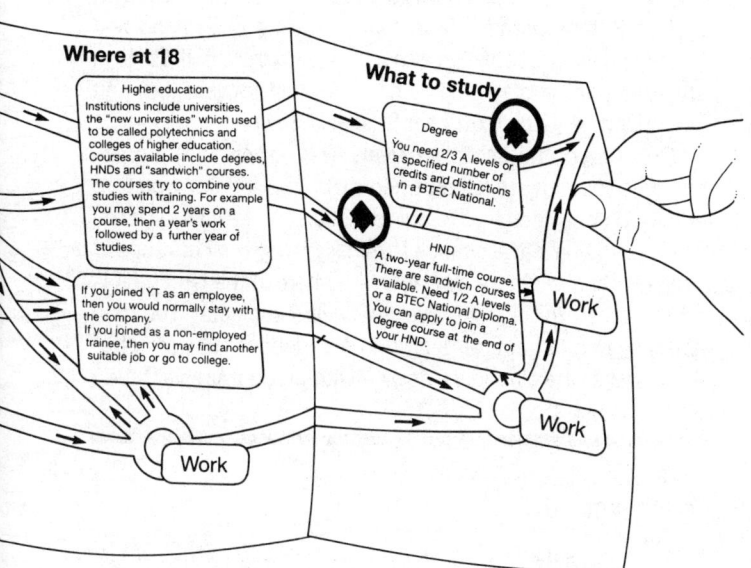

Where at 18

Higher education
Institutions include universities, the "new universities" which used to be called polytechnics and colleges of higher education. Courses available include degrees, HNDs and "sandwich" courses. The courses try to combine your studies with training. For example you may spend 2 years on a course, then a year's work followed by a further year of studies.

If you joined YT as an employee, then you would normally stay with the company.
If you joined as a non-employed trainee, then you may find another suitable job or go to college.

What to study

Degree
You need 2/3 A levels or a specified number of credits and distinctions in a BTEC National.

HND
A two-year full-time course. There are sandwich courses available. Need 1/2 A levels or a BTEC National Diploma. You can apply to join a degree course at the end of your HND.

Work

Work

Work

be absolutely specific at 16 but it is very useful if you pick from the 'stream' of subjects you want to study: arts, sciences, languages and so on. Studying for A levels will then further clarify the situation and encourage you to make a more definite decision. (It will not necessarily circumscribe that decision: every year many students decide to study for degrees in subjects they have not studied at school.) Having reflected on your interests, aptitudes and future aspirations, get a good idea of the range of subjects offered in higher education.

BOX 3.1 In Scotland

School students in Scotland usually take up to seven O grades at 15 or 16 for the Scottish Certificate of Education (similar to

GCSE). A year later they can take up to five subjects at H Grade SCE and, if successful, go on to university at 17. The Scottish system is thus broader than that prevailing in England and Wales and we probably have much to learn from it. If Scottish students want to stay on at school for a further year they can take a Certificate of Sixth Year Studies (CSYS).

Only one of the Scottish universities (Heriot-Watt) recruits students directly to departments. In the others you are admitted to a faculty. Except on courses like law or engineering, you have the chance to initially study a wider range of subjects than might be available elsewhere in the UK and it is often easier to change over between subjects. You can normally take a general degree in a variety of subjects after three years or an honours degree with greater specialisation after four years.

Which subject?

Start by consulting *University Entrance: The Official Guide* (Association of Commonwealth Universities for the Committee of Vice-Chancellors and Principals). *From 1994 a common entrance guide for all higher education institutions will be published replacing* University Entrance *and the* Polytechnic Courses Handbook. The following books are also useful:

- **The Scottish University Entrance Guide** (Scottish Universities Council on Entrance)
- **Guide to Colleges and Institutes of Higher Education** (Standing Conference of Principals)
- **Guide to Courses and Careers in Art, Craft and Design** (National Society for Education in Art and Design)
- **Design Courses in Britain** (Design Council)

These books will give you a grasp of the range of degree courses on offer and the kinds of grades you will need to be accepted. You can send off for them to the addresses at the back of this book. Some are free but some are expensive. Your school should have them; so should your local reference library. If you have difficulty obtaining them, try your local university or your local authority careers office. These publications are usually updated annually, so make sure you read the latest edition.

In addition there are a number of very helpful commercial publications, including

- **Which Degree?** (five volumes) (Newpoint Publishing)
- K. Boehm and J. Lees-Spalding, **The Student Book** (Macmillan Papermac)

Which course?

Once you have decided on a particular subject, you may find that there are various ways in which it can be studied at different universities.

- Can you combine two or even three subjects in a joint degree?
- Would you prefer to study one subject in depth?

The first approach leaves you with options open and doubles or trebles your repertoire but you may already have decided that you are a 'one subject' person.

- Do some of the courses in the subject that interests you provide a foundation year, or do you plunge straight away into specialised work?
- How is the pattern of the course organised – how many hours, lectures and classes and how much laboratory work?
- Is there scope for practical work or a research project?

To answer these and similar questions go straight to the horse's mouth: read the prospectus of the courses in which you are interested. This should give you most of the detailed information that you want on the syllabus and structures of each course, how the course is assessed, the amount of work involved – as well as where the course fits in to future professional examinations. Look at as many prospectuses as you can and make detailed comparisons. It is worth recalling that whilst most prospectuses are dispassionate, the institution is in the end trying to attract students. Student unions sometimes produce an 'alternative prospectus'. These give a 'student's eye' view of courses. There is also **Student's Eye**, an annual publication issued by the Careers Research and Advisory Council which gives pen pictures of institutions and courses as seen by students.

Your school or college should be on the mailing list for a wide range of prospectuses but do not hesitate to write off for more. The efforts put in will be handsomely repaid if you find yourself on a course tailor-made for your needs.

Which college?

Each institution has a different ethos and you cannot just stop at the academic. Do you prefer the city to suburbia . . . a new university to an old one? Sometimes painful decisions may have to be made: for example, if you discover a course which is absolutely ideal in a good college in what you regard as the back of beyond.

You may want to consider

- **The reputation of the institution and of the department.** Is the particular department flooded with applications? Are the staff well known? What is their research reputation? What kind of staff-student ratios are there and what degree of personal attention is given to students? What is the department's teaching reputation?
- **The course itself and the extent to which it is established and prestigious, experimental and innovative.** How popular is it? Is there a high success or a high failure rate? What happens to students when they complete their studies?
- **The college's facilities and resources.** What kind of facilities and resources exist? What are the teaching rooms, laboratories and libraries like – and the recreational and welfare facilities?

- **The location – and cost of living.** It may cost far less to live in Liverpool than in London. But be careful: it may cost much more in Aberdeen than in Exeter. What about accommodation? It is no good if everything else is marvellous but it is prohibitively expensive to get a roof over your head.
- **The size of the college.** Is it so big you get lost? . . . so small you live in each other's pockets? Is the site compact or are the buildings scattered? What about transport?

It is very useful if you can visit the college and talk to some of the students. Most institutions have open days when potential students are shown around. A recent open day at Manchester University attracted more than 6,000 visitors and almost all departments participated. There is nothing like seeing things at first hand: speaking to lecturers and students puts flesh on the pages of the prospectus. So do not be afraid to contact colleges and ask for the information.

Alternatively, you can always ring or make an appointment to see the Admissions Tutor, the person who will supervise the entry process. He or she will be only too happy to discuss the course with you and then show you over the department.

Most higher education bodies now have School Liaison Officers. They are usually lecturers on secondment to the college administration and they organise open days and are pleased to provide schools with a range of information and services such as arranging speakers to address classes. *Before you come to a final decision* about your course, it is vital that you experience at first hand, whether at an open day or at interview, the college and department in which you may spend the next three or four years.

Which qualifications?

Around 75% of students qualify for entry with A levels. The minimum requirement is two A levels and another three subjects at O or GCSE level. But this is very much a minimum. You

are almost certainly going to be asked for more. In recent years
under 20% of candidates with only two A levels were accepted
by the traditional universities.

Box 3.2   Entry requirements

If you are pursuing the A-level route you will need to meet

- **The General Requirement:** A *minimum* of two A levels and
  three passes at O level or GCSE or close variant.
- **The Special Requirement:** The above may need to be met
  by passes in specified subjects at A level and requirements
  for subjects such as maths at lower levels.
- **The Standard:** Because of competition you may be offered
  a place *if* you get certain grades in more than two A-level
  subjects – the general and specific requirements in practice
  may not be sufficient to get you in.

A levels hold the floor but remember

- Special conditions can apply to older students.
- All universities now accept the International Baccalaureate
  for the General Requirement, as long as you have the
  Diploma, not just passes in certain subjects.
- All universities now accept the European Baccalaureate as
  satisfying the General Requirement. Again, you need the
  Diploma.

And don't forget to check prospectuses for *age qualifications*. Normally entrants have to be 17 by 1 October of the
year they start their course but some institutions require new
entrants to be 18 at the date of admission.

The number of applicants for degree courses keeps on rising.
Yet only around 50% of applicants are accepted by the old
universities.

The position is a competitive one, and it still depends very
much on A levels rather than alternative qualifications.

Table 3.1 Qualifications of undergraduate entries

| | 3 A levels | | 5 Highers | | Other qualifications | |
	1988	1990 (% change)	1988	1990 (% change)	1988	1990 (% change)
Medicine/dentistry						
England	3461	3463(0.06)	—	—	275	325(18.0)
Wales	185	192(3.8)	—	—	17	21(82.0)
N Ireland	167	171(2.3)	—	—	15	15
United Kingdom	3813	3826(0.3)	—	—	307	371(20.8)
Scotland	338	348(3.0)	456	411(−9.9)	107	131(22.4)
Biological sciences						
England	3412	3934(15.3)	—	—	738	932(26.2)
Wales	345	504(46.0)	—	—	156	176(12.8)
N Ireland	102	181(77.0)	—	—	91	125(37.3)
United Kingdom	3859	4619(19.7)	—	—	985	1233(25.0)
Scotland	266	370(39.0)	481	490(1.87)	270	334(23.7)
Physical sciences						
England	4880	5469(12.0)	—	—	858	1044(21.6)
Wales	246	421(71.0)	—	—	104	148(42.3)
N Ireland	112	136(21.4)	—	—	91	90(−1.1)
United Kingdom	5238	6026(15.0)	—	—	1053	1282(21.7)
Scotland	150	280(86.7)	443	522(17.8)	256	291(13.6)
Mathematical sciences						
England	4112	4350(5.8)	—	—	795	954(20.0)
Wales	135	250(85.0)	—	—	61	105(72.0)
N Ireland	189	207(9.5)	—	—	104	151(45.2)
United Kingdom	4436	4807(8.4)	—	—	960	1210(26.0)
Scotland	112	150(34.0)	382	347(−9.0)	237	287(21.0)
Engineering/technology						
England	6386	6874(7.6)	—	—	2302	3226(40.0)
Wales	249	282(13.3)	—	—	227	87(26.4)
N Ireland	212	287(35.0)	—	—	168	227(35.0)
United Kingdom	6847	7443(8.7)	—	—	2697	3740(38.6)
Scotland	125	186(48.8)	666	683(2.5)	734	904(23.1)
Social studies						
England	7826	38728(11.5)	—	—	2433	2790(14.6)
Wales	471	814(72.8)	—	—	209	292(39.7)
N Ireland	291	280(−3.5)	—	—	126	88(−30.2)
United Kingdom	8588	9822(14.4)	—	—	2768	3170(14.5)
Scotland	179	289(1.4)	867	847(−2.3)	297	372(25.2)
Languages						
England	5908	6968(17.9)	—	—	1156	1360(17.6)
Wales	431	798(85.0)	—	—	138	180(30.4)
N Ireland	151	191(26.5)	—	—	80	83(3.75)
United Kingdom	6490	7957(22.6)	—	—	1374	1623(18.1)
Scotland	252	409(62.3)	247	293(18.6)	239	316(32.2)
Humanities						
England	3219	3931(22.1)	—	—	812	872(7.3)
Wales	224	477(12.9)	—	—	110	156(41.8)
N Ireland	104	129(24.0)	—	—	86	142(65.1)
United Kingdom	3547	4537(27.9)	—	—	1008	1170(16.0)
Scotland	165	266(61.2)	164	150(−8.5)	192	259(34.9)

Source: Committee of Vice-Chancellors and Principals and Universities Funding Council.

Table 3.1 shows that the number of successful candidates with
A levels is increasing across a range of subjects, particularly
languages and humanities. The number of undergraduates
with A levels on language courses, for example, increased by
around 23% between 1988 and 1990 compared with a rise of
18% in undergraduates with alternative entry qualifications.
In humanities the figures were 28% for A levels and 16% for
other qualifications. A levels are still very much the name of a
very competitive game and you need good grades.

A points system is often applied to A-level and AS-level
grades. The maximum applied is 30 points for three A-level
grades. The three best results are counted for those students
who take four A levels or three A levels and an AS level.

- The average points scored by the successful students who
  enter the old universities is currently 21.1 points.
- The average points scored by those who are unsuccessful is
  13.6 points.

Table 3.2   How the points system works

Grade	A level	AS level	Scottish higher
A	10	5	6
B	8	4	4
C	6	3	2
D	4	2	
E	2	1	

So you are looking for something like *two Bs and a C*. But
that is a rough average across subjects and institutions. The
average scores of those gaining places to study specific subjects
is as follows:

- Medicine: 26.6 points – something like an A and two Bs
- Law: 25.6 points – more than three Bs

- Economics: 23.7 points
- Maths: 23.5 points
- English: 23.4 points
- History: 22.7 points
- Teacher training and engineering: around 15 points – say two Cs and a D

More people are *getting* A-level grades and the numbers of those getting top grades is at an all-time high. Within these averages, some were accepted with far lower requirements and some with far higher ones.

Most prospectuses list the subjects you will be required to pass at A level and also 'offers in the range of' stating the *kind* of grades you will be asked to get to gain entry. These are not absolute requirements. The ultimate decisions will depend on the A-level results. Looking at one prospectus, I can see a range of differences in the offers. I am likely to be offered a place to study theology with CCC grades, and town and country planning with BCD. If I want to study plant science I might just get away with BCE – that looks like the lowest offer of all the courses. For mathematics, however, I must offer grades of ACC or BBC; for geography and archaeology grades in the range BBB to BCD; whilst to study law I will need a straight, no-nonsense ABB.

These grades cannot be simply in any subject I care to take. For example, to get in to study pharmacy I will need grades in the BBC to BCC area, but these passes must be *in chemistry and two from the three of maths, physics and the biological subjects*. And I am also told I will need a pass in maths at O level or GCSE. Close study of the prospectus is repaid, for I am also told a little about the grades obtained by final intakes of students. This is dependent on A-level results in a particular year and cannot be predicted with certainty. The prospectus says of one course, 'Present offers are usually for grades BBC/BCC, but the average intake is better than BBC.' So if I want to be sure then I have got to target myself for *at least* BBC. And if I do not think I will make those grades then perhaps I should go on looking for alternative courses. So read carefully and think hard about course offers and the level of grades of the likely intake.

If you cannot get hold of all the prospectuses or want a kick start, you will find guidance on offers across the range of institutions in the publications we have mentioned above. It is also useful to consult Brian Heap's **The Complete Degree Course Offers,** which is published annually by Trotman. This will give you up-to-date information on which A-level subjects you will need, and which grades, for all the degrees on offer. But if you are going for a particular course *be sure and check the prospectus of the particular department.*

You may eventually get offered a place with lower grades than those required by your offer. But at this stage you need to know the kind of target most people will have to aim at so check all entry requirements with the greatest care.

Box 3.3   Timetable for applying for a course

1 September	Application forms accepted
15 October	Last date for applicants who are including Oxford and Cambridge on their forms
15 December	Last date for other applications
16 December onwards	Late applications procedure
February	Interviews commence
	Applications to Art and Design Admissions Registry (ADAR) for art and design courses
15 May	Not more than one offer may be held after this together with an insurance offer

16 May	Interviews commence for those with a first choice of an ADAR application
27 May	Applications received from this date until late September will go into the clearing house scheme
16 June	ADAR clearing house procedure
30 June	All grant applications should be in – check your local education authority's cut-off date
Third week in August	A-level results
August – September	Clearing house procedure

3.4 Applying for your course

By the summer before your A-level year you should know exactly where you stand. Clarify your decision finally with parents, teachers, career advisers and friends. This is important because applications for universities and colleges have to be in between 1 September and 15 December in the year before you will start your course. Cambridge and Oxford require a preliminary application form to be submitted and an admission procedure application by 15 October (see Box 3.3). Use the *summer* to finalise your plans and, if you are not in full-time education, to send off for application forms. *Apply as early as you can. Most admissions tutors start filling places before the December deadline for applications.*

Until 1993 applications to the traditional universities were made through the Universities Central Council on Admission (UCCA). Application to polytechnics and some of the colleges was through the Polytechnics Central Admissions System (PCAS). From 1992 UCCA and PCAS used a joint form. Those applying to enter university in 1993–4 will use a new unified system. UCCA and PCAS have now merged to form the Universities and Colleges Admissions Service (UCAS). If you want to enter a new or old university or a major college or institute of higher education from October 1994 you should apply to

UCAS
PO Box 67
Cheltenham
Gloucester GL50 3SF

Remember: The admission system simply provides an application procedure. The decisions on your application will be taken not by UCAS but by the institutions themselves.

Cambridge and Oxford Universities

- **Application to** *Cambridge University* is through specific application to the college or through an open application to

  Cambridge Intercollegiate Applications Office
  Kellet Lodge
  Tennis Court Road
  Cambridge CB2 1QJ

Ask for a copy of the **Cambridge Admissions Prospectus,** which is available from that address. The Central Admissions System form must also be used if you are applying to other universities as well. It is also useful to consult the **Cambridge University Handbook.**

Application to *Oxford University* is also direct to the colleges although students must also meet the entry requirements of the university. The **Oxford Undergraduate Prospectus** is available from

Admissions Office
University Offices
Wellington Square
Oxford OX1 2JD

The Central Admissions System form must be used if applying to other universities as well. You cannot apply to Oxford and Cambridge in the same year – unless you wish to apply for an organ award at both universities.

UCCA/PCAS

PO Box 67, Cheltenham, Glos. GL50 3SF

Attach your application fee here with a paperclip

● YOU MUST READ THE ENCLOSED INSTRUCTIONS BEFORE COMPLETING THE FORM
● USE BLACK INK OR TYPE

APPLICATION FORM FOR ENTRY IN **1993**

222

9740694

1 SURNAME/ FAMILY NAME	2 PERSONAL DETAILS	Marital status
First name(s)		
Previous surname/family name		Sex
Correspondence address	Date of Birth	
	Your age on 30 September 1993: Years / Months	
		Disability: special needs
Postcode	Area of permanent residence	
Telephone (including STD code)	Country of Birth	
Home address (if different)	Nationality	
		Residential category
Postcode		Fee code
Telephone (including STD code)	Date of first entry to the UK	

3A INSTITUTIONS IN THE UCCA SCHEME

(a) Institution code name	(b) Institution code no.	(c) Course code	(d) Course code name	(e) Further requested details	Prev Applic'n (year)	Defer entry	Home

If you have previously applied through UCCA please give the serial or application number of your most recent application.

3B INSTITUTIONS IN THE PCAS SCHEME

(a) Institution code name	(b) Institution code no.	(c) Course code	(d) Course code name	(e) Further requested details	Prev Applic'n (year)	Defer entry	Home

4 EDUCATION FROM AGE 11	From Month / Year	To Month / Year	PT, FT or SW

5 PLANNING STATISTICS	SCHOOL CODE	A AS H C W P
A Occupational Background		
		BTEC HSC ILC M WR OEQ
B Ethnic Origin		

Page 1

Figure 3.2 Excerpts from UCCA/PCAS form
(Source: UCCA)
The UCAS form for 1994 will be essentially the same as the UCCA/PCAS form.

ACADEMIC QUALIFICATIONS

6A Examinations or assessments for which results are known.

Examination			Subject	Level	Result Grade or Band	Examination			Subject		Level	Result Grade or Band
Month	Year	Board				Month	Year	Board				

6B Examinations or assessments to be completed, or results pending

Examination			Subject	Level	(i) GCE/SEB/GCSE Examination centre address and/or centre number or (ii) title of examination	Institution Use	
Month	Year	Board				Req'd	Actual

6C Qualifications awarded by BTEC or SCOTVEC

Unit, module or component title	Month/ Year taken	SCOTVEC module number or BTEC level	value	Results (where known)

Title of Award held	Qual'n	Title					
Title of current qualification	Qual'n	Title					

BTEC registration number for current qualification

Name and brief address of college

Unit, module or component title	Month/ Year taken	SCOTVEC module level	BTEC value	Results (where known)			

Page 2

Figure 3.2 Excerpts from UCCA/PCAS form
(Source: UCCA)

7 Do you have an up-to-date (post 16) Record of Achievement?   YES/NO

8 Physical or other disability or medical condition including any which might necessitate special arrangements or facilities

9 FURTHER INFORMATION

10 Declaration: I confirm that, to the best of my knowledge, the information given in this form is correct and complete. I have read the *instructions, in particular paragraphs 72-74*. I understand what they say, and I agree to abide by the conditions set out there, which I accept as conditions of this application.

Applicant's Signature	Date	This form must be accompanied by the appropriate fee, either £7.00 or £14.00

Page 3

UCCA/PCAS

PO Box 67, Cheltenham, Glos. GL50 3SF.
UCCA/PCAS are Registered Educational Charities
Reference (strictly confidential unless stated otherwise by referee)

Name of referee

Post/Occupation/Relationship		Type of school or college		
Address		Total number of students in post-16 education		Full time
				Part time
	Telephone (including STD code)	Number normally proceeding to higher education each year		

Name of Applicant (block capitals or type)

Section 6 checked as correct?	Yes	No	Signed:	
Correct fee and stamped acknowledgement card enclosed?	Yes	No	Date:	HAVE YOU ENTERED YOUR SCHOOL CODE ON PAGE 1?

Page 4

Figure 3.2   Excerpts from UCCA/PCAS form
(Source: UCCA)

The Open University   Application is direct to
The Open University
Walton Hall
Milton Keynes MK7 6AA

Remember: The Open University academic year commences in February. Applications have to be in by the end of the previous September.

Colleges and Institutes of Education   Applications for most B.Ed. courses must now be made through the Central Admissions System.

Art and design courses   Applications for higher education courses in these subjects go to
The Art and Design Admissions Register
Penn House
9 Broad Street
Hereford HR4 9AP

Occupational therapy   You apply through the college clearing house:
College of Occupational Therapists
20 Rede Place
Bayswater
London W2 4TN

Physiotherapy   Candidates for qualifications in physiotherapy apply through the Central Admissions Unit for Physiotherapy Students:
Chartered Society of Physiotherapy
14 Bedford Row
London WC1 4ED

Social work You need to get full details from
The Central Council for Education and Training in Social
  Work
Derbyshire House
St. Chad Street
London WC1H 8AD

Filling in the form

Have a look at the form on pp. 85–7. Whilst forms differ slightly from year to year, the substance remains similar. So here are a few general tips.

- **Read the whole form through thoroughly.** Before you write anything, read the instructions and guidance again. Underline important points.
- **Make a copy of the form** so that you can use it **to make a draft** which you can then ask a teacher or friend to check. Make sure you keep a copy of the *completed* form for future use.
- **Check** well beforehand **with your chosen referee** that he or she is willing and able to act in this capacity. Check the time scale for submission so that you can get the form to your referee in good time.
- **Check you have got the college and course *code numbers* right and the correct *address for correspondence*.** If you are moving, it is safer to give your school or college address.
- **Put down a *phone number*** if at all possible. Some admission tutors prefer to ring, particularly if they have to rearrange interviews at the last minute.
- **Use black pen** or biro for ease of copying. **Print** in block capitals. Remember your form has to be readable when copied and reduced.
- **Check your spelling.** Misspelling can make a bad impression.

● **Enclose the required fees.**

Specific points about the form

Personal details   If you have a disability which may require special arrangements, mention it here as well as specifically later on.

Choosing institutions   Leave this until the end. (See 'Choice of courses' below.)

Details on ethnic origin and occupational background   These do not go to the institutions you choose. This information helps UCCA monitor how access is increasing.

Academic qualifications and exams   Admissions tutors will look carefully at this section. So be clear, specific and complete. Mention if you have a Record of Achievement. But do not attach it. Take it to interviews.

Further information   Admissions tutors will scrutinise this section in detail to see if it gives you an edge over other applicants. Project yourself:

● Write about: why you want to study your particular subject; your achievements and responsibilities at school or college; your outside interests – your hobbies, sporting activities, interests in drama, music, ornithology or whatever.
● Give brief details of work experience and sponsorship applications.
● Mention any awards you have received and the relevance of any travel undertaken.
● If you wish to defer entry for a year make sure you explain why here.
● Put down a brief word on how you see your future and careers which interest you.

- If you are an older student you may wish to include a brief curriculum vitae. This section is obviously of vital importance for mature students lacking conventional qualifications.

If you cannot get it all on the space provided, clip on a separate sheet. Make your statement a planned coherent piece of writing, not a series of swiftly jotted down notes. Sell yourself as a serious, committed and *interesting* person.

Confidential statement Here your referee will normally write about your academic achievements and likely progress, the contribution you have made to school or college, your personal qualities and how much of a success you are likely to make of the courses you have chosen.

Choice of courses

From 1993 you can make up to *eight* choices from the new unified university sector. Make sure your guide to courses is up to date, as codes can change. Think carefully before finally deciding on your choices. Remember to consider the popularity and degree of demand for particular courses and any advice institutions themselves give you.

- *Do not indicate an order of preference.*
- Put down at least one course which usually requires lower grades as a fallback in case you do worse than expected. If you apply for five top courses at top universities all requiring high grades you have no insurance policy against not achieving first-class results.
- Do not apply for too wide a range of subjects – English literature followed by zoology.
- Use abbreviations for the names of institutions and check code numbers.

In the end, it all comes back to knowing about the course and the level of offers, realistically assessing your chances and choosing *courses you have a reasonable chance of gaining admission to.*

Finally, do not forget to put down details of previous applications, and if you are willing to live at home, tick the appropriate column.

You will receive an acknowledgement of your form with an application number. Use this in all future correspondence.

The position with Oxbridge is somewhat different – you can apply in the year you are taking your A levels but this may place an additional burden on you. Interviews begin in September and for Oxford (no longer for Cambridge) there is an entrance examination in November. However, you may not have to sit this if you receive an offer after interview conditional on achieving certain A-level grades. None the less, many schools prefer to leave Oxbridge entrance to after A levels. Candidates will normally be expected to attain high grades in the absence of taking the exam. ABB is not uncommon. A decision to apply to Oxford and/or Cambridge will therefore require careful consideration.

Offers

What if you miss the 15 December closing date for applications? Until 26 May the admissions system will send your late application on to the institutions you have picked. It is up to them whether they are willing to consider your application. After that they will send your form to the institutions *for information* and you *may* get into the clearing house stage. So do not miss the 15 December cut-off point.

- You may receive offers on the basis of your application form alone or you may be asked to attend for interview.
- Offers may be *unconditional* – if you already possess suitable grades.
- More normally they will be *conditional* offers: you will be accepted if you attain certain grades in your exams.
- Or you may receive a rejection.

You may want to firmly accept an offer – for example, if you get an excellent offer from your first choice. This commits you – *so be sure*. If you definitely want to reject any offer you can do so by filling in the reply slip attached to the offer letter. After 31 March you will receive a statement of all your offers and you must indicate which you wish to accept. You can *hold two offers* (one additional offer should you not meet the conditions of your first choice). All the rest must be declined. You must respond or lose all offers. Select your preferred course and an insurance offer which requires lower grades.

Interviews

The colleges to which you have applied will be looking at your application to assess your potential. This is a competitive process; they will also be looking at the forms of other candidates. So a lot will depend on the popularity of the courses you have applied for. Applications will be studied by the admissions tutor. He or she will divide them into a number of categories – 'accept', 'interview', 'reject' – according to departmental policy. A second opinion from other members of staff will be sought.

- Some departments believe in interviewing everybody; some, only borderline cases.
- Some candidates receive offers *without formal interview*, although they may then be invited to an 'introduction' meeting at the department. It is important to attend this meeting as you will meet the head of department, admissions tutor and student representatives there.
- Other candidates are called for an interview. The style of this can vary, from the traditional position where you are interviewed by one or two members of staff to the admissions meeting where you are interviewed individually but then meet with other candidates, the staff and students of the department.

Admissions staff conducting interviews are aware of the

restrictions of a 20–40 minute talk and they allow for nerves. They know first impressions have their limitations. They will place emphasis on what you *have done*, and what your referee (who knows you better) forecasts you *will achieve*, not on the fact you are initially tongue-tied. The interview also provides you with an opportunity to see the department of your choice at first hand and quiz those at the chalkface.

If you *are* called for interview, some preparation is useful.

- Get your planning – arrangements for travel, overnight stay and so on – out of the way early. If in difficulty phone the college and explain.
- Carefully re-read the course prospectus and your application form.
- Arrive early. Remember college buildings are often scattered and rooms difficult to find, so consult any maps you are sent.
- Don't smoke.
- You are likely to be asked questions about what you have written on your form: 'Tell us more about the work you are doing in physics. Are you enjoying chemistry? What is the easiest area . . . what is the part you find hardest? Have you been pursuing your interest in chess?'
- You are likely to be asked why you want to study *this* subject in *this* department in *this* college. Remember, 'Because I like it . . . because it is interesting . . .' is not good enough. Before your interview think through why you like it . . . why it is interesting. Give as full and detailed an answer as you can to each question.
- You are likely to be asked about the kind of problems you envisage in your life as a student. You might be asked what you want to do with your degree.
- You might be asked about general interests such as what newspapers you read (so make sure you read them that morning!); what you think of some important event; what books you have read recently.

- You might even be asked what you think about recent developments in higher education.

Students are sometimes thrown by the fact that questions are so unspecific and broad. But as most of the areas you will be asked about are reasonably obvious, half an hour making a few notes and then asking a friend or parent to quiz you is well worthwhile. Do your best to appear confident and enthusiastic by thinking through the good reasons you have for wanting to take this course and the hard work you have put in already. Remember, your interviewer is simply trying to find out more about you, particularly how strongly motivated you are, how you think, how you respond to challenges. Tutors are asking themselves, will this candidate last the course and make a contribution to this department?

Finally, have to hand one or two questions to raise at the end of the interview.

If you are worried about interviews you may find it useful to consult *Coping with Interviews* by Martin Higham (New Opportunity Press, 1989), which is available from Yeoman House, 76 St James Lane, London N10 7RP.

The safety net

If your A-level results fall short of the grades required you may still get in, depending on the results of other applicants. If the worse comes to the worst and you have simply received a succession of rejection slips, do not lose heart. You will go into the clearing house scheme, so long as you have the minimum entrance requirement. August and September are hectic months in which the clearing house panels try to match your preference in terms of course, institution and region with what vacancies there are remaining.

You will have more forms to fill in, but having come this far, the journey is worth seeing through to the end. The system becomes very much a lottery and your future will depend on your A-level grades, the overall standards and the number of places unfilled. You may well have to show powers of adjustment and accept an alternative destination.

Help

There is a helpline for advice on clearing on (0242) 222444 and (0242) 227788.

You can also get in touch with institutions direct. Lists of vacancies are available at careers offices and are published in the quality press. The *Observer*, the *Independent* and *The Sunday Times* give detailed coverage of vacancies and run student support services. The electronic education networks Campus 2000 and ECTIS 2000 are also a source of vacancy details updated daily by the admissions system. Access is available through more than 1,000 schools and local authority careers offices.

When you are clear that there are vacancies for a particular course, telephone. Admissions staff prefer to talk to you, not your parents. Remember to quote your reference, your results and the course code. As soon as a department is interested, you must ask it to immediately put in a request to the relevant admission system for your application forms.

3.5   Special groups of students

Mature students

Box 3.4   Better late than never

Even the old universities are admitting a growing number of mature students. Since 1985/86 the percentage of full-time UK-based new entrants to first-degree courses aged 21 and over has grown – from 10.5% to 14.5% in 1991. Good but perhaps not good enough.

'Well I think I'm really ready for it now. I really feel I want to do something different. Whereas, if I'd stopped on at school and gone on to university then, I'd have been doing it for a job qualification more than anything else.'

'And what will you be doing it for now?'

Lucy had a sip of sherry before she replied,

'Because I want to.' It sounded like a child's answer.

'I feel as if I've been asleep for a long time and I'm just beginning to wake up.'

Barry Hines, *Unfinished Business*.

Much of the above may apply to students outside the 18–21 age group – except for the fact that if you are not at school you will have to be more self-reliant in digging out information and watching dates. However, whilst older people can pursue the conventional A-level route, there are alternatives. There is, just now, a greater interest in mature students because universities want to expand their base and minimise any decline in applications from the conventional age group, and because of the general emphasis on wider access. There are a number of helpful booklets about, such as **Mature Students and Universities** (available from CVCP and UCCA) and also books such as **The Mature Students Handbook** by M. Korving (Kogan Page, regularly updated) and **Making the Grade, Volume 2** by B. Jones and R. Johnson (Manchester University Press, 1990).

Many universities are now willing to admit older applicants without A levels. There are a variety of different routes.

- Some institutions will consider the existing BTEC qualifications instead of, or in addition to, A levels.
- More informally, some universities will admit mature

students on the basis of an essay, an interview and evidence of useful work experience. Others will require, in addition, some study experience and sometimes some qualifications. Basically they want evidence that you can make it.

● Some will ask you to complete a preparatory or access course successfully.

Almost all further and higher education bodies now mount a range of access courses, mostly part time, intended specifically to equip the mature student to enter higher education.

● Some are *subject specific*, intended to provide you with the basic knowledge and skills required to start a degree course in a particular subject.
● Some are *group specific*, intended to cater for women returning to study or ethnic minority groups.
● Some are *general* and based largely on study skills.

Your local education authority will publish a directory of access courses and you will find a variety mounted at your local university. You may want to go for *kite-marked courses* which are validated and which guarantee a university place upon successful completion.

A variety of 'crash' courses are also emerging. Greenwich University offers an intensive September bridging course to those who get a single A level but still want to take a science degree. The CVCP have given a lot of support to a four-year STEPS degree course on offer at more than 20 universities for those who have no A levels but want to take an engineering qualification.

Groups of universities operate more formal entry schemes. For example, the Mature Matriculation Scheme of the Joint Matriculation Board (which includes five of the older universities) involves a mix of interview, essay and written examination. A new development is *open learning*. To take one example, the Open College of the North West set out in 1979 specifically to provide alternatives to A-level study for mature students. Each credit recognises a unit of 50 hours; the accumulation of a number of credits qualifies you for entry to higher education. There is also now a credit transfer system by which you can build up credits through studying in different localities.

The important point is this: as a mature student do you really need to take A levels? There is an alternative, well-trodden, informal route with several paths. Would you not be better off following a route which is specifically tailored to your needs? If you take A levels and do badly, you would be worse off than before you started. Think carefully about which is the best approach for you. Follow the earlier advice on diagnosing which courses and institutions you would like to enter. And before doing anything further, write with a brief *curriculum vitae* and arrange an appointment with the Mature Students Adviser and the admissions tutors for the courses that interest you.

If it is a matter of having no qualifications at all, do not forget the Open University and its wide range of degree courses which require no formal qualifications.

Box 3.4   The Open University

This is one of higher education's recent success stories. To register you have to be over 21 but you can be 80 – and some students have been. The key features of the OU are

- No entry qualifications are required. You are admitted on a 'first come, first served' basis. Study is part-time.
- Study is through specially prepared distance learning materials – which attempt to combine rigour with clarity – and radio and television programmes, as well as tutorials and summer schools.
- Degrees are constructed on a modular system. Each course you successfully complete gives you a credit or a half credit. When you have built up six credits you qualify for a general

degree. With eight credits you get an honours degree.

The Open University is well worth considering. The educational materials are first class and *you can study at your own
pace*. But do not think you can sail in just like that! Serious
learning is involved. So if you have not studied before or for
some time, a preparatory course may be useful.

Research shows that many mature students worry unduly
about going to university. Reviewing the evidence in the
mid-1980s Alan Woodley found that, overall, mature students
did better in their finals than those from the conventional age
group; students in the 26–30 age group did best of all
(Woodley, 1985). An authoritative research survey found that
applications through the JMB scheme had doubled in ten years.
Moreover, the research report concluded,

Unqualified adults admitted through this mature entry scheme were
found on average to do rather better than other university students in
terms of the qualifications achieved and specifically in areas where
experience plays an important part, particularly education and the
social sciences and also law, mature entrants tended to come out on
top. (Smithers and Griffin, 1986)

Make a careful inventory of your domestic and financial
situation, your attachment to present or future employment
and the enhanced prospects a degree will give you. You may
not wish to give up a job which is rewarding – or be able to
afford it. You may have accumulated sufficient capital to take a
long job holiday – or you may be taking retirement early.

Part time or full time?

Part-time study can allow you to have your cake and eat it.
But if you take it seriously there is going to be less cake. You are
going to have to give up a lot of your spare time. Because study
for a part-time degree can take six years you are going to need
stamina. Time is vital, particularly when you start – and you
are going to have less of it than the full-time student. Your

studying will be lonelier; you will have less opportunity for educational and social interaction. On the other hand, you will hopefully come out at the other end with both continuity and progression in your job (not to speak of the income otherwise foregone) *and a degree*. All in all, this is a difficult decision which requires carefull discussion with family and those at work. It is also helpful to get some idea of the demands by talking to staff and admission tutors.

The largest provision of part-time degrees has consisted of the University of London External Degree programme. Birkbeck College, University of London has always been heavily involved in part-time degree work and has recently taken on an expanded range of courses for adults. So has the Open University. Now a wide range of universities are offering a variety of degrees specifically tailored for the part-time student on a mix of day and evening or evening-only teaching. These often operate on a flexible basis so that you can select from a large number of modules and gradually build up credits towards your degree.

A good book to get hold of is **Part-time Degrees, Diplomas and Certificates: A Guide to Part-time Higher Education Courses** by Malcolm Tight (Careers Research and Advisory Council). This book is regularly updated.

If you are particularly interested in sandwich courses, which mix study and work experience, then you should consult M. Brewer and G. Wallace-Hadrill's **Sandwich Courses: a Guide to All Courses in Universities, Polytechnics and Colleges** (Careers Research and Advisory Council), which is also regularly updated.

Overseas students

If you are a student from outside the UK there are a number of additional points you will have to take into account in choosing a course of study and pursuing your application. Your school or college should have a copy of **Higher Education** in the U.K.: A Handbook for Students and Their Advisers (Longmans for Association of Commonwealth Universities). This book is updated annually.

You will also be able to obtain a wealth of information and advice from your local office of the British Council. Make sure you get hold of their excellent publication **How to Live in Britain**. It is important to bear the following in mind.

- The university or college you are applying to has the final word on how relevant local qualifications are for obtaining admission.
- A good standard of English is required for degree studies and you may be asked to take a test in your own country or at the British Embassy.
- Some institutions also offer 'bridging courses' when students arrive in the UK.
- You will also need to be very clear on such issues as tuition fees and arrangements for entry to the UK.

Disabled students

Write as early as possible to the departments of your choice well before you complete your application form. Explain fully the nature of your disability and ask what resources and facilities will be available. Ask if they have had previous experience with students in your position and for details of access to the campus teaching rooms, libraries, and recreational and welfare facilities. You should try to visit the institutions prior to application.

Most institutions now judge applications from disabled people first of all on academic criteria. They then look at the nature of the disability and arrange an interview. There should be a policy statement on disability with your prospectus, which will state who is responsible for implementation. Progress has been made in the development of facilities but some institutions still lag behind. A very useful guide published by the

National Bureau for Handicapped Students is **Applying to Higher Education: Notes for Disabled Students, Their Parents and Advisers**, which is available from NBHS, 336 Brixton Road, London SW9 7AA.

Key points

1 As soon as possible start the process of self-assessment to decide whether you wish to go to university and which course you wish to pursue.
2 Study prospectuses and guidance books. Talk to friends, family and teachers. Link this process, if possible, to choice of A levels.
3 If you are a mature student, think and take advice as to whether the A-level or an alternative route is preferable. Decide on a full-time or part-time course.
4 Before the start of your pre-college year, review and clarify your decisions. Be clear as to exactly which qualifications and grades you will require for entry to the courses of your choice. Remember: for many courses competition is strong and standards are rising.
5 Be aware of the timetable for applications and how the system works. Spend time in filling in the application forms.
6 Prepare for interviews.
7 Think strategically about offers.
8 If you are unsuccessful, make one final effort using the clearing process. If ultimately unsuccessful, review prospects for the coming year.

Things to do

1 Discuss the arguments for and against an 18-year-old school student with adequate qualifications spending the next three years in higher education.
2 'It would be far better for most people if, instead of having a block of formal education from 18 to 21, they went to college for shorter periods throughout their life.' Do you agree?
3 Working in pairs, prepare a detailed analysis of your partner's ability and qualifications to do well on a higher education course.
4 Using prospectuses, make a report on the advantages and disadvantages of studying physics and history at three different universities.

5 Complete a copy of the UCCA/PCAS form. Discuss difficulties and problems and compare your responses with those of your fellow students.

6 Discuss the most important points involved in interviewing well.

7 Role-play this exercise in groups of three.

Each student has a copy of the same properly completed UCAS form. One student is an admissions tutor, another a candidate for entrance to Lovecity University. After preparation, role-play an interview on the basis of the form. The third student should assess performance and make a critical report back when the interview is complete.

Further reading

A lot of practical books are cited in the text of this chapter. So why not read something more imaginative? *My Cambridge*, edited by Ronald Hayman and *My Oxford*, edited by Ann Thwaite (both published by Robson Books, 1977) consist of recollections by distinguished artists and figures in public life. (It should be borne in mind, though, that Cambridge and Oxford are not exactly typical universities.)

Or why not try a novel? Whilst books as different as Kingsley Amis's *Lucky Jim*, C.P. Snow's *The Masters*, Evelyn Waugh's *Brideshead Revisited*, Howard Jacobson's *Coming from Behind*, or Mary McCarthy's *The Groves of Academe* are unlikely to deepen your understanding of how higher education operates today, they do contain insights and are worth reading in themselves. David Lodge's *Nice Work,* which is about an academic who 'shadows' an industrialist is (amongst other things) an illuminative satire on some of the issues we discussed in Chapters 1 and 2. It certainly shows how many academics are out of touch with life as most people live it. One of the best novels ever written about what it means to try to be a scholar is John Williams's *Stoner*. It is now out of print but you might find a copy in a good library.

4

Getting on

... money makes money as well as everything else

Charles Dickens, *Our Mutual Friend*

4.1 **Introduction**

In a recent survey three quarters of first-year students said that the biggest problem they faced was lack of money. At the end of their first year more than 50% had bank overdrafts and 10% were over £500 in debt (Higher Education Information Services Trust/PCAS, 1991). Over the last decade the system of student finance has been under strain – some would say it has cracked under that strain. The real value of grants has declined and part of the grant has now been replaced by the 'top-up' loan system introduced in 1990. The amount of student debt has increased dramatically. Several student unions have been reported as advising students to reconsider the possibility of full-time study: 'we are now in the position of having to ask students to seriously consider whether they might not be better off doing a part-time course and claiming benefits' (Tysome and Richards, 1991).

The start of every academic year now witnesses the sight of thousands of students with no accommodation, sleeping on the floor of university buildings. The squeeze on educational expenditure and the increase in student numbers has put pressure on hall of residence accommodation; this has gone hand in hand with the deregulation of the housing market and price increases in the private rented sector. The first six weeks of the autumn term are often chaotic; some students have been driven to squatting.

Unfortunately, it is often a case of shoes before Shakespeare! You cannot concentrate on your work as a student until you have a roof over your head and money to meet your basic needs in your pocket. Clausewitz, the great German military strategist, said money was the sinews of war: it is also the sinews of study. It is important, therefore, that as soon as you have a firm offer of a place you turn your attention to the mundane matters of finance and housing. The sooner you get these settled, the less likely you are to be diverted from your main object — studying for your degree.

This chapter provides you with basic information and commonsense suggestions on your financial position and accommodation. It will provide you with a basis on which to discuss your problems with others and confront specific difficulties.

- In Section 4.2 we talk about the system of student finance. Briefly we outline the present position on grants, student loans and access funds, scholarships, sponsorship.
- Section 4.3 then gives some advice on how to use banks and practise budgeting to manage the money you have, and goes on to look at some of the arguments about student finance.
- Section 4.4 deals with the problem of accommodation. In it we cover the different types of accommodation that may be available to you; a range of problems that arise in renting property; and the legal position covering various kinds of tenancy.

4.2 Getting support

Your local education authority (or the Scottish Office) will pay your tuition fees direct to your university. Your main source of income will come from grants and loans. You may be able to supplement these with grants from trusts and charities, scholarship awards or sponsorships. At some point in your student career you will probably want to generate more income through taking a part-time job. We will look at each of these in turn.

Grants

Your major source of income will be the maintenance grant paid directly to you from your local education authority. On being accepted by your college, you should become eligible for a *mandatory grant*. However,

- if you have already completed a similar course in the past for which you received a grant, or
- you started another course and dropped out at some stage, or
- you have not been resident in the UK for three years,

then the award of a grant to you is not automatic. The local authority can look at all the details of your position and decide whether or not to make you a *discretionary grant*.

Grants are available for degree and other higher education courses such as the Dip.H.E. The level of grants was frozen by the government from September 1990. Table 4.1 shows how the mandatory grant is now awarded.

Table 4.1   Mandatory grants

Accommodation	Amount
Parental home	£1,795
Own accommodation	£2,265
In London	
Parental home	£1,795
Own accommodation	£2,845
From Scotland	
Parental home	£1,660
Own accommodation	£2,200
In London	£2,780

Two points to remember:

1. Local education authorities may pay you the lower rate of grant if they feel you could conveniently attend the course from your parental home.
2. These figures include an element for travel, so you will have to pay any extra costs yourself.

Parental contributions

You will be treated as dependent on your parents unless

*   you are over 25 before 1 September in the year you start the course;
*   you have supported yourself for at least the previous three years; or
*   you have been married for at least two years before your course starts.

If you are dependent on your parents, in the sense that you cannot meet any of these conditions, their income will be assessed to see if they have to make a *parental contribution* to your grant. This is *means tested*. How much they have to contribute – if anything – will depend on their financial position and the extent of their other commitments. You may receive the full mandatory grant; at the other end of the scale, you may receive a reduced grant or even nothing at all – it is your parents, not the local education authority, who are now expected to pay the full amount of grant to you. If after assessment your parents are found to be liable for contribution it is *assumed* that this contribution will be paid.

The parental contribution is assessed on your parents' *residual income*. This is estimated by deducting the following from their total income:

*   allowances for dependent adults with income less than £1,810 (during the 1993–4 financial year),
*   interest payments, such as on a mortgage, and

● payments to pension, superannuation and life insurance schemes.

Further allowances are then made for other children dependent on your parents, for parents living abroad and domestic assistance in certain circumstances. If your parents' residual income is less than £14,345 then there is no contribution. If several children are attending university then the residual income will be far higher as the parental contribution will be divided proportionately between the children (see Table 4.2).

Table 4.2   Parental contribution to dependent students' grants

Residual income	Contribution
£14,344	Nil
£14,345	£45
£15,000	£101
£20,000	£589
£25,000	£1,195
£30,000	£1,890
£35,000	£2,642
£40,000	£3,394
£45,000	£4,146
£50,000	£4,897
£53,000	£5,349
£55,999 or more	£5,800

For residual income from £14,345 to £18,344 your parents have to contribute £1 for every £11.60 they earn. From £18,335 to £26,944 it is £1 for every £8.25. From £26,945 they are expected to pay £1 for every £6.65.

If you are an '*independent*' married student, an amount from your partner will be calculated as 'parental' contribution and deducted from your grant. If you have been married for at least two years and your partner has sufficient residual income, they will have to contribute on a fixed scale (see Table 4.3). If there are children dependent on you or your partner, the contribution is reduced by £75 for each child.

Table 4.3   Partners' contribution to dependent students' grants

Residual income	Contribution
£11,350	£10
£15,000	£427
£20,000	£1,074
£25,000	£1,874
£30,000	£2,796
£35,000	£3,796
£40,000	£4,796
£45,020 or more	£5,800

For residual income from £11,350 to £18,334 your partner has to contribute £1 for every £8.75 that he or she earns. From £18,335 to £26,944 the figure is £1 for every £6.25. And from £26,945 it is £1 for every £5.00.

Your local authority will provide you with a leaflet showing exactly how contributions are calculated for the coming year, as they are examined annually. You should also read thoroughly **Student Grants and Loans: A Brief Guide,** which is available free from your local education authority or DFE Publications, Despatch Centre, Honeypot Lane, Canons Park, Stanmore, Middlesex HA7 1A2 or **Guide to Student Allowances,** which is available from the Scottish Education Department, Awards Branch, Gyleview House, Redheugh's Brigg, South Gyle, Edinburgh EH12 9HH. Also useful is **Guide to Grants: Designated Courses,** available from DFE, Elizabeth House, York Road, London SE1 7HN. The National Union of Students (461 Holloway Road, London N7 6LJ) also produce helpful leaflets on grants

Personal contribution

The principle is that all students who receive income during their course will have at least some of it deducted from their grant. However, you are entitled to keep

- all income from a job you take, or the first £3,735 if your employer releases you on full pay
- £3,735 for any scholarship or sponsorship you receive
- £1,750 from a trust income
- £2,925 of any pension income
- DSS benefits, child benefit and non-taxable disability pension
- earnings you receive for work experience or placements
- the first £770 from any other sources.

Additional payments

These are various extra allowances you can claim on top of your basic grant. For example, the maintenance element is paid for 30 weeks of course time. So if your terms add up to more, you can receive additional grants of £71.20 per week (in London), £53.30 per week (away from home elsewhere) or £37.40 per week (living at home). As another example, if you are *studying abroad* as an essential aspect of your course for at least one term, you will be entitled to a higher grant.

Mature students

If you are 26 years of age or over at the start of your course and you have earned or received taxable social security benefits of £12,000 or more in the three years before you start your course then you are eligible for a *mature student award*. This is an annual sum paid *in addition to the basic grant* (see Table 4.4).

Table 4.4   Mature student awards

Age at start of course	Addition to grant (for 52 weeks)
26	£290
27	£515
28	£770
29	£1,005

Dependants' allowance

If you have dependants you will also be entitled to extra payment as shown in Table 4.5.

Table 4.5   Extra payments for dependants

Dependant Amount (for 52 weeks)	
Spouse/adult dependant (if single)/first child (if no other dependant)	£1,750
Children aged under 11	£370
Children aged 11–15	£735
Children aged 16–17	£970
Children aged 18 and over	£1,400

If you qualify for dependants' allowances and have to maintain two homes whilst studying, you are entitled to an extra £610 per annum.

Disabled students

Disabled students can receive extra allowances for travel and the following additional means-tested allowances:

● up to £4,550 a year for a non-medical personal helper

- up to £3,420 for special equipment
- up to £1,140 for other minor items necessary for the disabled.

Discretionary awards

These depend completely on the beneficence and goodwill of the local education authority; you have to convince them that you should receive an award. The best way to do this is to set out all your circumstances in full detail and argue for the money paid to be related to mandatory payments.

Applying for your grant

Contact your local education authority as soon as you have an offer. (In Scotland contact the Scottish Education Department, Haymarket House, Clifton Terrace, Edinburgh EH2 5DR.) They will tell you when to return your completed form and your parents' grant assessment form. Some authorities require it by the end of May; others, June. Do not miss the cut-off date. This will delay your grant.

Carefully check the figure for the coming year. Make sure your parents complete a grant assessment form. If you experience any problems in receiving your grant from the awards office at college or it is less (or more) than you expected, you should consult your Welfare and Information Office.

Student loans

In 1990 the government decided that grants would remain fixed at the levels outlined above. They would not be increased in coming years. Instead, a new system of 'top-up' loans would be available to students to compensate for the lost value of the grant and increases in the cost of living. For 1993–4 the maximum loan was

E

- £940 for London students away from home (£685 in the final year, as the summer vacation is not included)
- £800 for students outside the capital living away from home (£585 in the final year)
- £640 for students living at home (£470 in the final year).

The amounts available on loan will be increased each year until they reach the value of the mandatory award and the parental contribution. The government will then review the position.

The scheme works in the following way.

- The loans are available to students under 50 years of age on first-degree and equivalent courses and other courses for which mandatory grants are payable. You can apply for a loan between 1 September and 30 July the next year but colleges are not obliged to certify eligibility for loans after 30 June.
- Eligibility and application forms are available at your college. They will issue you with an eligibility certificate stating that you are on a recognised course. You do not have to borrow the whole amount available in a year but you can only make one application per year. You will need to produce a birth certificate – or, if you are an overseas student, a passport – as well as your award letter from your local education authority and details of your bank or building society account.
- Having received your certificate, send it and your application to

  The Student Loans Company
  100 Bothwell Street
  Glasgow G2 7JD.

  The loan will then be transferred to your bank account in one lump sum or three termly instalments.
- If you have problems, call the Student Loans Helpline, 0345 300 900. In the event of a dispute you can put your case to an assessor after letting the company have the complaint in

writing.

- You will have to start repaying the loan from 1 April in the year following the completion of your course. There is no fixed rate of interest on the loan, although the sum outstanding will be uprated in line with annual inflation. It is thus *not an interest-free loan*. And you will be charged interest at the rate of inflation registered when you took out the loan. Those taking out loans in 1993–4 will be charged interest at around 3%.

- Former students will be able to defer repayment on the grounds that their gross income is less than 85% of the national average wage, currently £15,000. In most cases, there will be a fixed repayment period of five years with monthly repayments.

Loss of benefits

As well as freezing grants, the government also ruled that most students are ineligible for state benefits. From 1990 students were no longer able to claim income support or housing benefit, although this does not apply to single parents, disabled students or student couples with dependants. *All* full-time students have lost entitlement to unemployment benefit the academic year is now deemed to last 52 weeks. The withdrawal of benefits has been an important and little publicised blow to many students.

Access funds

As some compensation for this, in 1990 the government introduced a system of access funds, which are provided to the educational institution in order to relieve student hardship. These are administered by the universities and colleges. If you are in difficulties, perhaps because you are not receiving either a full grant or a parental contribution or you have had to take high-cost, private rented accommodation, then you should contact your welfare officer to find how the scheme is operating at your college.

In the first year of operations, some institutions opted to dole out small amounts to large numbers rather than concentrate the funds on extreme cases. In 1990–1 12% of those eligible received payments. A survey at Brighton Polytechnic claimed that the average student applying for access funds was suffering a shortfall of approximately £36 a week.

For the second year of operation, access funds were increased by a little less than 1%, well below the level of inflation. A survey showed that by the end of the 1992 academic year 44% of institutions had used up their funds. The general view was that access funds have not compensated for the loss to students of £68 million state benefits.

Universities also operate *hardship funds* for students with financial difficulties, although these are usually geared to an easier financial climate.

Scholarships

Any scholarship you are awarded up to the value of £3,735 will be in addition to your grant. It is therefore worth keeping your eyes open for awards offered by your school, universities, professional institutions, trusts or charities. There are a number of (expensive) books you may wish to consult at college or in a reference library, including:

- Association of Commonwealth Universities, **Financial Aid for First Degree Study at Commonwealth Universities** (ACU, bi-annual)
- **The Grants Register** (Macmillan, bi-annual)
- Charities Aid Foundation, **Directory of Grant-Making Trusts** (CAF)

The Educational Grants Advisory Service, a division of the Family Welfare Association, advises students on problems and liaises with bodies which make grants to students. It publishes a valuable compendium which is expensive but which again may be consulted in a reference library: The Family Welfare Association, *Money to Study* (available from 501–5 Kingsland Road, London E8 4AU).

With the freezing of grants, the Department for Education advises students to apply to private trusts and charities. Some feel that this is government evading its own responsibilities in a situation where there is greater pressure than ever on grant-making bodies. The Educational Grants Advisory Service reported that requests increased by more than 50% in 1990 and that it will shortly be dealing with 10,000 applications annually. The service covers some 300 trusts but most have only very small budgets. At one end of the scale you might win an award of £1,000; at the other, £50 or £100. This is hardly going to solve the general problem of student maintenance.

Sponsorship

An increasing number of major companies sponsor students, normally with small payments of around £1,200 – and the guarantee of summer work. More than 5,000 new students are sponsored by companies every year and the number of sponsors has doubled over the last decade. Most sponsorships are available for the areas of science, technological and business studies. You need to be clear as to exactly what is involved and balance obligations – perhaps having to work for the company for a year on graduation or having to take certain courses – against financial benefits and useful, practical experience. For more information, you can send off for copies of

- **Sponsorships Offered to Students by Employers and Professional Bodies for First Degrees,** an annual publication from the Department of Employment, Department CW 1SCO5, The Paddock, Frizinghall, Bradford BD9 4HD
- **Industrial Sponsorship and the Universities,** an annual publication, free from the Universities and Colleges Admissions Service

- **The Which? Guide to Sponsorship in Higher Education** by Alan Jamieson (Consumers Association/Hodder and Stoughton)

It is useful to fully discuss the alternatives available and the specifics of any offered sponsorship with your admissions tutor.

Support for study abroad

COMETT   The European Community Action Programme for Technology. Grants are offered for students in relevant subjects who want to train or work in another EC country.

ERASMUS   The European Action Scheme for Mobility for University Students. Provides top-up grants to defray the cost of your study elsewhere in the EC as part of your cost.

LINGUA   Another EC programme to improve the learning of foreign languages. If you are taking a relevant course abroad you may be able to obtain assistance.

Further information is obtainable from

- U.K. ERASMUS Student Grants Council
  The University
  Canterbury
  Kent CT2 7PD
- The European Commission
  8 Storey's Gate
  London SW1P 3AT

Student finance

The introduction of the loans system prompted controversy over the whole question of student finance. Students suffering from the decline in the real value of grants (Figure 4.1) were also affected by the loss of social security benefits and the deregulation of the housing market in the late 1980s, which the

National Union of Students claimed increased rents by 10%. The initial national take-up rate for loans was low; 180,000 applied for loans in 1990–1 – less than 30% of those eligible. By the end of the 1992 academic year there were over 230,000 applications – approaching 40%. Many preferred to run up large overdrafts.

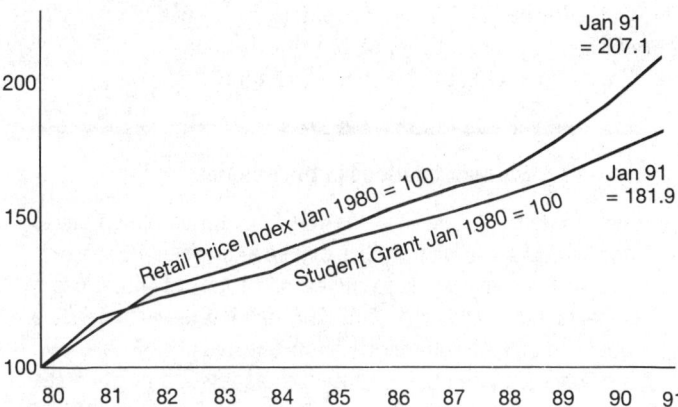

Figure 4.1 The decline of the grant
(Source: National Union of Students)

The new order was criticised by many who argued that access to higher education should be a right freely available to all who qualified for it. Loans involved students in paying for their own education. Yet this was a *social* investment, which should be a charge on the community through the taxation system. In the context of the low level of grants and their declining purchasing power, the introduction of loans would add new burdens to the student's financial load. In particular, it was claimed, they would deter students from underprivileged backgrounds from entering higher education. The Labour Party promised to abolish loans and replace them with a 'fairer system of grants'.

The government justified their decision by arguing that taxpayers were unable and/or unwilling to pay for the much

needed expansion of the education system. Loans worked in
other countries and would remain a limited and controlled
element in student finance. As students themselves would
benefit individually in increased earnings from a higher education, they should bear at least part of its cost. Working-class
people extensively used credit in other areas of their lives, why
not in education? Moreover, safety nets such as the access
funds would protect those in genuine difficulty.

For many the reality has been different.

Box 4.1   Student finances in the nineties

Karen Knott, 22, told how she was left with no option but to
drop out of a historical studies course at Sheffield Polytechnic
after just one year trying to survive on a total of £445. A loss in
benefits and allowances of £1,036 had left her with £8.80 a
week through the summer vacation. She had already taken out
a student loan and been refused an access grant. When she
wrote in desperation to Kenneth Clarke, the Secretary of State
for Education and Science, she received a reply from the DES
telling her there were no government funds for which she was
eligible and suggesting 'you may care to see if any of the
educational trusts or charities are prepared to help'.

Kim Tallie, a 32 year old single mother studying psychology
at the Polytechnic of East London, said a female friend had
taken up a job as a security guard which paid £2 an hour in an
effort to survive financially. 'We are turning into a nation of
part-time students in order to continue with our studies', she
said.

Times Higher Education Supplement, 12 July 1991

Whatever the advantages and disadvantages of loans – and
they do operate widely in other parts of the world – the real
problem is that they have been introduced into a under-

resourced system. They have been introduced to complement not a buoyant state award but one which already provided inadequate support.

4.3   Looking after the pennies

Students in the 1990s are in a very tough financial position. With the decline in the value of the grant, the majority of students are in a position where expenditure exceeds income. You therefore need to manage your finances extremely carefully. At the very beginning *make sure you have got every penny of grant to which you are entitled.*

Carefully scrutinise your entitlements and the parental contribution. Under 20% of students receive a full grant; the parents of the rest are expected to contribute. But there are no means of compelling them to do so and surveys show that only around 60% of students receive the full contribution. For the 40% who do not this is *the biggest cause of student hardship*. This question requires careful discussion with your parents. Whilst the sums required are often considerable, the full grant provides a *minimal financial basis* for students to organise their lives. If it is subject to parental deduction, problems inevitably increase; consequent difficulties can undermine your success as a student.

Banks

___

Box 4.1   Students and banks

The biggest bank in the student market is Nat West. It attracts 37% of student business, and with around 300 branches sited on or near college campuses it is the most accessible. But its policies towards students seem to have recently become somewhat less indulgent than of yore. Barclays has a 26%

market share whilst the Midland Bank with 115 campus branches has 23% of the student market and Lloyds has around 17%. In Scotland the Royal Bank of Scotland and the Bank of Scotland split 60% of student business between them. There is intense competition between banks for the student clientele, on the basis that today's students will be tomorrow's big earners and big spenders. If they treat you nice now you will stick with them when some real money is rolling in. Seventy-five per cent of students stay with the same bank when they graduate.

So maximise your position to find a bank which will suit you and give you a good deal.

Spend some time considering the best deal: then open a bank account quickly. (See Box 4.1). Find a bank used to dealing with students which has a branch near your college. It is best to shop around in your home town, where there will be branches of all the main banks, and discover what the position is. To ensure that your account will be open when your grant cheque arrives, open the account before you arrive at university.

Remember that whilst there is strong competition between banks they are always looking to cut costs. Introductory concessions on offer – cash gifts and Railcards, for example – can be useful, but look very carefully at what will concern you over the longer haul, such as bank charges and overdraft facilities. Most banks have a *student adviser*; ask to talk to him or her.

- Inquire as to the amount you will be allowed on overdraft and what the charges will be. Most banks allow a free overdraft of up to £400. But check: is it just for one year? In recent years banks have been tightening up. Establish what the position is if you go over your limits.
- Ensure that if your account stays in balance you will not pay any service charges.
- Ensure that your current account will earn interest and at what level.

- Check the facilities you will receive such as cheque card, cash dispenser card, immediate cash credit and commission-free travel facilities such as traveller's cheques.
- Ask what the position is regarding low cost loans.
- Compare the pros and cons of two or three banks before coming to a decision.
- Talk to friends about their experiences and periodically review your banking situation.

If you are lucky enough to be in credit for long periods, consider a building society account. Few banks pay interest; those that do, offer appallingly low rates. Make sure you receive regular bank statements: once a month is often too infrequent to allow you to keep up with your spending so that you may become unwittingly overdrawn.

When you get your bank statement, read it carefully and remember what your overdraft facility is. The banks have recently become 'charges happy'. Once you go over your overdraft limit most of them will start charging you interest. Some also start imposing charges of £15 for returned cheques and letters drawing your attention to your position – charges of £5 a day for monitoring accounts are becoming common. All this you can do without. You cannot afford it and it adds to your worries and eats into your time. So know how your bank account works, keep a keen eye on your 'ins' and 'outs'. Think carefully about standing orders and direct debit for regular payments such as rent or electricity. What about credit cards? Can you trust yourself with one? If so, keep a check on what you are spending and above all *try to plan your spending in advance*.

Budgeting

Careful spending in the first weeks of your student career will give you the practical experience to enable you to think realistically about budgeting. A number of universities produce material giving details of the likely costs of accommodation, food, clothing, energy, travel and so on for single students, a couple, and a couple with children, on an annual and weekly basis. See if you can dig out something similar to get you thinking about how much you will have to spend on different items.

Box 4.2   Budgeting

A. Cash in   £
                                    per week/per month/per term

- Grant
- Parental contribution
- Loan
- Scholarship
- Sponsorship
- Wages
- Any other benefit
- Other cash in
TOTAL

B. Cash out   £
                                    per week/per month/per term

- Rent/mortgage
- Local tax
- Gas
- Electricity
- Maintenance
- Food and housekeeping
- Laundry
- Telephone
- TV licence/rental
- Travel
- Clothes
- Books/equipment
- Insurance

- Entertainment
- Other
TOTAL
BALANCE

Work out how much money you will have coming in over the next term from your grant, loan and any wages and other benefits. (See Box 4.2.) Then look at your outgoings. Accommodation should be easy to estimate. Then think of any linked costs such as gas, electricity, insurance and telephone. And then comes food and clothing. And do not forget about books and equipment. You also need to think about travel and a fall-back 'contingency reserve'. Calculate your total income for the term and deduct estimated expenditure. Then divide the figure into weeks. You should now have an idea of how good or – more likely – how bad things are.

You won't be able to relate expenditure to income to the nearest decimal point. Nor would this be useful: unforeseen things come up. But if you do this exercise *after* a prudent two or three weeks, which will give you an idea of likely expenditure, it will provide a good general idea of your position. Of course you then have to cut your coat to the cloth available. *That* – involving, as it does, willpower, careful planning and an element of self-denial – is the hard part.

Exploration

Explore the facilities for food, drink and recreation around your college. Consult student guides which have first-hand advice on how and where to buy food, eat out, buy clothes, get your hair cut and watch films *cheaply*. Look for student discounts, a list of which will come with your National Union of Students membership card. Consider which form of transport is cheapest, and buy cheap student rail and coach cards. Remember that the bicycle combines economy and fitness. The more you work in the library rather than at home, the more you save on light and heating – but, of course, you can go too far with economising.

Working

Another approach is to attempt to *increase* your income by working. Working during vacation, when you have no classes or lectures, is traditional and unlikely to interfere with study. Your work period has a clear start and finish and if you relate it to your studies you can easily break vacation periods into work, study and play. Taking a part-time job during term-time causes far more problems. Many more students are being pushed into this position. It has advantages; work experience can help your development and increase your prospects with future experience. But the practice is being introduced piecemeal and informally into a system which is not built to cater for it. And much of the routine, low-paid work on offer may do little to help your future.

In other educational systems, where 'working your way through college' is a time-honoured practice, the college facilitates it in a number of ways, from helping students to get suitable work, to arranging classes and lectures on the understanding that students do have part-time jobs. If UK colleges adopted flexible timetables and job creation policies, the position would be different. At present they have so much on their plate that what they can do in helping with job opportunities is limited. But more universities and colleges should look at flexi-time for full-time students, given the introduction of more and more part-time and sandwich courses. Many universities are now splitting the academic year into two semesters rather than three terms with longer summer and Christmas vacations but no Easter breaks. Students will thus have better opportunities for job hunting.

Problems remain. In the recent years of high unemployment, most part-time jobs open to students are likely to involve long hours and low pay. Many – working in supermarkets, shops, bars, pubs and restaurants, for example – are the kind of jobs that take up a lot of your time, leave you fatigued, distract from your studies and reward you minimally. Job searching can be time consuming. A job at your college such as helping out in the library may be more suitable – but even here there may be problems. In 1991 Unistaff, an agency employing students for a maximum 15 hours a week at £3 an hour as cleaners, bar and catering staff, faced a challenge by campus unions which threatened industrial action.

Taking a through-term job is not advisable in your first year unless there are special circumstances – for example, it may relate to and help your course work – or unless it is financially unavoidable. On the whole, discuss pressing financial problems with welfare officers, grit your teeth and try to bear it. Coming to terms with and getting the best out of all aspects of your new life will need all your time and energy; it's hard enough without taking on the burden of working as well.

Tax and insurance

You do not pay tax on your grant. If you do get a job, you will not pay tax on your salary if you and your employer obtain form P38(S) from your local Inland Revenue Office; otherwise you will have tax deducted under the Pay As You Earn system and you will have to claim a refund. Once your earnings exceed the single person's tax allowance, you will start to pay tax on the extra income.

As a student you do not have to pay national insurance contributions but neither are you credited with them. You will pay normally, of course, if working in the vacation or on a part-time basis. Full-time students can increase their pension entitlement by paying voluntary class 3 contributions for the period they are studying. You can get full details from your local Department of Social Security Office.

A financial mess

If you are in a hole – stop digging! A small overdraft or a month's rent arrears can quite quickly turn into a problem you cannot see your way out of. Many students can cope quite competently with a limited level of debt. But as soon as it starts getting out of hand, talk to the welfare officers at your student services or student union (who will be experienced in debt counselling), your tutor and your parents.

4.4 'All I want is a room somewhere...'

Ideally, you are accepted for the course of your choice in April and you are able to begin looking for somewhere to live well in advance of term, which starts in October. This is the position of a few lucky people. In reality, for many more students, it may be August or September before they are sure of where they are going. All I can say is: *think about the problem of accommodation as early as you can*. A visit to the college accommodation office and a look at halls of residence, a wander around the area and a look at the local papers are useful as soon as you get a firm offer. Once you are definite on where you are going, you need to move decisively and quickly. Don't underestimate the importance of accommodation. Few people make a success of studying without a secure, comfortable base. And unfortunately, once again, do not underestimate the problem of finance. A National Union of Students survey in 1990 found that students were paying between £20 and £25 a week for accommodation in the North of England and £40-£50 in London and the South-East. That is a lot of your grant gone before you start.

Let us look at the range of possibilities.

Halls of residence

Until recently many well-resourced old universities had

something like a ratio of one place for every three students, which made it possible to house nearly all first years. Expanded recruitment means that ratio – it was never as favourable elsewhere in higher education – is crumbling. The advantages of living in hall are many. You live with people leading the same kind of life. You have a study bedroom in a hall with TV, a bar, laundry and games room, and usually, easy access to your college and its facilities. Most of your domestic needs such as meals and cleaning are catered for, which means you have more time for study and other matters. You know how much you are paying for accommodation, heating, lighting and some of your meals well in advance, which helps official forward planning. Halls are usually cheaper than private rented accommodation and you do not have to pay during the vacations.

On the other hand, some people find the 'total student' experience claustrophobic. It's students, students and still more students, and you may feel cut off from the wider community. You live with people you do not know, usually cheek by jowl, and the lack of an element of choice and self-selection can mean incompatibility. And, of course, there can be study difficulties, if your next-door neighbour is playing music all the hours God sends, particularly late at night. Rents in college accommodation have soared in recent years and competition for places has increased as student numbers have expanded.

Most institutions give preference to first-year students and to those – usually third years – studying for exams. Halls certainly have strong advantages for first-year students. You avoid what can be a time-consuming, stress-inducing hunt for private accommodation. Whilst you can do better, you may do a lot worse in private accommodation. In a hall you minimise the dangers of isolation and loneliness right at the start, when they are most likely to strike. And a hall enables you to find your feet in a protected environment and spend more of your time and energy in coming to terms with it. If you do not like it, you can move later when you have more knowledge of the area and alternative forms of accommodation. All new students would be advised to strongly consider a hall of residence place in their first term – if not first year – but there is strong demand and you may not be lucky.

The private sector

If you do not get into a hall of residence or you decide you do not want to live there, then you will need to consider alternatives carefully with your college accommodation office. The private rented sector provides a number of possibilities. You could

- live by yourself – probably in a small bedsitter;
- share a self-contained house or flat – you do not have a landlord on top of you but you have to cope with your fellow sharers;
- go into lodgings – most students rule this out because of the lack of freedom and autonomy.

But remember: you don't usually get value for money, good facilities or decent conditions in private rented accommodation – unless you really work at it.

To share or not to share

To some extent your decision on this will depend on what is on offer. One-person flats with good facilities are extremely expensive. The likelier bedsitter can become very claustrophobic – you are often relaxing, cooking and eating in a very cramped space. On the other hand, sharing a house or part of it has a better chance of success if you know the people you share it with. This may not be possible at the start of your first year. So again there might be something to be said for taking a bedsit at the start and then keeping an eye open for alternatives.

Sharing a house can be a successful venture. But it requires a clear understanding of what is involved. This may seem obvious, but it is important to be explicit from the start on who is to live there on what basis. What about smoking or late night parties? If your co-tenant's partner or friend takes up permanent residence, or another co-tenant decides to leave after a month, there can be problems. You need to talk in detail beforehand as to who will do what – cleaning, cooking, laundry (if relevant), gardening – when. And who will pay what bills when. And what will happen if they don't. If you are coming cold to an already established arrangement then a long talk may equip you better than a five-minutes chat over the phone. Be clear what you are committing yourself to before you take the plunge.

College tenancies

Some colleges complement their halls of residence with property *they rent* in the private sector. They then sublet it to their students. Here you have the buffer of the college between yourself and the landlord. There is some guarantee that the property will be halfway decent and you will have security of tenure and a sympathetic audience if you encounter difficulties.

Council tenancies

In many areas local councils have unfurnished houses or flats to let to students. Do not expect the Ritz, as these are normally properties no longer judged suitable for families. On the other hand, you can expect to pay less than you would to a private landlord. You will usually have to take on a *joint tenancy*. This means those remaining will still be responsible for the whole rent if one decides to leave.

Housing associations

If you have children, you may find very good accommodation through one of the housing associations operating in the area. It can take some time to get fixed up here, so budget for delays. Again, consult your accommodation office.

Buying a property

Values fell in the recession of the early nineties but during the last thirty years buying a house or flat has been a blue chip guaranteed investment. It may appeal, given the present state of rented property, and it can give you security through and beyond your student career. The big, big 'but' is, of course, *can you afford it*?

Purchase is normally through a loan or mortgage arranged through a building society or, less usually, a bank, with regular monthly repayments over 20 or 25 years. Building societies will normally allow you a mortgage of 2½ or 2¾ times your income. But you will normally need a deposit and . . . have you *any* income? If you have not, you will be dependent on the generosity of parents or relations. They may see this as a good investment, particularly if renting part of the property to fellow students helps to pay off the mortgage. There are some special mortgage packages for students, which enable group purchase. But you will still probably need parents as guarantors of the loan. And remember:

- The duties of house ownership can be time consuming. They can be more time consuming and sometimes worrying if you are acting as a landlords to fellow students.
- You have to think carefully if you are buying a property together with fellow students. You must all be clear on what you are letting yourselves in for: who is paying for what, who is responsible for what. Clarify at the beginning and avoid squabbles later on.
- There are additional charges to consider when examining prices – £150–200 for a survey, around 1% of the purchase price to solicitors who handle the purchase, and so on.

Therefore think carefully, take advice and look at the legal position before you get involved in purchasing property.

Squatting

At the other extreme, if the worse comes to the worst and

there is no alternative, some students consider squatting. If you are thinking of this, talk first to your accommodation office. You should also ensure you are doing nothing illegal. You are not doing anything illegal *simply by squatting* – although there are currently proposals to tighten up the law. But you will cross the line if you break into a property or damage it. Otherwise you will only get into legal problems if the owner of the property gets a possession order – this can now be done speedily in five or six days – and you fail to accept it. If you do squat, find an *empty* property (not one where the residents are away temporarily), don't break in, don't use gas or electricity without making proper arrangements, and look after the place. A useful source of information is the **Squatters' Handbook** which is available from the Advisory Service for Squatters, 2 St Paul's Road, London N1.

Looking in the private sector

Before you begin looking in earnest, try to get a good idea of the different areas – the pros and cons of each in terms of travel facilities, housing stock and cost. Weigh factors such as noise and higher prospects of burglary against price. Do look around and consider areas not previously colonised by students. Accommodation officers tell me they never cease to marvel at the 'lemming factor'. Students are willing to pay more for inferior accommodation in areas which are regarded as suitable and prestigious just because other students live there and they give easy access to college. As one officer put it: 'If students would look just a little further out of town, they would find both better housing stock and lower rents – with amenities which are just as good.'

Once again, the accommodation office is the starting point, but look also at noticeboards in the student union and your department, the first edition of the local newspaper, and newsagents' windows. Be careful of *accommodation agencies*; many are 'fly-by-night' merchants. Bear in mind that they cannot charge for registering your details, only for finding you suitable accommodation. However, the legislation allows them to make a small charge – around £5 – for costs they incur advertising your needs. It is common for agencies to make a small registration charge and then a fee of one week's rent if you decide to take the accommodation on offer.

What to look for

Always carefully inspect a property. Think and talk about it before you sign *anything*.

- Check the security and the locks on doors and windows.
- Check the property outside; look at the roof, gutters, drains and woodwork for disrepair.
- Is the house well lighted and well heated? Does the plumbing work? Try it. Are there adequate plugs? Do they work?
- Is there adequate furniture – fridge, television?
- Are there signs of damp – peeling wallpaper or paint – or pests?
- Are there adequate facilities for studying?

Deposits

You will be asked for a deposit to pay for any damage you do to the property. Under the Housing Act 1980 the maximum that can be charged is one sixth of the yearly rent. Make sure that you receive an *inventory* of furnishings provided. Check this before you sign it. Some landlords ask in addition for an extra premium. This is unlawful and a sign you have fallen amongst sharks.

The agreement

Do not sign anything you have not read carefully and fully understood. You should be clear about the following points.

- What type of letting and rent is it? Does it include payments for gas, electricity and other services? Or are these extra?
- What is the full name and address of the landlord, and what

are his or her responsibilities?

- What services is the landlord to provide – such as window cleaning or gardening? Basically, the landlord is responsible for keeping the structure and exterior of the property in good repair as well as maintaining sanitation, heating and gas, water and electricity installations. Tenants are responsible for the upkeep of the property, minor maintenance and avoiding damage. Any clauses that landlords attempt to insert limiting their responsibilities for repair are null and void.

Make sure

- you are sure **to whom you pay rent, the exact amounts and the due dates.**
- you have **a written agreement and a rent book.**
- you know **the length of the tenancy, the provisions to quit and any other conditions.**
- you have and **carefully keep a copy of the agreement.**
- you **pay over no money without a clear receipt.**

Types of agreement

There are four basic types of tenancy agreement.

1. **Assured shorthold tenancy** This agreement enables you to live in a property for a fixed period – longer than six months – stipulated in the agreement. Once the stipulated period is over then the landlord can repossess the property by giving you are least two months' notice to quit. For an agreement to be valid as an assured shorthold tenancy the landlord must give you a separate statement specifying that it is such a tenancy. For your part, if you intend to stay for the academic year then you must specify this in the agreement. Without a specific clause saying you can, you are not legally entitled to give notice within the fixed term. Under this tenancy you agree rent levels for the whole period covered. If you feel you are overpaying you can appeal to a rent assessment committee.

2. Fixed term assured tenancy   This gives you security of tenure for the fixed term you have agreed. The landlord can then either offer new conditions and increased rent or repossess the house by giving notice to quit equal to the period between rent payments – whether a week or a month. Again, you have to ensure the agreement covers the period you want to stay, and again, you cannot leave within the fixed term. Rent is set for the whole period and there is no right to appeal. This kind of agreement may have a clause stating what will happen to the contract at the end of the fixed term. It may say a new fixed term contract will be offered if new rent levels and conditions are agreed. If there is no such clause then at the end of the fixed period you operate under a *statutory periodic assured tenancy*. Under this you can appeal to a rent assessment committee if the landlord attempts to increase the rent or impose new conditions.

3. Assured periodic tenancy   This is an agreement under which there is no fixed date of termination. The period of tenancy is the interval between your rent payments. You have security of tenure as long as you stick to the agreement but after 12 months the landlord can ask for an increased rent. You can appeal but if agreement cannot be reached you can be evicted. If the landlord wants you out then he or she must give you *notice of proceedings for possession* in the proper legal form. *If you wish to contest this then it is important that you take legal advice*. The notice must state which of the allowed grounds for possession the landlord wishes to use. The landlord must then go to court and prove grounds for eviction.

For *fixed term tenancies* the landlord can go to court and get a possession order if

- a mortgage lender wants vacant possession to sell the property;
- there are at least three months rent arrears when the notice of proceedings for possession is served;

- there are rent arrears both when the notice is served and when the proceedings begin;
- the tenant has persistently delayed paying the rent whatever the existing arrears position;
- the property has been damaged or neglected or there has been a nuisance to neighbours.

For *periodic tenancies* the landlord must have the above grounds for eviction or one of a number of additional grounds. These include the situation where

- the landlord has previously occupied the flat or house as his or her only or principal residence and wishes to do so again;
- the tenant has demolished or reconstructed parts of the accommodation;
- suitable alternative accommodation is made available to the tenant; or
- the property is required for a minister of religion!

Normally the notice required will be two months. But where there are arrears or persistent delays or breach of the agreement as outlined above this may be reduced to two weeks.

4. No agreement at all   If you move in on the basis of an *oral agreement* then you are subject to an assured periodic tenancy. You must give notice to quit equivalent to the interval between rent payments. But remember that without a written agreement there may be problems in ascertaining what the landlord's responsibilities are. At the minimum, make sure there is a rent book and the landlord signs every time payment is received.

When somebody moves
It is safest to have individual agreements for each tenant sharing a property. If you have one joint agreement and one of your co-tenants leaves, the rest of you will be liable for the whole rent, and each will have to pay a bigger share. Although

the person who leaves will remain liable to those remaining, it may be difficult to enforce your legal rights. An alternative to individual agreements is a joint agreement which specifies the rent to be paid by each individual tenant.

Harassment If you fall amongst sharks, sooner or later they may bare their teeth and you may suffer harassment. Under the 1988 Housing Act you now only have to show that the landlord knows or *has reasonable cause to believe* that his or her conduct is *likely* to interfere with the peace and comfort of tenants to prove harassment. And do not forget taking out *insurance* on your possessions. The National Union of Students can be very helpful here. Ask for details of their insurance schemes from
Endsleigh Insurance Services
20 The Promenade
Cheltenham GL50 3NR.

Discrimination Many overseas students and students from ethnic minority groups suffer discrimination when seeking accommodation. There are often problems of providing proof but advice should be sought from Student Services as to the legislation.

Key points

1 Understand the system of financial support. Apply for entitlements as early as possible.
2 The value of the student grant has declined seriously and grants are now being gradually supplemented by loans. The consequent loss of state benefits has created real problems; some students are having to look to trusts, sponsorship and working in term-time.
3 In this situation it is important to plan. Think carefully about finance, banks and budgeting.
4 Student life involves problems with accommodation. Financial difficulties, the deregulation of the housing market and increased numbers of students have all increased the pressures of finding somewhere to live.

5 You should carefully consider the alternatives available: college accommodation, renting in the private sector, council tenancies, or even purchasing property.

6 Housing can be a legal minefield. To avoid difficulties have a good idea of your legal rights. Take advice if problems loom.

7 Having sufficient to live on and acceptable living conditions are important to maximise your experience as a student and you will need to organise yourself to secure them.

Things to do

1 Consider whether the current arrangements for financing full-time students in higher education are fair.

2 Discuss the statement 'More students should work while studying.'

3 Work out how much grant *you* would get if you started a higher education course. What would be your parents' contribution? Would you take out a loan?

4 Do a budget for your family's expenditure each month and each week.

5 Make a report on the cost of rented accommodation in the city or town in which you live.

6 Outline what you think will be the main problems you will encounter living away from home. What are the golden rules for living with other people?

7 Compare the main advantages and disadvantages of living in a hall of residence, a rented bedsit, a shared house.

Further reading

An excellent book on housing rights is the *Housing Rights Guide* by Geoffrey Randall (SHAC, 1991). If you are thinking of purchasing a property you might consult *Buying and Selling A Flat* (Which?/ Hodder and Stoughton, 1991). There are also a number of reference works by Andrew Arden, notably *Manual of Housing Law* (Sweet and Maxwell, regularly updated). More accessible is Arden's *The Private Tenant's Handbook* (Sphere, 1989).

Women students may find a book by Ann Dickson, *A Woman in Your Own Right* (Quartet, 1987), helpful. Overseas students and those from the ethnic minorities might find it useful to consult Duncan Forbes's *Racial Harassment* (Legal Action Group, 1989).

5

Getting organised

Time waits for no one
And it won't wait for you . . .

Mick Jagger, Keith Richards

5.1 Introduction

You will already have had some practice in organising
yourself and organising your time. You will have had to handle
private study and home assignments, integrating them with
your social life and your other interests and responsibilities.
The difference that quickly hits higher education students is the
greater amount of freedom and the greater degree of responsibility they now experience. When you are at school your
parents and teachers take a great deal of responsibility for
planning your learning and life. In higher education *you* are
expected to take responsibility.

Many new students have the feeling: 'it's just all too much.'
You can feel overwhelmed by the demands of your new course,
new friends, new social life – and of course having to look after
yourself.

- Section 5.2 suggests that you begin by thinking about the
  demands of your new environment. We then go on to look
  briefly at specific problems which may affect mature
  students, the disabled, overseas students, gays and women
  students.
- Section 5.3 draws some of these points together by providing
  a brief introduction to time management.

- Your course will be demanding in psychological terms; you may face problems of homesickness and adjustment. No term will ever be as long again as your first Christmas term. Basing itself on the view that a healthy body goes with a healthy mind, Section 5.4 discusses issues of health and confidence, stress and relaxation. These problems are secondary to learning but essential to its effective realisation.
- Section 5.5 notes research that demonstrates that your fellow students can constitute a valuable learning resource.
- Section 5.6 emphasises the usefulness of services for students universities provide and, finally,
- Section 5.7 outlines how you can influence your life at university through your student union and the National Union of Students.

5.2 Sorting it all out

Do some strategic thinking about how you are going to organise yourself over your first term – or longer.

Find your way around

Your first formal meetings in any subject are important ones and you want to get off on the right footing: do some homework on transport and the geography of the campus, the location and layout of your department, where tutors' rooms are, where your lectures and classes are held. When do buildings open and close – particularly libraries and study rooms? Have you got the telephone numbers of your department office and relevant lecturers whom you may need to contact? Do you know exactly the dates on which terms begin and end? Have you a *big desk diary*, a smaller pocket diary and an *address book* to note down information essential to your college life?

Looking at your course

You should have a very good idea of this but carry out a strategic review before you start work.

Syllabus   Make sure you have the detailed syllabus of each option. Look particularly at any statement of aims and objectives which distils what the course is trying to do and outlines the knowledge and skills you should have acquired upon successful completion.

Reading list   Study this carefully again to get some idea of course demands and the amount of work that will be involved. Don't buy books too early (see p. 205) but look at key texts to get some idea of how demanding they will be.

Assessment   What is the system of assessment? Does it all hang on final examinations in the third or fourth year of your course or are there other examinations on which final assessment will be based? Or will your degree depend partly on formal examinations and partly upon continuous assessment? When are your exams?

Lectures, classes, practicals   The number of contact hours differs from subject to subject. Students in science, engineering and technology tend to have more formal lectures and practicals than students in the arts or humanities. Science students may have around 30 classroom hours compared with, say, half that amount in the humanities. Areas like the social sciences tend to have more discussion groups and across subjects there is a tendency for more time to be allocated to student project work. Contact sessions are 'musts' – assume that you will be tied down at these times. Even if you think you are getting little out of a lecture or class, there may be ways of improving things and the little you are getting may be useful. Later, it may be advisable to miss some lectures or classes, but when beginning your course, budget for 100% attendance.

Essays, reports, projects   Whether these are part of your final assessment or not you will need to know how many there are, and when you are required to submit them.

Private study   The hours you spend in class are only the beginning. You can, on many courses, spend at least the same amount of time again on preparing for classes and writing essays and reports. Try to get some idea of what is involved here.

You will receive much of the information to deal with these matters before you start your course. You will receive more on arrival, in the induction classes many departments now run or in your first classes. Talk to your tutors; second-year colleagues can give you a student perspective. Think not only of the time demands of the coming term but of how it fits into your whole year. For example:

- Which subjects will be covered after Christmas and how will they relate to your first term's work?
- When does course work end?
- When do exams begin?
- How long are you likely to have for revision?

Domestic and social life

Think about the amount of time you will need for domestic activities and looking after yourself, shopping for food and clothes, looking for or maintaining accommodation, spending time with your family, thinking about your finances and paying bills. Are you likely to spend significant time in travel to college? Will you go away at weekends?

Although you have to try to put study at the centre of your life, you cannot spend all your time studying. Going into higher education can give you the opportunity for a rich social life and an intense period of personality development. The student who spends his or her days, Monday to Saturday, working from

9 am to 7 or 8 pm is neglecting that opportunity. Apart from anything else, you will need time to recharge your batteries. Sitting around chatting to other students can help indirectly with your work. And, of course, time spent playing an active role in your student union or particular societies is rewarding in itself and also helps many to develop the knowledge, skills and confidence which will help them tremendously in their future careers.

None the less your major aim is a good degree. You have to find a way to integrate learning, domestic life, social life and recreational or political activities, so that what should be central does not become a sideline. Think about your lifestyle. Will you be able to spend all or part of your vacations studying or will you need to work? Will your weekends be available for study or will you visit your partner? Are you content to limit social life largely to the weekend and concentrate on work during the week? Or do you need a mid-week break or like to get out every night? How does your social life affect your studying? A visit to the theatre or cinema takes up time; an evening in the pub can take up most of the following day if you have a hangover.

Box 5.1   Different lifestyles

Jill

- works in a pub as a barmaid 2 nights a week
- moved house last term and is still behind with her rent
- travels from Durham to London every other weekend to go clubbing with her pals

Joan

- contributes to her rent by cleaning the house 3–4 hours a week
- has a large quiet study bedroom in the house of Mr and Mrs Wilcox, who have no children

F

● goes out only on Friday and Saturday evenings

Which lifestyle is more conducive to studying?

5.3   **Are you different?**

Most students face similar problems whatever their age or sex. For example, some mature students are 28, others 48, some have family responsibilities, others do not. None the less, some groups may face specific difficulties.

Box 5.2   The support of your partner

Research currently being undertaken at the Open University by Helen Pearson shows how important it is for those studying for degrees to have the solid support of their partner. This is particularly so if you are a woman because women tend to support a male partner more fully as soon as the idea of their partner becoming a student crystallises. Some men feel they will be 'left behind' when their partner starts a course, or that their partner will neglect the housework or the children. Women have to justify their change of direction in terms of personal development; men's studies are seen more as being important to their career and thus the future of their families.

Lack of support can lead to serious tensions, stress, family break-up and drop-out from courses. It is important that those who have permanent relationships assert their individuality and right to development but discuss all aspects of their new course with their partners.

Mature students

We have used the term *mature student* as short-hand in this book but in reality it covers a variety of different students. The classification used in many colleges consigns all over 21 to this category. It can include those who left school early, those who deferred entry to college and those who dropped out of higher education and now wish to return. Some mature students will be very close in age to the 18–21 group; even for those who are older, most of what we have already said in this chapter will apply – only more so!

Those studying part time will need to exploit *every* opportunity for study. They will perhaps need to look at opportunities for time off from their employer and the possibility of flexitime, rearranged hours and early finishes. Mature students studying full time often have significant domestic responsibilities which necessitate detailed discussions with partners and family. It is difficult but important to try to give your family some imaginative understanding of the demands of your coursework. If they do not understand what you are doing and why you are doing it, feelings of resentment and neglect are likely to be intensified (Box 5.2, Box 5.3). Show them your university and the libraries where you work. Discuss with them your timetable and how you will plan your work. Their support will be vital to your peace of mind and motivation in the coming years.

Box 5.3   Problems

'Don't be like that, Phil. I'm only thinking about it.'

    'And what about me? Don't I come into it? It does affect me as well you know.'

    'I know it does. We shall have to talk it over. I'm not sure about it myself yet.'

    '... The best thing you can do is forget all about it. It's a ridiculous idea.'

    Lucy stayed where she was.

'Why is it?'
'Well because you're too old, for a start.'

Barry Hines, *Unfinished Business*

Your studies are likely to require some changes in your
domestic life. If others do not understand what you are about,
they are less likely to accept the necessity for the changes. See
whether it is possible for other members of the family to take
on some of your responsibilities. Many women students are
likely to be more successful if other members take on more
housework, shopping and child care. Universities cater largely
for full-time students with few responsibilities; provision of
child care is still poor. Mature students may feel that they are
restricted and are not able to get all they might out of the social
side of college. There will always be differences between what
those with commitments and those without can do; but all the
evidence shows (see p. 100) that older students can make it and
do just as well as, if not better than, their younger counterparts.
And surveys in the 1980s demonstrate that women students
gain better degrees than men in all age groups except the
18-year-old school-leaving group (Woodley, 1985). With
more women going to university at 18 in recent years, they will
probably catch up with men in that age group too.

Students with disabilities
Don't feel you are alone. There are six million disabled
people in Britain and some of them will probably be at your
college. Do make sure that you have got all the allowance you
are entitled to. *Skill* – the national bureau for those with
disabilities – is currently collecting information on the levels of
grant paid to the disabled. Make sure your college authorities
are aware of any difficulties and that you know what facilities
are available. Most institutions now

- provide special study facilities and assistance to those with visual or hearing impairment,
- will help with accommodation and tutorial difficulties, and
- make special provision for assessment and examinations.

You will have to make clear your special needs to fellow students and hopefully you gain a good deal of day-to-day support from those on your course.

Some institutions have disability advisers, although there is still a long way to go in this area. Some universities try to specialise in catering for particular difficulties, such as deafness or dyslexia. Others believe that they should try to cater for a range so that disabled people will have a wider range of courses. The National Union of Students believes that nearly 17% of students in higher education are disabled, yet an inquiry at one northern university found only 40 out of 8,000 students. But every year there are scores of success stories about those who persevere, such as Judith Smart, a woman born with cerebral palsy who was awarded a degree at Hatfield University in 1991 against all the odds.

Box 5.4   Gay and lesbian students

Most student unions now have a gay rights officer and charter a lesbian and gay society. Some students openly acknowledge a gay sexual orientation whilst others are still finding themselves and their sexual identity. Lesbian and gay support networks are there to help those who are coming out or who just want to talk about what being gay means, as well as activists and those who have been out for years. So if you feel isolated you can always go along to a meeting.

Overseas students

Despite increased fees, overseas students keep coming to our

shores. Since 1980 the number of non-UK residents studying
for degrees in Britain has increased by 11%, the biggest
increase being in the numbers coming from European
countries. At some universities today, students of 100 different
nationalities are pursuing courses.

Box 5.5   Discrimination

Students from overseas – as well as students from the UK itself
– might suffer discrimination and disadvantage because of
racist attitudes and activities. You might encounter this at
college or when looking for accommodation or part-time work.
The 1976 Race Relations Act proscribes

- **Direct discrimination**   treating a person less favourably
  than others because of their nationality or the colour of their
  skin, e.g. refusing to rent a room to a black person
- **Indirect discrimination** applying conditions which
  cannot be justified on non-racial grounds which affect members of a particular group disproportionately, e.g. sophisticated language tests as requirements for a part-time job
  stacking shelves in a supermarket
- **Victimisation**   treating one person less fairly than another
  because they have made a complaint under the legislation

   The legislation applies to educational bodies, employers,
landlords, estate agents and accommodation agencies.
Student unions and law centres are aware of problems that
affect students and able to advise on remedies.

Overseas students may encounter a range of difficulties
from language problems through to learning difficulties,
stemming from cultural differences to racist discrimination
(Box 5.5). A body which can help you with a wide range of
problems is the

United Kingdom Council for Overseas Student Affairs
60 Westbourne Grove
London W2 5FG.

Problems of adjustment can be more intense if you are away from home in another country for the first time. Do try hard to avoid isolation and to mix with other students on your course. You will wish to work hard to take advantage of an important opportunity but you should also try to benefit from the social life of your college. If you have any language problems, a range of courses are available; you may find study skills courses particularly useful. Your college will probably produce a guide for students from overseas – many are detailed and useful. Remember, if you are not a citizen of the Commonwealth or European Community and are staying more than six months, you will have to register with the police within seven days of arrival. And if you leave the UK to go on holiday, you will have to satisfy the Immigration Officers on your return that you still meet the requirements to enter Britain as a student.

If you come from a European Community country you will not need permission to obtain employment. If you are from other countries you will be given a stamp on your passport which either enables you to obtain employment with the permission of the Department of Employment or prohibits you from working unless you persuade the Department of Employment to move you into the first category. So don't take a job without permission.

There is race relations legislation in force in the UK although it is not particularly powerful; if you encounter acts of discrimination take advice on your rights.

Women in universities

The under-representation of women in teaching jobs contributes to the masculine ethos of universities in which there are increasing numbers of women students (Table 5.1).

This general picture is backed up by evidence on a subject-by-subject basis. For example, while almost 75% of students of

Table 5.1   Full-time non-clinical university staff, 1989

Academic staff	Men	Women
Professor	3,454 (97%)	95 (3%)
Senior lecturer	6,902 (94%)	449 (6%)
Lecturer	4,222 (85%)	2,481(14%)
TOTAL	24,578 (89%)	3,025 (11%)

Source: Association of University Teachers

English in traditional universities are women, only 23% hold lecturing jobs and only 14% hold senior posts (Griffiths, 1991).

Women students may thus be caught in a web of small disadvantages stemming from reflex male assumptions. Sexual harassment is more widespread in UK universities than many would like to believe (Stockdale, 1986). Your student union should have a women's officer with responsibility for issues like this (Box 5.6). It is worthwhile thinking about any difficulties you may encounter and talking them over with other women.

Box 5.6   Women students

Women students may encounter specific problems.

Safety   If you work late in the library or attend a function, avoid walking alone at night or standing at isolated bus stops. Look for special college minibus services and consider attack alarms.

Sexual harassment   Most universities now recognise that the pressing of persistent unwanted attentions on women students does occur. Your college should have a procedure for dealing with sexual harassment and if you experience problems you should quickly consult your student union's women's officer.

Other facilities   It is important to be aware of other issues and facilities which affect women students such as child care and reproductive rights.

Assertiveness training   If you feel you are too self-effacing and unassertive – as distinct from unaggressive – in your dealings with your tutors and fellow students; if, for example, you never get up the nerve to say what you really mean or you always get the worst assignments, then consider enrolling on an assertiveness course. Many universities now organise assertiveness training and it may help your confidence and your studying.

5.4   Managing your time

There are only 168 hours in a week. In this time, how can you maximise the efforts you put into studying whilst not neglecting other areas of your life? If you carry out even a cursory survey of your course and think about what it demands, the penny will drop. To do justice to your course, you will need to spend an awful lot of time on it!

The best way to ensure you can spend sufficient time on your studying and reconcile different demands is by *planning your time*. You already do this, if you think about it – when you plan a trip, a holiday or a shopping expedition. You might start by thinking about some of your basic needs and your social life. Or you may prefer to think about your course first.

Your time audit

Activity	Time spent
Sleep	
Household chores	
Cooking and eating	
Family obligations	
Exercise	
Private reading (including papers etc.)	
Watching television	
Social life	
Other entertainments	
Hobbies	
Personal (looking after yourself and your clothes etc.)	
Travel	
Miscellaneous	

Total time spent

When assessing time available, the key points are:

- the normal time you go to bed and get up (How many hours do you sleep?);
- the time it takes you to travel from home to college;
- the times of lectures, classes, practicals you have to attend;
- the amount of time you spend on breakfast, lunch, dinner and coffee or tea breaks.

Many students find this useful as a basis to block out a *timetable*. This focuses on the 'musts' – the compulsory sessions – so that you know *where* you should be *when*; but it also shows you the amount of 'free' time you will have available. Of course, in reality, it is not all free. You will need to spend time preparing for lectures and classes and reviewing them afterwards, as well as preparing and writing your essays, reports and projects and doing general background reading. So the next stage is to try to get some idea of the amount of time you will need for your assignments and 'private study'.

This should help you to get a general idea of the amount of time overall you will have to spend on your course. You must then start thinking in terms of how you allocate this time between different subjects and assignments. You must begin to *prioritise* – to allocate time to tasks in the order they are required, rather than on the basis of how enjoyable you find them.

- What are the *deadlines* for important tasks?
- Do you need to break tasks down into subdivisions with their own deadlines – for example, essay plan, first draft, completed assignment?
- How long can you spend on writing a report or preparing for a class? Your time is limited and the nature of academic work is such that in preparing a paper you can go on and on, reading more and noting more. You have to get to know what standard is required and when to stop.

Having looked at the demands of structured and private learning, you have to take into account domestic commitments and social life.

So you not only have to *manage your time* through planning but *allocate it to defined tasks*. Some students find it useful to block out detailed timetables on the basis of the coming week, month or term (see p. 156). But this is likely to be of little help unless you have thought through the problems of time organisation and are committed to carrying through plans which are realistic. *Make promises you can keep and plans you have a good chance of implementing*. Otherwise, detailed timetables can become sources of worry and guilt rather than motivation and efficiency.

Even if you find planning ahead in detail helps, be prepared for reverses. The real knack in life consists in getting back on track after you've had a week off through illness or had to spend 10 days away through bereavement. The key word is *resilience*, the ability to bounce back from a reverse.

Planning your time

Time	Mon	Tues	Wed	Thurs	Fri	Sat	Sun
9–10							
10–11							
11–12							
12–1							
1–2							
2–3							
3–4							
4–5							
5–6							
6–7							
7–8							
8–9							
9–10							

Many find it best to start planning on a two- or three-day basis and that it takes them at least a term to internalise a sense of how long assignments take, how much reading they have to do, and how best to plan it. Others find that planning a week ahead, sitting down every Sunday and thinking of the next seven days, is the best way. This is very much a personal matter. The important thing is to *think ahead about how you can most effectively utilise your time.*

Efficient time utilisation

You might think about some of the ways you can use your

time better as a student:

- **Sleep**   We all need a certain amount of sleep but many of us overdo it. An extra couple of hours of study can be generated by getting up just a little earlier.
- **Travel**   A long journey to college or away at weekends can sometimes provide the opportunity for intense effective reading or note making.
- **Waiting time**   Students who have a lecture or class often arrive early and hang around chatting. Why not use this time to read about the subject that is coming up?
- **Take a book**   Many students get used to carrying a book with them. The amount of reading you get done whilst waiting for friends or relaxing over a solitary drink can add up. Fit in background reading, rather than more demanding assignments, at odd moments.
- **Wasting time**   Try to be more calculating in what you do. Can you find more time for study by giving up going to the theatre or the football match just for this year? Do you aimlessly watch television rather than just switching on the programmes you really want to watch? Do you go down to the pub for an hour or two even though it's become a bit of an empty routine you no longer really enjoy?
- **Social breaks**   Getting together for a coffee after a lecture can be very useful. But often, as the talk turns to other things and new students join in, you are using time that could be better put to study use. And sometimes the more you chat, the less you feel like studying when the group *does* break up. You need breaks, but work out how long your coffee and lunch breaks should be and stick to the limits.
- **Social life**   Relate your social life to your studying. This does not mean eliminating the big occasion but *planning*. It is better to be up all night partying on Saturday than on Wednesday when you have a class on Thursday.
- **Vacations**   Use some of this time for study.

- **Targets** Don't forget that setting targets and deadlines can help you get the most out of your study time.

Subject	Length of study period	Target
	45 mins	
	1 hour	
	2 hours	
	3 hours	

It is not enough just to plan your time and tasks, you need to monitor how well you are doing. Always consider how you can *make more time* as well as how you can utilise more effectively the time you have. A comment by Lord Chesterfield, famous for the detailed advice he passed on in letters to his son, is instructive: 'I knew a gentleman who was so good a manager of his time that he would not even lose that small portion of it which the calls of nature obliged him to pass in the necessary house; but gradually went through all the Latin poets in these moments.'

5.5 *Mens sana in corpore sano*

There is a lot of truth in the old saw: a healthy body makes for a healthy mind. Although the young body can stand up to a tremendous amount of abuse – and often does – think a little about some very basic points.

Diet
Both new-found freedom and the exigencies of student life can combine to produce a poor diet based on fried fast food with a dash of curry, perhaps supplemented by snacking on crisps, biscuits and chocolate. This is sometimes washed down with large quantities of beer, tea and coffee. Fried food

increases weight and cholesterol. Alcohol is high in calories –
180 in a pint of beer – leads to a number of physical
impairments, and wrecks faculties essential to serious learning.
Caffeine in coffee and tea can also cause problems; so can the
sugar – rich in calories – you take with it.

'The student diet' makes for an unhealthy person. Over-
weight people are likely to succumb more to stress. You do not
need to discard it entirely but you do need to vary it and
supplement it. Eat less chips and hamburgers, drink less beer
and coffee. Stop taking sugar in your drinks. Try to drink a
glass of milk instead of coffee and eat fresh fruit with it instead
of crisps, nuts or biscuits. Try to eat a little more at home. Grill
rather than fry chicken and fish and have it with a baked potato
and fresh vegetables. Have a look at Katherine Whitehorn's
Cooking in a Bedsitter. Try at least to control your alcohol
intake. All of this takes a little more time. But it will work out
cheaper in the end and make you fitter.

Exercise

Health problems stemming from 'the student diet' can be
exacerbated by the fact that your work involves sitting down a
lot; life can easily become exercise 'free'. A little variation in
diet and a gentle introduction to exercise can help matters
immensely. Regular exercise can make you less stressed, help
concentration and improve the quality of sleep. If you are out
of condition, start by walking part of your journey to college;
or get a bike. Jogging and swimming are two gentle forms of
exercise. But remember you need to exercise regularly and in a
sustained fashion. You could start, for example, by a regular
session of swimming 40 minutes once a week, combined with
two periods of serious jogging per week. This is likely to be
more successful than running a fast three miles which could put
you off exercise for the rest of the term. Visit the gym at your
college and try some exercise routines there. Build exercise into
your timetable at a suitable time.

Sleep

Good studying requires good sleeping! We all need a different amount of sleep but a regular regime helps. A couple of drinks will help you get to sleep but alcohol impairs the quality of the sleep so that tiredness is one ingredient in a hangover. You also need to unwind before going to bed if you have spent the evening studying. So take time out to listen to music, watch television or go for a stroll. And of course the caffeine in coffee which may help late night studying is likely to keep you wide awake. Don't worry about an occasional sleepless night. But a pattern of sleeplessness will impair your work efficiency and you will need first to consult your personal tutor (see Box 5.7) and/or your student union welfare officer.

Box 5.7   Your personal tutor

If you do encounter problems your personal tutor is there to help. A good personal tutor will be your *mentor*, a friend and adviser, a confidante and advocate if you hit serious trouble. Academics are not, for the most part, trained therapists or counsellors, but they should be prepared to help students with problems beyond pedagogic counsel where they can put you in touch with professional counsellors or the student health service if that is required. There are fine, indifferent and poor personal tutors just as there are excellent and mediocre teachers. Good personal tutors remember what it is like to be young and a student. They will take this part of their job seriously rather than regard it as an irritating sideline. You will find them ready to listen sympathetically, make constructive suggestions and pass on the benefits of their own experience. Their experience and observation will mean that they will usually know more about your college, typical student problems and the difficulties of organising your life than you do. And they will try and educate you in your subject, your institution

and the ways of the world. So if you see a problem looming talk
it over early with your personal tutor.

Stress

Study for a degree may not be as stress inducing as piloting
an aeroplane or running a company. But during your career as
a student you *will* worry, you *will* be anxious, you *will* be under
pressure. Pressure can help us. It can key us up, motivate us to
deliver the goods. At times, however, it can turn on us and
become stress. When stress hits us hard we feel tense, tired,
unable to cope. The natural anxieties and tensions which arise
in student life from deadlines for essays or looming exams turn
into headaches, indigestion, eyestrain, hypertension, diar-
rhoea. We cannot concentrate, we feel rushed, constantly
under threat. Our work suffers.

The job of a student, the new-found freedom, the demand
that you manage your own time and offer yourself for assessment and criticism in a variety of ways, particularly to your
peers, can easily create stress. In many cases you are deprived of
your key support systems, your family and your school friends.
Although you might not be prepared to admit it, you find you
really miss your mum and dad! Coping in this new world can
be difficult. Self-pity and anxiety can quickly find a place in
your mind. Crutches – too much to drink, experiments with
drugs, neglecting work – can be appealing when new challenges replace established landmarks.

Most of us encounter stress at some time. A small example is
the panic we often feel when we lie awake at night thinking of
all the things we have to do. What we often do is look
negatively at the situation. Running the next two weeks
together, we think as if we had to have all our outstanding
assignments, not just one, completed by this Friday; we forget
that after handing the first one in, we will have 10 more days to
work on the other two. We create a malignant tutor as well as a

malignant deadline. *We distort reality and lose perspective.*

We can only overcome this by thinking positively and coherently. If we cannot talk to a helpful friend we have to summon up that friend *from within ourselves* and hold the conversation with him or her. Positive thinking means looking on the bright side. Think how a reasonable person would disparage the lack of evidence we have for our fears and laugh them out of court. Blackness and panic can be fought with light and reason. We have to cut our worries back down to size.

You may also have to look at more radical solutions. Perhaps you have too much on because you have not planned your work properly. Or you have had too good a time in the recent past. If stress is becoming a real problem then you need to review how you are organising yourself – and perhaps thoroughly *reorganise* your life. Are you cutting back too much on leisure? 'All work and no play makes Jack a dull boy' is still true, and it can also make him a tense boy. Make sure you keep up the outside interests that relax you and 'take you out of yourself'. But on the other hand, are you working hard enough and efficiently enough? There is no greater dispeller of stress than *success*. After giving a successful talk to your class or getting a good mark in your essay you may feel drained but you should feel 'up' and more confident. Congratulate yourself. Take pleasure in your achievement.

It is important to review how you have organised your work and your life style to see if long-term factors are at work. Track down why you feel stressed and how you can displace the source of the stress. Is it overwork? Or a tough class with an unsympathetic tutor? What can you do about it? Talk to him or her? Take advice from your personal tutor? Transfer to another class? Drop that option in your course? Ask yourself what exactly is the problem and what you can do about it by reviewing your work schedule and leisure activities.

Perhaps you should consider relaxation techniques (see Box 5.8). Some students use relaxation tapes or attend classes on yoga or meditation. Some feel that these methods also improve concentration. Others swear by breathing techniques. Exercise, fitness, friends and a little less alcohol and cigarettes can also help. But studying can be stressful and the incidence of nervous disorders in students and academics is greater than in the general population. If you have real problems, do not hesitate to talk to your personal tutor or union welfare officer, or consult the student health or counselling services.

Box 5.8   Relaxation

Once or twice a day:

1. Sit in a comfortable position in a quiet place. Support your upper neck and head.
2. Slowly and deeply breathe in and out. Allow your shoulders to fall into a relaxed position. Draw in again and close your eyes.
3. Where do you feel tense or tight? Try relaxing your muscles in each area.
4. Starting with your feet and working upwards relax your muscles. Imagine warmth and sun flowing into each area. Focus on your hands; say to yourself, I feel warm, heavy, relaxed.
5. Try to return, when your thoughts wander, to the ideas of relaxation, isolation, quiet, dissipation of tension.

Carry out these exercises for about 20 minutes. (You might start with periods of, say, 10 minutes.) Always end each session with several deep breaths. After opening your eyes maintain the relaxation position for three or four minutes.

Cary L. Cooper, Rachel Cooper and Lynn Eaker, *Living with Stress*

Confidence

If you have been admitted to university, it is because the staff feel you have the ability to complete the course successfully. We have already mentioned the success story of those mature students who possess the confidence to see their course through and the high grades they get (see p. 100) and surveys demonstrate a correlation between A-level results and your chances of getting a good degree (see Raaheim, et al., 1991, pp. 70–1). Overall drop-out in the universities is around 13% and research suggests that more than half those who drop out do so for personal and emotional reasons. If you get your study environment and techniques right, organise your life efficiently, work hard and stay honest, you should get a decent degree.

5.6 **Working with other students**

Studies show how important the social groups that emerge amongst students can be in providing moral support and stimulating educational development. Researchers concluded that 'a student's colleagues often represent the least recognised, least used and possibly the most important of all the resources available to him'. Your student peer group can provide a support network which can see you through a range of practical and emotional problems and strengthen your academic motivation and goals (Tinto, 1975).

Informal discussions with fellow students are important opportunities for learning. There will always be *somebody* who has grasped a point that has passed you by or who, because they are your friend, can take you through a difficult problem in a way you feel your tutor could not. Discussing classes and lectures, comparing notes and essays, talking your way through projects with your fellow students can be very useful. And so can talking to them about the different ways you approach learning. You will realise that your problems are not unique. Others face similar difficulties. How do *they* overcome them?

Students attest to the influence of their peers as well as their tutors in changing their attitudes and developing their learning during their college years. Where students have been involved on a semi-formal basis in teaching fellow students, the 'teacher' who has to come to terms with 'learning how to learn' enhances his or her understanding. The other students in the group also 'appear to learn as much as under conventional instruction, but to remember it better, and to develop more highly the capacity for creative thinking and problem solving' (Wilson, 1981, p. 88).

Student self-help groups, where you get together with your friends to discuss study problems, lectures and assignments are well worth considering as your course gets under way. But such groups require careful planning, agreed agendas, and a spread of tasks and effort between the group. They may be particularly useful before examinations (see p. 390). Such groups can also provide a basis for feedback to staff as to how the course is going and can present proposals for change or development.

5.7 Student services

You should quickly familiarise yourself with these as they can help immensely in getting organised.

Accommodation officers These are trained experts who will advise you generally on where to live, try to help you find somewhere, and then be on call should you have problems with your rent or your landlord.

Student health You will need to register with a local doctor as soon as you arrive but you will also usually be able to draw on a student health centre and the advice of skilled counsellors.

Child care Facilities here are still very poor. A recent survey of new universities showed that the biggest creche had only 40 places, and cost ranged from 'free' to £22 per day. Nursery facilities are often on a small scale.

Careers office   No need to wait until the final year of your degree. Towards the end of your first term, it is worth finding out where the careers office is and what it offers.

Student counsellors   Your university or college may provide specially trained counsellors to help you with a range of problems, from learning difficulties to stress, caused by a bad relationship, to debt counselling.

Learning advisers   There is an increasing attention to study skills and many institutions now have a study skills centre or education adviser.

Chaplains   There will be chaplains to cater for the needs of students from a number of different religions.

Services for disabled students   There will be somebody to advise and help on any problems disabled students may encounter in the institutions.

Student services are there to be *used*. Make sure you acquaint yourself with what you need as early as possible. Student services often work closely with the student union.

5.8   Your student union

Student self-organisation can represent you at two levels.

The student union

Student unions exist:

- To provide a channel for representation of students' views to the teaching and administrative staff. The union will often be involved in nominating students to represent their colleagues on faculty boards, academic boards and senate.

- To promote the welfare of their members by dealing with student problems, personal and academic, and providing a range of facilities from entertainments to creches to advice on health, accommodation and finance. In your college career you will almost certainly attend socials organised by the union, drink in the union bar and benefit from specialist advice over grants, loans and housing.
- To promote scientific, artistic, cultural, political and recreational activities by chartering a series of societies. You will have the opportunity to join a range of societies financed by the student union from the film society or the drama club to mountaineering and rugby clubs and the Socialist Workers Student Society.
- To promote co-operation between students locally, nationally and internationally through affiliation to the National Union of Students. This gives students a voice in the wider decisions which determine the size of grants, the standard of accommodation, and the quality of the education they will receive. Locally, student union representatives are often asked to sit on committees with other campus union representatives to discuss issues which affect every body in the college.
- To provide training in the issues and skills of democracy for those willing to take an active role within the union. These life skills can be valuable after university.

Student unions are as old as universities. In a sizeable institution today the union may

- employ 30 or 40 staff;
- finance a well-resourced welfare office dealing with grants, accommodation, child care and legal problems – with lawyers in attendance;
- charter more than 150 student societies; and

- publish their own weekly newspaper

as well as own and administer a range of bars, eating and entertainment facilities, with a turnover of over £1 million. Particularly important is the union's input to educational matters and discussion of the structure of courses, its role in representing students on wider union bodies, and its welfare function.

Its income is derived from a grant paid through the university and profits on trading. All students are automatically members of the union and it operates through a democratic representative structure. In 1991 the European Court refused to accept that automatic membership of student unions in the UK was contrary to freedom of association as enshrined in Article 11 of the European Convention on Human Rights.

Any student can attend general meetings which determine union policy and stand for election to the executive committee or to council. Council is directly elected and has powers delegated from the general meeting to deal with all issues affecting the union. It elects a number of committees to deal with elections, services, societies and so forth. Representatives to university committees are elected from Council. Together with the general meeting it supervises and controls the executive committee, in whose hands rests the day-to-day running of the union.

The union executive is directly elected to posts of specific responsibility. The academic affairs officers, welfare officer, campaigns officer, women's officer and so on are elected, as is a General Secretary. The executive's job is to implement policy decided at general meetings and oversee the union's administrative staff.

In 1992 the government promised to introduce voluntary membership of student unions so that individuals could opt out. Where this was on a large scale the union's service functions would be privatised.

The National Union of Students

The NUS is a federation of the student unions in some 800 universities and colleges. It was established as long ago as 1922 and, with 1.5 million members and 80 employees, it is the biggest such union in Western Europe. The NUS, with an annual budget of around £3 million, tries to do on a national and international level what student unions do locally. It has acted as a pressure group over grants, housing and, of course, the education system itself, forcefully presenting the views of students to the universities, politicians and the public. It also provides legal, research and training services – invaluable to the smaller unions. Its commercial services and the discount schemes it runs, offering cheap travel and consumer products, have been particularly successful.

Affiliation to the NUS is *voluntary*; decisions are taken by the general meeting of individual student unions. The NUS holds two conferences each year. Delegates are elected from the affiliated student unions and policy is decided on the basis of motions submitted by affiliates. Such motions must first be adopted as policy by a general meeting of the affiliate. The elected NUS executive will campaign for policies decided at conference; but whilst such policy acts as a guideline for affiliated student unions, it is not binding upon them.

In recent years there has been intense criticism of the NUS from the press, Conservative students and Members of Parliament. In the run-up to the 1992 general election, for example, there was a row over the NUS campaign 'Target 70'. The NUS argued that the 1987–92 Conservative administration had pursued policies which were to the detriment of student welfare. However, they claimed that their campaign to persuade Members of Parliament in 70 marginal seats to support increased financing of students was bi-partisan, affecting Labour as well as Tory Members of Parliament. Conservative students argued that, as Labour supported increased grants, the campaign was in essence an electoral intervention on behalf of the Labour Party. The government's 1992 declaration of intent to make membership of student unions voluntary led to co-ordinated opposition by the NUS. They argued that the majority of student resources was devoted to service functions rather than political campaigns and a strong NUS was indispensable to efficiency and democracy on campus.

There will always be tensions when an organisation funded by taxpayers' money goes into the realm of politics. Yet student unions and the NUS are essential to give students a collective voice – which will inevitably be heard in the political arena. Whilst they lack the muscle of ordinary trade unions, students acting together can exercise more influence than if they act in an individual or fragmented fashion. Despite criticism from politicians, they perform a useful and thankless role. As with any other organisation, their strength and democracy depends on participation. You will undoubtedly benefit from student union services. Why not read the constitution, attend meetings and get involved?

Key points

1 Think about your course. Analyse curriculum, timetables, reading lists and assessment systems. How much time will be involved in lectures and classes and how much private work?
2 Think about the time your course work will take up in relation to your domestic responsibilities and your social life.
3 Different categories of student need to think about particular problems they may encounter.
4 Time management is essential for all students.
5 Draw up schedules, timetables and targets which suit *you*, not elaborate, unrealistic blueprints which look wonderful but last a few days.
6 Think about diet and exercise. Studying for a degree can be stressful. Prepare the weapons to minimise its impact.
7 Working on problems with your fellow students can help your learning. Consider establishing student study groups. Understand how student services and your student union work and how they can help you.

Things to do

1 Compare notes with fellow students to assess whether you work hard enough. How many hours do you spend on your studies each week? Do you make plans for the work you have to do and other commitments?
2 Using your timetables, booklists and diaries, make a plan of your work for the coming month. Compare notes with fellow students.
3 Consider whether 'You simply cannot combine a good social life with getting a good degree' is a fair statement of facts.
4 Outline the good points and bad points of developing a student study group.
5 If you worry about your work, think about what produces stress and how you can cope with it.
6 Discuss whether the National Union of Students is too involved in politics.
7 Discuss the main problems likely to beset women students in their college career.
8 Assess whether there is discrimination against overseas students and whether it can be combatted.

Further reading

You should find a number of guides to time management and self-organisation in any large library.

John Adair's *Effective Time Management* (Pan Books, 1988) and Michael Haynes' *Making Every Minute Count* (Kogan Page, 1987) are popular. On stress, the best book is by Cary Cooper, Rachel Cooper and Lynn Eaker: *Living with Stress* (Penguin Books, 1988). Another useful text is Richard Lovelace's *Stress Master* (John Wiley, 1990). Both of these books discuss relaxation techniques. You might also like to look at Patrick Holford's useful books *The Whole Health Manual* and *The Family Nutrition Workbook* (both published by Thorson, 1988).

There are a number of cheap and useful cookery guides on the market such as Jenny Barker's *The Student's Cookbook* (Faber and Faber, 1985), Katherine Whitehorn's *Cooking in a Bedsitter* (Penguin Books, 1986) and Delia Smith's *One Is Fun* (Coronet, 1987).

6

The learning process

'... Carpe Diem,' Keating whispered loudly.
'Seize the day. Make your lives extraordinary.'

Dead Poets Society

6.1 Introduction

We now get to grips with the central purpose of higher education – *learning*. That is what your job will be in the immediate future. Like all jobs it repays some thinking about. At school you often tend to carry out learning tasks without perhaps thinking too much about what it is you are doing. However, if you are going to spend an important chunk of your life as a professional learner then it is helpful to know a little about what experienced professionals have written on the processes of learning – and address some of the practical lessons. Hopefully this will stimulate you to reflect on how *you* learn.

- Section 6.2 considers some of the aids to learning and how you can use them. Some of the points made here are developed in more detail in succeeding chapters. We talk about the need for a stimulating study environment, when to study, the need to organise your study materials and the use of computers.
- In the last 25 years a number of researchers in the USA, the UK and Scandinavia have begun to research the learning process. Section 6.3 outlines and discusses some of the main findings and conclusions of academics, who have studied how learning takes place in higher education. Many of these

studies are limited and some are still developing but they provide some evidence as to the state of the art.

- Finally, Section 6.4 suggests some basic lessons from this research, which may be useful to you in assessing how you learn and how your learning can be deepened.

6.2 Tools of learning

Let us look at some of the tools you will need before you begin systematic learning.

Where to work

You will probably want to do some of your learning at home. The advantage of working at home is informality as well as direct access to tea, coffee, chocolate biscuits and other study aids! Have you a room where you can be relatively insulated from the activities of others? Is it properly lighted, quiet and ventilated, with adequate study furniture, desk and chair? Most people find it best to be comfortable but alert. Although relaxing on a bed or sofa can usefully break up study sessions, if you do it for too long, you may drop off.

Some people, particularly if they are living in cramped conditions, prefer to get out of the house and study in the more formal setting of a library or student workroom, on the campus. Some students find it useful to read and take notes in libraries but are more comfortable writing up their assignments at home. Logistics dictate that you will have to work in college at certain times. So it is useful to develop a secure home base whilst also exploring your college and other nearby libraries for a study setting.

Be prepared

Remember our discussion of time management in Chapter

5. Different students have different planning horizons, but you should know in detail your study schedule for the following day – not just your lectures and classes but what you will study in detail in your own time. You must also be aware of deadlines and set yourself targets: 'I will complete my report *tomorrow*', 'I will fully understand this problem *by tomorrow evening*.'

Distractions

Some students feel that they must study at home, in a part of the college or town away from their colleagues. They feel they cannot resist the invitations to go for a 'quick' coffee or drink which takes hours and then puts them in a frame of mind for further recreation. Other students swear they can study whilst watching television or listening to rap music. You may feel you need to have the radio or tapes on to study. Try switching them off and working undistracted for 20 minutes – you may see an improvement in your concentration. On the other hand, it may be better to study at a slower rate or in a more shallow fashion with music then not to reach your desk at all. If you tend to get distracted, take the phone off the hook for an hour. Remember, one interruption can lead to another . . . or get you thinking about something completely different from studying . . . just when you've got yourself into the right mood.

When to study

Many of us work best when we have a relatively long stretch – three hours or so – in front of us and when we can get at it early in the day. Others work well when they have an hour or so available and are night owls. There are no absolute rules or perfect blocks of time. But give yourself adequate time for the task. Don't try to cram two hours' learning into half the time. Again, we all differ on the length of breaks and the kind of breaks we need. But bear in mind how long you can study effectively without a break, even a brief ten minutes for coffee.

Routine

It helps many of us to know that if it's Tuesday at 5 o'clock, it must be time to write our reports or essays. If we have a routine and study certain subjects at set times, we develop a rhythm. Studying different subjects throughout the day, week-end or week, rather than in large blocks, provides variety. Some students find it useful to give themselves incentives and rewards: 'I will get this done . . . then tonight I will take my partner out for a meal . . . or spend the evening with a friend.'

Concentrating

The watchword is *study*. OK, make yourself a cup of coffee, clear your desk – but then get in the chair, *write, read, underline*. You may actually come to in quarter of an hour and find you are working. The famous novelist Arnold Bennett used to offer the following advice: 'How do I begin? Dear Sir, you simply *begin*. There is no magic method of beginning. If a man standing on the edge of a swimming bath wanting to jump into the cold water should ask you, "How do I begin to jump?" you would merely reply, "Just jump!" '

Forward planning can help. If you know well in advance that you are going to be at your desk doing a specific task from 9am to 11am, then you tend to clear your mind of other distractions, mentally arrange to do other things earlier or later.

Learning to concentrate depends to a degree on interest, achievement and routine and on *proper learning strategies* (see p. 181). The more you get into a subject and the more you produce pieces of work, the more you will get into the pattern and rhythm of serious study. Perhaps you are not taking an active deep learning approach which is more satisfying and efficient (see p. 183).

Perhaps you are studying at the wrong time or for too long

or in the wrong place. Perhaps you have left it to the last minute with the deadline for submission looming. Good planning means less last minute panics and paralysing stress. Or are you biting off more than you can chew by trying to work through an area for two or three hours at a go? Sometimes a more incremental approach is useful. Start working for half an hour rather than an hour. Once you have got into the habit of concentrating in half-hour blocks you can gradually increase this to an hour. Your concentration for your next task may be improved if you *review* what you have achieved at the end of each session. Link it to previous learning and plan your next session. Plan, always asking yourself: why am I studying this? What do I want to get out of it?

Basic study tools

Your notes and assignments are valuable to you and worth making easy to access. Some students spend almost as long looking for notes, reports and essays they produced last term as they did writing them in the first place! A good filing system is essential and worth investing some time on.

- **Folders or wallet files**   This is perhaps the simplest system.
- **Ring binders**   Have one for each subject with cardboard inserts to break the subject down into topic areas or to separate lecture notes from reading and essays.
- **Box files**   These secure your notes and may look attractive in your room but it is sometimes more difficult to find exactly what you want once your box is full.
- **Hanging files and filing cabinet**   You hang the files marked with a tab on the steel frame inside each cabinet drawer. You get an awful lot into a four-drawer cabinet. Keep one drawer for personal letters, bills etc. and it will probably see you through your student career. But filing cabinets are relatively expensive and difficult to move.

- **Index cards** They can be particularly useful if you are studying certain subjects – you can use them to note different cases in law, for example – but if you have that kind of mind they can be used in any subject to break down and cross-refer concepts, events, great thinkers. They come into their own when you are doing a project or keeping bibliographies with details of, and notes on, important books.

Box 6.1   Always have notebook and pen with you

The great novelist Thomas Hardy was once infuriated by his over-confident reliance on memory.

He had once been pruning a tree when an idea for a story suddenly entered his head. The best story he had ever conceived and it came complete with characters, setting and even some of the dialogue. But not having pen and paper with him, and wishing to finish his pruning before the weather broke, he took no notes. By the time he sat down at his table to recall the story it was utterly gone.

Robert Graves, *Goodbye to All That*

Computers

Tutors increasingly welcome reports and essays which are *typed*. They are so much easier to read. When you come to do longer projects, typed copies may be required and this can involve another strain on your finances. Today, however, it is probably best to think about gaining access to a computer you can use for *word processing*. Writing for most students is about drafting and redrafting. The great advantage of the word processor is the way that it adds, deletes and re-arranges. Many people find they can see the structure of the essay better on the word processor. It provides an easy introduction to typing and – a great advantage – to working with computers in general.

Some students who are used to the mental processes associated with handwriting find they start to lose confidence on the word processor, but the initial time and effort involved in learning to use one can be a good investment at the start of your student career. Why not see if there is a word processor you can practise on?

Computers are also useful for getting information. You will have to get used to using them in the library. More and more catalogues are computerised; more and more data banks are being put on disk. We talk about the use of computers for searching out information in Chapters 7 and 11. During the next decade there are likely to be great strides made in learning through computers: computer packages are already being used for programmed learning, and with computer conferencing you can 'attend a class' by typing in responses to other students and academics via a central computer telephone link.

Computer skills will also help you in your future career. So why not get in on the ground floor? Find out what provision your department makes for access and training, think about attending a class and at least find the time to practice using computers.

6.3   How students learn

We have talked quite a lot about some of the pre-conditions for efficient learning. We have not yet said much about *what* learning is and *how* you learn. Broadly speaking, you might say learning involves

- understanding – not just being able to regurgitate – new theories, ideas and information;
- making this new knowledge our own by integrating it with our existing understanding, so that our overall understanding of a problem or topic develops;
- making this new knowledge our own by being able to

explain our new theories and ideas, understand them and teach them to others. This is a good test of how far we have really learned.

Research on how students learn has been neglected. Even today we have far from a complete picture. Let us look briefly at the conclusion of some of the recent pioneering investigations of student learning.

How students develop

William Perry, the father figure of research into student learning, interviewed students at Harvard University (where he was a Professor of Education) and Radcliffe College from the early 1950s to the early 1970s. He interviewed students in each year of their course to see how they developed intellectually. He found that students' perception of their learning environment passed through nine main stages.

Position 1 The student views the world in dualistic terms of we/right/good v. other/wrong/bad. Right Answers for everything exist in the Absolute known to Authority whose role is to teach them. Knowledge and goodness are perceived as quantitative accretions of discrete rightnesses to be collected by hard work and obedience.

Position 2 The student perceives diversity of opinion, and uncertainty, and accounts for them as unwarranted confusion in poorly qualified authorities or as mere exercises set by Authority 'so we can learn to find The Answer for ourselves'.

Position 3 The student accepts diversity and uncertainty as legitimate but still temporary in areas where Authority 'hasn't found The Answer yet'. He or she supposes Authority grades him or her in these areas on 'good expression' but remains puzzled as to standards.

Position 4 (a) The student perceives legitimate uncertainty (and therefore diversity of opinion) to be extensive and raises it to the status of a realm of its own in which 'anyone has a right to his own opinion', a realm which he or she sets over against Authority's realm where right–wrong still prevails, or (b) the student discovers relativistic reasoning – it all depends on the context, one view is as good as another depending on what your values are – as a special case of 'what They want' within Authority's realm.

Position 5 The student perceives all knowledge and values (including Authority's) as contextual and relativistic and subordinates dualistic right–wrong functions to the status of a special case.

Position 6 The student apprehends the necessity of orienting him or herself in a relativistic world through some form of personal Commitment (as distinct from unquestioned or unconsidered commitment to simple belief in certainty).

Position 7 The student makes an initial Commitment in some area.

Position 8 The student experiences the implications of Commitment, and explores the issues of responsibility.

Position 9 The student experiences the affirmation of identity among multiple responsibilities and realises Commitment as an ongoing, unfolding activity through which he or she expresses a life style.

(Perry, 1970)

Perry then compressed his scheme into three main divisions. In the period of *dualism* (Positions 1–3) students moved from 'When I went to my first lecture what the man said was just like God's word . . . I believed everything he said, because he was a professor' to 'In physics you get definite answers to a point. Beyond that point you know there are definite answers but you can't reach them.'

In the period of *relativism* (Positions 4–6) it was a matter of 'anything goes'. There are a number of theories, interpretations or approaches and one is as good as another. But students were now looking deeper: 'I'm looking for the ideas rather than plodding over the words . . . I tend to generalise the thing and get the main ideas and concepts.'

By the period of *commitment in relativism* (Positions 7–9) students were taking up positions, establishing their own philosophy of life; they were increasingly aware that studying and life involve continuous addressing of alternatives, redefinition and learning. Not all students developed in this way and for those who did the process was complex and discontinuous (Perry, 1970).

Perry's scheme is a valuable one, even if, like all such typologies, it simplifies matters and magnifies the difference between the school leaver and the mature university leaver. Moreover, it does not take account of differences which may apply between the arts and the sciences and, like other studies in this chapter, it is restricted in scope and geography.

Although Perry said it is important to see and understand alternative answers to problems, students need to go *beyond relativism*. One answer is *not* as good as another. Whilst it is important to look critically at 'one-dimensional' explanations, in the end students come back, in a different sense, to the right–wrong, good–bad position they started with. But now they have thought for themselves about the range of alternative answers, about which explanation has the greater power, about which argument is best supported by the evidence, about what is right and wrong. They have now arrived at *their own* answers, which they accept may in the future require revision. If we simply stop at relativism we will never fully educate ourselves.

Different learning strategies

Whilst he provided many useful examples, Perry did not look in detail at the way students approached their learning. Gordon Pask and his colleagues, in contrast, carried out a series of experiments under controlled laboratory conditions.

They used students and paid volunteers from the general public.

Pask found that some people learned through taking one step at a time, grasping each new step or link in the chain before moving onto the next. Others operated by looking at the whole chain first to establish the broad picture. They then moved from the large overview to the individual detail. From this evidence Pask distinguished two categories of learning strategy. *Serialists*, he argued, learned, remembered and reviewed a body of information through an item-by-item approach, working their way through a series of sub-topics and examining the structure of an idea or argument and its evidence in sequence. *Holists* learned, remembered and recapitulated the topic as a whole and then looked at the detail and supporting evidence. They made comparisons between this topic and others.

Pask argued that students only possessed a full understanding of a topic when they had so absorbed it that they could explain it to others by reconstructing it and applying the principles learned to a completely different situation. They needed to be able to draw analogies between what they had learned and other areas of learning and understand the steps they had taken in learning. Pask saw learning as a *conversation* in which we develop a deep understanding of ideas by testing them out and asking questions of a tutor or fellow student or another part of our mind: we learn through interaction and dialogue.

Pask saw two major problems or pathologies in his learning styles. A major danger for the *holist* was of seeing the wood but not the trees, to neglect the hard, uninteresting work of detail. Some holists jumped around from topic to topic and drew poorly based analogies. These 'globetrotters' were also too ready to generalise and reach conclusions from inadequate evidence. *Serialists*, in contrast, had a tendency to see the trees but not the wood. The danger for serialists was what Pask termed *improvidence*, the tendency not to relate topics, to be too careful, too immersed in detail so that they missed seeing the big picture.

Pask termed the holist style *comprehension learning* and the serialist style *operation learning*. An architect, for example, has to do comprehension learning to get his overall plans. But he also has to do *operation learning* to establish the detailed processes for making his plans operational. Pask (1976) concluded

> Some students are disposed to act 'like holists' (**comprehension learners**) and others 'like serialists' (**operation learners**), with more or less success. There are also students able to act in either way depending upon the subject matter, and if they excel in both pursuits, we refer to those students as **versatile**. It is these distinctions which can more appropriately be referred to as learning style. (p. 133)

Surface learning and deep learning

Some of the most important and influential work on student learning has been carried out in Sweden at the University of Gothenburg by a pioneering group of researchers. Students were asked to read articles, taking notes if required, and were then interviewed on what they remembered, how they had studied the article and their normal approach to learning. The students' approaches could be divided into two kinds. Some 'sort of memorised everything I'd read'. Others 'tried to look for . . . you know . . . the principal ideas . . . I tried to think what it was all about.'

The first group of students were characterised as adopting a *surface approach*. They thought about what questions they would be asked later and essentially tried to memorise answers. They looked at the words on the page and only skimmed the surface. The other group of students took a *deep approach*. They tried to get beyond the words on the page to the meaning of what was being said. They tried to understand what the writer was trying to say by actively entering into the ideas and relating them to their existing knowledge. They tested the author's conclusions by scrutinising the evidence given for them.

In the case of *surface level processing* the student directs his attention towards learning the text itself (*the sign*) i.e. he has a 'reproductive' conception of learning which means that he is more or less
forced to keep to a rote-learning strategy. In the case of *deep level
processing* on the other hand, the student is directed towards the
intentional content of the learning material (*what is signified*) i.e. he is
directed towards comprehending what the author wants to say about,
for instance a certain scientific problem or principle. (Marton and
Saljo, 1976, pp. 7, 8)

Later researchers subdivided the two categories into *surface
active* and *surface passive* and *deep active* and *deep passive* –
according to the extent of activity demonstrated by students.
Deep processors worked longer hours and were more
successful than surface processors. There were difficulties
moving from a surface to a deep approach although students
who felt threatened by the situation they were in, worried by
the amount of reading they had to do, inadequately prepared
for the difficulties of this level of work, tended to adopt a
surface approach (Fransson, 1977).

One of the Gothenburg researchers, Roger Saljo, argues that
the differences between surface learners and deep learners go
beyond particular contexts and assignments to personal conceptions of what being a learner and being a student means. He
outlines five conceptions of learning:

1 Learning as increasing knowledge
2 Learning as memorising
3 Learning as the acquisition of facts and procedures which
  can be retained and/or utilised in practice
4 Learning as abstracting meaning from material
5 Learning as an interpretative process aimed at understanding reality.

This scheme, which is similar to Perry's, gives us an overview of the Gothenburg experiments. The first three conceptions are clearly related to surface learning and points 4 and 5,
to deep learning.

UK researchers (Entwhistle and Ramsden, 1983) working at the University of Lancaster have taken up the distinction between surface and deep learning. They have attempted to refine the two categories and relate them to motivation and context. They suggest three approaches.

- **Personal meaning** is related to intrinsic motivation to study the subject, a desire for independence and a deep approach to learning.
- **Reproducing** is associated with extrinsic motivation, anxiety, following the syllabus closely and the surface approach.
- The **strategic approach** involves an attempt to maximise performance in study and a desire for success.

Box 6.2   Categories of approaches to learning

Deep approach	Intention to understand
	Vigorous interaction with content
	Relating new ideas to previous knowledge
	Relating concepts to everyday experience
	Relating evidence to conclusions
	Examining the logic of the argument
Surface approach	Intention to complete task requirements
	Treating task as an external imposition
	Unreflectiveness about purpose or strategies
	Focus on discrete elements without integration
	Failure to distinguish principles

	from examples
	Memorising information needed
	for assessments
Strategic approach	Intention to obtain highest
	possible grades
	Gear work to perceived
	preferences of teacher
	Awareness of marking schemes
	and criteria
	Systematic use of previous papers
	in revision
	Organising time and effort to
	greatest effect
	Ensuring right conditions and
	materials for study

Source: Raaheim, Wankowski and Radford, 1991

The student, the syllabus, the department

Research undertaken in the USA has demonstrated the importance of *context*: the approach students take to learning is strongly influenced by their teachers and the ethos of their department. Becker and his colleagues (1968) demonstrated some of the ways in which students adjusted to the situation they found themselves in, seeking success with a minimum of effort. Snyder (1971) emphasised the idea of the *hidden curriculum*. Students find it difficult to adopt deep approaches because of the crowded curriculum and the demands of assignments and preparation. The formal goals of the university – independent deep learning and the development of the mature creative individual – were displaced and students adopted a variety of expedient tactics to get good grades and pass exams.

In the UK, researchers (Miller and Parlett, 1974) have

observed the way some students conform to perceptions of what they feel their teachers really want in assignments and exams, as distinct from what they formally say they want. This makes for surface, reproductive learning and an opportunistic approach.

- **Cue seekers**, amongst students, actively looked for signals from teachers as to the kinds of approach and answers they liked. As one of them put it: 'I play the examination game. The examiners play it, so we play it too . . .'. Cue seekers sought to make a good impression on staff and were active in classes. They got the best results.
- The **cue conscious** were aware that there was a 'hidden curriculum' and that staff dropped hints about it, but they tried to combine the formal demands of the course with, for example, spotting questions on exams and studying a wider range of topics than those they felt might come up. They were not so successful as the cue seekers but more successful than the next category of students.
- The **cue deaf** ignored hints and informal contact with staff and trusted that hard work rather than tactics would pay off.

More detailed work on the interaction between student learning and the learning context has been produced by a group of educationalists around Noel Entwistle, first at the University of Lancaster, later at the University of Edinburgh. These studies showed that factors associated with academic success centred on motivation, work habits, personality and approaches to study. Not surprisingly, the successful student worked long hours, was well motivated, had done well at A levels, practised effective study methods and exhibited satisfaction with the course (Entwistle and Wilson, 1977).

Further research involving more than 200 students drawn from a wide range of departments emphasised the powerful role of the teachers and the learning context in influencing student learning. Entwistle's three approaches, the *deep*

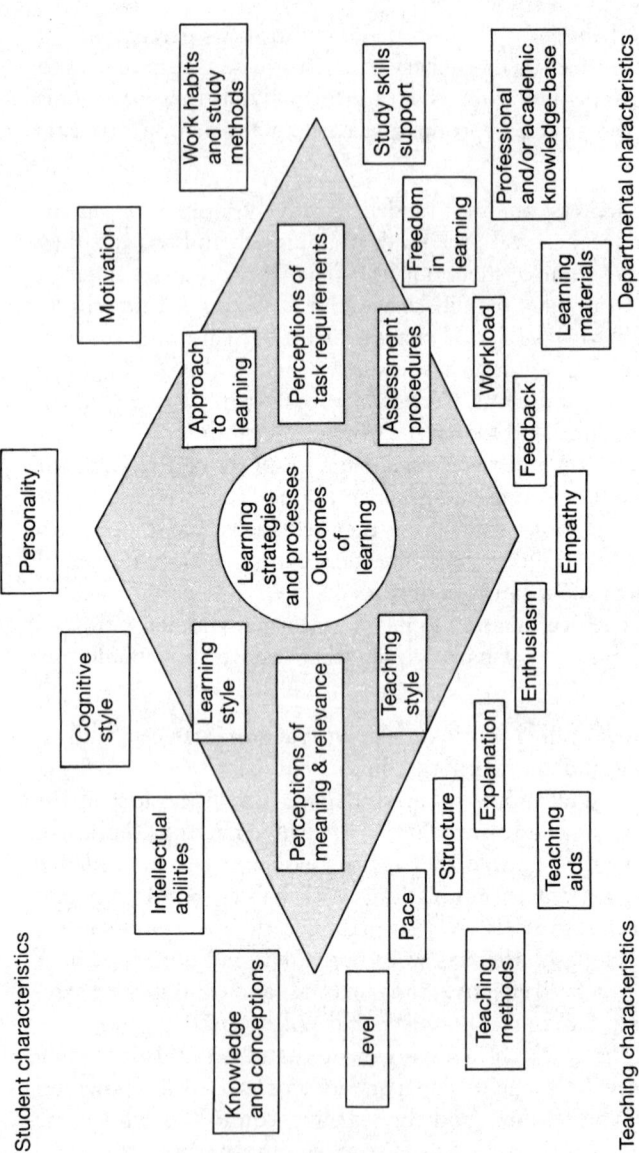

Student characteristics

Departmental characteristics

Teaching characteristics

Figure 6.1 A model of the teaching–learning process in higher education
(Source: Entwistle and Tait, 1989)

approach (seeking understanding), the *surface approach* (based on reproducing) and the *strategic approach* (related to Miller and Parlett's 'playing the system' to maximise advantage) represented relatively consistent individual differences. But these approaches were related to motivation and course organisation.

'Good teaching' was related to deep learning in students. The good teachers were effective lecturers, able to stimulate understanding by enthusiasm, striking analogies, cogent exposition and relevant illustration. They pitched their material at the right level, went through the course at a pace students found appropriate, let the students know where they were going and followed these initial directions. Students had a clear picture of the course objectives and the course map. Tutors provided support and sympathetic feedback and students felt they were regarded as important. Poor teaching, in contrast, included inefficient lecturing, unclear goals, too heavy a workload and lack of a student-centred approach. It was associated with a reproducing approach from the students and produced poor learning.

6.4 Lessons for learning

These innovative studies tell us a lot about how we learn. They represent, despite their small scale and sometimes artificial experimental conditions, a small breakthrough in this field. Higher education is at last critically examining itself and its methods. As usual, a lot lies in the detail and you may wish to read more about these experiments. The researchers differ in emphasis and conclusions on some points, but you might like to turn back to Chapter 1 and see how the findings of the researchers on what learning is and how we learn compare with our outline of what would be expected of you in higher education. Does the outline fit with these findings?

The outline is an ideal to strive for; its attainment may be foiled, to some degree, by how our universities operate in practice. Below are some fundamental lessons drawn from the research.

1   Real learning is deep learning

You will have observed that there are two pairs of concepts running through these studies. Learning approaches are categorised on a *surface–deep* line. At the surface pole, students skate over the ground attempting to routinely absorb material so they can regurgitate it. Deep learners, in contrast, attempt to extract meaning from what they are studying, draw out the general principles, relate them to their existing knowledge and critically address the evidence and the alternative possibilities. And learning is also described within a *serialist–holist* framework where learners either try to see the subject as a whole or attempt to incrementally build up a complete picture, detail by detail.

Surface approaches focus on the facts and the primary theoretical building blocks of our discipline that we need before we can go on to more sophisticated theorising. But Perry characterises some students who try to learn largely in a surface manner as dealing in *cow*: they pile up mountains of data without awareness of its framework and context. They are not learning in terms of understanding. Others deal in *bull*: they 'discourse upon the contexts, frames of reference and points of observation which would determine the origin, nature and meaning of data *if one had any*' (Perry in Wilson, 1981, p. 37). But because they have 'no data' – they have studied frames of reference and interpretations without direct sifting of the data – *they are unable to test the meaning for themselves, their interpretations and understanding are secondhand.*

The effective deep learner, in contrast to those who deal in either 'cow' or 'bull', will understand both data and the wider frame. The efficient surface learner will always remain only a sponge, assimilating and reproducing. *The learner in higher education must strive to be a deep learner and a holistic learner* even though some of the techniques utilised by the surface learner may be integrated within that deep learning approach. The surface learner *per se* is not really learning.

2 Learning is active ... a conversation

I cannot learn unless I am interested, involved, active to at least some degree. Pask's statement that we learn through *conversation* is worth underlining. We learn through talking to the author we are reading and through talking to ourselves. We learn through being *active*, we learn through thinking about what is being said or what we are reading, through relating it to our existing knowledge and experience, through asking, 'Is that so?' We learn through asking questions, not only in class but when we are reading and writing. We learn through interrogating not only our teachers but our texts and ourselves. We must all strive to become Grand Inquisitors. Socrates had the right idea when he saw education as based upon a dialogue. We question . . . and then we question the answers we receive . . . and we receive a new response . . . which we question in turn.

If we never stop questioning we will never stop learning. That's why babies learn so much so well. Our typical response to our teachers, texts, written assignments should be 'That's so, isn't it?', 'What does that really mean?', 'What's the evidence for that?', 'But surely X is contradicted by Y?' Talking to yourself used to be popularly viewed as a sign of madness. It is in fact a manifestation of profound sanity, a demonstration that an educated mind is at work.

3 The student can grow

The work of William Perry remains of fundamental importance for two reasons. His painstaking analysis spanning generations of students shows students *can* develop through a process of cognitive growth and transformation – although, of course, many do not. His work did not differentiate between students in different disciplines. Yet many have observed that the way science is often taught with the emphasis on established authority and the orthodoxy of the textbook can limit the growth of critical learning in the student.

4   **The context is important**

Going on from this point, the studies demonstrate that students react to the environment they have entered.

> Talk by lecturers of students developing their critical abilities is just cant when students are obliged to adopt atomistic and surface approaches just to assimilate and reproduce the course content and where they are expected to spend many hours every day in the laboratory or to complete an essay every week and to sit ten or more three hour papers in two weeks. (Barnett, 1990, p. 157)

The Lancaster research emphasised the importance of the motivations students bring to their studies. But they also showed that the context in which learning takes place can generate problems for students. These include bureaucratic, impersonal departments, whose staff have minimal interest in students and learning techniques, whose curricula are overloaded and whose students lack understanding of assessment principles and control over the pace of their work. But lecturers, in their turn, are often the prisoners of their own environment. 'Teacher training' has developed in recent years in higher education but it remains optional for staff and limited in its intensity. Promotion and the reward systems in universities remains strongly based on research. This remains the position despite widespread verbal support for reform. The pressure is thus on lecturers to be research-based, subject specialists rather than versatile pedagogues whose central concern is student learning and educational practice. The squeeze on resources and the increase in student numbers has made change more difficult and, if anything, led to a greater recourse to traditional formal methods. *Yet it is clear that any wider programme for improving student learning has to involve the teachers.* And it has to involve broader change in the way higher education bodies function as learning institutions. We cannot simply focus on the student in isolation.

5   But the student is not a prisoner of the environment

There is no need for fatalism. Entwistle and his colleagues, you will recall, showed us how important your motivation, your attitude to work and your work habits are. They added to the surface and deep approaches a third category, the strategic approach. This involved students aiming to maximise their grades by managing their time efficiently, organising their study and relating their learning to examinations. Student motivation and their perception of the situation they found themselves in were factors as important as the situation itself. Students did not simply respond in Pavlovian fashion to the situation in their department. *They developed strategies to deal with it.* Those who used a deep approach and those who used strategic thinking, the researchers felt, would achieve success. They concluded, 'Students in the interview study, for example, who used constantly deep approaches and those who used highly strategic methods to handle assessment tasks were more likely to achieve First or Upper Second class honours degrees' (Entwistle and Ramsden, 1983, p. 195).

The commonsense approach would be to go for deep learning but

- polish up your learning skills,
- organise your time,
- examine why, what and how you read,
- scrutinise your writing techniques and
- relate your learning to your system of assessment.

The researchers summarise it: 'Students who were oriented towards both meaning and achievement were apparently less

affected by adverse teaching and assessment conditions'
(Entwistle and Ramsden, p. 204).

6 So you should critically examine your learning
approach and your learning skills

We have talked a little about how students learn in order to
enable you to think about how you learn – so that you can
think about what you do and what you want to do and develop
for yourself learning strategies which are satisfying and
successful.

You can help yourself by thinking about the points raised in
this book and by attending learning skills courses. One fundamental problem is the neglect of how students learn and the
emphasis on *what* they should learn. The assumption that you
learn how to learn *unaided* – 'After all, that's how I did it' –
means that there are too few courses in this area. There is also
some argument about *how* learning skills courses should be
organised.

- Does your university organise induction courses and/or
  skills courses?
- Does your department organise such courses?
- Are they *general*, looking at research on student learning and
  discussing general approaches to problems taught by educationalists or trainers in the institution who are interested in
  this area?
- Are they *specific*, using materials and exercises which come
  up in your course, and taught by the staff who will be
  teaching your course?

There have been criticisms of some approaches to study
skills on the grounds that they ignore published research on
learning, operate on an idealised picture of the student, impli-
citly assume a 'one best way' and are too broad and general
(Gibbs, 1981). Against this it has been asserted that study skills
can be developed in a formalised and systematic way, that

'common sense', 'ordinary knowledge' and direct experience have much to teach us – if we reflect on them. Criticisms of study skills courses, it is argued, particularly some of those made by researchers, can disillusion teachers and make the battle for a greater emphasis on learning more difficult (Dunleavy, 1986).

The limited evidence appears to suggest that programmes linked to the students' own courses and taught within their own departments represent the best approach (Martin and Ramsden, 1987). But there are not enough of these courses. Overworked staff sometimes resist new and potentially difficult responsibilities. The matter should not rest there. But more general courses, reflecting on recent research, supplementing it with reflections on 'common sense' approaches and actively involving students in thinking and doing about learning, fill a gap today and hopefully create pressure and support for more specific provision tomorrow. The danger is that they may, on the contrary, take pressure off individual departments, but this can be avoided. Our advice to students would be *attend whatever general and induction courses are available but press for specific provision in your department.*

7   And you should critically examine the approach of your teachers

If existing staff development programmes in higher education are often too limited and optional, they also often assume students as givens and concentrate on 'how to get it across'. Not enough attention is paid to the problems of student learning. Not surprisingly, students themselves rate research lower than their lecturers and want more attention paid to teaching, which they feel 'has never been of primary importance in universities' (National Union of Students, 1987, p. 8).

The National Union of Students can press their case in collaboration with higher education reformers. As staff assessment programmes develop in higher education, students are increasingly involved in the rating and review of courses and teaching. You should use all the avenues open to you to bring your difficulties, your criticisms – and what you think should be done in terms of changes to study skills courses – to the attention of your tutors and your representatives. However, fundamental change is likely to be an uphill battle. In higher education today limited resources, cutbacks and classes with more students hardly provide the best setting for experiment and innovation.

Key points

1 Think about how you learn, where you work, when you work, the need for planning learning and the tools of study, from books to computers to filing systems.
2 Students can develop from models of right–wrong, good–bad, authoritarian teacher–empty vessel student, through uncertainty to relativism – the idea that different theories may be useful in explaining different things or be justified in different circumstances. And they may then progress further to critical commitment to particular theories and ways of looking at their subject.
3 You need to develop *deep learning*, understanding the whole map of the problem, and eventually of the discipline. Nuts and bolts are important but you have to be able to see the whole machine, in its entirety and in operation, not just a disaggregated series of bits and pieces or parts of its operation.
4 Successful learning requires you to enter *actively* into contention with tutors and learning materals. We learn by questioning.
5 How we organise our work is important but so is *how it is organised for us*. The quality and kind of teaching, the commitment of staff to teaching – as against research or consultancy – assessment systems and a range of other factors over which we have limited control can constrain or stimulate successful learning.
6 You need to adopt *strategies* to deal successfully with your total learning environment. Take account of the *real* curriculum – as distinct from the formal curriculum – and prepare for actual assessment tests as well as trying to meet the formal goals of the course. On the one hand, you need to scrutinise and develop your own learning abilities and attend learning courses; on the other, you

need to try to influence the wider environment through discussion with teachers and representation on course committees.

Things to do

1 Define the way you study by making a list of the most important things you do when you are approaching an assignment such as writing a report or an essay. Compare notes with fellow students.
2 Think about an assignment you handled particularly well, a book you read which has influenced your work, or something you wrote that you enjoyed and which received a high grade. Compare this with a book you gave up on after a chapter or two, an essay that bombed. Can you learn anything by thinking about what you did differently in the two contrasting situations?
3 Describe your working environment. Can you improve the conditions in which you learn? Make a list of some of the positive and negative things about working at home or in a library.
4 Discuss this statement: 'Every student should have access to a computer.'
5 Discuss William Perry's scheme of cognitive development. Do students really develop like that at college?
6 Ask yourself whether you are a surface learner or a deep learner, a serialist or a holist, a 'cow' or a 'bull'.
7 Consider whether 'All learning is a conversation.'
8 Discuss the statement, 'The people to blame when students do not learn are not the students but their teachers.'

Further reading

Most books on learning are written by researchers for lecturers, but you may like to look at some of them. Ruth Beard and James Hartley's *Teaching and Learning in Higher Education* (Paul Chapman Publishing, 1984) is extremely valuable. New students may find it, like the other books in this area, a little difficult, but if you are interested it repays effort. Graham Gibbs has some trenchant things to say about study skills courses and is interesting on learning in general. His book is *Teaching Students to Learn* (Open University, 1981). Many of the articles recounting the research into how we learn can be found in a book edited by Ference Marton, Dai Hounsell and Noel Entwistle,

The Experience of Learning (Scottish Academic Press, 1984). Other books you might like to look into are Noel Entwistle and Paul Ramsden's *Understanding Student Learning* (Croom Helm, 1983) and John D. Wilson's *Student Learning in Higher Education* (Croom Helm, 1981). *Brain Train*, by Richard Palmer and Chris Pope (Spon Publishers, 1984), has a section on using computers.

7

Books, libraries, reading

Polonius: What do you read, my lord?
Hamlet: Words, words, words.

Shakespeare, *Hamlet*

7.1 Introduction

You might think that students entering higher education would already possess a lot of experience in using libraries and reading books. Yet a detailed, comprehensive survey carried out in the 1970s found that 15% of students never used libraries, that students as a whole lacked knowledge of how to access, handle and benefit from books and that, in many cases, their lecturers failed to remedy deficiencies (Mann, 1974). Problems still exist today. Half-way through the 1990–1 academic year a survey made by the Publishers Association showed that 17% of students had not yet bought a book, while 9% of undergraduates said they had never received a reading list (Tysome, 1991).

In this chapter we explore the use of the printed word and some of the problems students encounter.

- Section 7.2 looks at the different kinds of printed materials you will use on your course as well as radio and television.
- Section 7.3 covers the basic points about use of the library. It is essential that you get to know your way around sophisticated, large libraries quickly. Familiarity with the way libraries operate breeds understanding and better studying.
- Section 7.4 concentrates on reading skills – discussing the reasons why we read and the different techniques we can

adopt for different purposes. It emphasises that a critical, questioning, purposive approach to reading is the key to deeper, more efficient learning.

7.2   **Different kinds of text**

A library is thought in cold storage.

Lord Samuel

Let's begin by noting the wide range of materials you will need to use in your student career.

Survey books   Before you start your course it is worth trying to get a general overview of the history and development of your subject, its current scope, some of its current concerns and contemporary controversies. You should receive a pre-liminary reading list which should contain introductory, historical and survey texts which will help here. For example, Blackwell publish a series called 'Invitation to. . .', introducing a wide range of subjects. I have in front of me now Glyn Daniel's *150 Years of Archaeology*, a brilliant historical intro-duction, and two other survey books: David Crystal's *What Is Linguistics?* and Keith Brown's *Linguistics Today*. Look for titles that start with *What is . . . ?* or *An Introduction to . . . .*

Some introductory books are just that. They help you find your way into your subjects but you will not use them later on in your course. Other books, such as E. H. Carr's *What Is History?*, have attained the status of classics. They will repay periodic reading throughout your course and pondering once it is over.

Specialist dictionaries   These give brief summaries of the thought and contributions of your subject's most distinguished proponents, the key texts, major theories, concepts and controversies. They are useful to peruse in conjunction with a survey text.

Reference books   Some wider reference books, such as the *Fontana Dictionary of Modern Thought*, cross subject boundaries; others, such as the *International Encyclopedia of Education*, cover a range of subjects.

Bibliographies   These list books and articles in particular disciplines and particular subdivisions of disciplines. The best are annotated bibliographies, which assess the status, content and, thus, the utility of the item cited.

Textbooks   Many courses involve intensive use of a small number of textbooks which attempt to synthesise in an accessible way the various primary and secondary sources of knowledge in your subject. They provide an understanding of current debates and an overview of the discipline. Textbooks are useful because they are expert commentaries on important primary and secondary sources. But their secondhand nature is also their weakness. Gradually you have to start going to the secondary and primary sources *themselves*. A textbook should be a mentor and stimulus, not a substitute.

Secondary works   These are the books, monographs and articles in learned journals where an author directly addresses, criticises and assesses primary materials or analyses and interprets raw data to produce new arguments. In many disciplines they include works which review, reformulate or revise old theories and positions.

In the subject of law, for example, the primary sources will be law reports, legislation and proposals for legislation. Secondary works will be monographs or books which seek to analyse and assess the premises of a particular strand of case law, review public attitudes towards an Act of Parliament and its impact, or theorise on the role of law in changing human

behaviour. Tertiary works will be textbooks bringing together
cases and commentary. But primary works may also be books
which involve the collection and analysis of raw data on attitudes towards, and the implementation of, legislation or a
tightly argued innovative book on the philosophy of law. Some
of them become classics which in their own right will attract
works of commentary and criticism.

Primary sources, primary works These are the *raw
materials* – novels and poems, law reports, scientific reports,
economic statistics. But, to take one example, great political
economists such as Marx, Marshall and Keynes worked on the
primary sources of their day to produce major works of
economic analysis and philosophy which still dominate their
subject and have in turn attracted commentary, reinterpreta-
tion and revision. We can call them primary works because
they constituted breakthroughs which could be mined by those
following.

These are the classics and they often intimidate us. Mark
Twain called them the books everybody wants to have read but
nobody wants to read. But they repay effort. When you go to
primary sources and primary works you are not listening to
somebody else's opinion of them but going straight to the
object of praise, criticism or clarification itself. You are finding
out for yourself at first hand. This is where learning can be
exciting. A real induction into your subject demands an understanding of the raw materials themselves, not just other
writers' commentaries on them.

Readers These stand halfway between textbooks and the
primary sources. They consist of extracts from key commentaries or primary sources with commentary by the editors.
The difference from textbooks is that you get more directly
from the horse's mouth. The difference from the source itself is
that you only get part of it, taken out of its context. None the
less, readers can be useful as tasters and samplers to lead you to

the real thing. They can be particularly useful in bringing together a variety of material over a long historical period, assembling extracts which debate crucial issues from different viewpoints or republishing pieces now out of print.

Journals   You will probably find that in your subject there are three or four major academic journals. Academic journals often come out three or four times a year. They are edited by and contain the publications of the professionals in your field. They have the great advantage of being more up to date than most books. Sometimes academics will publish new research findings only in a journal or in a journal in preliminary form before they are polished to appear in book form. A glance through the last two years' issues give you a good idea of the present state of play in a particular area. Many journal articles consist of reviews of the recent literature and will usefully supplement your usual texts.

You should gradually start reading articles in journals. Not all the articles will be useful or relevant: you must select. But regular dipping into journals will help you find your way into your discipline, see how it is developing and give you an idea of how its high priests – and their acolytes and critics – approach problems and build up knowledge.

Abstracts   These outline in about 200 words the contents of useful articles from a range of journals in particular subject areas. Later on in your course you should find your way around these abstracts which are very effectively cross-indexed.

Reviews   Some journals have a very strong review section. This alone makes them worthwhile. Good reviews by academics not only tell you what new books are being published but give you a good synopsis of what they cover, who they are for and their merits and weaknesses.

Periodicals   As well as academic journals, you will find one or two periodicals which are intended for the practitioner or the general reader but often contain high quality work in accessible form, ideal for the student. *New Scientist, The New Statesman and Society* and *History Today* are classic examples.

Newspapers   If you are studying economics or politics then regular reading of a quality newspaper may be essential. But even for those studying other subjects each day's paper often contains relevant articles which illuminate our understanding of issues we are thinking about, as well as keeping us abreast of scientific and technological development. They also keep us informed as to what is happening in education itself.

Film, television and radio   Statistics on viewing and declining newspaper sales suggest that more and more of us rely on TV and radio for our information as to what is happening in the world. The synchronisation of script and pictures makes TV and film powerful learning devices. The increasing spread of video recorders minimises some of the disadvantages of printed materials, such as the lack of control over the pace of work. The use of film and the broadcasting media is undervalued in higher education. Yet as long as they are used in conjunction with more conventional methods such as handouts and note making, advance preparation and subsequent revision (as at the Open University), they can help our learning tremendously. Audio and video recorders and cassettes are important equipment for the student of any subject: they give you control over the pace of your learning. Much of what we will have to say later about lectures in Chapter 8 will apply here – although, despite the fact that it is more important, active involvement is often more difficult to attain. Moreover, viewing certain films and TV programmes can fulfil the same functions as background reading – strengthening your knowledge base and opening up areas of your subject that more sustained active study can consolidate.

Box 7.1 Citation terms used in books

There is, nowadays, an attempt to discourage the use of Latin citation terms. But you will still come across the following:

et al. Short for *et alii*, 'and others'. Where there are more than two authors of a book or article, they are usually all mentioned in the first citation, but thereafter referred to in this way. For example, J. Smith et al., *The Continuing Crisis of Almost Everything*, London, Catastrophe Books, 2001.

ibid. Short for *ibidem*, 'in the same place'. This is used to refer to the text already fully cited immediately above in the references.

op. cit. Short for *opere citato*. Where you have already cited the J. Smith et al. book, you do not need to give the full reference again. Simply state J. Smith op. cit., p. 72.

passim Used where the point you are referring to in your book or article is not simply made on p. 81 or pp. 81–3 or in Chapter 3 but is made, emphasised or developed 'here and there' throughout the book.

7.3 Access to books

'The library is testimony to truth and to error,' Jorge said.

Umberto Eco, *The Name of the Rose*

Now you have some idea of the different kind of materials you will need on your course. But which are the most important, which will you need to buy and how can you get hold of the less essential materials?

Your reading lists

First stop is your reading list, which should provide answers to some of these questions. Your reading list is essential – a key document. Yet the Publishers' Association survey referred to earlier (p. 199) found that 32% of students who responded had received a reading list *after* their course began and 12% never received a formal list. Your reading list should give *alternatives*, given the price of books, cut-backs in library budgets and the decline in student grants. This can make it a long and intimidating document. The earlier you get it, the more slowly and effectively you can digest it.

Box 7.2   Elements of the good reading list

Topics   It is broken down into different areas of your syllabus. It describes what is to be covered, outlines key issues and then suggests what you should read.

Questions   It either confronts the topic as a series of questions or, having outlined the issues, gives you some specific questions you should address in your reading.

Kind of books   It distinguishes clearly between textbooks, primary sources etc.

Annotation   It briefly tells you what the book is for.

Student centred   It mentions which books are best from your point of view, not necessarily your professor's.

Priorities   It tells you which materials are fundamental and which are optional; which you should read first and which can come later; which are essential reading and which provide useful background.

Alternatives   'If you can't get hold of Smith, Johnston is the next best alternative, although it does not cover ...'

Publication details   Author, title, publisher, date. A kind tutor might give library references and some prices, others feel this is spoon feeding.

If you do not receive a reading list or if it is seriously inadequate, then take it up with the lecturer involved or your personal tutor. Through more information from your teachers, self-help or a mix of both, *you have to build up a good reading list* (see Box 7.2). It is an indispensable tool to prepare for your coming lectures and classes, essays and reports.

Using your reading list

How do you get hold of important texts? For a start, get used to the way lecturers and authors cite details of books and articles.

Book: Eagleton, T., *Literary Theory: An Introduction*, Oxford, Basil Blackwell, 1983.

Journal article: McIlroy, J., 'Continuing education: do the universities mean business?', *Studies in Higher Education*, vol. 14, no. 3, 1989, pp. 331–45.

Jot down the price of books. You will want to buy some books – textbooks, primary works – which you will use frequently, which will be difficult to get from libraries, and which you will want to mark. But in the present financial situation you will want to think carefully, discuss the position with colleagues, see the book and survey it (see p. 215) before putting down your cash. Can you buy key books *secondhand*? Have a look at the notice boards in your department and the student union as well as your college bookshops. You should look at textbooks before primary sources, more modern before older texts. But look closely for *edition* and *date*. Has a new edition of the book been published in the last year or is one imminent? This can be important with textbooks and 'must' reading, less so with substitutes or background reading. It may be useful to wait a week or two before buying certain texts so that you can find out more and discuss with colleagues what they are buying, whether they are willing to share certain texts, whether you can establish a lending pool.

Libraries

Intrinsic to your decision on what to buy is what you can borrow. Check out the libraries where you will have user and/or borrowing rights.

- **Your department library** A good place to start.
- **Your college library** This will be bigger and more difficult to handle so start finding your way around it as soon as you can.
- **Other colleges** Can you dig out in the libraries of other institutions books difficult to get hold of in your own? Can you get access and/or lending rights?
- **Public libraries** You are likely to have access to a number of public libraries. Join them and explore them. Central libraries in cities and big towns are comparable with libraries in colleges, but do not neglect the small branch library. These may be under less pressure for certain categories of non-fiction books and sometimes specialise in particular subjects.

Time spent early on in establishing how libraries work will save time later. You will probably have a guided tour of your college library but most people need to follow up *quickly* and use the library intensively to assimilate how things work.

The Dewey Decimal System

The most common system for classifying books used in the UK was first published by a librarian, Melvil Dewey, 1876. You will find it on the wall in most good libraries. Dewey felt that all human knowledge could be broken down into ten major divisions. Each division can then be broken down into further divisions so that 500 – Pure sciences – covers Mathematics (**510**), Astronomy (**520**), Physics (**530**), Chemistry (**540**), and so on. Each subdivision can then be broken down in turn – for example, **540.1** Early Theories, **540.2** Textbooks and so on.

You should get to know the classification numbers of your subject or subjects and the physical location of the books and periodicals. The best way to do this is to start annotating your reading list with the classification numbers and then going to find the books.

Catalogues

Armed with your reading list, start at the *author catalogue*. This lists all the books in the library alphabetically under their author you will be able to quickly discover whether the library has the book. Remember to have the author's full name, if at all possible. In the earlier citation we just used initials. But there may be hundreds of J. Smiths listed. Is it John Smith? There may be scores of John Smiths listed. Is it John A. Smith, John B. Smith or John O. Smith? The fullest information gets the quickest results.

When you find the entry write down the full details and the full classification number. Not just 378.1, but 378.1 S107. If you miss the last bit then you have to wander through all the 378.1s, or at least 378.1 Ss, rather than being able to go straight to 107.

You will normally be using the author catalogue as you will have details of the books you want. But later on you may want to consult the *subject catalogue* to discover the wide range of books which exist in a particular subdivision of your subject. If you know the classification number you want, you can go straight to that subdivision of the subject catalogue, where you will find listed all the books the library has in that area. If you do not know the classification number then you will need to look at the shorter *subject index* or, as it is sometimes called, *classified catalogue*, under the name of your subject. Comb through until you find the subdivision you want. Armed with the classification number return to the main subject catalogue.

More and more libraries are now complementing the card catalogue with on-line computer terminals – where you type in the author's name and the book's title or keywords – and microfiche readers. Get used to using the computer terminals: they work fastest and can also quickly tell you whether a book is on loan or on the shelves.

Loans

In some libraries, all books are on the open shelves but you can only borrow certain volumes. In others, loan volumes and library-access-only volumes are segregated. Some books may be 'on reserve' or 'on short loan', as they are in great demand. Some college libraries favour loaning the majority of books, others feel it is fairer to keep them in the library. It is important to find out quickly which books you can borrow, how and when. What are the loan periods? How can you recall books? What is the fines system? Don't forget photocopying facilities. Sometimes it may be easier to copy a key chapter rather than note or borrow a book. Copying is particularly helpful with key journal articles which are nearly always in use. And do not overlook the inter-library loan system through which you can order books and copies of periodical articles from other libraries.

Going a bit further

Become as familiar as possible with the literature of your subject and how you can get hold of it. This entails a gradual build-up. But it is summed up by the phrase 'use your curiosity . . . always do a little bit more'. When you look up a book by John Q. Smith, have a look at what else he has written. When you get to the shelves and you find the book you wanted by Jill Jones is not there, then have a look at the other books on that shelf or section to see if others will do. When you look up the back volumes of a periodical, have a look at its shelf neighbours. At first you will probably want to take the references cited in many of the books and articles you read as given. Later on you should start at least having a look at them in the library.

You cannot treat your reading lists as holy writ. Lecturers might be pushed for time, overlook a recent text, allow dislike of a particular book to override judgement. So add to and develop your reading lists (see Box 7.3). It is often useful to look at textbooks other than those you habitually use, read for alternative viewpoints to those put forward by your lecturers and even read again what you know for the novelty of different formulation. If you encounter problems, *ask the library staff*.

Box 7.3 Pushing forward the frontiers of your knowledge

1. Shahida, a first-year law student, reads the chapter in her textbook on the law on cat licences.

2. Shahida attends a lecture on the subject.

3. Armed with the case references, Shahida goes to the Law Library and works her way through the reports on six key cases. She finds that many of the ideas she formed from the textbook and lecture were partial or mistaken and that whilst it takes a lot more work to read through the actual judgement, her understanding is greater.

4. Shahida goes to Her Majesty's Stationery Office and gets a copy of the Licensing of Tabby Toms (Amendment) Act 1990. As she goes through it, she does not have to rely on secondhand interpretation; she can see what it says, aided by her notes from a textbook and lecture, and make her own mind up.

5. Having read brief comments about the policy of the 1990 Act in her textbook and heard what her lecturer thinks, Shahida now digs out from the library the White Paper setting out in detail why the legislation was introduced. This is more hard work but Shahida is now not only able to write a successful

essay on recent developments in cat licensing, she has set herself up in a small way as an original researcher. She is beginning to get some idea of how judges reason and interpret the law, how governments make policy and create legislation. She is starting to get a first-hand insight into how her subject works.

You will find more information about using libraries and tracking down material in Chapter 11, 'Handling your research project'.

7.4   Reading for understanding

... reading is a sort of rewriting.

Jean-Paul Sartre

William Perry, whose work we looked at in Chapter 5, asked a group of students to read a chapter of a book. After twenty minutes the students were asked to stop and answer questions. Many of them had whisked through at the rate of a page a minute. They were able to answer all sorts of questions about the detail of their reading, but less than one in ten were able to tell the lecturers what the chapter they had been reading was *about*. Many students read a lot and they read fast. But they do not read for *meaning*, so they do not read with *understanding* and they do not read *effectively*. The problem is not, as some students think, the speed at which you read. Speed itself may be counterproductive. As the comedian put it, 'I took a speed-reading course. It worked. I read *War and Peace* in twenty minutes. It's about Russia.' It is the kind and *quality* of your reading that is central. So let us look briefly at some of the ways you can make your reading more effective.

Some new students believe that with all their reading they should start at the beginning and work through to the end. In higher education you have to cover a lot of ground. But often this involves covering a little bit here and a little bit there. This kind of coverage is essential but it means that you simply do not have the time to work through every book from page 1 to page 250. You will do much of your reading to prepare a class or to write an essay. This often dictates using *parts* of books or articles and summing up their message in a few lines. Students often experience difficulty with reading for understanding, because they are reading material which is too far ahead of their development. The key thing is carefully phased development, block building. We read most efficiently when our reading represents the next link in our developing chain of knowledge. If we try to jump two or three links we come to grief (Calfee and Drum, 1986). Academic writers are sometimes to blame here. They tell you to practice clarity in your writing. They themselves write in 'academese'. They use jargon for the sake of it rather than for precision.

We need the right knowledge base for our reading. We also need to be *interested*, which means being active and purposive in our reading. Our reading should go hand in hand with our essays, lectures and classes – because similar things are going on in all these learning activities. When we read we should try to locate and unpick the author's structure, the kind of structure we will be attempting to reassemble in our essays or reports. So the more interaction we get between writing, reading and our formal sessions, the better we learn.

Reading for a reason

You will need to use different kinds of reading at different times. Many books – though not all – should be read as means, not as ends. At times you will have to violate their integrity, turn them inside out and upside down, pillage some and quarry others. In contrast you will need to know important primary works like the back of your hand, from start to finish. But your reading should *always be purposive*, always *for* something – whether an essay, report, lecture or class or background reading to build your basic knowledge. It should always link up with what you know and need. Always ask yourself: Why am I reading this? What are my goals in reading this? How does it relate to my existing knowledge and understanding?

Reading as conversation

When you read you are entering into a collaboration with the author: trying to find out what he or she has to say and relate it to what you already know. As in any conversation, your mind has to be working, linking, processing. As you read you will be looking for meaning and clarification, asking questions of the author, assessing the evidence he or she presents, plugging it into what you know, measuring it against your existing understanding, making a mental note to check up on this point or that. The questions you will be asking will be specifically conditioned by the purpose of your reading – whether it is to prepare a report or get yourself in trim for a lecture. As well as being active and questioning, your reading is therefore likely to be selective. However, you must always remember that different students may justifiably place different interpretations on their conversation with the author. There is *not just one interpretation*. We all make different meanings from what we read. As David Lodge puts it: 'in every decoding there is an encoding'.

The conversation should not be *too* leisurely. As well as your goals for the conversation, what you want out of it, you should try to estimate *time targets*: how long should it take?

The activity involved in conversation and your time targets help maintain interest and concentration. But the conversation is also likely to be punctuated with periodic silences. At times you will turn away from your companion – the text – murmuring, 'Let me consider that'; stopping whilst you weigh up what is being said; recapitulating what has been said so far; making a note of key points; reflecting on how all this is related to your reading goals.

A structured conversation

All authors worth their salt lay down a path for you to follow and signpost it. Sometimes this will be explicit. If you take this book as an example, there is an introduction at the start, telling you what the book covers, and a contents page which directs you more specifically. Each chapter begins by stating what will be covered in sequence and ends by summarising what has been said. In between, each section is numbered and there are numerous headings and sub-headings. Some of the literature you will read will have less explicit signals and signposts. But there will be a planned structure there for you to uncover. A preliminary task is to get a general idea of what a book or article is about, what it has to say and how it is organised to say it. This is to establish its relevance to our essay, class or project – whether we will buy the book or borrow it from a library, use it habitually or on a one-off basis.

Finding what to read

We need first to make a *survey*. We look at the book as a whole to see if it is worth looking at further. Here we ask: Why is the author writing? What are his or her motives in producing the book, chapter or article? Is the author trying to

- provide a critical synthesis of the field, as in a textbook or literature review?
- provide new information, as in a scientific report?
- propose a new way of looking at the subject or debate?
- critically qualify or reformulate an argument?
- knock down and replace an established way of looking at things?

Here are some points to look for in your survey.

- You will have already taken in the **title** and the **author**.
- The **date of publication** will give a hint as to its utility.
- The **number of reprints** may give you some idea of the demand for the book, but remember many popular texts are also limited in scope and approach.
- Read what the **blurb** on the jacket has to say about the book and the author. This, of course, is written by the publishers to sell the book. It may be a fair comment or an inflated statement of the volume's value. Are any **reviews** quoted?
- There may be more information on the inside jacket and occasionally on the **title page**. Is the author an experienced teacher in his or her field? What is his or her discipline and what is the approach within that discipline? What else has he or she written?
- Now have a look at the **contents page**. Are the topics you are interested in covered?
- Flick through the **chapter headings**.
- Return to the **introduction,** where the authors normally state what they *intend* the book to be about and how it is organised. What level is it at – who is it for? Have the authors been helped by distinguished colleagues in the field, who have thoroughly read the text? Was it a Ph.D. thesis (in which case it will presumably have had close prior scrutiny)?
- Flick through the **chapters**, reading the first and last couple of paragraphs or looking over the introduction and conclusion to each, if they have one. What does it cover? How deep does it go? How readable is it? Is the style vivid and easy, cumbersome, plodding, hard going?
- Look for a **conclusion** at the end of the book.
- Glance through the '**Further Reading' section** or **bibliography** to see what literature the author has covered.
- Is there a **glossary of terms**?
- Browse through the **index,** checking names, events, theories that are of relevance to you.

Most of us do this, or rather *some* of this, in a semi-automatic fashion. It is useful to think about and develop this kind of survey technique. Always survey texts *interrogatively*. What do you need out of this book, how does it relate to your report or your class? Is it likely to be excellent to good, fair to poor in answering your needs? What ground does the book cover? Is it worth your while ploughing through the whole book or are there just one or two chapters or even pages that are useful for the task in hand? Or have you already traversed all the ground it covers? If so, it may be a waste of time going over it again, unless of course the way it arranges material, its style and presentation make it worthwhile.

Different kinds of reading

In surveying a book you will have already used some different approaches to reading.

Skimming   As when you glanced through the headings and sub-headings, the first and last paragraphs of chapters, introduction and conclusions. *Purpose*: to survey, establish status, establish structure.

Scanning   Looking through a text for particular pieces of information or explanation. *Purpose*: to dig out smallish nuggets or as preliminary targeting.

Gutting   Where you deconstruct the text and then take out and read carefully in detail the passages you want. *Purpose*: to isolate and capture key areas of relevance in a text.

All of these methods are of use with secondary texts, often in combination. Having skimmed a book to establish its general status, you may then home in and gut certain key passages. Always skim what comes before and what comes after to place the passage within the general argument and avoid misunder-

standing. Then read quickly through the key pages, once without stopping to puzzle your way through difficult passages.
Then read through a second time. This time stop and confront
problems.

Box 7.4   Reading critically

Some critics have tried to dismiss the film as little more
than an affected mystery but that does not account for
its continued popularity after forty years. *The Thirty-Nine
Steps* stands alone in the genre as a survivor of time and
fashion. In its simplicity, economy and pure cinematic
technique it surpasses even *The Maltese Falcon*.

Thus the respected critic Donald Spoto begins his analysis
of *The Thirty-Nine Steps* in his book *The Art of Hitchcock* (W. H.
Allen, 1977). This passage comes at the beginning of the
chapter so you should suspend final judgement. But already a
series of tentative questions should crowd your mind. *Which*
critics have tried to dismiss it? What have they said, why are
their dismissals inadequate? Surely the *popularity* of a film is
not the test of its *quality*? Aren't even *bad* films popular over
many years? Spoto states that the film 'stands *alone*' as a
survivor of its era but then mentions another survivor, *The
Maltese Falcon*. Are there not other 'survivors' such as John
Ford's *The Informer* (1935) or Marcel Carné's *Quai des Brumes*
(1938) or Jean Renoir's *La Bête Humaine* (1938)? *Why* does
The Thirty-Nine Steps surpass *The Maltese Falcon* in its
simplicity, economy and pure cinematic technique? Surely this
is a contentious judgement. Isn't it arguable that if we go back
to popularity John Huston's *Falcon* has lasted better than
Hitchcock's *Steps*?

Many questions like this may be answered to your satisfaction as the chapter or article unfolds. Or you may feel arguments are evenly balanced but, in all fairness, the author has a
case. Spoto does not justify many of his initial assertions with

detailed substantiation in the pages which follow the passage quoted. But the real point is to be sure that right at the beginning you are active and entering a critical dialogue with the author and his material. Only then are you reading successfully and efficiently.

A formula for reading?

Many exponents of study skills have suggested a formula for reading secondary texts which combines and integrates many of these points – the SQ3R Approach. This suggests that with sections of a book or with an article students should survey, question, read, recall and review the text.

1 **Survey**   We have outlined how to survey a book. The method can be adapted for a chapter or an article.
2 **Question**   Confront the text with a series of questions, operationalise your reading goals. What essentially is being said? What is the structure of thinking? How does it relate to what you know? What are the key concepts, ideas and arguments?
3 **Read** the section of text from start to finish, patiently and scrupulously with your questions in mind. As you go through you should ask a *procedural* set of questions. Is the author
   - *defining* terms; establishing concepts;
   - *describing* key features of phenomena;
   - *evaluating* theory and argument?

And simultaneously a *quality* set of questions:

   - How internally consistent is the passage? Do the arguments or explanations logically follow? Is the structure coherently built?
   - Can I clearly distinguish evidence from interpretation? It is argued, isn't it, not asserted? Can I clearly distinguish the authors' views from those of others?

● How convincing is the overall argument?

And finally a *learning* set of questions:

● Boiling it down, what is finally being said?
● What does it mean?
● How can I use it?

You may well subconsciously ask these questions out of habit; with practice they will become an organic part of your reading. At this stage you may also wish to jot down key points or phrases but not full notes.

4 **Recall** Not how much you memorised but how much you understood. How far have you grasped the structure of thought and feeling of the text? How much have you translated? How successfully have you developed new meanings through your conversation with the text? How far has your dialogue produced something new in your mind? How well have you translated the text into *your own* understanding and your own language?

Turn away from the text and think about it. Recall the answers you got to your questions. Chew the whole thing over in your mind, précising what you have read.

● *Talk to yourself*, argue with yourself and the author, remembering, clarifying, drawing analogies between new learning and what you already know.
● *Teach back*, explain to yourself *in your own language* what you have just read and then criticise it. You *know* when you can teach others.

Some people feel it's best to think deeply and take the new ideas into your mind before making notes. Others feel you think and clarify your ideas through making notes.

5 **Review** This is the assessment, 'bringing it all together' stage. How good was your teach-back? Read through the passage again in conjunction with your notes, establishing what you have recalled and what you have missed and the kind of answers you have received to the ques-

tions you have asked. Check how your notes reflect your new knowledge and how well you have achieved your reading goals. Put them in a form you can now use. Are you in a position to teach others what you are learning?

Alternatives

An alternative approach is suggested by Tony Buzan.

Overview: Survey the text by dipping into it and looking at chapter headings, illustrations, tables, contents pages, conclusions.

Preview: Selectively trawl through the book looking at the beginning and ends of chapters and paragraphs, the information-heavy areas.

Inview: Fill in what you have missed. Read quickly, leave out difficult bits which will stop you in your tracks, perhaps never to resume.

Review: Go back to the hard parts. You should now find difficulties minimised because of the wider contextual information you have gathered. Make notes on the material.

(Buzan, 1979.)

Whether or not you want to follow mechanically the SQ3R formula or Buzan's technique, you will undoubtedly want to apply *some* of these techniques in your reading strategy. The real usefulness of these approaches is to get you to formulate objectives and methods of your own, perhaps using some of these methods in a different way. What is important is not a particular sequence or when you take notes. Rather it is how you begin to develop skills through this kind of active approach. If you always *read for meaning* and attempt to *grasp the structure* of the author's thought and argument, the detail falls into place. Cultivate the skills of

- *interpreting, focusing and concentrating*;
- translating the author into your own language and your own understanding;

- learning how evidence and arguments are presented;
- comprehending how theory is built;
- gaining insight into what standards of quality apply; and finally
- linking this reading to your earlier knowledge and evaluating it.

Box 7.5   Questions in reading

1 Am I clear as to the author's *motives*? What is he or she *trying to do*?
2 Am I clear as to the *structure*? How the author is attempting to achieve his or her objectives?
3 Am I clear as to the *commanding ideas* and the *key sentences* in paragraphs and chapters?
4 How important are *details, examples, comparisons*? Which part of the trees can I prune the better to see the wood?
5 Do I need to use a dictionary to get through the *difficult language* here?
6 What *characterises what the authors are doing*: describing, explaining, discussing, evaluating, presenting evidence?
7 What are the *standards* for judging what the author is doing? Does the evidence support facts and conclusions? Is it partial – or out of date? Do conclusions stem from facts and evidence? Are alternative conclusions addressed? Can I see contradictions, counterarguments?
8 How would I evaluate overall
   a. the *substance* of what the writer is saying?
   b. the *methods* the author has used to treat the subject and express arguments?

Detailed reading

You will certainly not want to use SQ3R reading Shakespeare! Or dealing with primary sources: 'big books', novels, poems, scientific treatises, *The Origin of the Species, Das Capital* or *Finnegan's Wake*. With works like these you often have to toil slowly and precisely, detail by detail, paragraph by paragraph, to quarry out their meaning. Don't use works of explanation, commentary or criticism as a substitute but as a way in.

With key works which are closely integrated it is important to get a sense of the overall structure and argument – the detail follows once you have 'learned' the author's structure of thought. Many literature tutors insist it is vital to read literature, at least initially, first hand, otherwise works of criticism will come between reader and text and form or deform reactions. So it is best to start by struggling with the original, by reading the text through once or twice and noting down your reflections and difficulties. *Then* consult secondary works of interpretation to help your understanding. Go back to the primary text for a more intensive scrutiny, worrying away at key problems, making notes, marking the text – which should be your own – and making important comments on it. Only do this at a stage where you have worked through problems and feel you have something *substantial worth recording*, not something superficial. If you jot down 'first thought comments' on a first reading they may well later seem superficial and ephemeral and your text will soon become covered in writing.

Getting stuck

Each subject possesses its own specialist language and you can get impatient with this. Sometimes the language is justified – words are used because they convey meaning more precisely. At other times a certain use of language may have more to do with making academics feel superior, more professional. Some of what you read will be written for other academics and reflect a little 'plumage and preening'. Tortuous sentences sometimes reflect the fact that the authors are not good writers or are not clear as to what they think.

However, if you are to develop in your subject then you need to understand its language. Have your dictionary and subject dictionary handy. Note new words and new meanings. Perhaps a card index could come in useful here.

If you start getting bogged down, read back a little from the tough passage . . . or read forward a little where you may find summaries, a different formulation of the ideas, or a simple expression that you can grasp. Underline difficult words, and look them up; try to break down complex sentences into their component parts. Become more active. Read aloud. If you have done all that and you are still in the dark, talk it through with a colleague or tutor.

Box 7.6   Does the evidence support the conclusions?

The fact that they lack solid evidence for their theories does not stop well known authors sometimes expounding them! In a book published in 1963, Lorna Packer asserted that an important incident in Christina Rossetti's life was a love affair with William Bell Scott. Some 18 years later this was demolished by Georgina Battiscombe, who concluded her survey of the evidence:

For the theory that Christina was in love with Scott is based entirely on supposition. It is not impossible, but not one jot or tittle of factual evidence exists to prove it true. To read Mrs Packer's book is to be reminded of the old saying 'If "if and ans" were pots and pans there'd be no need for tinkers' – or for biographers who believe in the importance of historical facts. The expressions 'must have', 'could have', 'would have', bespatter her pages and the rhetorical question is one of her favourite devices – 'Christina must have responded to "the singularly penetrating and deliberate gaze" of the magnetic blue eyes'; 'He would certainly have wanted to see her again'; 'It could not have taken Christina long to discover Scott's new friendship'; 'Was it at Penkall that Christina told Scott that she loved him?' And so on and so forth.

Mrs Packer explains and excuses this total absence of historical proof on the ground that William [Rossetti], *the primary authority for everything concerning Christina*, knew of her love for Scott and deliberately omitted or falsified any evidence which might point in that direction. One of the great difficulties in the way of Mrs Packer's theory is that in order to believe her it is necessary to disbelieve William, and that he appears on balance to be the more credible of the two.

Georgina Battiscombe, *Christina Rossetti*

Background reading

Most of your reading will be for specific learning tasks. But before your course, with introductory books in the in-between times, perhaps at weekends, on journeys, in the vacations when you need a change, you need to do general background reading, often of whole books or articles. The purpose here is to read entire texts to get the core of the contribution the book makes to your debate in your subject. But it is also to build up your sense of how knowledge is assembled and presented, and how theory is taken forward in your discipline.

Background reading is for anchorage and ballast. It gives you more directly purposive reading, a broader context and a stronger base. The more you do this background reading, the more you jack up your starting point for your next assignment. You are better able to progress with key primary materials and the important secondary books you will read for your assignments because you are better read – *you know more* to begin with. Background reading can be more of an armchair job, reading a book all the way through. Popular books on your subject, books for the lay person, novels or plays can also aid your understanding. The important thing is to keep up wider reading from a variety of perspectives outside your formal study sessions. It can be pleasurable, and it will aid your development.

Key points

1 Your reading list is central to your learning. Be clear as to the status and role of the different books and materials you will use on your course.
2 Familiarise yourself early with all aspects of the operation of a number of libraries.
3 Push out from your textbooks to the original work cited, summarised and discussed there. Relate your reading to your lectures, classes and writing and ensure you are at the right level for major reading assignments.
4 Read selectively. Consider the different techniques of surveying, skimming, scanning.
5 Consider the SQ3R approach. But always read actively, interrogatively and critically.
6 For primary works and big books you will need more detailed reading utilising commentaries and critiques.
7 Try to do background reading throughout your course to jack up your general level in the subject, immerse yourself in the techniques of knowledge development, and develop your overview of the discipline.

Things to do

1 Have you a reading list(s) for the course you are following? How does it compare with the points made on p. 206. Discuss with your teachers its purpose, strengths and weaknesses.
2 Try to get some idea of the amount of reading your course requires each week. Is it too much . . . or too little? How does the reading prescribed relate to your lectures, classes and writing assignments?
3 Working in pairs, survey a book in three minutes and give a report on it to your partner. Repeat the exercise, first taking five minutes then taking ten minutes.
4 Look at three or four books. How effective are the contents pages, introductions, chapter headings, summaries and index of each in signposting what the book is about and how it is organised to the reader?
5 Working in pairs, each read a short chapter of a book using the SQ3R method. Then teach back the chapter to your partner.

Compare the notes you made. How useful do you think this method is?

6 Working in pairs, pick out a section of a book or article of 1,500–2,000 words. Précis the section to half the text. Then try to summarise your notes in two or three paragraphs. Compare your notes with your partner's. Did you succeed in boiling down the essential ideas of the section?

7 Using the libraries available to you, track down examples in your subject of textbooks, readers, dictionaries, academic journals, popular periodicals.

8 Determine what the key books in your course are. Why are they key?

Further reading

Reading to Learn, by Sheila Hari-Augstein, Michael Smith and Laurie Thomas (Methuen Education, 1982), is well worth looking at and takes up some of the points we have discussed here. You may also want to look at Tony Buzan's *How to Study: Brainpower* (Encyclopedia Britannica, 1979). If you do want to go into the speed reading game, Tony Buzan has also written *Speed Reading* (David and Charles, 1977). Terry Eagleton's *Literary Theory: An Introduction* (Blackwell, 1983) is already a classic. It should be read by students in all disciplines. If you want to look a bit wider Luciano Canfora's *The Vanished Library* (Vintage, 1991) is a fascinating detective story tracing the rise and fall of the first libraries. *The Strange Rise of Semi-Literacy in England: The Dissolution of the Libraries*, by W. J. West (Duckworth, 1991), looks at the problems we face today.

8

Lectures, classes, making notes

Term began. She went into town each day by train. The cloistered quiet of the college began to close around her.

D. H. Lawrence, *The Rainbow*

8.1 Introduction

Lectures, which developed centuries ago as a response to the lack of books, continue in higher education in the age of high technology. They still constitute the spine on which the majority of courses are built – witness the continuing use of the term *lecturer*.

- Section 8.2 discusses lectures and how you can get the most out of them. It suggests that you can maximise their impact by forward planning, previewing the topic and taking an active approach to the lecture itself. Once more it stresses the importance of the teaching staff facilitating optimal benefit through the provision of well-constructed lecture lists, readable handouts and visual aids.
- Section 8.3 looks at communication skills, discussion techniques and listening strategies. It discusses some of the problems in small group learning and how difficulties can be overcome. It concludes with a section on practical work and sessions in laboratories.
- Section 8.4 deals with skill in note making, which is vital to getting the most out of your lectures and classes, making knowledge your own and preserving learning benefits. Students generally attest to the importance of note making and the problems created by lecturers who are unprepared,

or lack the skills of exposition and structuring material (Brown and Atkins, 1988, pp. 165–6).

Box 8.1   Little and Large

The **lecture** is simple to organise ... but the speed of speech can mean that masses of information or complicated argument can be hard to retain. The lecture offers the advantages of economies of scale ... but it is hard to maintain attention for almost an hour and make good notes. The good lecturer provides an exciting experience ... but the poor or mediocre exponent makes the lecture eminently forgettable. It is ironic that the lecture, which developed because of the lack of books, today is maintaining its hold with ever larger audiences partly because of the pressures on books.

The **smaller class** seems more appealing. But its success depends upon the participants' being at a similar level and being adequately prepared. The class

- can help in unmasking difficulties students are having with learning
- provides an opportunity for intense tutor–student inter- action
- helps staff to track student progress
- helps to develop skills of verbal fluency, quick thinking and reacting to pressure
- can improve confidence and skill in interacting with others.

Our belief is that the more student-centred and discussion-based the class, the better. This seems particularly important at a time when increased student numbers will probably entail more classes being taken by postgraduate students.

Both lectures and classes can be useful: it is important that they are interrelated and reinforce each other.

8.2   **Getting the most out of lectures**

Curious joy she had of the lectures. It was a joy to hear the theory of
education, there was such freedom and pleasure in ranging over the
very stuff of knowledge and seeing how it moved and lived and had its
being.

D. H. Lawrence, *The Rainbow*

Some critics would agree with Albert Einstein that 'It is in
fact nothing short of a miracle that modern methods of instruction have not yet entirely strangled the holy curiosity of
enquiry . . .'. First in the firing line they would put the lecture –
if, that is, it can be termed a *modern* method of instruction! The
lecture has had numerous critics – yet it survives, it thrives and
many students find it useful.

Arguments about lectures

The advantage a lecture has over reading is that, instead of
having to construct an imaginary conversation, you are
actually hearing advanced students of your discipline talk their
way through key debates and arguments. You can listen and
watch a trained exponent deploying the language of your
discipline. Speech – vocal thinking – is more immediate and
more mentally combustible than reading. The lecture may give
you a clear overview of a problem or topic. Your lecturers may
put things in a more accessible fashion than your textbooks:
out of the difference can come good learning. Even if you are
simply hearing what is in essence a repetition of the chapter of a
textbook, you hear it differently. At its best, the lecture demonstrates how your subject works in practice – the key issues, the
key questions, the key debates.

Critics see reading, videos and computers as preferable
means of imparting information, although they concede the
virtue of the lecture in providing an overview of an area and the

immediacy of the spoken word. The disadvantage of the lecture, they insist, is that it is a one-way process, not a two-way exchange. It is based upon the idea of learning as transmission, the lecturer actively pumping information and ideas into the passive, listening vessel of your mind. If we believe the best learning requires *interaction*, then we will still need to *construct a conversation*. A major difficulty is that we cannot control the lecturer or the flow of speech. When we are reading, in contrast, we can stop when and where we want to. We can look forward or go back over what has been said when we want to; we have more control over the flow of the author's thought.

Some researchers conclude that lectures are useful for drawing maps of topics, backing up learning, and imparting certain kinds of information rather than developing deep learning (Bligh, 1971). As there are ways of conveying information which give students more control over their learning, lectures may be seen at best as trail blazing or reinforcing, at worst as redundant. Others conclude that they *can* convey the skills of thinking through problems, handling evidence and analysing conflicting arguments (Beard and Hartley, 1984).

Obviously, different lectures provide different experiences, depending on the lecturer and the student. The lecturer who follows a clear pre-planned structure, deploys strong powers of exposition, pauses, emphasises, summarises, utilises handouts and visual aids and introduces up-to-date research, sometimes not covered in basic texts, is likely to elicit a more effective response than the lecturer who simply reads an outdated script in a dull monotone (Brown and Atkins, 1988). The 'good lecturer' can link up your existing learning to new knowledge and show you, more vividly and permanently than a written text, how new areas work. One study characterises the good lecturer in terms of *expressiveness*, enthusiasm, empathy, humour, energy and charisma (Abrami, Levanthal and Perry, 1982). Another study describes the good lecturer as having the ability to relate to the students' existing learning and experience and take them forward through the use of analogy (Entwistle and Ramsden, 1983).

But how many good lecturers are there? Are defenders of the lecture making the best of a bad job? Shouldn't the still predominant 45 to 50 minute talk be broken up into smaller blocks? Lectures continue substantially unmodified for a variety of reasons external to their utility as learning methods. These include conservatism, the fact that today's lecturers largely benefitted from them, and the fact that large attendances are cost-effective. Nor are students overly critical of what is undoubtedly, in terms of both pedagogy and technology, an anachronism (Beard and Hartley, 1984, p. 154). It seems likely that the lecture will be with us for some time to come.

How to get the most out of lectures

Key words are once again: *planning, active, questioning, conversation.*

1 *Attending* lectures will usually be voluntary. Unless they are absolutely hopeless, attendance should help learning development. Initially at least, make strict attendance part of your study regime. Once you start missing lectures there may be a snowball effect – you missed the last one so you won't benefit from this one, so you miss that, too! Regular attendance keeps you in touch with other students and with what is happening on your course. OK, you have read the book but now you can see how those who are teaching you – and who will *examine* you – think.

2 *Plan* at least a little. Make sure you have a note which lists your lectures, tells you a little about the topics of each, and suggests reading. Some students skim the literature cited before a lecture. They like to get *the general idea*, to see the skeleton they hope the lecture will flesh out. Others tend to think the more you already know, the more you learn. These

students intensively work over the suggested reading so that they can concentrate more in the lecture itself by starting at a higher level. Having already absorbed much of the detail, they feel they can concentrate on the shape of the argument. Find out which approach fits you. Some degree of preparation is a worthwhile investment.

3 *Question* Formulate a series of questions you wish to answer about the topic of the lecture.

4 *Structure* All competent lecturers will follow some kind of structure. Gradually you will build up experience in recognising and responding to different categories within the lecture.

- **Icebreakers** Getting started with an anecdote or humorous comments
- **Setting** Relating this week's topic to what has gone before
- **Introduction** What the lecture is about and how the material will be sequenced and handled
- **Key points** Often emphasised by pauses or repetition or '. . . and this is absolutely vital', 'Finally and centrally', 'But what is really crucial . . .'
- **Extensions** 'Now let me take this a little further . . .'
- **Another direction** Signalled by a pause, or change of tone, 'OK, now let's look . . .', 'I'd now like to turn . . .', 'In contrast . . .'
- **Examples** Vital as illumination, or keys-in, or different illustrations to those in your reading
- **Asides** May be irrelevant or cast a striking light on substantive argument
- **Critique** Having outlined argument and evidence, the lecturer puts it under the critical microscope
- **Summaries** A good lecturer will briefly recapitulate – throughout the lecture as well as at its end
- **Conclusions** Firm, tentative, interim
- **Preview** Looking ahead to the next lecture

5 *Handouts* If you have prepared and know your way around the material it will be easier to plug into the speaker's structure. A handout outlining the main points helps in this. Can you encourage lecturers to give you handouts? Can you encourage them to give them out the week *prior* to the lecture to facilitate preparation?

6 *Activity* Some students relax during lectures. They feel safe in the knowledge that nobody is going to confront them with difficult questions, or ask them to do anything. But you will get a lot more out of the lecture if you don't expect the lecturer to pump you full of knowledge during the hour. You learn best through a struggle to critically engage with what is being said. Some students find it helps concentration to sit at the front. Others avoid sitting with potentially distracting friends. *Concentrate. Listen. Question.*

- What is the lecturer saying?
- Is he or she arguing, justifying, documenting or simply asserting?
- What is the evidence?
- What are the criticisms?
- What are the alternative theories or viewpoints?
- How does the lecture square with what you already know?

7 *Listen* Concentrate on your questions and whether the lecturer is answering them, not on what you are doing tonight. Try to concentrate on what is *new* and what challenges your assumptions and premises. Some of us listen actively to the reinforcing or confirmatory statement. But we shy away from what we interpret as the hostile challenge. You have to get used to receiving and assessing views which disturb or threaten your existing assumptions or scheme of knowledge. Listen to and distinguish evidence and opinions. Practise by listening to tapes and making notes.

8.3   **Small group learning**

This tutorial, the first of the new academic year, had already
assumed a characteristic tone of embarrassment and
uncertainty...

Malcolm Bradbury, Eating People Is Wrong

Groups included in the phrase *small group learning* can
number up to thirty; small group work is sometimes used by
lecturers to get students to discuss points after a period of
lecturing.

A variety of terms are used to cover learning in small groups.

Seminar Normally involves between ten and twenty
students. It is usually used in a research context – a speaker
gives a paper and other colleagues comment, question and
criticise – or as an alternative term for a *class* where as part of a
course a student or tutor gives a paper or introduces a topic for
general discussion.

Tutorial   In its pure Oxbridge form, a meeting between a
tutor and one or two students, where a student reads an essay
which is then discussed. The term is sometimes now used for
small classes of five or six students.

Practical classes Where groups of students undertake
exercises in a laboratory or on a field trip to train them in the
techniques of scientific enquiry.

The terms do not suggest the growing diversity of learning in
groups which can involve buzz groups, brainstorming sessions,
discussion syndicates, role-play and ongoing project and
report work. Traditionally, groups were tutor-led but there is a
movement towards student leadership–tutor supervision.

If the lecture has often been used as a means of conveying
information the small group has the advantage of developing

thinking by providing the opportunity for a real *conversation*, with its clash of ideas and theories, and direct *application* through exercises and case studies. Psychologists suggest the optimal size for this kind of creative interaction is five or six and that once class sizes are over twenty the advantages diminish (Argyle, 1983). Surveys demonstrate that students and tutors welcome the informal atmosphere small numbers can encourage as well as the flexibility, the opportunity to participate, and the chance to give and receive instant feedback. Students feel they get more individual attention and are trained in developing discussion, exchanging ideas and learning to analyse problems and produce solutions. Difficulties include the silent or dominant student, the demands of preparation and participation, the sometimes threatening nature of direct, intense interaction with tutor and other students, and the anxiety of being in the direct firing line with 'no hiding place' (Brown and Atkins, 1988).

Small groups can act as effective learning mechanisms by:

- fostering and utilising *group identity* – you realise other students are grappling with the same problems as you are and that you are not alone and can learn from others;
- providing a small learning forum where you can explain your difficulties, ask questions which may solve them, use your colleagues as a sounding board, practise what you have learned, understand what you have not;
- providing a first-hand opportunity for you to learn the skills of *constructing argument* and also *defending an argument* or theory and *reacting to criticism*;
- giving you the opportunity to *practise communication skills* – listening, explaining, questioning and answering – the techniques of discussion and debate.

Box 8.2   At the start of the series of classes

Be clear as to the purpose of this part of your study programme, how it relates to lectures and assignments, what role it plays in assessment. Discuss the way classes will be conducted. Will they involve tutor-led or student-led discussion, be introduced by a brief talk or written paper, developed through smaller groups discussing problems? Ensure you know what your future responsibilities will be. A good lecturer will want to involve you in discussing how classes should be conducted. So here are some points to think about:

The first class should be an ice-breaker, a chance for getting to know each other and finding out what you have to do in the coming weeks. How about suggesting to get going:

Naming circles The first student introduces herself, the second herself and the first student, the third himself and the previous *two*.

Pairs You talk briefly to the student next to you and then introduce each other to the group.

Interviews You take longer to interview your partner about their background, courses they are taking, what they want out of this programme. This then leads naturally into a discussion as to how classes should be handled.

Even groups where the tutor is dominant, which are instruction-based, essentially punctuated lectures, still have advantages over the larger lecture. They offer more direct contact and an opportunity to address in detail problems arising out of lectures or reading. They allow for Socratic questioning, dialogue and intense discussion. You will undoubtedly encounter the tutor-led class. But some would argue that the tutor's domination of discussion is a constraint on the full exploitation of small group work and that small groups work best when the tutor becomes less dominant and the students move centre stage. In this view the small group is more effective when there is greater interaction between *all* its members, not just the student–tutor, student–tutor couplets. It then provides a marvellous opportunity for students to talk through ideas produced by reading and lectures, to test what they have learned through questioning and answering each other, to start speaking the language of their discipline, and to prove and polish their learning through *articulation*: 'I didn't know I understood that till I said it.'

> The group system aims to emancipate the student from the authority–dependence relationship and to help him [or her] to develop intellectual independence and maturity through interaction with peers, by glimpsing not only the context in which a more experienced scholar sees the problem but the various contexts in which several equals see the problem. (Abercrombie, 1979, p. 6)

Such contexts may be best established where the tutor relinquishes some of the authority role, attempts to ensure students take greater responsibility for their own learning and acts as a *primus inter pares* facilitator rather than a dominant instructor. Tutors should shed *some* of their authority, certainly – but they cannot divest themselves of their *scholarly responsibility*. If they do, they may let any old rubbish pass in the hope a student will question or correct it, or let the group stumble around for a time in the hope they will find their own way out of the impasse. At some stage the tutor *must* intervene. Good tutors recede a certain distance – according to the group and approach – into the background. They re-emerge when required. They are learning facilitator *and* learning resource.

Box 8.3   Behaviours in group discussion

Introducing   Suggesting a path for exploration; starting the ball rolling

Informing   Providing the group with *information*, relevant facts or experience

Stating opinions and arguments   Addressing the facts and evaluating them

Questioning   Testing   or   seeking   clarification   or statements

Refining   Restating with more precision what someone has said

Building   Expanding on previous comments or connecting them up with others

Criticising   Probing, assessing, comparing, evaluating

Ordering   Chairing the class so that a rush to irrelevance or a dominant speaker or an excess of humour is set to rights

Planning   Asking how far have we got? Where next?

Confidence building   Showing friendliness. Being receptive to comments, encouraging students

Pulling together   Relating different ideas to each other, extracting meaning, summing up progress

Testing   Assessing whether the class understands the point reached and agrees on where to go next

Summarising   Building up and expressing progress so far

Concluding   Reviewing class at end and extracting key points

---

The small group at work

'Well', said Bates, 'let's see what the others think . . . '.

'What do other people feel?' he asked.

Immediately all was embarrassment. Feet were shuffled, faces reddened, useless notes were consulted diligently. No one spoke.

Malcolm Bradbury, *Eating People Is Wrong*

The tutor may assign different students to introduce the class each week on a rota basis. It is important that all students are clear as to what is required, what the assignment is and the style of introduction required – a 10- to 15-minute outline of series of key issues and problems in their settings is far preferable to the extended paper or essay as way of stimulating discussion.

What you should expect from a good tutor

Students are increasingly asked to comment on how classes are run so that they can be improved. The National Union of Students wants a greater voice for students in how classes are organised, and more participation. You should expect your tutor to

- know the existing state of the group's development;
- allocate manageable tasks;
- only intervene if necessary;
- answer questions only if members of the group cannot answer them;
- respond to questions by putting another stimulatory question;
- state views tentatively rather than rigidly so as not to choke off discussion.

Preparation

It is vital that *all* – not simply the student introducing the topic – prepare thoroughly. Otherwise time may be wasted by questions whose answers would have been disclosed in the early stages of preparatory reading.

Learning inter-relations

Groups work best when they develop on lectures and writing assignments. A system of regular reading, lectures, classes, writing and then back round the circle again, integrates and reinforces learning.

Introductions (see Box 8.3) are best kept short, accompanied by a brief handout listing key points, or a brief outline on a flip chart or blackboard. The student assigned the role should thoroughly research the area. He or she should take on a 'steering' role in discussion ensuring relevance and treatment of all aspects of the topic and be prepared to briefly summarise at the end before handing over to the tutor for concluding reflections.

Seating arrangements The circle or horseshoe shape increases interaction. So does ringing the changes in who sits where within it, seating dominant students near the tutor or speaker and quieter students opposite the speaker (Argyle, 1983).

The dominant student may be constraining the development of discussion, inhibiting or irritating others or taking up more than a fair share of questions. Others may be silent, the class may be less effective, because the dominant student is noisy. If you feel you may be one of these, ask yourself: Do I really need to make this point? Has it already been adequately made? Is this contribution relevant? Even though it *was* pertinent five minutes ago will it interfere with the way discussion has developed now? Am I listening properly to what others are saying? Can I be briefer, more specific, more relevant? Have I prepared thoroughly enough?

The quiet student is often shy or worried. If you are, think about why this is so. The more you prepare, the more confident you will feel. Break the ice early by asking a simple question or making a simple statement. We all become inhibited because we feel we need to impress others with some blinding insight or startling new formulation. The longer you hold off, waiting for great thoughts to come, the more nervous you will feel and the more authoritative the statements of others will appear. Confident speakers become able at putting their ideas together by *practice* – by starting to speak in a simple, sometimes stumbling, fashion. When they realise that their fellow students are pleased that they have made a useful contribution, not sitting there trying to catch them out, it all becomes worthwhile. We learn when we get involved. You will remember points far more vividly if you ask about them, rather than if you sit passively. You will lose the opportunity of utilising the knowledge of the whole group if you do not explain a difficulty or learning problem. Gradually becoming a participating member adds to the purpose of your attending.

Helping discussion   Students can help develop a friendly atmosphere by reacting and giving feedback. If the person opposite you is obviously trying hard to make a point, nod or mutter 'yes', rather than stare stonily at the floor. Use other students' names when talking to them. If a good point is made, say so. Smile; don't yawn. Try to relate your contribution to what has just been said by, perhaps, briefly restating it in your own words. If you disagree with a colleague, say, 'I see what you are trying to get at *but* . . .'; 'You're right, Jane, in relation to X. But, surely, more generally . . .'; 'But Razina, the problem I have with this . . .' All are much better than 'Rubbish,' or 'You've completely misunderstood what I'm trying to say.' To say, 'Rubbish,' is not really much help as you have to then go on to explain in a reasoned and civilised way, *why* you think it is rubbish – having, in all probability, made your colleague less receptive to your eventual explanation. Don't get personal – criticise the message, not the messenger. As time goes on and you get to know each other better, discussion may become more informal and vigorous. And, of course, politeness must never stultify thought or stop an argument being pursued to its conclusion.

Listening   The quality of discussion and the degree of progress in a class turns on how well people listen. If you get a chance, listen to tapes of discussion. Are people responding to statements or questions they actually heard? Or are their responses pre-formulated? Jot down (a) what is being said and (b) your response. In class, follow a similar procedure. This helps focus concentration. Do not erupt into a reaction whilst others are in mid-sentence. Relax, slow down, wait until their message is finished, absorbed and you have your response. *Then* come in. Somebody else will get in first? With what? If they make your point – fine. If not, a good chair will ensure you get your chance. You can expect to hear statements you strongly disagree with. Learn to take them calmly. The calmer you are, the better you will be able to articulate your response.

Procedures for discussion

- **Don't interrupt** even though you think you know what is coming next . . . at least until you know each other very well or the person is waffling or piling error on error. Unjustified interruptions disrupt dialogue; the well timed intervention can strengthen and lubricate discussion by keeping it relevant and interactive.
- **Listen to the speaker,** don't interject to the person next to you . . . one singer one song.
- **Relate to what has been said.** A major problem here is listening to the speaker while formulating a point you want to make at the same time – particularly if somebody else makes a point and the discussion flows past you. The question is – and it is a matter of judgement – how important is your question or argument? If you think it is vital you may say, 'Could we just go back a little?' But sometimes this can disrupt a fruitful vein of discussion.
- **Be constructive** in form even if you have to be destructive in substance: 'True, Liz, but another way of looking at it . . .'; 'You put that very well, Betty, but haven't we also got to look at . . .?
- **Be succinct.** Try to keep questions and comments brief and to the point. If you ask three or four questions together or combine questions with comments, you make it difficult for the discussion to proceed coherently. So raise one or two *specific* questions at a time.

- **Avoid pairing** – classes becoming one-to-one interchanges. Sometimes a student may be justified in coming back at a point, but if the class starts turning into a two-way conversation move it on.
- **Don't worry about pauses.** They are sometimes necessary so that the group can think about a problem or recharge batteries. If the group is stymied and creaks to a halt, why not suggest smaller groups to address different aspects of a problem?
- **Take remedial action if necessary.** For example, if one or two students are dominating – and some students *do* need shutting up at times – say, 'I'd like to hear what other people think' or 'If I could just get a word in.' With the quiet student – and some students *do* need prompting – say, 'Don't you think that's the main point, Paul?'
- **Summarise** – not only at the end. If you have, or look as if you have, reached some conclusions then stop and let someone stick your conclusions on the flipchart.

The substance of discussion   Listen not only closely but critically to what others say in discussion. Subject comments to the following mental questions:

- Is that argued or asserted? Where is the evidence? Does it stand up?
- How is that relevant? Why is that important?
- What do your arguments imply? Can you give us an example?
- What is the underlying principle?
- Is there an alternative point of view?

Note making   Don't feel that notes (see p. 246) should be dispensed with in classes. Some students find noting down comments essential to their response. Brief summary jottings may be useful when you pause to summarise, and again when the class reaches its conclusion.

Laboratory classes

At some point in your course you may have to undertake some practical work – field trips, placements or small projects. This will be particularly true for science and engineering students, who often spend more than 50% of their contact hours working in laboratories. Practical work in the sciences is intended to develop in students a number of qualities:

- An understanding of **the application and development of theory**
- The acquisition of **skills of inquiry and a critical approach to experimentation**
- **The acquisition of skills of observation and data interpretation**
- The development of **problem-solving techniques**
- The development of practical **skills of utilising and organising equipment,** measuring etc.
- The development in the student of **professional attitudes and autonomous learning**
- The development of the **skills of report writing**

It is sometimes questioned whether practical work in science degrees meets these objectives. Researchers find that laboratory work is less effective than lectures in imparting factual knowledge and concepts but better at improving manual and observational skills (Brown and Atkins, 1988, p. 93).

The principle in practical work is that you learn *by doing*. However, learning is sometimes impaired because demonstrations, experiments and case studies are not properly thought out and devised in terms of learning goals nor fully explained to demonstrators and students (Beard and Hartley, 1984, p. 201).

- Are you clear as to explanations and instructions for practical work? As with lectures and classes, it is useful if lecturers prepare handouts.

- Are demonstrators and technicians fully briefed to help you in your work in laboratory sessions and clear up difficulties?
- Is there a manual which deals clearly with laboratory organisation and layout, explains each experiment in terms of your course, tells you where apparatus and materials are and outlines procedures?
- Do your tutors provide you with a list of questions? As with other areas, you are programmed best for learning when you are seeking answers.
- What feedback and evaluation do you get of your practical work? We learn best by doing if the quality of our doing is assessed afterwards so we can learn from our mistakes.
- Take care with writing up reports (see p. 313).
- Be clear as to the role practical work plays in your course and how it counts towards final assessment.

8.4   Noteworthy notes

Let's look at this aspect of your studying in a little more detail. Several studies show that students find note making important and wish to improve their skills in this area (Beard and Hartley, 1984, p. 121).

Throughout your course you will probably make notes to:

- help you concentrate on a book or lecture;
- facilitate your response in a class;
- help you to understand a particular problem or a difficult passage in your literature;
- see what you have understood as in reviewing books or lectures;
- remind you of key points or materials you need to read;
- provide you with a permanent record of what happened in a class or lecture or the main ideas in an article or book that is difficult to get hold of;
- provide you with a *personal record* which fuses what the

lecturer or author was trying to communicate with your purpose, understanding and viewpoint.

This last point is particularly important. We use the phrase *making* rather than 'taking' notes to emphasise the creation or re-creation element. A secretary *taking* a letter is transcribing, copying down his or her boss's thoughts verbatim. A student *making* notes should be transforming, to some degree, what the lecturer or author says by rearranging it and recording his or her own impressions and ideas as well as the lecturer's or author's. Understand what is being said and *express it in your own words*. The purpose of note making is *learning*, not recording, translation, transcription nor simple repetition. Your notes should be the product of the lecturer or author *and you,* a personal record made in a personal language, which means we will all make notes differently. What follows is for individual consideration; it is not a general prescription.

However, it is safe to say that a watchword in making notes is *compression*. Because of the demands of your course – this week's lecture soon gives way to next week's, the reading never seems to stop coming – you will want notes that are more in the nature of brief skeletal references rather than detailed volumes you are going to peruse exhaustively through your course.

Making notes in lectures

Making notes in lectures is tougher than making notes from written materials. The 'material' is continually in motion, moving in ways you are not sure of or cannot directly control. You have to think, sift, criticise and write in a limited time. You, too, have to be in motion, moving quickly from one to the other. You are under greater pressure than when reading a book; locating the signals and signposts and grasping the structure of thought is harder, although you can be helped immensely by a good handout. Particularly with the poor lecturer, you have to uncover the structure yourself and plug into it.

- Use one side of the paper only to allow for later amplification, review and translation into diagrams.
- Prepare for each lecture and know what it will cover. Refresh yourself by looking over your notes from your last lecture and class, and do any preliminary reading.
- Don't *even try* to write everything down. You'll go into overload and then miss key points. You must learn to discriminate between *the structure, important ideas, arguments and illustrations* and setting, repetition, waffle and jokes. The basic structure is most important. If we remember that, the details quickly follow. But, once again, all generalisations are fallible. An anecdote which at first appears irrelevant might turn out to encapsulate a way into the subject.
- *Critical questioning* will facilitate sifting and selection because it facilitates concentration and real listening.
- Look for *signposts and signals* that tell you what is coming, how important it is, and how it relates to what has gone before.
  1 Wait for the speaker to move from the preliminaries to the **introduction to the day's structure**.
  2 Concentrate on the **summing up pauses** and the changing of gears from one area or argument to another.
  3 Listen for **emphasis** which means 'Note this, it is important.'
  4 You have to burn with concentration *at the end* when many lecturers distil the substance of the last 40 minutes and emphasise their conclusions.
- Practice in writing will help you in note making but when making notes in lectures throw out of the window conventional notions of neatness or coherence for anybody other than yourself. Your notes may look a mess to others. Do they ignite your understanding when you come to review them?
- Use shorthand, headings, indentations, underlinings, highlighting. Get used to making an effective mess in plenty of space. Polish up your use of abbreviations such as e.g., n.b.,

viz., i.e. and etc. Use initials, symbols. Above all compress material and relate it to your reading. If you know what is being said, know it is fully documented in a book or article you have, don't let writing interfere with thought, simply jot down the reference.

- And always keep thinking. Bang down your own thoughts on what is being said, your own comments, your own criticisms, you own links with what you already know.

Forms of note making

Some of the numerous methods of making notes are listed below.

Prose summary   This is prose in sequence and paragraphs but using compression, abbreviation etc. to make a précis of the lecture.

Linear logical method   Here you record an outline of the lecture, shearing off the flesh and leaving the bone structure, with headings and numbers, indentation, lists and so on. In Figure 8.1 you can see notes I made in this way on a lecture entitled 'The Background to 1916'. I had done some reading beforehand and was able to isolate the main points.

Diagrammatic notes   If you already know a lot about the subject or it suits your way of thinking, you might like to use diagrams to cover at least part of the ground in lectures. These are useful because they highlight interrelationships and inter-connections and provide you with an overview of a topic – often vividly. Most of us would use the linear logical method in lectures or talks. But it is sometimes useful when later reviewing our notes to translate linear logical notes into a diagram. Figure 8.2 on page 252 shows how I have done this with my notes on 1916. I take the main concept or core idea to be explained and bang it down in the middle of my page – as I

20th century Ireland Lec.⑤ 12/3/93

Background to Easter 1916

A. | Background features 1900-14 |

① New Nationalism —

'Cult. rev.' - eg Gaelic League,
Gaelic Athletic Assoc; Celt.
Lit. Rev.; Irish Feminism

② Boer War —

1900 → anti-imperialist mobilisation
          vs govmt.

③ Labour Unrest and Labourism

Dublin - living conditions, low wages,
class conflict, 1912-13 strikes.
Larkin/Irish T&WU. James Connolly.
Internat. Soc. /Irish Nat

④ Sinn Fein (Ourselves Alone)

Broad front. Irish Parl. Party still in
control but anti-Eng/anti-Prot. in
New Nat. Irish Republican B'hood=

Figure 8.1   Linear logical notes

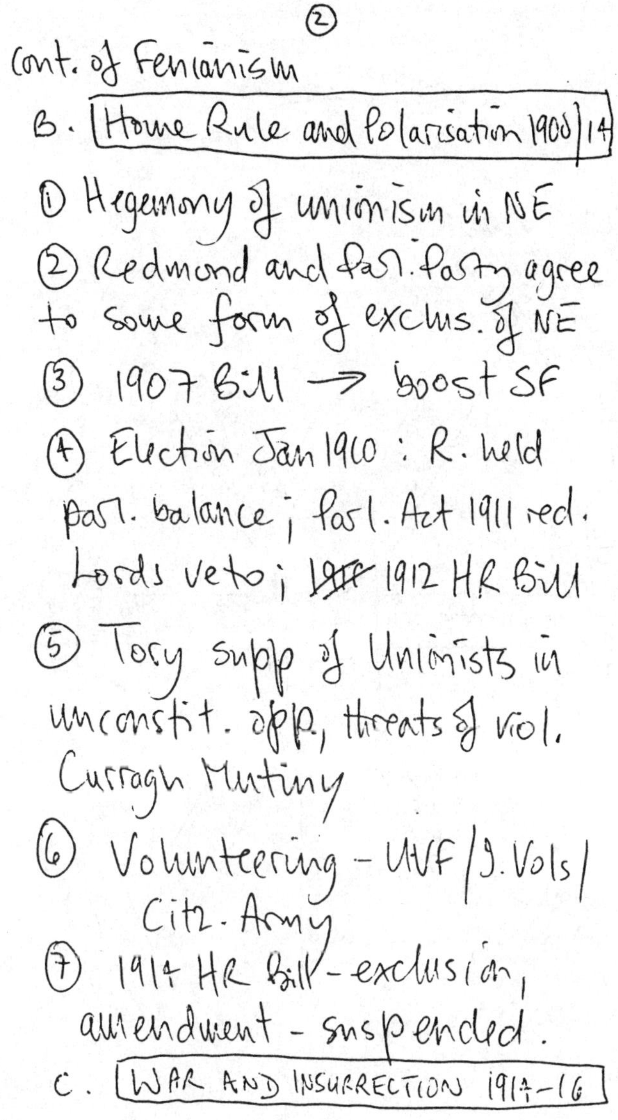

②

Cont. of Fenianism

B. [Home Rule and Polarisation 1900/14]

① Hegemony of unionism in NE

② Redmond and Parl. Party agree
to some form of exclus. of NE

③ 1907 Bill → boost SF

④ Election Jan 1910 : R. held
Parl. balance ; Parl. Act 1911 red.
Lords veto ; 1912 HR Bill

⑤ Tory supp of Unionists in
unconstit. opp, threats of viol.
Curragh Mutiny

⑥ Volunteering – UVF/I.Vols/
Citz. Army

⑦ 1914 HR Bill – exclusion,
amendment – suspended.

C. [WAR AND INSURRECTION 1914–16]

Figure 8.1 Linear logical notes

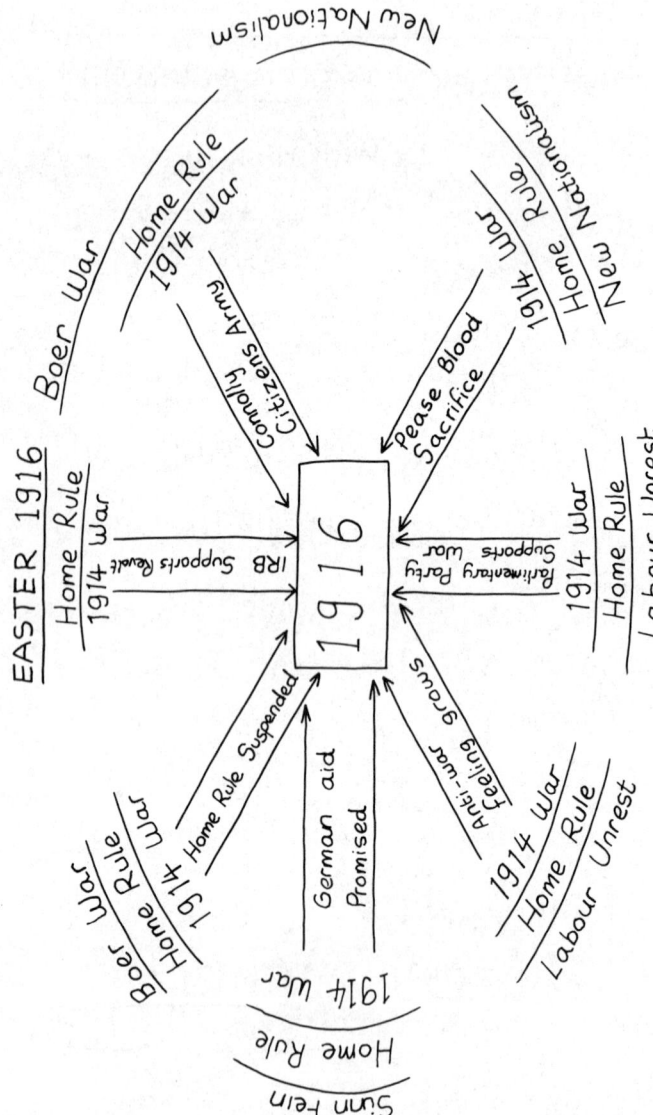

Figure 8.2   Diagrammatic breakdown of background features to Easter 1916 uprising

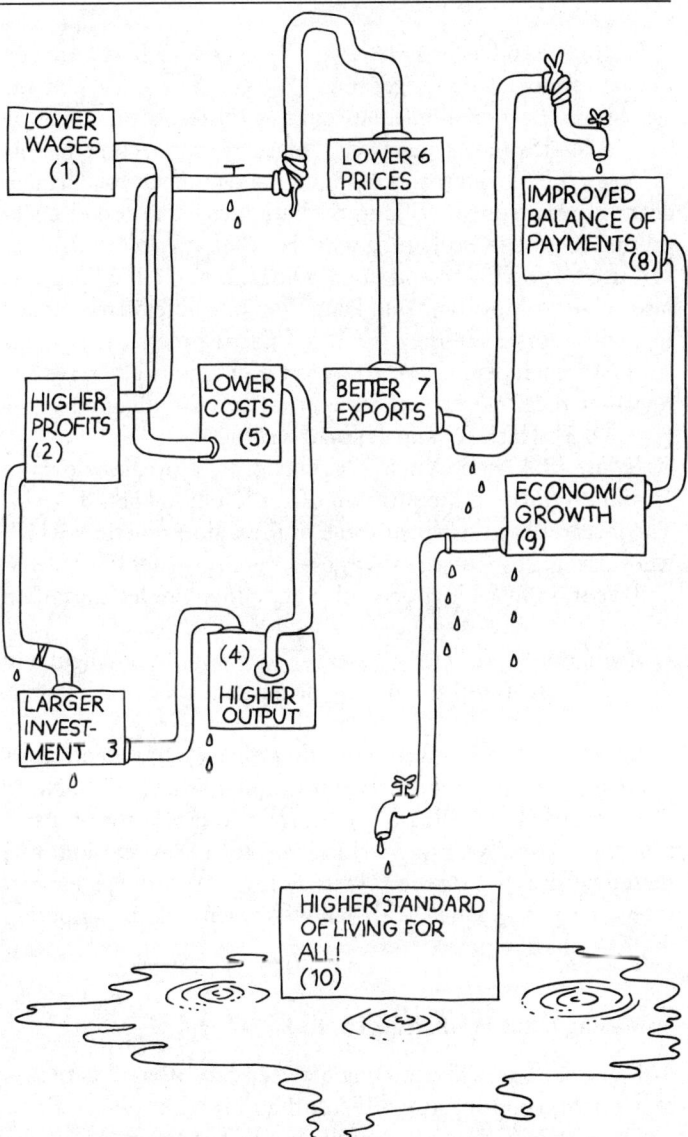

Figure 8.3 Flow diagram illustrating stages in theory of economic growth

have done with Easter 1916. I then jot down furthest away, on the periphery of my page, major longer term causes of the rebellion. The more immediate igniting causes, such as the way the 1914–18 war developed, I place as connecting factors between the rebellion and more fundamental causes. The diagram moves from specific immediate factors to broad background factors in explaining why the rebellion occurred.

I use lines, arrows and double lines to make the links and interrelationships stand out. Diagrammatic notes can be added to easily. For many they produce effective recall as patterns stimulate memory. If you really get going, particularly when revising linear notes, you can produce vivid diagrams (see Figure 8.3) which sum up pages of writing.

Figure 8.4 is a quick diagram which breaks down a 15-minute talk on the position of trade unions before 1979. The lecturer then outlined some of the union practices which were affected by Conservative government policies (Figure 8.5) and went on to look at one policy, employment legislation, in more detail.

If you don't like diagrams, leave them alone! You might find they are more useful as a device for revision.

Review   Some studies show that nearly 10% of students never subsequently read their notes (Gibbs, 1981, p. 59). Notes help immediate learning but they are also useful for preparation for classes, for essay writing and for exam revision. It is therefore useful to review your notes soon after a lecture, perhaps over a coffee with fellow students and comparing impressions and notes.

Making notes in small group work

Making notes when moving between the different activities of a small group is more difficult than in the lecture, for you have to listen, think and respond as well. Your notes are likely, therefore, to be shorter and more skeletal. However, if you

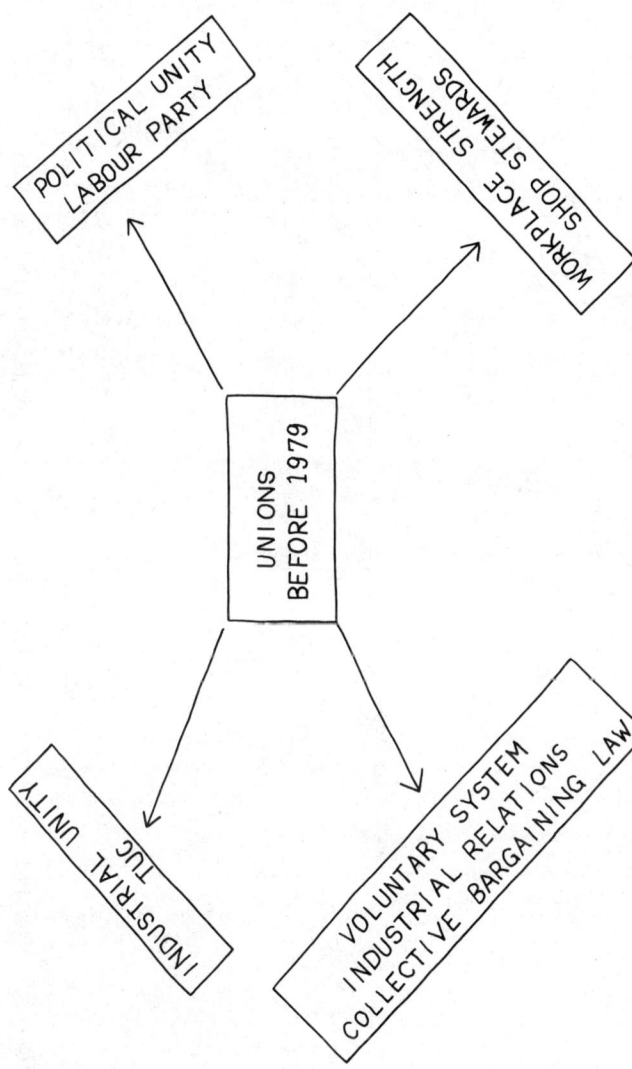

Figure 8.4 Diagrammatic breakdown of lecture on trade unions before 1979

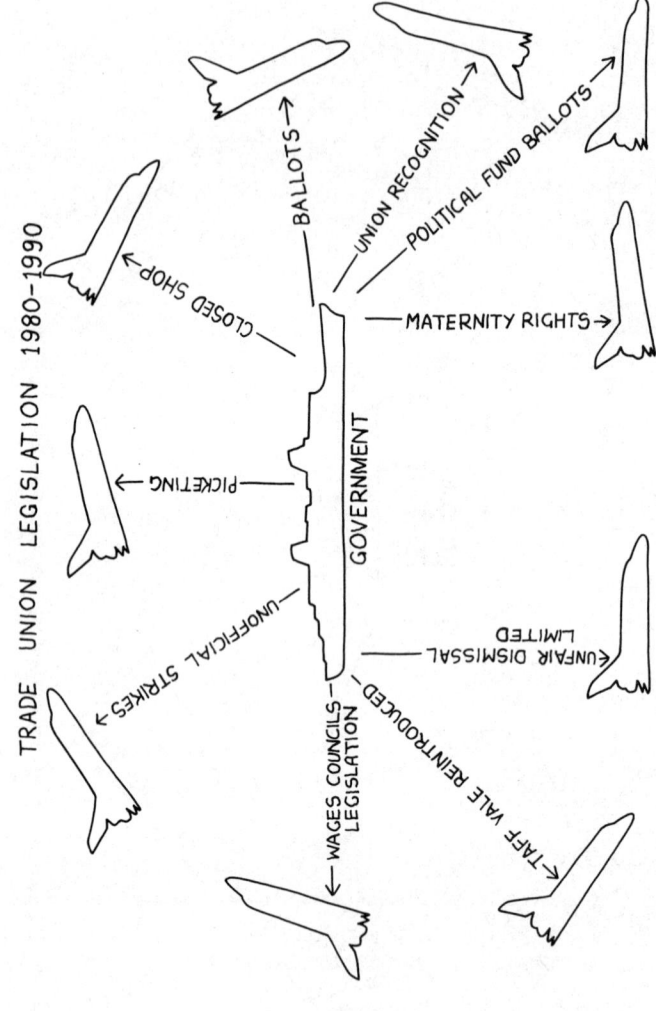

TRADE UNION LEGISLATION 1980–1990

BALLOTS

UNION RECOGNITION

POLITICAL FUND BALLOTS

CLOSED SHOP

MATERNITY RIGHTS

PICKETING

GOVERNMENT

UNFAIR DISMISSAL LIMITED

UNOFFICIAL STRIKES

TAFF VALE REINTRODUCED

WAGES COUNCILS LEGISLATION

Figure 8.5 Diagrammatic representation of Conservative government policies towards trade unions

have prepared well for your class you will not need to make complete notes. Only make note of clarifications, new points and corrections, so that you can make a full contribution to discussion. But review your class and notes as soon as possible afterwards while your memories are fresh.

Making notes from reading

You may make notes to help you understand as you read, notes which are instantly disposable. You may make notes to help you concentrate on your reading which you also dispose of or you may make notes to keep of important chapters, passages or articles. Before making these 'lasting' notes consider whether underlining, highlighting and making margin notes in a book (if it is your own) will suffice. Or whether you can photocopy key pages of a book and article and give it this treatment.

If you do need to make notes follow the guidance on reading given earlier (p. 217) first. Make sure you can recall the material and have a grasp of it before you start making notes. Don't make notes just for the sake of it (see Box 8.4). Avoid transcribing rather than translating what is on the page into your own language and your own knowledge. Transcription may be a means of avoiding work. Note making is harder: it is always part of thinking and learning. Use direct quotation from the text only where it is vital or expresses a point superbly. Having located the passages you want, skim read the connecting passages before and after them and familiarise yourself with the key part you want. You may find that note making from reading lends itself more to the use of diagrams than note making from lectures. But once again the key is: what works for you?

Box 8.4   How long a note?

Don't make notes for the sake of it.

If you just need a brief note of a book then just make a brief note.

Arno Mayer, <u>Why did the heavens
not darken?</u>   Verso 1990

Controversial. Argues final sol'n
not necess. logical outcome
of Nazism. Rather failure of
invasion of Sov. Union. Genocide
product of both ideology <u>and</u>
circumstance.

or if you need to say more

Crit. of view Fin. Sol. inherent
in Nazi ideol. Anti-comm.
and anti-sem. permeated
Nazi practise and <u>Mein Kampf</u>
Ideas of N'm prod. by
gen. crisis of Europe 1914 →

persec. of Jews rel. to polit.
events 1933 - dramatic change
with war - mills. more Jews
under Nazi control. So
long as N's winning, persec.
of Jews limited. <u>Hitlerism</u>
<u>necessary but not sufficient</u>
for Holocaust. Impasse of
attack on S.U. ⇒ Final Sol.
Jews pay for defeat. Genocide
prod. of brutalisation of total
War. View that all ordained
from 1933 or MK divorces ideas
from historical ideas - anti-history
[But what if H. had won?? !]

This is a longer note which starts to raise questions. Making notes is like playing the concertina. You have to decide how much you push in or pull out to get the length and detail of note you need.

Storage and retrieval

Clearly label and date your notes and file them carefully (see p. 176).

Key points

1 Lectures are likely to play a key role in your course. Prepare, attend, develop an active role, make notes.
2 Small group learning can play a major role in your development, particularly where a degree of autonomy and activity passes from tutors to students.
3 Small group work requires careful design and explanation by tutors, detailed preparation by all students, and cultivation of the skills of listening, active thinking, discussion and note making. Learning by *doing* – discovery work or role-play – can be particularly useful.
4 Making notes requires preparation and the ability to absorb the speaker's structure of exposition. Learning can be helped by handouts and explanation of structure.
5 Notes are a personal matter and should be related to handouts, books, articles. Discussion with fellow students after lectures and classes can be an important learning aid.
6 Note making from reading provides for more student control; diagrammative methods may be useful here.
7 Have an effective means of storing notes. If their use is to be maximised they should be reviewed periodically.

Things to do

1 Compare the advantages and disadvantages of lectures and classes in learning. Which do you prefer?
2 Discuss with another student a recent class. What were the good points? What were the bad points? How could the class be improved?
3 Plan and hold a 40-minute discussion with five or six fellow students on an important topic in your course. Tape-record the discussion, play it back and analyse problems.
4 Record 20 minutes from a discussion programme whilst making notes. Compare your notes with the playback.

5 Swop the notes you made from a recent lecture with the notes one of your friends made. How helpful do you find his or her notes? Can you understand them? Why did they note down certain points and eliminate others, emphasise some areas at the expense of others, use certain methods rather than others? Discuss together the rationale, advantages and disadvantages of each set of notes.
6 Make notes of a chapter in a book and compare them with those made by a colleague carrying out the same exercise.
7 Take two sets of prose notes you have made recently. Translate them into diagrams.
8 Take ten key words used in the chapter of a book or article. Find the *synonym* (key partner word which means the same) and then the *antonym* (word which means the reverse) of each.

Further reading

A thought-provoking book on teaching is Donald Bligh's *What's the Use of Lectures?* (Penguin Books, 1971). More difficult is Minnie Abercrombie's *Aims and Techniques of Group Teaching* (Society for Research into Higher Education, 1979). *Effective Teaching in Higher Education* by George Brown and Madeleine Atkins (Methuen, 1988) is well worth looking at if you want to see the good advice on teaching being given to your lecturers. Jean Rudduck's *Learning through Small Group Discussion: A Study of Seminar Work in Higher Education* (Society for Research into Higher Education, 1978) is a useful primer on classes and seminars. You might also like to look at *Learning in Groups* by David Jaques (Croom Helm, 1984) for more background information.

9

Writing well

Proper words in proper places, make the true definition of a style.

Jonathan Swift

9.1 Introduction

This chapter stresses the desirability of a good written style. You might question this emphasis by arguing that it is content which is the more important: that what is in the parcel is more important than its wrapping. I would respond by making three points.

Firstly, the parcel metaphor is inappropriate: style is not just the wrapping, it is also part of what's inside. If you have something interesting to say, good style makes it even more interesting. Style is a combination of form and content. It doesn't just ornament what you have to say, it helps you achieve greater clarity and subtlety of thought. An unusual way of expressing something often sheds new light upon it. Good style then, reflects good thinking and encourages it.

Secondly, good style gives you a crucial advantage in the battle for your reader's interest and sympathy. At university your most important readers are your tutors and success will win you higher grades. In the outside world your readers could be colleagues or superiors; persuading them will help achieve success in your chosen profession.

Thirdly, writing well provides its own rewards. Great satisfaction can be derived from expressing yourself with clarity and felicity. When you are an undergraduate words become your trade: a good writing style means you have mastered it.

Even scientific reports – often thought of as irrevocably dry – can be elegantly articulated through concision and correct choice of words. (See Chapter 10.7).

- Section 9.2 probes the inner mysteries of style by taking a short diversion into the domain of literary criticism;
- Section 9.3 goes on to address punctuation;
- Section 9.4 looks at sentences;
- Section 9.5 deals with paragraphs;
- Section 9.6 considers quotations and references; whilst
- Section 9.7 looks briefly at the vexed topic of spelling.

9.2   What is good style?

The answer to this question is not easy, and literary critics debate it with some passion. From one point of view, judgement of style is essentially personal. You may like a particular writer; your friend might not. The critic F. R. Leavis thought *Middlemarch* by George Eliot was one of the finest novels in the English language; another critic might prefer a different classic – say, Virginia Woolf's *Mrs Dalloway*. Neither is necessarily right: despite their intellectual distinction, critics merely apply differing criteria in their individual ways. Does this mean that all judgement is personal, that there are no objective criteria and that any writing is as good or bad as any other? The playwright David Hare said as much in 1991 when he maintained that, for his admirers, the lyrics of Bob Dylan were as good as the poetry of John Keats. This provoked a furious response at the time from Michael Ignatieff and others who attempted to refute such heretical relativism and argue for objective standards of excellence. The details of this debate need not concern us, but beyond a certain point the relativist position clearly breaks down: the scribblings of a child, for example, cannot be judged in the same light as Shakespeare's plays. A piece of writing has to fulfil certain basic requirements before questions of its literary merit can even begin to be asked.

Firstly, it usually has to *obey the rules of grammar, punctuation and syntax*. David Hare would presumably not seek to equate the following piece of writing with that of Dickens.

> Well, I mean like its gott to be stoopid hasnt it. You no, the quality sort of thing, I mean like wheres the quality in this kind of riting.

You might respond by pointing out that some noted writers have breached these rules – but they have always done so from a position of maturity. Even then, some of these experiments – the writings of Gertrude Stein, for example – have been judged failures by readers and critics alike. Such avante-garde excursions are certainly not advised for the average under-graduate.

Secondly, the style and tone employed has to be *appropriate for the context*. For example, a letter of commiseration to someone whose mother had died would be unlikely to be considered well written if it adopted a chatty, jokey style.

If it is assumed that a piece of writing is both technically accurate and contextually appropriate, what further qualities must it have to be classed as good writing? A few examples will help provide the answer.

1 **INCREDIBLE Ian Botham led England to a superb eight-wicket victory over Australia in today's big World Cup showdown.** The amazing 'Beefy' roasted the Aussies with a three-wicket maiden over which ripped the heart out of their innings as they crashed to 171 all out.

You will recognise immediately a sports report from a popular newspaper (the first two sentences on the back page of the *Manchester Evening News*, 5 March 1992). As a piece of writing this is notable for its prodigal use of superlatives ('incredible', 'superb', 'amazing'); its use of a feeble pun (' "Beefy roasted the Aussies" '); and its use of con-frontational, dramatic images ('big World Cup showdown', 'ripped the heart out').

Is this good writing? It's clearly not Shakespeare and even as journalism it would not win any Pulitzer Prizes, but in the context of tabloid sports reporting it is quite effective. The author wishes to attract the attention of readers in the bus queue or during the coffee break and there is a sense – particularly if you are a cricket fan – in which he grabs you by the lapels and insists you read on. The style then is appropriate for the context.

2 'Come on up,' she said.

As Keith followed her heavily into the apartment, Nicola did something right out of character: she cursed her fate. Then she swivelled and inspected him, from arid crown to Cuban heels, as he cast his scavenging blue eyes around the room: Keith, stripped of all charisma from pub and street. It wasn't the posture, the scrawniness of the shanks and backside, the unpleasant body scent, the drunken scoop of his gaze – unappealing though these features certainly were. Just that Nicola saw at once with a shock (I knew it all along, she said to herself) that the capacity for love was extinct in him.

This extract, fairly obviously, comes from a novel – *London Fields*, in fact, by Martin Amis. He is seeking to describe someone who is physically and morally degenerate and achieve his effects via a variety of literary devices. He uses *alliteration*, the repetition of consonants at the beginnings of words ('crown to Cuban heels'); *assonance*, the repetition of similar vowel sounds ('shanks and backside') and evocative *imagery* ('the drunken scoop of his gaze'). He uses short words and short phrases to good effect ('she cursed her fate', 'Keith, stripped of all charisma from pub and street.') Notice also how the use of the colon gives both phrases added force. Is this high quality writing? Most certainly it is, in the sense that it reflects considerable literary skills; whatever his shortcomings as a novelist, most critics argue that Amis is a consummate stylist. Whether he is as 'good' as other writers – Ian McEwan, say, or Doris Lessing

– is a matter of fine individual judgement.

3   Andrew rose to the dispatch box to cries of 'Answer, answer,' from
    the Opposition benches. He had checked his crib sheet while sitting
    on the edge of his seat. Andrew had prepared answers for medical
    facilities, old-age pensions, supplementary benefits, food allow-
    ances, medical charges – but nothing for TV licences. As he stood
    stranded at the dispatch box he was aware for the first time of the
    pitfalls that a minister encounters when he is not fully prepared.
    Such a system might appear wonderfully democratic to onlookers,
    he thought, until you are the Christian facing the 300 hungry lions.
        A handwritten note was quickly passed along the front bench to
    him from one of the civil servants who sit in the official box to the
    left behind the Speaker's chair. With no time to consider its impli-
    cations Andrew crossed his fingers and read the note out to the
    House.
        'This was a decision taken by the last administration, of which
    the Honourable Gentleman was a member. We have seen no reason
    to reverse that decision,' he read, thinking how much like a parrot
    he sounded. He sat down to polite Government murmurs and some
    considerable relief.

    This extract is from *First Among Equals* by Jeffrey
    Archer. The style is devoid of any sophisticated literary
    devices and the images used fall into the category of clichés:
    'Christian facing 300 hungry lions'. One also wonders if a
    minister under such pressure would have time for such
    biblical reflections and would he *really* cross his fingers? The
    final sentence, moreover, does not make it clear who
    experienced the relief: the Government or Andrew? The
    style employed, however, is effective in advancing the
    narrative; whatever his stylistic shortcomings might be,
    Jeffrey Archer is a competent story teller.

4   One would hesitate, however, to sip from the same poisoned
    chalice as those who would speciously crusade the assertion that
    literature is quintessentially socially functional. Pose the following
    interrogative: would Dante, Shakespeare, or Milton, from their
    own peerless pinnacles, have sullied their art, prostituted the muse

which their endeavours had enthroned, by indicating something as trivial, as unworthy, as a social purpose? The art of such as these argues another view; that at the heart of all great creative achievement lies a self justifying, eternally fathomless and sacred mystery.

This extract appears to be from an article or book. It is written in the ornate, self-consciously intellectual style peculiar to a certain kind of literary criticism. It speaks of 'a poisoned chalice', 'peerless pinnacles', and 'a prostituted muse'. It uses the word 'crusade' instead of 'argue' and 'interrogative' instead of 'question'. What precisely is it saying? This is not easy to decide but it seems to be something along the following lines: 'Literature should not have a social function but should seek to be great art, an objective which is impossible to define precisely'. The extract says badly in 82 multisyllabic words what our paraphrase says simply in 22. Such verbosity represents the worst kind of academic writing. It is the substitution of sound for meaning, pretention for learning. It betrays the second-rate academic who believes form is a substitute for content. You gather that we are not impressed by this kind of writing.

The four extracts examined are all different, but all have illustrated how the quality of prose has to be judged within its correct context. By gaining some appreciation of the criteria by which prose is judged, you will, we hope, become more sensitive to the style of others and be able to examine your own in a more discriminating light.

To help you analyse written style, use the following checklist of questions when confronted with a piece of writing.

Purpose   What is the writer's objective?
Vocabulary   What kind of words are used?
Syntax   How are phrases and sentences built up?
Grammar   What kind of punctuation is used?
Imagery   What figures of speech are used? Are they original or clichéd, poetic or down to earth?

Literary devices   What use is made of alliteration, assonance, and so forth?
Tone   What kind of tone does the writer adopt – witty, grave, condescending?
Quality   To what extent is the writing appropriate for the task attempted?

Whilst studying at university you won't need to write in tabloidese or like Martin Amis (even if you could). It is not unknown, however, for some students to aspire to the style illustrated by the fourth example. This is not a style to be cultivated; if you have already edged towards it, we advise you to edge back again in the direction of clarity and economy. The high priest of both of these qualities in the English language was George Orwell. His six elementary rules of good English first appeared in his 1946 essay, 'Politics and the English Language'. They easily survive the test of time.

1   Never use a metaphor, simile or other figure of speech which you are used to seeing in print.
2   Never use a long word where a short one will do.
3   If it is possible to cut out a word, always cut it out.
4   Never use the passive where you can use the active.
5   Never use a foreign phrase, a scientific word or a jargon word if you can think of an everyday English equivalent.
6   Break any of these rules sooner than say anything outright barbarous.

(Orwell's purist objections to clichés (rule 1) are perhaps excessive for most undergraduate purposes.)

9.3   Punctuation

This section looks at punctuation, but first a few words in general on the subject of grammar. Half a century ago grammar was taught in such a dry, mechanical fashion that it developed a fearsome reputation for driving pupils insane with boredom. It was also mistakenly thought at that time that English grammar followed the rules of Latin. After the war a reaction set in against such rote learning: less attention was paid to grammar and more to communicating meaning. It was assumed pupils would pick up the rules of grammar naturally and gradually through regular writing practice and help from their teachers. This shift was doubtless justified but it did lead in some cases to a downgrading of grammar teaching and to its virtual absence from the curriculum. This has meant that some teachers themselves are none too clear about the rules of grammar. The only real contact that many pupils have with grammatical rules occurs when they learn a foreign language. It comes as quite a shock then to discover that the language which five-year-olds imbibe and speak quite easily follows fairly regular and complex rules. But if we absorb them naturally, why bother to learn anything about them? 'I know whether something is grammatically correct or not just by how it sounds' is a frequently heard assertion from undergraduates. And there is much in this: we do develop an intuitive sense for detecting something which is wrong – just as we have a sense for a wrong note in a piece of music. Moreover, some pupils give grammar an undue emphasis which smacks of pedantry: those who take it upon themselves to correct the world's grammar are often, quite rightly, condemned as royal pains. But after all the qualifications have been made, grammar still matters. It helps to be aware of it and to take pride in getting it right. If, as Orwell believed, the purpose of good style is to make your meaning absolutely clear, then grammar plays a crucial role. Good knowledge of it greatly extends the range of how you can express yourself and gives your writing a precision and authority it would otherwise lack. It follows that poor grammar can blur your meaning and undermine your authority.

Your tutors at university may not correct your mistakes – it is widely, and perhaps wrongly, assumed that once you are at university this is more your responsibility than theirs – but their acknowledgement of them will be reflected in your marks. In this section we can only touch on a small part of this extensive subject, but our experience suggests that they are especially important elements.

Punctuation for pauses

In one sense, good written style is spoken English properly formulated. When we speak we make regular pauses: for breath, to separate one piece of information from another, and for effect. Punctuation enables us to replicate these pauses and to allow our writing to sound and flow more like spoken words. Everyone makes different pauses and it follows that this kind of punctuation is to some extent a matter of personal taste.

There are four main punctuation marks used to indicate pauses in the sentence: the comma (short pause), the semi-colon (longer pause), the colon (slightly longer pause) and the full stop, which marks the end of the sentence.

The **comma** is used chiefly to separate adjectives, clauses and items in a list. Most students use commas correctly though some tend to overuse them, which is unwise because this can interupt the flow of the prose. Commas separating clauses can often be dropped without any loss. The following sentence would still be acceptable without the commas, for example:

The record flopped, but the extent of the failure was not admitted by PMI, which wished to protect its image.

On the other hand, commas can crucially affect the meaning of a sentence. Consider the following:

Raymond walked in rapidly drawing the curtains in one dramatic move.

A comma after the adverb 'rapidly' would mean that it

described the manner in which Raymond walked; a comma before it would relate it to the way in which he drew the curtains.

It is the semi-colon and the colon which are probably most often misunderstood and misused, largely because the pauses they represent have specific meanings.

The **semi-colon** is commonly used in two ways:

1 *To join two short but related clauses or sentences*, especially when the second represents a development, elaboration or contrast to the first.

- I always prefer to write with an expensive fountain pen; it seems to produce a higher class of prose.
- When the war finished the families reassembled; they needed to count their dead and account for what property remained.
- Albert always went on long walking holidays in Iceland; his wife invariably took hers studying dung-beetles in East Africa.

In all the above cases the semi-colon joins what could be shorter complete sentences but too many short sentences produces a stuttering, halting effect; semi-colons help improve the fluency of your prose.

2 *To separate phrases which themselves contain punctuation*, as in the example below:

To regain its buoyancy the housing market needs: more first time buyers, especially young ones, to come on the market; a reduction of interest rates – currently the highest in Europe; and a slowing down of repossessions, something which keep house prices high.

The beauty of the semi-colon in this context is that it enables you to pack a great deal of information quite manageably into a single sentence. It saves words and reading time, and adds an extra gear to your written style.

The **colon** is more often used:

1 *To introduce a list*:

> Roy stepped up to the bar and ordered drinks for us all: a whiskey, a brandy, a half of lager and a pint of bitter.

> It can also introduce a list of points or reasons or otherwise complicated clauses as in the 'housing market' example above.

2 *To register a pause before a closely related additional comment is made*:

> After much internal debate with his left wing principles, John made up his mind: he decided to send Tiffany and Sybil to be privately educated.

3 *To indicate that the second clause explains the first*. The colon in this context effectively means 'that is to say':

> Gordon stormed in, turned on the lights, switched off the music and turned to face them: he was furious.

4 *To register a marked contrast between two statements*:

> Graham loved the soft red wines of the Loire Valley: Rachel hated them.

The **exclamation mark** is, of course, used to indicate alarm, surprise, anger, irony or sarcasm, but it needs to be used sparingly and never in its double or, even worse, triple form.

The **dash** is often overused and misused. There are only two forms of correct usage.

1 *As an alternative to commas when marking off a clause inside a sentence*:

> I refuse to believe that Jenny – a highly competent, experienced and professional nurse – could have made a mistake like that.

> You might well ask why dashes have been used here instead of commas: the answer is that they give added space and emphasis to the clause and – as in the example – allow the clause to have some internal punctuation.

2 *To add an additional clause or afterthought to a sentence*:

I threw myself onto the bus and sat down beside Mary – it was my last chance to see her.

When I finally got to see him I did not at first recognise him – he looked so old.

The **apostrophe** is used in two main ways:

1 *To indicate possession*:

> The child's pocket money
> The dog's tail

The apostrophe is not used in the case of possessive pronouns like *his, hers, theirs, its, ours* and *yours*, but remember that it is used in the case of 'one' as in 'one's feelings'. But what do you do when the final letter is *s*? If the noun is singular then it's still apostrophe *s*:

> The mass's opinions
> Markus's computer

But if plural, the apostrophe comes *after* the *s*:

> The students' grants
> The cats' baskets

2 *To indicate contraction*, usually when a letter is missing:

> I don't like. . .
> You're a complete idiot.
> It's a terrible shame.

(Note that in the case of *can't*, two letters are missing.)

Abbreviations

There are a great many of these – *e.g.* (for example), *i.e.* (that is), *viz.* (that is to say), *etc.* (and so forth) – but whilst they are very useful when taking notes they are not generally regarded

K

as being part of good written style and should not be used in academic essays.

Inverted commas

Single inverted commas usually indicate direct speech:

I shouted, 'Get out of my house!'

But what do you do when the person whose speech you are reporting also quotes someone? The usual practice is to use double inverted commas inside the quote.

The man said, 'I asked him whether he wanted to buy some religious literature and he replied "Clear off!" '

Some prefer to use double commas for quotations and single ones for internal quotes but the rule here is to decide what you prefer and stick to it.

9.4   Sentence construction

A sentence represents a complete unit of meaning: even though it may be given wider significance by surrounding sentences, it should still make sense on its own.

It is fairly obvious that the following words do not constitute a sentence:

Sat on the mat.

The proverbial cat is clearly absent and the result is a meaningless collection of words.

The cat on the mat.

is equally nonsensical: this time it is the verb, 'sat', which is missing. Finally,

The cat sat on the

leaves the 'mat' hanging somewhere in the air.

To be grammatically correct, sentences usually need a **subject** – in this case the cat – a **verb** ('sat') and an **object**: 'the mat'. There are exceptions: for example, an order or imperative can be just one word: 'Go!'

Here the subject – it might be 'you' – is implied but not stated. 'I laughed' is also clearly a complete sentence even though it has no object. But the rule of *subject – verb – object* – generally applies.

Martin	ate	his breakfast.
subject	verb	object

What follows the subject is also called the *predicate*, for which a verb is essential but not the object, as we saw in the 'I laughed' example. (A verb which needs an object is a *transitive* verb: see p. 287.) The subject does not have to be human, of course; it can be a pronoun ('He got down off his horse'), a noun ('The table was black'), abstract noun ('Love is good'), a phrase containing a noun ('The tiny multicoloured bird ate the bread'), or many other possibilities. The way to remember these relationships is to think of the **subject** as *the thing you want to talk about* and the **predicate** as *what you wish to say about it*.

The above sentences are all very simple; they become more complex when **phrases** or **clauses** are added. Phrases comprise a group of related words which don't make sense unless they are within a sentence:

His delicious muesli breakfast

Clauses are more complex. Take at look at the following sentence.

I went to see the headmaster although I was nervous.

'I went to see the headmaster' is called the **main clause** and could, of course, stand as a sentence on its own. 'Although I was nervous' has both a subject and a predicate but it only means something when attached to the main clause: it is therefore a **subordinate** or **dependent clause**.

The above comments may seem a bit too theoretical and unnecessary, especially if you already write well, but being aware of the inner workings of a sentence can help to improve your own technical skills as a writer.

Common mistakes

The overlong sentence

Bernard Levin, who writes for *The Times*, is famous for his long sentences, but they are invariably skilfully managed and, as proved by his success as a journalist, a pleasure to read. Consider the following example (containing over 60 words). Levin, a cat-lover, is lamenting that he only has model cats in his flat,

> ... but never a real cat to rub itself against my leg, to sleep in my lap while I listen to music, to stretch out its chin to be tickled, to be stroked so long that the purring is as loud as a car's engine, to demand to be let out and to change its mind and insist on being let in. (*The Times*, 21 March 1992)

Levin is always in control – but the author of the following example is clearly not:

> The problem with Marx's theory of growing monopoly capitalism and the immiseration of the masses is that it was predicated on a metaphysical basis which meant that it was inevitable and almost like an iron law of nature but in practice the economic polarisation of the nineteeth century has not continued into the twentieth and a substantial increase has occurred in the size of the middle class and the wealth of the working class.

Too many ideas are being included here: one per sentence should normally be enough. The sentence just seems to go on and on and the substantive points are lost; too many 'ands' are always a sign that the sentence is out of control.

We have seen in Section 9.2 how good use of punctuation

can enable you to write perfectly acceptable long sentences but this is not always appropriate and takes time to learn. If you feel your sentences are prone to ramble and lead you into vagueness and convolution, there is an easy answer: keep them short. As we have already noted, too many short sentences can produce a staccato effect but as long as you remember to vary sentence length you will be better off with clear short sentences rather than unreadable long ones.

The back-to-front sentence

Sentences sometimes do not quite ring true or run into trouble when a constituent phrase or dependent clause follows rather than precedes the main clause. The following sentence is acceptable:

As he entered the room he was smiling broadly.

However, it was not clear whether 'as' here means 'because' or 'at the same time'. It also sounds slightly better if the dependent clause comes second:

He was smiling broadly as he entered the room.

The following sentence indicates how the back-to-front sentence can founder:

Slipping in the mud as I said 'Hello', he shook my hand.

In this sentence it isn't clear who has slipped. Assuming it is 'you', the subject of the clause, who has slipped, a superior, amended version would be:

He shook my hand as I said 'Hello' and I slipped in the mud.

The present participle is no substitute for an active verb

A common mistake amongst students of all ages is to confuse the present participle or 'continuous' sense of the verb with the 'active' form. The following is not a sentence:

Parliament being in session.

To be correct, a sentence needs an active verb; for example:

Parliament *was* in session.

Incorrect case agreement

If the subject is in the singular, it is important that the verb should not be in the plural form:

The Conservative Party are opposed to this measure.

This too is an easy error to make because a political party is made up of many people; it is, however, a collective noun and so 'are' should be 'is'. The word *none* presents a problem because strictly speaking it is singular, as in the following example:

None of the news bulletins has mentioned this fact.

But where *none* means 'no person' the plural – though strictly speaking incorrect – *sounds* right and is acceptable, as in:

When we interviewed the candidates, none were suitable.

9.5   Paragraphs

It comes as a surprise to some students to discover that not only do essays need a good structure but paragraphs do too. They are not just a device to break up the page into digestible bites, important though this function is. Just as a sentence needs to express a complete unit of sense, so paragraphs should deal with a single topic. What actually *constitutes* a single topic might be difficult to decide but this is only a general rule so don't agonise over it unduly. There are two elements, however, which paragraphs usually need.

1   The topic sentence

This is the sentence which expresses the central point, idea or argument of the paragraph. It usually comes, and is best placed, at the beginning of the paragraph, but occasionally it can be tucked away in the middle. The important thing is to have one, otherwise your paragraphs will tend to lack theme and structure. Have a look at the following paragraph.

Elsewhere the press was critical. The *Daily Telegraph*'s editorial asked whether the Prime Minister should be asked such questions 'before a camera that shows every flicker of the eyelid'; the *Observer* worried lest 'the television screen begins to by pass the House of Commons'; and the *Daily Mirror*'s Cassandra opined that 'the Idiot's Lantern is getting too big for its ugly gleam'. But between them Day and Macmillan had forged a new relationship between broadcasters and politicians and a new distinctive kind of media event which would play an important part in British politics from thereon.

The short first sentence introduces the topic sharply and concisely. Often a topic sentence is followed by another which offers some elaboration but this is not necessary here: the examples follow in a long sentence held together by semi-colons before the paragraph moves towards a concluding sentence.

2. A linking device

The above paragraph's topic sentence is particularly useful as an illustration as it employs a 'linking device' in the form of the word 'elsewhere'. This word clearly refers to the previous paragraph and facilitates 'flow'. This is very important if you wish to achieve a good written style. The importance of flow and cohesion has already been emphasised in this chapter and well-joined paragraphs are the key to giving your essays that 'seamless robe' effect. Observe how the linkage is effected in the following example:

. . . By this time Wilson had become so much the television professional that he had learnt the technical command used to start filming and was thereby able to project his prepared sound bite from the podium into the news bulletins.

This event struck one young member of the news team as

worryingly significant. Now at Granada Television it was he who suggested it might provide a starting point for an essay on the changing relationship between broadcasters and politicians over the last two decades. . . .

The word 'this' provides the simple link into the topic sentence. The final sentence of one paragraph can set up the link to the next one:

Macmillan was always scrupulously courteous. Not all politicians, however, have been so polite to interviewers.
    Mrs Thatcher's style was more confrontational.

Useful linking words include the following:

Nevertheless . . .	Despite . . .
Another . . .	Also . . .
Notwithstanding . . .	However . . .
Moreover . . .	Furthermore . . .
To sum up . . .	Finally . . .
In contrast . . .	Paradoxically . . .

Making sure that paragraphs are neatly linked together can be very difficult at first but with practice you will find yourself doing it naturally – just as you do when explaining an argument verbally.

A final note on paragraphs. Our advice on structure has covered the following:

- Topic sentence
- Elaborating sentence
- Example sentences
- Concluding sentence
- Linking device

All this sounds a little mechanical; and if you try to follow such a structure too slavishly you run the risk of losing the very flow and coherence we have been trying to encourage. Moreover, there are all kinds of paragraphs where such a structure will be inappropriate. Our advice is rather to be generally aware of paragraph structure when you write your first draft. Then, when going through your draft afterwards, check that your paragraphs deal with discrete topics, and that you have employed topic sentences and effective linking devices.

9.6 Quotations and references

Quotations are regularly used in academic writing to inform, enliven and provide authoritative reference. Quotations over three lines are usually 'indented' or 'inset' but short quotations are usually included in the main text. Make sure you blend such quotations smoothly into your prose, as in the following example:

> Harold Wilson once said, 'Most of politics is presentation and what isn't is timing', and his observation is even more relevant in the present day.

You may prefer a colon to introduce your quotation:

> Mrs Thatcher's most famous line was probably: 'You turn if you want to; the lady's not for turning.'

Be sure of the following, however.

1 Do not overuse quotations, otherwise your tutors will criticise your essays for being too derivative and not sufficiently your own work.
2 The grammar of an embodied quotation should accord with your own grammar. Students sometimes fail to ensure this producing the following kind of result:

> There was no way in which 'You turn if you want to; the lady's not for turning' was going to change her position on the Falklands.

3 If you exclude some inessential words from a quotation to save space, follow the convention of using three dots:

> But without a revolution or a coup d'état our constitution has been used not to establish a real dictatorship . . . but to allow a manner

of government that must be the least democratic among Western democracies.

References

In the foregoing chapter the point was made that arguments made in essays should be backed up by authoritative evidence. In academic books and journals great care is taken to acknowledge the source of such evidence with accurate references. University tutors ought to look for rigorous notation in undergraduate work. Some do not, however, and others have their own preferred systems. Check with them to be sure of their expectations. Larger, research-based projects in particular *will* always require accurate referencing which of course is *de rigueur* for work at the Master's and doctoral levels. Each academic journal has its own 'house style' of referencing – as indeed does each and every academic. Phlegmatic scholars can become quite passionate over which referencing style is the best. However, if we talk about *systems* rather than style, there are only two major ones.

1 **The numeric system**   You put a number in the text instead of the reference, then give the full reference at the foot of the page or the end of your essay. The usual order is Author – Title – Publisher – Date of publication – Page reference. See Chapter 7, p. 207 for examples.

   Do you place your references at the foot of each page or at the end of your essay or chapter? Should you use 'footnotes' or 'endnotes'? From one point of view, it is easier for the reader to glance down to the foot of the page than to turn to the end; from another, constant looking down interupts the reader's flow. Most readers are more interested in the text than the references and are usually happy to wait until the last page is reached before checking them through.

2 **The Harvard system** is an alternative which provides a short reference *embodied within the text* with the full details given

at the end of the piece. This extract (from T. Bilton, *Introductory Sociology* (Macmillan, 1987)) illustrates:

Moreover there is no guarantee that all young people will receive a similar 'training'. 'All manner of types and levels of provision will exist' determined not by informed planning but rather by the accident of where they live and the short term preferences of employers (Muncie, 1984, p. 146).

The reference at the *end* of the chapter is as follows:

Muncie, J. (1984) *The Trouble with Kids Today*, London, Hutchinson.

Apart from the house style punctuation, the major difference is that the year of publication is given directly after the author's name. This is because it is the chief means of identifying the particular work to which reference is being made. If another book by Muncie – written, say, in 1987 – had been cited in the same chapter, the reference in the text might have read: (Muncie, 1987, p. 127).

If two references by the same author occurred in the same year they could be differentiated by 'a' and 'b'.

The Harvard system is increasingly popular as it gives a brief mention to the chief source, the author, within the text itself. But you must make up your own mind as to which system you prefer and in addition bear in mind the following:

1 Whichever system and style you choose *be consistent*: don't chop and change within the same piece of work.
2 Try to be scrupulously accurate, even pedantic, over references but avoid overkill just to impress: only give a reference when it is genuinely required.
3 Avoid giving supplementary information along with your references. If something is worth mentioning, include it in the main text.

9.7 Spelling

English has developed almost organically from several

sources including German, Latin, and French, not to mention the eclectic influences of an imperial past. Our spelling reflects this diversity and is both complex and idiosyncratic. Everyone makes spelling errors occasionally and we all have words over which we habitually stumble.

Research undertaken in March 1992 by the RSA Examination Board revealed that up to half of Britain's office workers regularly misspell simple words. The 20 most misspelt were as follows:

Word	Percentage of workers who misspelt it
practice/practise	54
withhold	52
occurred	52
innovate	52
benefited	48
principal/principle	45
incur	44
grievance	40
concede	40
transferred	39
competent	37
calendar	35
warranty	35
acquire	34
liaise	34
truly	34
expedite	33
discrete/discreet	33
affect/effect	32
accommodation	32

Does it matter? The short answer is, yes, it does. For many readers, spelling mistakes leap out of the page and, just like grammatical errors, call the authority of the writer into question. In response to the RSA survey, Peter Morgan, Director General of the Institute of Directors, remarked, 'Where spelling and the use of language are inadequate, the effect can be disastrous for a company. It creates an image of poor quality which costs business.' University tutors who responded to a Queen's English Society survey (July 1992) were not sanguine either about the spelling prowess of their students: up to 40% of them could not spell properly, 60% had only a tenuous grasp of grammar, and 25% were very weak on punctuation. Mrs Anne Shelley, the Chair of the Society, argued that 'this dismal situation goes right back to teacher-training'. She could be right. In 1990, teachers at a professional association conference were asked to spell the following words: *allegiance*, *abscess*, *accommodating*, *occurred*, *surprise*, *attached*, *misspelt*, *vacillate*, *instalment* and *licence* (noun). Only one in ten got them all correct and the average score was seven.

Even if it is unattainable you should aim for the Holy Grail of perfection with your spelling. The following guidelines will help.

Systematic practice   Compile a list of your spelling *bêtes noires* and try to implant them in your long-term memory.

Does it look and sound right?   Intuition is sometimes the most reliable guide.

Mnemonics can help, for example:

Only one *c*
In necessary.

Syllables   If in doubt, try to simplify the word by breaking it up into its constituent syllables: pos–ses–sive.

Rules   There are some basic, though heavily qualified, spelling rules which you will absorb with profit.

● *i* before *e* except after *c* when making the sound E: *receive*, *achieve*, *grief*. But it's *e* before *i* if the sounds A or I are being made: *eight*, *neither*.

- Plurals of nouns ending in *f* or *fe*: nouns ending in *f* usually add only *s* to make the plural: *handkerchiefs*. Some, however, end *ves*: *wives*. In other cases, either plural form is correct: *hoofs/hooves*.
- Plurals of words ending in *o* usually add *s*, but some have an extra *e*: *potatoes*. Strictly speaking, *manifesto* has an extra *e* in its plural form but in recent years this has been dropped by many journalists.
- *all* at the beginning of words has only one *l*: *already*. Note, however, that *all right* is preferable to *alright*.
- *full* at the end of words loses one *l*: *helpful*, *useful*.

Use your dictionary

Words are the trade of the university student: you need to develop a feel, even a fascination for them. Don't feel satisfied until you have clarified the meaning and/or spelling of a new or difficult word. Make sure you have a dictionary of your own. Avoid the small, pocket versions as well as the very big ones which can confuse rather than enlighten. *The Concise Oxford* or Collins *Concise English Dictionary* are good, clear compromises. Below is a sample entry from the *Collins*.

> *pos-sess* (pezes|) vt.[⟨ L. pp. of *possidere*] **1.** to have as something that belongs to one; own. **2.** to have as an attribute, quality, etc. [to *possess* wisdom] **3.** to gain or keep influence or control over; dominate [*possessed* by an idea] **4.** to cause (someone) to have property, facts, etc. (usually with *of*) **5.** [Archaic] to seize; gain – **pos-ses|-sor n.**

As you see, the syllables are separated by hyphens in this dictionary. Following the word is a bracketed phonetic version indicating the pronunciation (according to the prefatory guide) found in the 'normal, relaxed conversation of educated speakers'. The full phonetic guide is found at the beginning of the volume. 'vt.' indicates this word is a transitive verb ('n.' means noun; 'adj.', adjective; 'adv.', adverb; etc.).

Then follows a little history of the word. The symbol ⟨ means 'derived from'. '⟨L. pp. of *possidere*' means that the word 'possess' derives from the past participle of the Latin verb *possidere*.

Then follow the definitions with bracketed examples. The fifth definition is an older (archaic) sense of the word and the final entry gives the noun – 'possessor' – derived from the verb. There are many more possible abbreviations in this particular dictionary: to learn the full list and the full variety of what you can learn about words, read the guide which precedes the word list. The *Collins Dictionary* contains 85,000 words; the *Oxford English Dictionary*, half a million, but only 10,000 words are used in normal written communication and a mere 3,000 in everyday speech.

Adapted from B. Jones and R. Johnson, *Making the Grade*, (Manchester University Press, 1990), pp.101–2.

Key points

1 Appreciation of literary style helps improve your own. You are encouraged to study the vocabulary, syntax, imagery and other literary devices used by good writers as a means of achieving some critical distance from your own writing practices.

2 Good understanding and use of punctuation can give your style an 'extra gear'. The semi-colon and colon in particular are useful (though not essential) devices which will provide you with this advantage. The importance of accurate use of apostrophes, dashes, inverted commas and other punctuation is emphasised.

3 It is useful to be aware that sentences have a grammatical structure entailing a *subject* and a *predicate*. The need to avoid pitfalls like overlong sentences and incorrect case agreement is stressed.

4 Paragraphs should deal with a single topic and, like an essay, should have a beginning, a middle and an end.

5 Good use of quotations is essential in good academic writing: they need to be properly blended into your prose and accurately

referenced.

6 Inaccurate spelling is sloppy and unscholarly: every effort should be made to remedy deficiencies.

Things to do

1 Examine short passages from Jane Austen, Joseph Conrad, Norman Mailer, Margaret Attwood or other well-known authors. How do they achieve their effects?

2 As a secondary exercise to the above make a particular study of how these authors:
　　(a) use punctuation
　　(b) vary sentence length
　　(c) link paragraphs.

3 Study some extracts from the work of Gertrude Stein or (easier to find) James Joyce's *Finnegan's Wake*. How does the style used depart from the usual conventions? Is the result successful?

4 Compare the style used in a *Times* editorial with that used in a *Sun* editorial.

5 Write up a recent event in your family, street or community in the style of a tabloid newspaper.

6 Punctuate the following:
　　Labours defeat in 1992 can be attributed to a number of factors the failure of Neil Kinnock a very competent politician to win the respect and sympathy of a broad swathe of the populus the enduring distrust which remained within the electorate over Labours economic competence and a last minute realisation by a crucial minority that even though they had flirted with the idea they did not want a Labour government.

You will find a punctuated version at the end of Chapter 13.

Further reading

Making the Grade, Vol. 2 (Manchester University Press, 1990) by Bill Jones and Roy Johnson deals in more detail with 'grammar and punctuation', 'sentences and paragraphs' and 'appreciation of written style'. It also provides exercises and a study guide at the end of the volume. Roy Johnson's *Studying Fiction* (Manchester University Press, 1991) is also recommended for its clear, in-depth treatment of literary style. H. W. Fowler's *Modern English Usage* (Oxford University Press, 1988) and Eric Partridge's *Usage and Abusage* (Penguin, 1991) are both well-established guides, as is *The Oxford Guide to the English Language* (Guild Publishing, 1988). Michael Temple's little book, *The Pocket Guide to Written English* (Michael Joseph, 1990), is excellent on punctuation. If you are investing in a dictionary, *The Concise Oxford Dictionary of Current English* is recommended along with Collins' *Concise English Dictionary*.

10

Writing good essays

Nothing goes by luck in composition. It allows for no tricks.
The best you can write will be the best you are.

Thoreau, *Journal, 1841*

10.1 Introduction

The importance of being able to produce high quality written work hardly needs stressing. Most of the study skills we
have covered so far in this book – reading, note taking and so
forth – are in one sense secondary to writing or preparatory to
it. Written work represents the culmination of all these skills; it
is what comes out of the process involving the other skills and
provides evidence (or otherwise) that the process works in your
case. What you write is the outward and visible sign of what
you have learned and what you can do. As far as some of your
examiners are concerned, what your write *is* you.

According to Henderson (1980), essays are widely believed
to provide proof of the abilities to 'select, relate, integrate,
organise and evaluate materials learned, use learning creatively
and use language to express ideas'. He shows, however, that
there is no evidence to suggest the essay is a reliable measure of
such skills or a more effective test than, say, multiple choice
questions. He concludes that 'the case *for* the essay must still be
regarded as not proven, but so must the case *against*'. Such
judicious scepticism is not shared by most academics, who
believe coursework and examination essays together with
written scientific reports are the best means of assessment
available. As long as they believe this, writing good essays will

continue to be of key importance for A-level students and undergraduates.

Writing well is important for another reason: it is a skill directly applicable to the world of work. Most of the jobs graduates go into require them to write letters, memos, papers or reports which are well structured, clear and forceful. University provides the opportunity to nurture, develop and refine your writing skills: it is an opportunity which should not be missed.

Chapter 9 addresses the question of written style but this one concentrates on the essential requirements of structure.

- Section 10.2 discusses the elements which constitute a good essay;
- Section 10.3 explains the 'for and against' variety;
- Section 10.4 goes on to look at the straightforward Strategy One approach, whilst
- Section 10.5 describes eight other strategies and types of essay.
- Section 10.6 looks briefly at what should go into introductions and conclusions;
- Section 10.7 takes you through a ten-point plan of writing good essays and
- Section 10.8 looks briefly at how to write good scientific reports.

10.2   What makes a good essay?

Many students enter higher education without any clear answer to this question. If they are students of the arts and social sciences, they will almost certainly be able to write competent essays, otherwise they would not have got into university in the first place. But they will still be hazy on the criteria by which quality is judged. One of the best ways of achieving clarity about this is to read something which plainly fails to meet such criteria. Consider the opening section of the essay quoted below in response to the question 'Politics is essentially concerned with the harmonisation of conflicting interests. Discuss.'

Politics

I don't think politicians should be trusted. History proves that they are only interested in themselves, their egos and the power they can get hold of. Look at Napoleon, Stalin, Hitler, Pol Pot and Thatcher. Politicians anyway are less important than the forces which control them. They are just the tip of the iceberg. Below the surface you get the big industrial barons who pull the strings and call the shots. Politicians are drawn from the fat cats class and ensure all the laws in the country and the way in which it is run benefits those who are already privileged and wealthy and keeps down the mass of poor people who do most of the work and create all the wealth in the first place.

The faults in this (mercifully short) extract are glaring.

- The essay is clearly not going to answer the question. The full title has apparently been forgotten in favour of a single word abbreviation and an essay has been started which is almost certainly going to miss the point entirely. The germ of an effective counterthesis – that politics is not essentially about harmonisation of interests but more about the defence of certain interests and the suppression of others – is perhaps present, but it seems unlikely that the author is going to elaborate such a case with any vigour or persuasiveness.
- It is also unlikely that this essay will display much in the way of a structure or systematic ordering of arguments. Within a few sentences, it is clear that the essay has omitted any proper introduction and the focus has rambled hopelessly.
- A series of assertions and unsupported generalisations have been made which are more appropriate for the saloon bar than an academic essay.
- The written style is poor and convoluted; it overuses the first person and falls into tired clichés.

- There is no evidence that the literature of the subject has been absorbed or that the author's head has in it anything more than a random collection of half-baked ideas.

We could go on.

The criteria for a good piece of writing should now be as obvious as the above criticisms. A good essay should reflect the following qualities, the first two being the most important.

1 **Answer the question** In our experience the majority of essays receiving a low mark do so because they fail to address the question. Usually this is because the question has not been understood and its inner meaning teased out. In these circumstances, it is typical for the student to fasten lazily on a simplified version of the general topic rather than the precise requirements of the title. Whilst such an approach will suffice at a lower level, it will risk failure in higher education where one of the main purposes is to produce convincing, well thought out responses to testing questions.

2 **A clear structure** This more or less follows from the above. To produce such a response your essays need to have their arguments clearly distinguished and ordered in a logical fashion. A good structure gives you control over the subject matter rather than letting its complexities baffle and hence control you. Try to look on writing an essay like building a house. It needs a solid foundation (good understanding of the question) and a number of well-organised rooms (logical structure) filled with appropriate furniture (arguments, ideas, information, etc.). Establishing this structure should be one of your first objectives.

We reckon that answering the question and devising the kind of sound structure which will help you achieve this objective is more than half the battle in writing good essays. If you succeed in these two areas it is likely that other requirements will be met as well but we list them just the same.

3 **Presentation**   This requirement is obvious but often over-looked. Researchers show that essays can lose up to 10% when they are untidily written and presented. This may seem unfair but tutors are only human; it is hardly surprising if they unconsciously 'punish' students by awarding lower marks to irritatingly untidy work. It has also to be realised that poor handwriting breaks up the reader's concentration and the natural flow of your essay: there is little point in developing a good written style if poor handwriting prevents anyone appreciating it. Typed essays are always welcomed by tutors, so if your handwriting is a problem try acquiring this very useful skill (which will also serve you well in virtually every area of graduate employment).

4 **Wide reading and understanding of the subject**   At univer-sity, studying a subject is very largely a matter of familiarising yourself with the literature, absorbing theories and arguments, and developing your own ideas upon their validity. Your essays therefore need to reflect an awareness and understanding of a wide range of relevant writings.

5 **Evidence used to support arguments**   You don't need to go to university to issue forth with unsupported generalisations – they are freely and abundantly available on the bus and in the bar. The purpose of university study is not to make assumptions but to establish the truth. Ask yourself after every point you make in your essays, 'Have I established this point sufficiently well?' If you cannot be emphatic then qualify what you write accordingly. There is no shame at all in not reaching clearly defined conclusions – the state of knowledge in most disciplines seldom allows such luxuries in any case – but you must explain the reasons why.

6 **Appropriate style**   If you can make your writing exciting, witty and inspiring then don't hesitate to use your skills. But be reasonably sure of them before you unleash them on tutors who might not prove especially receptive to them. If

you cannot make the words sing then settle for expressing what you wish to say grammatically. Adopt the calm and friendly tone of someone explaining a complex problem to an intelligent but not especially well informed person. (For more on style see Chapter 9.)

7 **Clear thinking** If you have met the above requirements, you will already have demonstrated commendable clarity of thought. But there will be other opportunities for critical analysis, maybe of a particular school of thought, which will enable you to display the quality of your thinking. Much of this training comes from reading ('reading is to the mind what exercise is to the body') and from writing essays. If you work hard and regularly, straining your own limits, you cannot fail to improve the quality of your thinking.

8 **Originality** Just occasionally at university you will encounter someone with a genuinely original mind who can produce ideas which startle and illuminate. Quite possibly most of us would secretly like to be such a person and some of us might even think we are. You will find that attempts at original thinking are always encouraged and appreciated at university. But beware. Trying too hard to be original and failing often results in pretension. Playing safe can have its advantages.

Our experience suggests that you probably did not find the above especially revelatory; you almost certainly were aware of such criteria even if you had not articulated them. Our experience also suggests that heightened awareness of such criteria produces better essays; if you need to remember them use the acronym ASPRESCO.

Answer (the question)
Structure
Presentation
Reading
Evidence
Style
Clear thinking
Originality

10.3   The 'for and against' essay

Essays, more usually set in the humanities and social sciences, can take many forms. It follows that different subjects tend to have different requirements. It is obvious, for example, that an essay in literary criticism will be a different kind of species from the historical or sociological essay. A unifying thread through written assignments in many subjects, however, is the requirement for discussion or debate. The precise instructions in the essay title might vary. You might be asked to *discuss* a proposition, *consider* a certain view or *assess the strength* of a particular theory. But the essence is the same: you are being asked to develop something: to match the arguments 'for' against the 'againsts'.

The debating requirement may not be that explicit, as in the following example: 'Should traffic be banned in city centres?' If you agreed with the statement and merely elaborated the reasons why such a ban should be imposed, you would almost certainly receive a lower mark than if you had also identified and discussed the case against. The debating requirement therefore is often implicit and you need to tease it out carefully.

Why is the 'for and against' essay employed so frequently? Essentially because it is a format which reflects an important part of the intellectual process involved in the pursuit of new knowledge. Truth, that much stated objective of university research, is something of a Holy Grail; its pursuit can be unending and, often, just when it appears ready to be captured it floats away again to hide in the mists of our ignorance. 'Truth' is seldom unvarnished, plain and simple. To achieve the (often temporary) status of truth, a proposition has to withstand the sustained assaults of informed doubt and scholarly counter-proposition. This is the case in every subject studied in universities. In history, scholars debate propositions like 'Hitler's rise to power followed a carefully worked out master plan'; political scientists debate (furiously) whether 'British voters still vote according to class divisions'; sociologists debate whether ' "commonsense" attitudes to authority merely reflect the values which ruling élites have subtly persuaded us to accept'. In each case, ideas are put forward and their strengths tested against criticism. In such disciplines results are not clear-cut and knowledge exists in a constant state of 'becoming'. In subjects like English literature, moreover, there is no truth, merely a constant debate; but even in the natural sciences the process – and indeed the result – is not dissimilar. Scientists put forward hypotheses which they then test against all kinds of counter-hypotheses. And even when they believe, supported maybe by universal acclaim, that they have seized that Holy Grail, some other scientist can come along and replace their 'truth' with something radically different. Debate then is central to what goes on in universities. The 'for and against' essay reflects this dialectic process and draws you into it. It is useful for two other important educational reasons.

Firstly, it enables you to expose the strength of arguments in your discipline, to hold up their underlying assumptions to a scrutiny which is organised, systematic and comprehensive rather than haphazard and partial like most lay approaches. After all, outside the areas they know well, most people do not think things through carefully but distribute judgements liberally on a host of issues on the basis of prejudice, misinformation, habit and partial information or no information at all. Secondly, the 'for and against' essay forces you to take up positions you may not agree with and to think them through. Whether we realise it or not, we become attached to our points of view and they often harden into prejudices which we would rather not disturb. A junior minister in the Thatcher government used to have a ruler on his desk bearing the legend 'Don't confuse me with the facts: my mind's made up.' Allowing for the humour (we assume he was being humorous), such an approach is antithetical to that encountered in universities (perhaps explaining some of the hostility between government and universities during the Thatcher years). Within these walls it is recognised that in all important controversies, powerful cases can be mounted both for and against. It is the objective of the educated mind to seek a dispassionate familiarity with all the arguments involved. The 'for and against' essay provides valuable training in such an approach.

10.4   The Strategy One approach

Let's become more specific and practical and look at what we call the Strategy One approach to the 'for and against' question. Consider this question:

'Advertisements for smoking should be banned.' Discuss.

This straightforward question cries out for a 'for and against' treatment. If you were answering it you would have to think of all the relevant arguments and organise them accordingly.

Brainstorming

Here's a tip which might help you at this stage of the essay: if you have difficulty in summoning up ideas, write down the title in the centre of a blank page and try to let your mind reflect solely upon it for a few minutes. As facts, ideas and arguments come to you write them down quickly. You will soon find that your page has been filled up. This technique is called *brainstorming* and it can be very helpful. In this instance you may find it useful to divide the page into two and write 'for' ideas on the left: 'against' ideas on the right.

The arguments likely to be adduced in this instance could be as follows:

Arguments for advertising

1 Companies and individuals should be allowed freedom of choice even if the results of such choices can be harmful to smokers.
2 Government interference and control is potentially tyrannical.
3 The medical link between cancer and smoking is still questioned by some.
4 The Exchequer gains huge sums from taxes levied on smoking which are spent on socially useful functions like welfare services.
5 A ban would cause unemployment in both the advertising and tobacco industries and remove sponsorship from sport and other activities.
6 It would be politically and legally difficult to achieve such a ban.

Arguments against advertising

1 The medical link has been established beyond any reasonable doubt.
2 Smoking-related diseases kill one in four smokers: advertising for such an addictive, deadly pastime cannot be justified.
3 Advertising affects the vulnerable, especially young people who do not yet know their own minds.
4 Medical and other expenses incurred by the welfare services as a result of smoking-related diseases far outweigh taxation and other income.
5 Government revenues from smoking place government in

thrall to the tobacco companies.

6 Political and legal difficulties have been overcome in other countries.

Such a set of arguments, properly introduced and concluded, provide the basis for a solid response to the question set. This essay structure – introduction, arguments for, arguments against and conclusion – is simple to remember, simple to apply and easy for the reader to follow.

Analysing the question

However, the example given above is quite simple and we would be misleading you if we didn't ask you to read every question set with great care. Even the question on smoking involves a double negative: if you consider arguments *in support of the statement*, you are arguing for the ban and not for advertising. This is an easy mistake to make. Other questions can be more difficult to interpret. Consider the one below:

Has the problem of poverty has been solved in Britain?

This seems straightforward but a moment's thought will reveal that the word 'poverty' lends itself to two major interpretations: absolute and relative. Is it true that 19th-century levels of poverty have been removed in the present day? The levels of deprivation are not the same today but there is enough of it about to deny the assertion that the problem has been 'solved'. If we define poverty relatively, however, by comparing what the poor have in comparison with the rich, then poverty increased markedly during the eighties as a result of unemployment and benefit cuts on the one hand and reductions in upper levels of taxation on the other. This title really requires *two* 'for and against' essays in one. The following title presents similar problems:

Should sex and violence on television be curbed?

The temptation is to lump sex and violence together, but in reality they pose different problems; once again they need to be treated separately in your essay structure.

It's a good idea to go through the title first identifying the *instruction word* and then the *key concepts*, especially when they are complex and open to several interpretations. An attempt at a *paraphrase*, writing the title out in your own words, is not a bad way of deriving the kind of in-depth understanding you invariably need to acquire. Five minutes spent analysing the question can be worth hours of misdirected reading later on.

Paraphrasing instruction words is particularly useful. You may think you know what 'discuss' means, but can you express it precisely? A good definition would be 'debate the pros and cons of'. Other instruction words you will encounter and possible paraphrases are as follows:

Compare   Look at the similarities and differences between two or more things.

Contrast   Focus on the differences between two or more things.

Criticise   Analyse sceptically and give your judgement.

Define   Explain clearly the meaning or meanings of something.

Evaluate   Judge the worth and truth of . . .

Justify   Give adequate reasons in support of . . .

Review   Provide a general survey and analysis of . . .

10.5   Other approaches

The Strategy Two approach

Strategy One is ideal for the shorter essay, especially in the context of examinations (see Chapter 12). But is it so appropriate for the longer course-work essay of, say, 2–3000 words? A more sophisticated approach, what we call Strategy Two, might be more suitable for this kind of assignment. This approach focuses on the *kinds* of arguments being set or matched against each other. A quick look back to the 'smoking' example reveals common themes uniting both the 'fors' and the 'againsts': medicine, freedom of choice, finance, political factors, the law. The Strategy Two approach entails contrasting like with like, dealing with the medical arguments both for and against in the same section followed by the legal arguments, then the political, and so on. In a longer, more complex essay or short dissertation this makes sense because the reader might well forget elements of the 'fors' by the time the arguments against have been reached in the text. This approach also provides a natural structure to the essay which is easy to follow. It is often more difficult to think through, but the less complex Strategy One approach can help as a preliminary exercise. A useful hint for social studies essays is that, a bit like the smoking example, many of them can be analysed under the headings: economic, political, legal, moral and social.

Strategy Three: The comparative 'for and against' essay

Some questions ask you to weigh the pros and cons of two or more sets of arguments or perspectives. For example, 'Which philosophy is best suited to solving the problems of the nineties: an ecological approach or liberal capitalism?' The potential for getting lost in this title is immense. A simple approach would be to call on Strategy One: advantages of ecology followed by disadvantages; then the same for liberal capitalism. You might, however, wish to consider the advantages of *both* before looking at the disadvantages. A more ambitious strategy might be to employ elements of Strategy Two: break down the problems to be faced – economic, environmental, social etc. – and consider how well each philosophy would cope under each heading. The key is to spot quickly the type of question you have been asked and to analyse its requirements clearly.

Strategy Four: The 'multiple perspectives' essay

Academic debates are often very complex and entail more than mere 'for and against' arguments. Consider the following example:

> Criticise the view that inequality in society is both inevitable and desirable.

This statement expresses a right-wing Conservative view. It could be answered in a 'for and against' fashion, but a more scholarly approach would consider a range of critiques including, say, the Marxist, ecological, social democratic and feminist perspectives. Note that such an approach would clearly require close familiarity with a wide variety of relevant literature, plus an ability to summarise your knowledge into short essay sections. It often follows that the deeper your understanding of a subject the easier it is for you to express it simply and clearly. Long, prolix essays often disguise lack of understanding and can try the patience of your tutors.

Strategy Five: The 'analyse the reasons' essay

This kind of essay is often encountered in historical subjects and the appropriate strategy is not especially difficult to follow. For example:

> Analyse the reasons why Germany invaded Poland in 1939.

Here you would need to consider in turn the economic, political, diplomatic, military and other reasons for the start of the Second World War. Another might be

> Why did the most powerful postwar Prime Minister feel she had to resign on 22 November 1990?

The reasons here are many and complex and need to be

carefully managed; they would include: the economy, the poll tax, Europe, prime ministerial style and opinion polls in 1990.

It should now be obvious to you that there are an infinite number of potential questions you can be set. Each requires a purpose-built answer. No formula can provide you with a ready-made approach but the strategies outlined here should certainly help you to handle frequently encountered question types. It might also be helpful at this point to mention briefly one or two other kinds of essays which you might come across in your studies.

The literary appreciation essay   None of the strategies considered above would be suitable if you were asked to write, for example, 'An Appreciation of the "Ode to Autumn" by John Keats'. If you are a student of literature you will know what is required; but you may not be and you will need to start from scratch. You would need to consider what the poet is saying and how it relates to what is known of his own philosophy and the climate of his time. You would also need to make a close textual analysis of the poet's choice of words, his tone, use of grammar, punctuation, and literary devices. Especially important would be a discussion of the poet's use of metaphor, the provenance of his images and their multifaceted connotations. There is no particular way in which such an essay should be structured, apart from the requirement for an introduction and conclusion. What you put in the middle might, for example, be a line-by-line analysis, or a thematic approach based on the whole poem. You may also wish to discuss the poem from some of the various different perspectives which currently occupy literary theorists: structuralism or post-structuralism, Marxism or feminism or, indeed, deconstruction, new historicism or cultural materialism.

The philosophical essay   Naturally if you study philosophy all of your essays are likely to be philosophical and some might well be suitable for treatment by Strategies One to Five.

Others, such as 'What is happiness?', might not. There are no rules to the answering of such questions: you need to construct your own response based on your own thoughts and those of others who have written on the topic. You need to begin by analysing the question very thoroughly; the insights you gain at this stage often determine your eventual essay structure. You need to ask yourself: is happiness something you feel yourself (subjective), or is it defined by others (objective) or is it a combination of both? Is it a momentary sensation or a general state of mind? Is it always the concomitant of pleasure or is it possible to achieve happiness when suffering? What relationships between the physical and spiritual are involved? You need to select your lines of enquiry and structure a coherent answer.

You may easily find, however, that philosophical questions are set in a number of different subjects. For example, in the social sciences you will often be posed moral or ethical problems. Such titles often involve words like 'should' or 'ought'. If you are studying education, you might be asked, 'Should corporal punishment be allowed in schools?' A student of sociology might be asked, 'Should capital punishment be reintroduced?' and a student of politics might be asked, 'Should the private lives of politicians be investigated by the media?' All these questions involve important moral dimensions and to that extent are philosophical essays.

The polemical essay This is when a particular point of view is vigorously asserted or a particular position attacked. This is the preserve of journalists and politicians rather than undergraduates but your university tutors from time to time may encourage you to write in such a style to encourage your powers of argument. If you are interested in student politics you will find plenty of opportunities for exercising this particular skill. Again, there are no rules regarding structure, although an arresting introduction will help and a powerful conclusion is advisable. Just because the aim is to be committed rather than objective, it would be a mistake to overstate your case. The purpose is to *persuade*; most people don't like being bludgeoned by aggressive, one-sided arguments. The same goes for the use of sarcasm or personal attacks.

The classical essay   This literary form was established by writers like Hazlitt and Lamb and sustained by George Orwell and others in the 20th century. The aim is to write a short piece which explores a theme or an argument in a stimulating or entertaining fashion. The approach is usually discursive and relaxed rather than tightly organised. The classical essay is no longer popular but it repays a little retrospective study and arguably still exists in the form of the longer feature articles in serious newspapers.

10.6   Introductions and conclusions

Introductions

The need for an arresting introduction to a polemical essay has just been mentioned. This advice merely reflects a necessary emphasis: all essays need an introduction which seizes the often fickle attention of the reader. This is part of journalists' trade: headlines are specially confected to claim our interest, as are the opening lines of articles. These often summarise the main story in a way which emphasises its news value. Any newspaper will display this skill in action as the following examples, chosen from the *Guardian*, 11th February 1992, demonstrate.

A Question of Intelligence
   Whitehall, not before time, is conducting a wide-ranging review of the role of Britain's security and intelligence services . . .

Students' say on lecturers' pay scheme scorned

Students and dons combined yesterday to condemn a Conservative Party initiative to link pay awards for lecturers to customer views of their performance in lecture hall and seminar room ...

Feature articles – little essays on some aspects of the news – employ slightly different strategies but strive for the same effect. Consider this piece on the Barlow-Clowes financial scandal, written by Daniel John and Ruth Kelly in the same *Guardian* issue:

Peter Clowes: The Specialist in Guilt

For viewers of the slick corporate video the message was confidently reassuring with its images of security, trust and caution.

'Grandpa,' said a small boy on the film, 'how did you get so rich?' The grey haired actor replied, 'I saved and I invested carefully ... I've worked hard for my money and now I want it to work for me.' As his words faded out they were replaced by the comforting tones of a voice-over announcing 'Barlow-Clowes, the gilt specialist ...'

This introduction exploited the ironies contained in the corporate video of a crooked company and, in typical journalistic fashion, played on the pun between 'guilt' and 'gilt'.

The opening lines of George Orwell's essays are also worth studying for the way they irresistibly draw the reader in. Consider the following examples. From 'Marrakesh' (1939):

As the corpse went past the flies left the restaurant table in a cloud and rushed after it, but they came back a few minutes later ....

From 'England Your England' (1941 – during the Blitz):

As I write, highly civilised human beings are flying overhead, trying to kill me.

An apt quotation can also provide that strong start, so look out for them when you are doing your preparatory reading.

What else do you include? It's not a bad idea to indicate that you have understood the question thoroughly. You can do this by explaining any key terms in the title; the recommended paraphrasing exercise might come in useful here. Make sure you use your own words: dictionary definitions can often seem dry and pedantic. You may also wish to add a few sentences which place the topic in some kind of context – comparative, historical or theoretical. Finally, you might decide to sketch out briefly the strategy you are going to employ. This gives an impression of being well organised and in control of your material – but don't overdo such 'signposting'.

Conclusions

Conclusions are usually briefer than introductions and should include a brief summary of the main arguments covered in the body of the essay, possibly re-emphasising key points which you judge to be especially important. If you are requested to reach a personal judgement, be sure to do so. If not – if you are merely asked to 'discuss', for example – then you are not obliged to do so, although we would suggest that you do offer a judgement if possible. Sitting on the fence does not usually impress: one of the purposes of university education is to train you to make up your mind. However, if the evidence or the weight of argument does not justify anything more than a tentative conclusion, this is the proper position to take. You may wish to end your essay with a flourish – another apt quotation, perhaps, or a return to your opening theme. The authors of the article on the Barlow-Clowes scandal quoted above chose to conclude it in the following (perhaps too pre-dictable) way:

> Now nearly four years after the scandal broke, the real guilt that he [Peter Clowes] and Barlow-Clowes had specialised in has finally been established.

Box 10.1   A tutor's eye view of student essays

How will your tutors judge your essays? With some variations they will apply the ASPRESCO criteria explained in this chapter but you gain an additional tutor's eye view by reading this advice to new academic members of staff issued by Professor Michael Moran and Bruce Wood of the University of Manchester Department of Government. Note in particular the warning against plagiarism.

Essays vary as widely as the personalities of their authors, but particular kinds of 'problem' essays recur. Here are some common types, and hints about how to respond:

The Perfect Essay. It is wonderful to read an essay that in 2,000 words of beautifully written prose displays wide reading, judiciously sums up evidence and arrives at a clearly argued conclusion. But what do you write after giving it 80 per cent? Three things: give high praise, because even bright students need reassurance; register disagreement, if there is any proposition in the essay against which you can raise an argument; and suggest some further reading on the topic for what is obviously a highly motivated student.

The 40 Page Essay Covering Everything from a conscientious student. Praise their industry, and then go to town on the structural faults. Set them a target for the next essay: to write no more than 1,000 words; and suggest that they write it under 'exam conditions' having put their books and notes away.

The Illegible Essay. Decline to read it until it is either typed or written out legibly. You should have emphasised the importance of clear presentation in your initial guidance to students.

The Polemical Essay. Unless you have asked for a polemical essay, go to town on the importance of balance in the presentation of argument. You may also consider requiring the student next time to write a polemic – but against the position which he or she holds.

The Appallingly Written Essay. If English is not the student's first language, check that (s)he is attending remedial classes; any large university or polytechnic should offer this facility. If the student's first language is English make plain that correct grammar, spelling and punctuation are not irrelevant. Tell the student to buy a simple style primer and a dictionary.

The Idler's Essay. When an essay appears which is plainly the result of a couple of hours' hurried scribbling, return it with a nil mark, and draw the attention of the student to the minimum standards of work and presentation which you have set out.

The Plagiarised Essay. Most institutions have rules governing plagiarism, but judgement in particular cases can be difficult. Crude plagiarism is quite rare. Issue a general reminder to the group about the dangers of plagiarism, and a reminder that a plagiarist has no help in an examination.

10.7   The ten-point plan for writing good essays

Much of what has been written so far about studying and writing might seem a little theoretical or hard to take in. To help you we have, by way of a conclusion to this chapter, distilled much of our advice into a ten-point plan of action, beginning when you receive the title and ending when you hand in the completed piece of work.

1 **Understand the title** The title is vital. Remember to identify the *instruction words* and the *key terms*, paraphrasing the title into your own words if this helps reveal its inner meaning. Think about the title as much as you can, asking yourself: What knowledge have I already got? How much more will I need to acquire? And what kind of essay structure will be most suitable? Try to keep the title in the forefront of your mind whilst you are writing the essay. It sometimes helps to write it out and prop it up in front of you on your desk or table.

2 **Generation of ideas** If you have difficulty in summoning ideas and information at this (or indeed any other) stage the *brainstorming* technique can prove invaluable. Write the topic in the centre of a clean sheet of paper and scribble

down ideas in any order as they come to you.

3 **Preliminary essay plan** This is an extension of your title analysis and is a useful way of clarifying your thoughts and gaining a sense of direction before you start reading. Your plan need be no more than a number of headings or half a side of paper. Many students dive straight into their reading in the belief that they do not yet know enough to even start thinking about their essay structure. Producing an initial plan, however, will help you take stock of what you know and identify the gaps in your understanding and knowledge. *Five minutes' hard thinking at this stage is worth an hour's undirected reading later on.* You will almost certainly find that your plan proves inadequate and you may scrap it altogether, but it will have served its purpose in enabling you to reach a higher level of understanding and planning.

4 **Assembly of sources** Unlike at school, where sources are usually concentrated in a single room or building, at university you will often need to do quite a bit of legwork and this can take time. You may have to do a trawl of libraries (university, local, city) and bookshops as well as gathering together relevant lecture notes, or borrowing from friends and so forth. If your course is popular, all the library books for particular assignments will be snapped up at once so you need to be quick off the mark. Much of your reading may also involve library-based back copies of learned journals. Most libraries have photocopying services, so you can acquire copies of key articles, but as this can be expensive you may need to allocate considerable slabs of time for library study.

Remember

a. An ability to *preview* (checking the title, author, dust jacket, contents, etc. in a few seconds) enables you to identify your sources quickly and efficiently.

b Don't overwhelm yourself with reading: four or five relevant books are probably sufficient for most essays.

5 **Reading** Once you have assembled your sources you need to use the full range of reading techniques including skimming; search reading; detailed reading (see Chapter 7).

6 **Note making** This is especially important during lectures, any of which could be of key importance to your essay – remember, a book can always be re-read but lectures cannot be re-listened to (see Chapter 8). You might find with your detailed reading for essays, however, that the briefest of notes or even page references will suffice.

7 **Detailed essay plan** As you proceed through your reading you will find yourself constantly re-assessing your preliminary plan, adding new ideas and redesigning your framework to accommodate the complexities of your subject. After a certain amount of reading and thinking, time limitations will demand that you stop and begin writing. This is when your *detailed plan* needs to be constructed. It needs to be as comprehensive as possible, with page references and relevant quotations. The more work you put into the plan, the more likely it is that the essay will be easy to write.

8 **First draft** For many students this is the hardest part of writing an essay. You need to bear in mind the imperatives of *answering* the question and sticking to a clear *structure* as well as *presenting* your work clearly, showing evidence of wide *reading*, supporting your arguments with *evidence*, writing in a a lively and appropriate *style*, displaying *clear* thinking and, if possible, a degree of *originality* (ASPRESCO). The discipline of expressing yourself clearly will almost certainly cause you to rethink elements of your plan as you work through, so whilst following the plan, appreciate that you will simultaneously be developing it. Writing good essays will be difficult at first and may seem to take an unconscionably long time but, as with any skill, practice will enable you to speed up and do automatically things which at first you found hard to master.

9 **Second draft** Many students believe they are sufficiently clever to submit their first draft and save the fag of writing out a second one. They are not usually justified in their assumptions, and they receive lower grades than they might deserve. A second draft enables you to improve your style and presentation (remember, your tutors will welcome a typed essay) and also to benefit from the insights which further reflection upon the by now familiar topic has allowed. You can also tidy up quotations, the bibliography, and footnotes (if you have used them) and generally make your essay a more convincing, persuasive and professional piece of work.

10 **Final reading** Once you have finished your second draft, you may be so sick of the essay you cannot bear to check it through before handing it in. This is an error. You will astonish yourself at how many minor mistakes you will spot when doing this final run-through. Don't spoil all the hard work you have put in by skimping on this final effort.

You may have read the above and concluded that your own system of writing essays is superior – which is fine. 'If it ain't broke, don't fix it' is a sound philosophy. However, the above strategy has been tried and tested over 15 years in our classes at the University of Manchester, and large numbers of students have benefited. It might be worth giving it a try and seeing whether your performance improves.

10.8 Writing good scientific reports

Science students do not have to write as many essays as their fellows in the arts and humanities, but they do have to write a large number of scientific reports. 'It is no longer the exception but the rule', wrote F. Peter Woodford in 1968 'that scientific writing is heavy, verbose, pretentious, and dull.' It is a matter of opinion (and some dispute) whether this situation has changed significantly since then. T. R. Henn, a Cambridge don writing in 1960, traced the problem to the point when 15- or 16-year-olds choose to specialise. At that time those who opt for science lose contact with 'linguistic discipline'; at university this is exacerbated by long periods of practical research rather than practice at prose. His somewhat old-fashioned (but in our view still quite sensible) solution was a 'therapeutic course of reading, particularly of those authors who are masters of control . . . Addison, Swift, Jane Austen'. An additional reason for poor scientific writing can be adduced: the widespread assumption amongst scientific students that 'writing-up' is relatively unimportant and that the bald facts will suffice.

This assumption is misplaced. It is true that literary quality is more important in a history or English literature essay than in a scientific report, but this is not to say that scientific writing should be devoid of any literary merit. Such writing is designed to achieve effective communication: as a science student you need to express your findings with clarity, accuracy and, if you can manage it, style. Scientists need to communicate with each other and the rest of society. It is a mistake to think the arts are to do with 'words' and science with 'facts'; this is the frame of mind which produces C. P. Snow's 'Two Cultures' in which graduates of the sciences and humanities regard each other with mutual incomprehension and bewilderment. Bridging that gap should begin in the sixth form and continue at university with the active connivance of your teachers and tutors. Furthermore the quality of your reports, the care you have shown, the precision you have achieved, will be judged as an important part of your scientific skills.

Most of the essay-writing elements discussed earlier are directly applicable, but there are significant differences. In the humanities, you are usually asked to respond to a particular question. In science, questions are answered through practical experiments: your written report records and comments on the process. Whilst a humanities essay is based on notes from lectures and books, scientific reports are based on notes taken during practical work, very often in the laboratory or the field.

Notes

You should write your notes with great care, using a proper notebook rather than odd bits of paper. Be systematic and disciplined; record every detail of your apparatus and the observed process in chronological order. Numbers are particularly important so make sure you write them legibly. If ideas occur to you during the course of your practical work, write them down too (possibly in square brackets to differentiate from your other observations). Get into the habit of writing as you work and write up your findings as soon as possible whilst the work is still fresh in your mind. At the time you might not think it possible that you will forget but even a few days later the details will become blurred. If you have been working in a group or team, prompt writing up is particularly important: it may be difficult to re-assemble the same group at a later date. Remember also in this situation to check and verify your notes with your colleagues.

Structure

There are no hard and fast rules on structure, as each discipline and each task will have specific requirements. As with all written assignments, you need to find the framework which will best accommodate what you have to say. If you are writing an analysis based on secondary sources, let's say, an analysis of theories of evolution, you will essentially be writing an essay and the advice given earlier on in this chapter will apply. If you are writing up a laboratory experiment, however, you might well divide it up as follows.

1 **Title** Make sure your title is both an accurate description of your set task and of what follows.
2 **Abstract** Scientific papers usually start with an 'abstract'

which offers a brief summary of what will follow (The Royal Society's rule of thumb on abstract length is not more than 200 words or 5% of the whole piece) but drafting the abstract is probably best left until last. Writing good summaries, comprehensible to non-specialists without any reference to the text needed, is not easy: it requires practice and some literary skill.

3 **Purpose of experiment**   This will often entail the testing of a hypothesis; if so, make sure you state it clearly. You may also need to make some reference to relevant literature – journal articles and so forth – but try to be brief.

4 **Methodology employed**   This needs to be explained with great precision, especially your measurement techniques. You may need to point out briefly the strengths and weaknesses of your methodology, once again making reference where necessary to relevant literature.

5 **Apparatus and materials used**   This section needs to be like a good recipe: sufficiently detailed for someone to replicate your experiment. Diagrams or drawings might well assist when describing your apparatus.

6 **The experiment**   The sequence of events which occurred in the experiment or in the field needs to be meticulously recorded.

7 **Results**   This section often requires the use of tables, graphs and other devices for displaying quantitative data in a clear and comprehensible fashion. You will not always need to show every measurement made. In some cases, the *range* of findings will suffice; in others, the *mean* of several readings will do.

8 **Discussion and interpretation of results**   This is the most important part of your report and might be its longest. This is where your qualities as a scientist – your powers of logical thought, your scientific imagination and judgement – will be on display. It will also show your ability to express yourself coherently and concisely. Reference to other work might need to be more extensive in this section. Remember

to include a *critical* evaluation of the limitations of your experiment, including, for example, possible sources of error or the percentages of error within which your results have to be understood.

9 **Conclusions** This should not be a summary of your experiment but a brief statement arising from your discussion. The focus will be on what conclusions can reasonably be drawn from the work you have undertaken. If your results are inconclusive, you should say so: negative findings can be just as important scientifically as positive ones.

10 **Bibliography and references.**

Style

The poet chooses words for their sound, rhythm and complex emotive connotations; words are thrown into the pool like pebbles, for the ripples they will make. Scientists are close to the other end of the word-usage spectrum; they tend to choose words for their technical precision, for their low ripple effect. This does not mean, however, that scientists are uninterested in words except for the technical terms of their discipline. Good style is defined by how appropriate it is for the context. Science does not offer the same scope for stylistic virtuosity as the arts but it is quite possible for an economical, concise style to be highly readable – even elegant. The prime requirement is to say *exactly* what you mean without ambiguity or any possibility of misinterpretation. This is easier said than done: when you know what you mean, it isn't easy to realise that other people might not. 'Keep it simple' is the best advice: short sentences, short paragraphs, short words instead of long ones.

But scientists also need to interest and persuade. Like anyone trying to communicate effectively in writing, they have to pay attention to the rudiments of good style (covered at length in Chapter 9) such as a wide vocabulary, accurate use of grammar and punctuation, correct spelling, well-balanced sentences of varying length, and effective linkage of sentences and paragraphs to ensure flow and coherence.

Writing characterised by monosyllabic technical terms, jerky short sentences, grammatical errors, laboratory jargon, slang and acronyms will undermine your authority, however brilliant you might be in the laboratory or in the field.

Here's some more specific advice on scientific style.

- Be careful not to use carelessly words which could have a precise scientific meaning – for example, 'positive' or 'significant'.

- Try to use prose rather than technical symbols and formulae unless they are reasonably well known, such as $6CO_2 + 6H_2O$ $C_6H_{12}O_6$ $+6O_2$ which is easily recognised by biologists and chemists as the formula for photosynthesis – its use saves time. Avoid contractions ('won't', 'can't') and abbreviations like $\therefore$ for 'therefore' or $\because$ for 'because'.

- Explain or define new terms or symbols when they are first used in your report.

- Follow the Royal Society's advice and use the third person rather than the first.

- Use analogies and metaphors where they can elucidate or enrich but be sparing, and beware of misleading your readers with inappropriate usage.

- Be cautious rather than over-expressive: 'These findings suggest that . . .' rather than 'these findings are very important in that . . .' (also see Box 10.1).

- Make sure you are familiar with the conventions of your discipline and of your teachers and tutors. The Royal Society, for example, advises you to write 0.25 rather than .25 and that figures with many noughts be expressed in the shortened form: 3.92×10^7 instead of 392 00000 or 0.25×10^{-4} instead of 0.000025. If you are supplying references, the Royal Society advises using the Harvard rather than the numeric system (see Section 9.5). Be sure to be consistent in such usage, as lack of uniformity, like poor spelling, will impair your credibility.

Box 10.1   Phrases that scientists should not use ... but often do

Phrase	Possible meaning
As is well known ...	I think
It is evident that ...	I think
It is perhaps true to say ...	I don't know what to think
It is generally agreed that ...	Some people think
It is likely that ...	I have not got enough evidence
For obvious reasons ...	I have no evidence
There is no doubt that ...	I am convinced
There is no doubt that ...	I still have no evidence

From A. Trinci *et al., How to Write a Thesis*, p. 6.

Drafting and editing

You have to accept that writing is a complex and difficult process. Anyone who thinks they can dash off a long report in an hour or so is in for either a rude awakening or at best mediocre marks. You will need to rework rough drafts very carefully ensuring that:

- you have reported all aspects of your work, especially the key passages, accurately and clearly;
- your figures are all correct;
- excessive verbiage has been excised; and
- grammar and spelling are all in order.

It is worth waiting a few days before producing your final draft, as a little distance can help you spot mistakes which you would have otherwise have missed – but don't wait too long.

Presentation

Neat presentation is important as it enhances the clarity of your work. Reports typed on word processors, now available in many schools and most university science departments, create a particularly impressive end-product. They also make corrections and revisions less traumatic when you are anxious to meet your submission deadline.

Key points

1 The two most important requirements of a good essay are that they answer the set question directly and thoroughly and they display a clear logical structure.
2 The acronym ASPRESCO – answer the question, structure, presentation, reading, evidence, style, clear thinking, originality – is a memory aid for all eight key elements in a good essay.
3 Many essays require you to follow a 'for and against' structure. The Strategy One approach entails a consideration of all the 'fors' followed by all the 'againsts'. The Strategy Two approach is more sophisticated and prescribes a structure which requires you to match like against like in a 'for and against' fashion in, for example, economic or moral arguments.
4 Brainstorming is a useful technique for generating ideas.
5 Analysing the question is a key preliminary activity which requires you to consider carefully the *instruction words* and the *key concepts*.
6 Introductions need to claim the attention of the reader whilst conclusions should sum up in a memorable or persuasive fashion.
7 The processes of writing a good essay can be broken down into ten clear stages: understanding the title, generation of ideas, preliminary essay plan, assembly of sources, reading, note making, detailed essay plan, first draft, second draft, final reading.
8 Writing scientific reports requires similar skills but has other distinctive requirements.

Things to do

1 Look through some of your earlier essays and apply the criteria

explained in this chapter. How do your essays survive the test?

2 Plan an essay in response to this question: ' "The banning of private cars in city centres would be as socially equitable as it would be environmentally beneficial." Discuss.'

3 Now write an essay – it could be course work or something you have set yourself (or even the one mentioned above) – that follows the ten-point plan. If you are a science student follow the advice given in 10.8. Try to get some feedback from your tutor or teacher.

4 Practice 'brainstorming' the following subjects: 'nuclear power', 'Elton John', 'communism', 'global warming', 'hamsters', 'ideas for Christmas presents'.

5 Read some feature articles in the serious newspapers and analyse how they are structured. Study also how they are introduced and concluded.

6 Dig out some classical essays by William Hazlitt or Charles Lamb and note how they are constructed and written. Make an attempt at writing one yourself on the subject of 'The Two Cultures'.

Further reading

Making the Grade (Manchester University Press, 1990) by Bill Jones and Roy Johnson covers the subject of this chapter at considerable length. The booklet by Roy Johnson, *Writing Essays* (Clifton Press, 1991; PO Box 100, Manchester 20), is also a useful summary.

T. R. Henn's 1960 volume *Science in Writing* (Harrap) gives a selection of classic scientific writings. The Royal Society leaflet *General Notes on the Preparation of Scientific Papers* is recommended for those with scholarly standards and ambitions.

11

Handling your project

The outcome of any serious research can only be to make two questions grow where only one grew before.

Thorstein Veblen, *The Place of Science in Modern Civilisation*

11.1 Introduction

At some stage in your student career you are likely to have to work on a research project or dissertation. This may involve reviewing and analysing literature, or reporting on a case study, fieldwork or laboratory experiments. In some courses, choice of project is left to the student guided by a supervisor. In others, students are asked to select from a list of topics or areas drawn up by tutors. A project report is increasingly likely to count towards your final degree (see Chapter 12). In at least one case we know of, the student project now counts for 25% of finals marks.

Project work developed from the methods of teaching in science which involved identification of problems, the rehearsal of a range of solutions, and the formulation and testing of hypotheses. By the early years of the 20th century 'the project method' was taken up more generally. It was popular in the USA where it was associated with the famous thinker John Dewey and discovery learning – the belief that we learn by *doing*, particularly when we direct our activity to solving problems we perceive as important. In the UK, the first book on project work was published in the early 1930s (Gull, 1933), whilst there is 'evidence that a small number of British university departments were using the project method as early as the 1920s' (Adderly *et al.*, 1975, p. 13). Project work has now spread across the higher education curriculum, colonising most subjects. Renewed emphasis on the practical, and initiatives such as the Enterprise in Higher Education scheme, which is intended to provide students with 'work awareness', promise an increase in the importance of student research.

Project work has a number of advantages.

- You pick a problem that *interests you*. You answer your own questions rather than those imposed by others.
- You actively test out what you have learned in your course work.
- You learn how to handle a range of skills: the techniques of investigation, analysis, communication and collaboration.
- You learn how to learn by organising your own activity. You take responsibility for the management of your own education.
- The active element is fully deployed. You understand and make your own what you grasp actively yourself, rather than what you passively imbibe from others.
- You produce a report which is useful evidence of your work to your teachers and future employers.

You receive an induction into how the research activity, which is at the heart of higher education, works. You get some understanding of how researchers create new knowledge. Your appreciation of the research of others and your ability to analyse and evaluate it should be enhanced. Your project can help to demystify research. You should now see that it is far from the prerogative of a small elite of very clever people. Research is, after all, only *an organised strategy for gaining more knowledge about problems that concern us through using commonsense tools of investigation in an organised way.* The word derives from the French *recherche* which means 'quest' or 'pursuit'. It helps, I think, if we conceive research as detective work, as critical, disciplined inquiry designed to clarify or solve problems.

The extension of project work is important in extending

research skills beyond a minority of postgraduates to all students. The more citizens educated in organised problem solving, the stronger our society is likely to be. Social and economic progress requires continuing research. But, of course, its social application can raise questions for its creators. Albert Einstein, whose work made nuclear weapons possible, remarked, 'If only I had known, I would have become a watchmaker.'

Your project work can be an exciting part of your course.

- Section 11.2 examines the need to establish the part project work plays and the process of selecting a problem and developing a synopsis.
- Section 11.3 deals with how you search for relevant previous studies. You may like to look back at Chapter 7 before working through this section.
- Section 11.4 examines some of the different approaches to research and some of the different techniques of investigation.
- Section 11.5 makes some general points about the craft of research and the virtues you need to cultivate.
- Section 11.6 stresses that you should keep the necessity for a well written report in mind throughout the earlier stages of your project: the more writing you get done early on, the less the danger of the last minute pile-up. We outline ways in which you can organise your report; emphasise once more the need for good expression to reflect clear thinking; and stress how essential the process of rewriting is to good organisation and exposition.

Box 11.1   Handling your research project

1 Establish area of interest
2 Establish topic of interest
3 Review literature and course work
4 Formulate a research problem

    5 Generate a hypothesis
    6 Discuss with your supervisor
    7 Carry out thorough literature review
    8 Write a research proposal
    9 Decide on research design
   10 Carry out research
   11 Collect and record data
   12 Interpret results
   13 Write up research report

11.2 Planning your project

Project work on your course

As soon as possible, check:

- when you start and the deadline for submission;
- the proportion of marks awarded for your project;
- who assesses your work and the weight given to different factors: clarity and accuracy of exposition, style of present-ation, critical understanding of the literature, research design, originality;
- the position as regards group projects;
- who supervises your project, what say you have in this, whether and when you have to agree a title with your supervisor;
- what guidance exists on the format of your final report: what the requirements are as to *length*, layout, number of copies and binding;
- where you can find copies of previous project reports.

Talk about the requirements with friends and students who did their projects the previous year.

Talk to your tutors

When you have worked through the above checklist, discuss your results with your teachers. What role do *they* see project work playing in the course? Which aspects do they see as most important? In general, do they emphasise book work (mastering the literature) or fieldwork (getting you out of the university and amongst the practitioners)? Do they have any specific preference for *you*, arrived at through observation of how you have worked recently? Do they place more emphasis on skills development (*process*) or on knowledge development (the quality of your final *product*)? Is collaborative work encouraged? Try to get some idea from tutors as to the time and effort involved. Sometimes projects are based on a number of hours' work; in other cases they are open-ended. Explore whether there is any set of typical problems staff have seen emerging in the past.

A key question to consider is the *kind* of research you will undertake:

Descriptive research essentially involves filling in gaps in our factual knowledge. A piece of descriptive research might seek to elicit the number of immigrants living in Newtown, the number of burglaries over the last 18 months, what proportion of the population supports Tranmere Rovers.

Explanatory research seeks to develop explanations and make connections between phenomena. It asks why immigrants are coming to Newtown, why the number of burglaries is increasing, decreasing or static. It endeavours to relate patterns of child rearing, religious affiliation or propensity to delinquency, to support for Tranmere Rovers. Its aim is to close gaps, not primarily in our factual knowledge, but *in our understanding*.

Higher education should seek to train you in explanatory, problem-solving research, but you may also do some projects seeking to gather information and to describe attitudes, behaviour or conditions.

Relate projects to coursework

The best projects often stem from problems you encounter in your course work. If you think about your project from the start, it is in your mind as you work through your reading, classes and assignments: 'Couldn't I take this further ... haven't we only dealt with that superficially . . .?' Which areas seem to you to be controversial or under-researched? Beware the area that is heavily documented. Look for what is *not* known, at areas where there is a dearth of published work.

Have a preliminary look at what has been written relevant to possible projects. See what your tutor has to say. Think broadly about what methods you might use. This kind of preliminary work can pay dividends, particularly for those of us who only start thinking when actively confronted with a problem.

Selecting a problem

Even before your first meeting with your supervisor you should have done some work on the ideas you will discuss together. From a supervisor's point of view nothing is more irritating than 'I haven't really thought about it. What do you think would be a good topic?' Next most irritating is 'I'd like to do something that involves interviewing people.' You may be advised to apply for work at the Job Centre ... or join the police force!

Before you see your supervisor *work on two or three specific proposals* and have a go at fining them down so that they are of operational precision. If you approach your supervisor with 'I want to do a project on unemployment' the response will be: 'Which aspect of unemployment? How it is measured and debates about statistics? Or how unemployment develops and diminishes, its impact on the economy, on companies, on families or individuals?' Think through these kinds of questions yourself. Get off on the right foot by accepting from the start: *this project is my responsibility.*

Your proposal must have a manageable, limited ambit – a *precise focus*. Academics spend years and thousands of pounds writing books on one particular aspect of unemployment. With your limited time and resources, you must cut your coat according to the cloth available. Get your project topic in the context of available resources and competing demands. Remember, anyway, that you are not being asked to write a book. You may be told your report should be 'between 5,000 and 10,000 words', 'up to 10,000 words', 'not more than 15,000 words' – although limits vary, you will rarely be asked for more. If you translate this into typescript, you are talking of between 15 and 50 pages of double-spaced A4. This should give you some help with selecting a manageable problem to research.

Box 11.1   Picking a problem

Key words: *choice, commitment, interest, motivation*

- A topic in the course which could yield a testable hypothesis?
- A study in the literature which could be developed?
- An area in which I have past experience?
- A topic my supervisor is researching?
- An aspect of a study my department is mounting?
- A problem suggested by my tutor?

Question words: *accessibility, controversial, dangerous, detachment, existing literature, interest, viability*

- Has the work been done already?
- If I work on a project selected by another will I be adequately motivated?

- Will I have adequate access?
- Is the problem viable – am I likely to clarify it and propose a solution? Am I being too ambitious?
- What is the state of the existing literature?
- Am I sufficiently detached to produce a rigorous study?
- Is the problem controversial and likely to cause difficulties of access, a hostile response or unwanted publicity?

Plane the problem down

With an undergraduate project it is important to stretch yourself whilst avoiding over-ambition. 'Unemployment in Merseyside, 1989–91' is obviously an improvement upon 'Unemployment', 'Unemployment in Britain', 'Unemployment in Britain in the 1980s', or even 'Unemployment on Merseyside, 1979–90'. You have restricted the problem in temporal and geographic terms. But it still covers too wide a range: at this level it constitutes not a problem but a collection of problems. Related to your time and resources it probably still falls under the heading 'Megalomania' rather than 'Realism'. See if you can shave it down further.

For example, Kirkby – a small, reasonably demarcated part of Merseyside – has always constituted an unemployment black spot. And you might further restrict the problem to the youth. So you might refashion your title: 'The Impact of Unemployment on 16- to 18-Year-Olds in Kirkby, 1989–91'. If you want to narrow the angle further you might focus on crime, illness, nervous breakdown or suicide. What about: 'The Relationship between Unemployment and Criminal Conviction amongst 16- to 18-Year-Olds: A Case Study of Kirkby, 1989–91'? You have now homed in on something that is more manageable. It is also, in a way, more difficult – you have less room for manoeuvre, you are entering the field of explanatory research and preparing to grapple with complex questions of causation – but your subject is potentially more valuable and more rewarding.

You are trading off breadth (but would it, in practice, mean superficiality?) for the opportunity of an in-depth case study. Fine, you might think, but the specific local focus places limitations on the utility of the study, even if it is done well. Would the project not be more valuable if it offered a comparison of working-class Kirkby with a bourgeois locale either in the North or – to give a starker comparison – in the more prosperous South East – say, Hampstead? The answer is clearly 'yes' – *in the abstract, if you could pull it off.* But look at the difficulties expansion generates. You double the work, you introduce a range of practical problems involving time and resources. The wider problem may be just too ambitious at this stage. Thinking your way through a project proposal in this way teaches you that you cannot cover everything. Research is about resources and getting the scale right. With small-scale research you are dealing in imperfection. Each proposal has to lose something to make it more realisable.

Objectives and method

You now have your *provisional* title. It may change as you work: 'The Relationship between Unemployment and Criminal Conviction amongst 16- to 18-Year-Olds: A Case Study of Kirkby, 1989–91', 'The Influence of James Joyce on the Novels of Samuel Becket', or whatever. These titles, however, may seem to lie somewhat inertly and passively on the page. Can you make your title more active so it tells you more precisely what you have to do and how to go about it? If I say to you, 'What are your objectives in doing this project?' you might reply: 'To find out all I can about the relationship between Joyce and Becket and analyse what comes out of my work'. This approach may work well for you. But the problem for many students is that this objective is insufficiently specific and directional. The danger is you assemble masses of information without structuring and shaping it as you go along. Doing so later is difficult. You get lost in the data.

We have spoken in terms of 'selecting *problems*' for project work – this focuses the mind and helps to structure and organise the work from the start. To take this a stage further, you might *make a guess as to what the solution to your problem is*. For example, as you read *Murphy* you may be taken by the similarity of style in Becket and Joyce. You may have heard that Becket worked for a time as Joyce's secretary. Your guess may be that the influence of the great modernist on Becket was a strong one, that Becket was essentially an epigone of Joyce. This may help in directing and structuring your work. But you must avoid the self-fulfilling prophecy. Your guess is just a guess, to be modified or disproven if the evidence justifies doing so. As you read Becket's novels more closely you may detect a bleaker vision, a more pessimistic view of humanity than is found in Joyce. You might conjecture the relationship of this to what Becket did not have in common with Joyce – his loss of God, his Protestantism – and start testing this tentative connection. But always remember that with well-known figures and controversial issues you must check out the state of the art. Has this issue already been dealt with adequately? Your project must say something *new*.

When students say to me, 'I want to find out all I can about . . .', my response is often 'But you already know something about this topic . . . *what do you think you will find out by further inquiry?*' My experience is that the problem-guess framework sharpens up the objectives of a project by recasting them in a more active way. It seems to work best for first-time researchers in a wide range of subjects.

Give some preliminary consideration to the techniques you use. For example, the following might cross your mind as ways of developing the Kirkby project:

- the need to work on analysis of employment statistics and regional differentiations

- the need to analyse criminal statistics
- the need to use questionnaires
- the need to interview economists, personnel at job centres, criminologists, a cross-section of local youth

Polish the problem up

In real life, the planing down process will run parallel with

- spadework on existing literature;
- a consideration of research design and methods;
- thinking about access and resources.

You may reduce, expand, transform or discard proposals as you find out more about these matters. Just as you are getting things together you may find that an article comes out which reports that Jill Bloggs has just done what you wanted to do – or contrarywise, suggests a new and fertile line of inquiry. But hopefully the generation of a number of possible problems and work on their refinement now gives you and your supervisor something to get your teeth into.

Your hypothesis

At this stage your supervisor may remark, in relation to the ideas you have come up with, 'Sounds fine . . . What's your hypothesis?' This goes back to our earlier points about the problem–guess framework for projects. *A hypothesis is a hunch, an informed prediction about the relationship between variables, that the researcher makes.* The assertion is made on the basis of a look around the problem and the literature, your intuition and imagination. A hypothesis is a *tentative proposition which will be found to be true, modified or disproved, which will guide the student as he or she works through the research puzzle.* You might begin to fashion your hypothesis by writing:

My guess is that as unemployment increased amongst young people in 1991–2 so did the incidence of certain kinds of crimes, specifically crimes against property such as burglary. My assertion is that these two factors are related. The former is causative. I shall begin to see whether this guess holds true by examining the crime and the unemployment statistics . . .

Research manuals usually say that a hypothesis should be clearly enunciated, limited in scope and grounded in existing knowledge. It should state the relationship between variables and be testable. In practice, many research hypotheses are rough, fluid and constantly changing. Sometimes they come after some of the research is completed. For new students, however, formulating a working hypothesis at the start is very useful. It can commit and guide you and give your project structure and interest, so long as it is clearly understood that it is an expedential and disposable instrument which requires testing, not justification. It would be fatal if you simply looked for and took on board evidence which upheld your hypothesis and ignored or downplayed evidence to the contrary. The point about grounding a hypothesis in the literature can be particularly important. You should cast off from the dry land of existing knowledge but remain in the shallows. Launching a hypothesis into an area of which you know little can result in the shipwreck of the new researcher.

Expand your topic

A definite runner may now emerge from your shortlist. Your supervisor may ask you to go away, have another look at the literature and come back with a more detailed statement, *a research proposal*. This helps you to clarify where you are going and what the problems are. It commits you. It provides something for your supervisor to endorse, improve, criticise – a basis for negotiation – and helps to avoid future misunderstanding about what is involved. Suitably rewritten and subject to reasonable redirection in practice, it can constitute a contract of expectation between you and your supervisor.

Your synopsis should state the *research problem*, your *hypothesis* and the *methods* you are going to use to test it. It may be useful to use a format where a general introductory statement of problem, purpose and method is followed by a heading for each section or chapter of the proposed report with a couple of paragraphs explaining the coverage of each. In conclusion, list key literature. Do not allow the idea of writing a synopsis to freeze you. Write a rough outline. Go over it and write a revised outline. Discuss it with a friend and try again. Your supervisor may suggest further amendment.

You and your supervisor

A good supervisor – who may act as a mentor, questioning, steering, suggesting rather than imposing – should try to educate the student's judgement without substituting his or her own. The supervisor should advise without insisting: the student should be left some scope to make mistakes, an essential part of the research experience. Perhaps *facilitator* describes better what the lecturer should do. There may of course be personal problems.

> The lecturer may be shy, absorbed in his [*sic*] own research, impatient of student demands, a habitual dampener of enthusiasm, or just plain lazy. A student may be shy, intolerant of criticism, insecure about putting forward his own ideas, unable to articulate them in a form his supervisor can understand or just plain lazy. Added to this there will probably be a few clashes between different types of personality. Despite some consequent difficulties it may be good for the student to realise that lecturers are only human. (Adderly *et al.*, 1975, p. 51)

To minimise difficulty and stimulate partnership, ensure that the supervisor allocated possesses expertise in the area of your project and is going to be available for its duration. Bear in mind that he or she will not be available full time. Listen carefully to advice. Remember: your supervisor has been here before.

Research confirms that differences of approach between student and supervisor can cause difficulties. Some students like to meet often, some supervisors only feel it is necessary when something is achieved; sometimes it is the supervisor who wants lots of meetings and the student who is reluctant (Phillips and Pugh, 1987, p. 8). It is important that the expectations of both parties and their understanding of what is involved synchronise. Talk about your expectations, establish procedures for contact and think about *time* (see Box 11.2). You must establish a clear work schedule with deadlines to motivate you (see Box 11.3).

Box 11.2   Timing is vital

Time will be restricted. Moreover a delay in completing one stage can knock a big hole in a tight timetable. If you don't carry out the interviews on time you won't have the questionnaires ready when you have been allocated time on the computers. So: *draw up a realistic timetable*, taking into account likely delays, and *then stick to it*.

1 Think about how long you will be able to spend searching out and reading the literature, refining your problem and working out your research design. Clear time limits will prompt entry into the action phase.
2 How long will data gathering and analysis take? Remember how time consuming preparing questionnaires, attending meetings, mounting interviews can be.
3 It helps to write up results as you go along. Your final report may be the longest writing assignment you have yet undertaken. Many supervisors would suggest that you budget 25% of your overall time for the writing-up process. Writing up and revising will be time consuming. Don't use all your time

for doing the research itself. Budget for dependence on others: your report may have to be typed up or wordprocessed by somebody else. The typescript will require revision and correction, binding takes time.

4 Think clearly about the availability of others and the need to give advance notice, and allow for waiting periods. If you give your supervisor 10,000 words on Monday you cannot expect to have the draft back by Tuesday.

5 Be realistic. If you have to submit your report at the end of the long vacation, have you *really* got the whole three months to spend on your work?

6 If you run into difficulties, talk to your supervisor. There may be a case for cutting down the scope of your project or changing tack.

Box 11.3

If you are doing a project in your second year when you have no exams to be completed for the start of your third year, your first attempt at a timetable might look something like this:

Date	Action
Sept/Oct	Think about topic
	Look in library
	Do some preliminary reading
Nov/Dec	Refine and specify problems
	Meet supervisor
	More reading
Jan/Feb	Write research proposal
	Agree title and approach with supervisor
	Begin literature search
March/April	Complete literature search
	Begin writing up
	Arrange visits and interviews
	Meet supervisor

May/June	Carry out write-up visits, interviews
	Begin writing of final report
	Meet supervisor
July	Complete first draft of report
	Meet supervisor
September	Produce final report

Report in to your supervisor even when you have no progress to report. Projects go wrong when students who have made little progress fail to contact their supervisor and let things drift. It is your job to maintain contact, not your supervisor's job to run you to earth.

At every stage, criticism and feedback are crucial. If you do not let your supervisor see your work as it unfolds, you will lose the opportunity to refashion and improve it. Deliver on your promises if you expect your supervisor to do likewise.

Group projects

A group of students may wish to work on a collective project.

Advantages

- The project may be more intensively developed or its scope may be extended. For example, the comparison between two locales, as suggested earlier, would become more viable if two or three people were involved.
- Different minds generate different views: the project may be multi-faceted, interdisciplinary and richer.
- There is the possibility of specialisation: different abilities and talents may be brought to bear on, for example, research design, interviewing or writing up.

Disadvantages

- The problems of co-ordination are greater. A lot of time can be spent on meetings.

- This can lead to slow progress – *everything* must be discussed.
- People who see eye to eye at the start might see things differently once the project develops. Some students become concerned that their contribution is greater than that of others.

Group projects can work well. Breakthrough research often requires collaboration: through a group project you receive an early training in the difficulties and potential. Against this it may be argued that a prerequisite for effective co-operative research is that all the collaborators possess a good individual training; the hard, somewhat solitary, process of doing your own project is a good start on this. In this view group work comes *next*. Certainly successful group projects require

- equal commitment, by all involved, to the problem under investigation;
- a clear-cut understanding of who will do what;
- a good, mutually agreed timetable; and
- at least a limited compatibility of interest and temperament amongst those involved.

11.3   The literature: search and review

The existing literature is the map which shows you the ground that has already been charted and the territory which awaits discovery. The existing literature may also be rich in suggestions as to which methods you should use in your journey of discovery – and how you should organise your final report. Your literature review may not be completed before you begin your substantial investigation, but the more high grade fuel you can take on board and assimilate at the point of embarkation, the speedier and more comfortable your journey is likely to be.

The literature search

To recall advice given earlier in this book: request assistance from librarians and use one, two, three, *many* libraries! With your essays and shorter reports your main bearings were taken from your reading lists. Now you have to construct your own lists and your guides will be more diffuse. Comfort yourself by noting that assembling materials at first hand is a central component in a training in research.

We have emphasised the need to examine previous projects and dissertations. But it may also be useful to look at a list of *theses* completed for Master's degrees and even Ph.D.'s relevant to your work. A general problem will be the need to be up to date. New work may have been completed since relevant books were published; the time span between submission and publication of journal articles can be up to two years. So ask your supervisor about *conference papers* and *working papers*. The proceedings of recent conferences related to your project and the first drafts of work in progress circulated in some academic departments may help to overcome the problem of time-lag in publishing. Keep up with recent issues of journals and pay particular attention to book reviews.

You will need to use all the available tools in your search for materials.

1 Library catalogues Now you will get your chance to use the *subject catalogue* to track down books, reports and pamphlets you are not aware of. Note down the class numbers of items – unemployment, theories of . . . Great Britain . . . regional . . . and so forth – and then work through the *classified catalogue* to see which publications are available in each subdivision in this library.

2 Bibliographies No single library will have everything. Bibliographies will help you find out about books your library does not stock. You may want to look at general bibliographies, such as the *British National Bibliography (BNB)* which list books under key words, and then at specialist subject bibliographies. The *BNB* should be available in your college library and its organisation follows the Dewey classification.

3 Abstracts and indexes   Rather than hunt through the individual index of journals in your field you should see if they are covered in abstracting and indexing journals. The latter list under subject headings bibliographic details of journal articles. Abstracting journals tell you a little more about what the article says. The journals are usually published monthly and aggregated annually. The best way to discover what is available in your area of concern is to look at *Ulrich's International Periodicals Directory*, an annual publication.

4 Theses   Your library should have a catalogue of theses awarded by your institution. If you wish to search further afield you should consult ASLIB's *Index to Theses Accepted for Higher Degrees by the Universities of Great Britain and Ireland* and the Council for National Academic Awards and the British Library's *British Reports, Translations and Theses*.

5 Official publications   HMSO produces monthly and annual catalogues. A more general guide is D. R. Butcher's *Guide to Official Publications* which your library should have for consultation.

6 Conferences   The British Library publishes an *Index of Conference Proceedings Received*. This contains a list of the papers available from their Document Supply Centre.

On-line computer search

Your college library should have facilities for an on-line search based on search words. But there is likely to be a charge which can be expensive. Some academic libraries do not encourage undergraduates to use these facilities although the ice is starting to break. You will usually be unable to do the search yourself but you should be able to 'sit in' with a trained searcher – otherwise you will have to take a great deal of time and care in explaining exactly what you want to the searcher. Data bases are still better in the science area than they are for arts and humanities subjects. Some research results do not favour the efficiency of the on-line search compared with traditional methods. One study showed on-line searches identifying 25% of references established manually from bibliographies and 50% of those retrieved from abstracts and indexes (Gash, 1989, pp. 47–8). A awful lot depends on how good the data base for your subject is.

None the less, the movement is towards computers. It is increasingly important to know about these facilities and how they work; consider utilising them even though most undergraduate projects can still be adequately resourced through the conventional literature search as outlined above. A knowledge of the bibliographic tools is useful in itself even if you are going to use the computer later.

The literature search is an indispensable prerequisite for a good project. But it can eat up time. To some extent you need to be all business: having selected your search words, stick to them. But you have to combine this with a little browsing. As you work through bibliographic materials a little wandering from the main path may disclose other relevant headings and references which you would otherwise have missed.

Keep records

Always write down *full* bibliographic details, including classification numbers. There is nothing worse than having to spend hours looking up a reference when writing your report. Be precise with titles and authors. It is now time to stop jotting references down on stray bits of paper and open a proper system of project files – one for the work on your title and proposal . . . another for your literature search.

Following up your references

You now need to get the books and articles on your desk. Some of them may be sitting on the shelves of your 'home' library. You may need to locate others elsewhere. You may find in your college library the published catalogues of other important libraries. *The British Library General Catalogue of Printed Books* and *The National Union Catalogue* listing the holdings of a range of libraries are useful but intimidating publications. Many academic libraries are now part of 'regional unions' which produce microfiche catalogues of the holdings of all libraries affiliated. Check up on this as it can save visits/telephone calls to individual libraries. There is also in some fields a *Directory of Periodical Literature* which lists journals and periodicals and which libraries stock them. The Joint Academic Network (JANET) maintains an on-line catalogue of the holdings of most academic libraries which your librarian can utilise.

Most students will at some stage use *inter-library loans* to get hold of articles or books unavailable in their locality, with materials or photocopies normally being sent via the British Library Document Supply Centre at Boston Spa. Most libraries have introduced charges for this service, so use the system with discrimination.

Box 11.3   Records again

Weed your file of infertile references, and make notes on those which have yielded fruit. File these in a card index so that you can extend and re-order your bibliography as the research develops. Keep your index regularly updated; in a section at the back, record items you are pursuing. Some students are fascinated by the idea of using a computer data base: this is more logical when you are dealing with a greater volume of items than is likely on most undergraduate projects. Make full use of photocopies and store them carefully. Having separated the sheep from the goats, study in depth and make notes on the useful items.

- Recall earlier advice on note making (see pp. 246–60).
- Start to allocate the evidence you are generating from your reading and notes into sections of your literature review and/or chapters of your final report.
- Spot when the generation of evidence requires you to *revise your initial synopsis*.
- Look for illuminating *summaries* of evidence and striking *quotations*. Keep quotations carefully referenced and distinct from your own commentary.
- Keep a *personal notebook* in which you note down as they occur thoughts about the literature: how it relates to your project and new lines of investigation it suggests.

The literature review

You will have followed through a number of 'hope' references, going on bare details such as the title of a book or article or knowledge of its author. You will now have to get used to skimming and scanning a lot of material, ruthlessly disregarding the irrelevant. *Look at everything you can.* Err on the side of examining sources where the title suggests only a 50–50 chance the work will be in the frame. Titles are sometimes deceptive and you could be passing up a gold mine. But deal summarily with material that does not live up to expectations.

Writing up your review

Some projects consist simply of a literature review. Others

use the review as the bridge or introduction leading into the main body of the report which deals with the empirical testing of the problem. In this case the purpose of the literature review is twofold.

1 It enables you to explain to your readers *why you are doing this project*. Your aim is to demonstrate that there *is* a problem worthy of your attention by demonstrating gaps, limitations, incorrect approaches in the available evidence. The rehearsal of the existing literature gives you something to react to: it gives your work focus. And it keeps you honest.

2 The review demonstrates *your grasp of the relevant literature* – your knowledge of what exists, your understanding of it, your ability to effectively deploy it.

Some students produce elaborate and abstract reviews but supervisors find, moving from a magisterial analysis of the literature to the student's own findings, that there is little connection between the two. The mountain has produced a mouse. Eschew padding. Keep your review lean and sharp-edged. *Select*. Do not write about 'everything I have read'. Write about 'the most important things I have read that *shed light on my research problem*'. It is your *own findings* which are important and require most emphasis. You need to state as briefly as possible – in a sentence or two – the contribution a relevant book or paper has made to the state of the art, unless it is a major work, in which case substitute 'paragraph' for 'sentence'. But leave out comment on works which add little to clarifying the research problem. Your review can easily turn into a descriptive list with little analysis applied to its contents. Don't write a slightly annotated bibliography. Always ask: *In relation to my problem*, what does the author achieve? What does the author not achieve?

The key lesson is not to start a literature review by reviewing the literature.

- *Start with the research problem* – a brief introductory statement – and *then go into the literature*.
- Alternatively, by taking a key piece of literature and writing about it analytically you can *bring out of your consideration of the book or article the nature of your research puzzle*, how it has been treated, how aspects of it have been neglected and so forth.
- Another way of dealing with the problem of a literature review is to divide it into two. In Part I, 'The Literature', briefly note the argument of each important contribution and then in Part II, 'Discussion' or 'Critique', analyse its strengths and weaknesses in relation to the solution of your problem. In a brief Part III, sum up by stating the present status of your problem and outlining how you will take the research on it a stage further.
- Yet a fourth way of handling a literature review is to divide existing research into a number of typologies or approaches. In some cases your problem may have previously been analysed from a variety of theoretical or methodological standpoints and you may be able to group the literature under each of these. This will help you to organise the first part of your review but you still have to bring everything together at the end, summing up how each approach has contributed to problem resolution and the difficulties that remain for you to pursue.

Review articles in journals should give you an understanding of the technique of the literature review. Try the direct approach: 'The reason I wanted to do this project was that I saw that the available evidence was clearly inadequate. For example, Smith (1982) . . .'. Whenever you feel yourself floundering, take the bull by the horns and explain *directly* what you are about.

11.4   Research methods

We believe that it is useful for undergraduates to go beyond commentary on existing work and run the risk of undertaking small-scale practical work. It is now time to look more closely at some of the techniques you might employ.

Different approaches to research

Investigators sometimes group their methods into a number of different approaches or styles of inquiry. They overlap and your study may draw on a number of them.

The case study approach   This involves an in-depth examination of a problem in one or a small number of specific contexts. Rather than studying the problem of study skills in universities across the board you focus on one university. You lose breadth – how representative is what you learn? – but gain in intensity – you can study the problem in close detail. By limiting the scale, you can see how things operate under the magnifying glass with a clearness of delineation lost in a wider investigation. Case studies also lend themselves to *comparing* two or more specific instances of a general case. This approach is attractive for undergraduate work: it enables you to get to the coalface and examine in manageable fashion how more general findings relate to one specific case.

The survey approach   This approach offers a loss of depth but a gain in breadth. You will not have the time to study 101 different situations close up. Using this broad-brush approach examining, for example through the use of questionnaires, a wide range of instances, you hope to get a better understanding of what is happening across the board. What happens in A or B studied in depth may not happen in C, D, E, F, G, . . . The case study stops at A or B. Surveys can generate a mass of information which can be analysed for patterns, consistencies and differences. Case studies can give you a sophisticated picture of individual situations; surveys give you more superficial understanding.

The experimental approach Here you set up an experiment to test a hypothesis. It is central to the natural sciences; it is also used widely in psychology and the social sciences. Experiments involve an attempt to test the interrelationship of variables in an overall system. In a laboratory experiment the proposition that variable A depends on variable B is tested by varying the value of B, the independent variable, and measuring the change in A, the dependent variable, holding all the other variables in the system constant. If you are dealing with people, it is more difficult to hold other variables constant so that they play no role in the outcome. So researchers developed the use of the control group. The experimental group and a control group are matched. The experimental group is treated differently from the control group and any consequent differences attributed to the treatment. But even with changes in physical conditions, variables not controlled by the experiment may be at work. Moreover, the attribution of behavioural changes to the difference in treatment raises complex questions of causation. The experimental approach usually entails close supervision and careful construction.

The action approach This combines research with social action. A researcher might study, from the standpoint of a participant, community action to improve local social services, halt the closure of a hospital ward, attract jobs to an area or attempt to improve adult literacy. Action research is usually problem orientated and can involve studies of organisational change – the introduction of a new system of payment in a workplace or the introduction of a new degree in a college. Sometimes it involves trying out an innovation for the purpose of researching how it works in practice and generating feedback for future use. This approach can again raise questions of reliability and validity, over-involvement and partiality. It may appeal to mature students or those studying part time who still identify themselves as part of a professional or vocational community.

The ethnographic approach *Ethnography* means the direct observation of people. Here the researcher is a close observer, sometimes a participant in the situation under investigation. This approach is based on the view that if you *go through the experience* all the time in the same way as those you are studying, you will understand more fully what is going on. A major problem is that the account of the observer is particularly subject to his or her values, perceptions and idio- syncracies. This raises questions of the reliability and validity of the research. The ethnographic approach may be beyond the resources of an undergraduate project. In a better resourced, more ambitious project it may well be an effective approach to inquiry.

Research methods

Your supervisor will help you to assess first the *reliability* of different methods – the degree to which methods of data collection, if used again, in the same conditions, would pro- duce the same or similar results. How different, for example, would be the response to the same question if two different interviewers asked it? If the answer is 'very different' you need to do something about it. They may also talk to you about the difficult problem of *validity* – whether methods of collecting data are sound and produce findings which truly measure and reflect the phenomena being studied.

Questionnaires

You might want to use questionnaires with standardised questions intended to elicit standardised responses: 'Tick Yes/No'. Or you can use open-ended questions which leave your respondents to formulate their own response. The first is likely to produce shallow black-and-white reactions: the second can chart a more complex response and allow for follow-up questions. Think carefully about the *substance* of your questions and the information they are intended to elicit. Make a list of what you want to know and then frame questions around each point. Think, too, about their *form*: are they drafted in such a way as to ring the right bell in the respondent's mind?

Avoid the 'wide open' question, 'What do you feel about . . .?', and the double question which can involve different responses: 'Are you happy with your lectures in semiotics and Hungarian epistemology?' Look out also for the jargon question, the leading question, the question inviting agreement ('Why do you like history seminars?'), the too-long-by-half question. The questionnaire should be

- reasonably brief – most people are not prepared to spend a lot of time on answering
- clear – people give up if it becomes difficult; and
- well laid out with plenty of space for responses.

Questionnaires may be postal, self-administered or administered by an interviewer. In each case they should be accompanied by an introductory exposition of their purpose and a request for co-operation. With postal questionnaires, budget for difficulties with response and the need for reminders.

In designing questionnaires you should be able to draw on specialist expertise in your college. Remember that you need to build into your design the method for collating and analysing the completed questionnaires. Consider whether you need to pilot your questionnaire and revise it on the basis of a dummy run?

Sampling   The group whose attitudes you wish to test may be a big one. You can't administer your questionnaire to everybody so you have to try to involve a representative sample of the wider group. This is termed *representative sampling*.

Random sampling involves a method of choice which ensures each member of the group being studied has the same probability of being included. Representative and random samples can be developed quickly and efficiently on computer with guidance from your supervisor.

Students often become very enthusiastic at the thought of using questionnaires, but they are most effectively used in conjunction with other methods. Anybody who has witnessed respondents filling in postal questionnaires, for example, will have serious doubts as to the quality of response. Moreover, non-response can be a big problem.

Interviews

Face-to-face interviews can go into greater depth. You might use

- the standardised interview with no schedule, where a number of uniform questions are asked but in no strict order;
- the semi-structured interview, where you list a range of issues or concerns but improvise specific questions; or
- the unstructured interview, where both questions and answers develop out of the face-to-face situation although, of course, they are influenced by research design. To the outsider the interview may appear a spontaneous conversation. But the interviewer always has a light hand on the steering wheel.

The advantage of interviews is the ability to follow up and explore: the dialectic of dialogue. Interviews are likely to yield deeper material than questionnaires. There may still be a 'response effect': you are told what the respondent thinks is the respectable orthodox response. The presence of the interviewer and his or her initiative in structuring the interview can also influence the outcome. In-depth interviews are time consuming and can only involve small numbers. None the less, interviews are a vital weapon and can take you important steps into the universe of those under scrutiny. They require careful preparation – even with the unstructured interview you must have a good idea of the path you wish to pursue – careful recording and analysis. If it is a key interview, tape-recording is ideal but remember transcription takes time.

Study of documents

You will want to talk to those involved. But you will want to scrutinise the *records* of their activity.

- This will involve study of primary sources: reports; minutes of meetings; correspondence; memos; policy statements; diaries; statistical analyses; company accounts.
- You may also be involved in analysing government reports, official statistics and the minutes and reports of official bodies.
- Nor should you forget about newspaper and magazine reports, and radio and TV programmes.

Documentary research is often essential in combination with other methods of investigation as a prelude to their use or as a control on what they yield. The written record can vindicate, amplify or lead us to question or doubt what people say happened; as such it is an indispensable general research tool. More specifically it is the tool of *historical* research – where the *dramatis personae* are no longer available to be interviewed.

There may be problems in locating documents. Local libraries sometimes house a range of archives and universities sometimes have collections of the papers of prominent public figures. Specialist journals often publish details of such deposits. You may need to consult the catalogue of the Public Record Office for government papers or the National Newspaper Library at Hendon.

Box 11.4 Testing documents

Authenticity Is it what it claims to be – sound, undoctored, complete, author verified?

Credibility Was it written sincerely for a genuine purpose rather than constructed to mislead; is what it states accurate?

Meaning What is its literal meaning? What wider meanings can we decode by interpreting the document? What light does it shed on individuals, events, culture?

Witting evidence What did the writer want to say? What story did he or she intend to recount?

Unwitting evidence What wider meanings can we decode by a deeper analysis of the language, assumptions, references of the text?

Documents may require *verification*. Are they what they seem to be? (The notorious *Hitler Diaries* – forgeries which even the famous historian Lord Dacre failed to verify before announcing they were genuine – spring to mind.) They require close, critical analysis. How reliable an informant is the document in front of you? The unreliability of many newspaper accounts is a good warning. An analysis of the differing reports of a single incident in five or six different newspapers should make the point: never take documentary evidence as gospel, carefully interrogate each document.

Consider who wrote each document, who it was written for, in what circumstances. What is its message and its relevance for your research? What was the standing of its author in relation to the events under consideration? Did they have an axe to grind and is it ground here? Was the document written at the time of the events or years later? How does it check out with other sources? If there is bias, how does it affect the situation? In studying documentary sources, key words are *question* and *relate*. Probe each document, read it critically, relate it to the picture built up from other sources.

Box 11.6   Working on the documents

Randolph Henry Ash's Proserpina, 'gold-skinned in the gloom' was also 'grain-golden'. Also bound with 'golden links' which might have been jewellery or chains. Roland wrote neat cross-references under the headings of grain, apples, chain, treasure. Folded under the page of Vico on which the passage appeared was a bill for candles on the back of which Ash had written: 'The individual appears for an instant, joins the community of thought, modifies it and dies; but the species that dies not, reaps the fruit of his ephemeral existence'. Roland copied this out and made another card, on which he interrogated himself.

Query? Is this a quotation or is it Ash himself? Is Proserpina the species? A very C19 idea. Or is she the individual? When did he put these papers in here? Are they pre- or post-*The Origin of the Species?* Not conclusive anyway – he cd have been interested in Development generally . . .?

That was 11.15. The clock ticked, motes of dust danced in sunlight. Roland meditated on the tiresome and bewitching endlessness of the quest for knowledge.

A. S. Byatt, *Possession.*

Observation

Ethnographic research can range from the situation where the student attends one or two meetings to the situation where he or she lives and works in the group or organisation. The researcher may 'sit in' on activity or shadow an important player. There is either no direct participation or the observer can fully participate. Other methods tell you what respondents say they think and do; observation tells you what really happens. It provides a means of checking on other techniques: you see for yourself. Observation also provides an important means of understanding interaction and how actors relate to each other, which may be difficult to gauge from questionnaires, interviews or documents.

On the other hand, those studied may feel on stage; they may suppress certain aspects of behaviour and exaggerate others. This 'participation effect' can be minimised if participation continues over a period; it then becomes very time consuming. And the degree to which the experience is generalisable is questionable. Perhaps the key advantage is the opportunity to assimilate to and comprehend the world of those being researched: it can provide crucial insights and 'inside' material. Against this there are difficulties in maintaining an effective ratio between dispassionate observation and becoming committed to the world under study. And researchers can encounter hostility and suspicion.

Recording the phenomena under observation also presents problems. If an unobtrusive role towards the non-participant end of the spectrum is being adopted, there is a range of grids, checklists and charts to facilitate observation and analysis (Bell, 1987, p. 89). Where the involvement is at the participant end of the spectrum, good recording requires more long-term activity and is likely to involve a greater element of recollected reconstruction.

Other methods

A variety of other techniques are sometimes used.

Oral history   Long, tape-recorded, unstructured interview accounts of the past recollected by actors. At their best they make your work vivid and authentic. But they need measuring against other sources.

Life histories   A mixture of personal accounts and documentary sources: letters, diaries, newspaper accounts are assembled to provide a personalised cross-section of a slice of history.

Diaries Where you have a sympathetic respondent you might request them to keep a diary of key activities over an agreed period and then follow up with interviews.

To repeat: there is no one best technique of investigation. The best research draws on a range of methods, probing the problem in different ways, the yield of one technique providing a check on the results of the others. Each method has its 'pros' and 'cons': *triangulation*, the combination of several methods in one project, thus offers the best chance of validity. You may already feel a disposition for or against certain methods. But the best way to develop a quite justifiable predilection is by using a number of methods.

Getting going

Having selected appropriate techniques, you can now put them into practice. Problems will undoubtedly occur. But as your project develops, *keep writing, keep reading and keep reporting to your supervisor.* By now you should have gathered momentum and things should be flowing naturally.

> You do not really have to *study* a topic you are working on; for as I have said, once you are into it, it is everywhere. You are sensible to its themes; you see and hear them everywhere in your experience especially, it always seems to me, in apparently unrelated areas. Even the mass media, especially bad movies and cheap novels and picture magazines and night radio, are disclosed in fresh importance to you. (Wright Mills, 1970, p. 232.)

11.5 Becoming a researcher

Good research requires more than mechanically following the procedures outlined in this chapter. As Professor Anthony Giddens (1989) points out, the good researcher eventually moves beyond the textbook approach. 'The difference is a bit like that between the procedures outlined in a recipe book and the actual process of cooking a meal. People who are experienced cooks might not work from recipe books at all, and their work is often much more creative than those who do' (1989, p. 662). Research is not always meticulously planned in advance; sometimes plans develop out of the research itself. Rigidly following accepted procedures may cramp and restrict inspired improvisation, the sudden, informed hunch, the switch of tack in relation to new circumstances that can be maximised by the sensitive researcher. Successful researchers often go their own way; much outstanding research would not follow the kind of sequence we have outlined above (Orenstein and Phillips, 1984).

Successful scientists argue that there is no scientific procedure as such: the mind must be used 'no holds barred'. It is difficult to generalise about the process of discovery as it is so tied up with individual approaches (Wright Mills, 1970, p. 69). Scientific discovery often involves short cuts, compromises and muddling through; the research process is very different from idealised accounts given in research papers (Medawar, 1963). In the social sciences, arts and education, too, research is often more messy and complex than research manuals suggest. Progress can be the product of happy coincidences, rivalries between researchers, and successful reactions to unforeseen circumstances (Bell and Newby, 1977). Researchers may test a sample first and then formulate a research problem; they may quickly change from one problem to another; they may formulate a hypothesis towards the end of the project.

Initially follow the approach suggested above in gaining the experience good improvisation is often based on. But you should supplement this advice by reading some of the accounts of how researchers operate in practice (Bell and Newby, 1977; Roberts, 1981; Walford, 1991).

Qualities to cultivate

At the last minute I move my head the smallest bit and the punch

comes so close I can feel the wind but it misses me. How do I know to
move just enough? How do I know which way to move?

Muhammad Ali.

Formal approaches and established methods must be the
servant, not the master, of the good craftworker. The serious
researcher needs to develop intuition and insight, to know
when to move and when not to. Good research depends not
only on disciplined methods but also on developing a range of
intellectual and human qualities. You need to consciously try
to become a shrewd observer, a good listener, a good organiser,
a good companion interested in others, evoking their trust and
confidence. Like Muhammad Ali, good researchers often
possess an 'indefinable something'; often this stems from hard
training and long thinking about their craft. Let us look at
some of the qualities you should try to cultivate.

Ten commandments of research

1 Be sensitive. Communicate your own enthusiasm and
belief in its importance when seeking co-operation; point out
advantages for those involved. Be painstaking about seeking
permission to carry out research; don't take things for granted.
After informal discussion seek co-operation through a detailed
letter explaining precisely what help you want and why. Make
clear what will happen to your report and its availability.
Explain the position regarding confidentiality and anonymity
of respondents.

2 Be straight. Don't make promises you cannot keep – to
circulate 100 copies of your report will take time and money.
Don't say one thing to one person and a different thing to
another. Stick to agreements. Don't overstay your welcome.
Remember that your project is unlikely to be at the top of other
people's priorities. Turn up on time; if problems intervene,
ring! Once your work is finished, don't forget about those who

made it possible. Thank all participants, librarians, computer staff and your supervisor.

3 Be patient.   You will often be awaiting the arrival of a key book, a phone call from a typist who never works fast enough! It will come. Meanwhile there is always something else to be done. If you allow impatience to take over you may not use the waiting time fruitfully. Patience also applies to the work itself. Do not give up easily: if Avenue A is closed, try B. The good researcher is tenacious. Interviews particularly require self control. You must be a good listener. You must know when to keep your mouth shut. Be understanding about respondents' difficulties in recalling events, explaining their attitudes . . . or finding a date on which to talk to you. *They are doing you a favour*. The end result of impatience is frustration, loss of motivation; it can also annoy others and minimise their co-operation.

4 Be imaginative.   Mentally construct what it's like for the other person, the kind of world they live in. Do not transpose your own values and assumptions to those you are studying. There *is* a common humanity. But a 20-year-old under-graduate, an unemployed black 16-year-old, and a novelist of the 1880s are different people with different experiences. Try to empathise with their world rather than simply pressing them into yours. It is *you*, the researcher, who has to make the leap in imagination and sympathy. Applying your own values and experience may sometimes hinder rather than facilitate under-standing of motives and action. You have to research case studies not as isolated phenomena but in the context of the wider processes which mould and constrain them. Your reading can never be limited to the specific focus under study.

A judicious blend of hard evidence and intelligent controlled surmise may produce fascinating work, as in Claire Tomalin's imaginative rekindling of documentary sources to reconstruct the story of Nelly Ternan and Charles Dickens in *The Invisible*

Woman (1990). Where you encounter gaps, a cautious elaboration of what factors *may* have influenced actions *can* be helpful − as long as you make clear what is fact, what is interpretation and what is imaginative reconstruction.

5 Be flexible. If your research is going nowhere consider a change of tack. Important contacts can move, change jobs, be taken ill. Questionnaires may be lost or not distributed. Sometimes a blinding flash occurs: you see a way you could examine your hypothesis more successfully in another context. Do not be afraid to consider changes of approach; as we have said, that is how a lot of good work gets done. But, of course, time is the enemy and it depends what stage you are at. Sometimes a final report bears little resemblance to the project proposal: students have not got the results they wanted. Don't despair. An essay in failure describing how far you got, what you found and what you didn't find can be instructive.

6 Be honest and balanced. Researchers may bring a variety of preconceptions to a project: these may influence the choice of problem. Facts rarely speak for themselves; they require interpretation. In many cases there is no one compelling interpretation but a variety of competing interpretations. The researcher's own values may influence the weight attached to each. This has to be acknowledged and controlled for. Total impartiality may be a mirage. The student's values and opinions may energetically drive the search. Bias, which occurs when the researcher's views *illegitimately* influence the deployment of evidence or weighing of conclusions, is a different matter. Strong predilections may fuel research; they can contaminate it. The good researcher will interrogate his or her partiality. If impartiality is impossible the avoidance of bias is realisable. It requires scrupulousness in the selection of facts and materials and an acceptance of a hypothesis as a guide to be tested, not a dogma to be established at any cost. Control of bias requires imaginative empathy with other viewpoints, a critique of counterarguments where they are at their strongest, not their weakest, a scrupulous attitude to quotation and sometimes an explicit statement of your own position and standards of judgement.

7 Be accurate and precise. Always ask yourself: am I being specific enough? When I use 'most', 'some', 'a good many', can I be more precise? Try to cultivate concentrated, active thinking. Train yourself to get titles of books, dates, places just right; read carefully what writers are saying. The habits of exactitude will stand you in good stead throughout your career.

8 Be careful. Do not take statements at face value. There are numerous cases of faulty conclusions repeated at second, third, fourth hand becoming established orthodoxy. To take one example: many study skills books talk about 'a learning plateau'. They state that after a certain period of study cognitive progress comes to a halt. This comment is often accompanied by a graph but no attribution. Gibbs (1981) traced the statement back to a work by Book in the 1920s. On examining the original he found that the relevance of the experiment to conceptual learning was very limited indeed. Yet it had attained the status of a law of learning simply through repetition (p. 65).

9 Be ethical. The results of research may not please those who feel they are portrayed in a bad light or that information useful to competitors or opponents is disclosed. Experiments have been mounted where all participants have been informed that they are receiving the same treatment: half of them are not. Some researchers use their membership of organisations to carry out research surreptitiously. Others adopt less than honest means to gain access. In general, research should be open and agreed. But all generalisations are fallible. There will always be powerful or controversial groups which will seek to avoid dispassionate scrutiny. Yet the health of society often depends on discussion of important issues on the informed basis only third-party insider research can provide.

10 Be writing. The tenth commandment is *write*. As soon as your work of empirical verification is under way start thinking about your final report.

11.6   **Writing your report**

If you are unable to explain clearly and fluently what you have achieved and how you did it, your achievement will lose in impact. A very good research project can be marked down because of its author's failure to successfully present the results of hard imaginative work. The ability to write well-organised, clear reports is a fundamental research skill. Look again at the advice on good writing in Chapters 9 and 10. Here are some key points to reflect on as you prepare your report.

Length   Most requirements will possess flexibility. For example: 'The dissertation or report should be around 12,500 words. It should not fall very much short of this, although allowance will be made if there are special circumstances relating to methodology; the maximum number of words is 15,000 and this must not be exceeded.' Read such requirements carefully. Where you are allowed the privilege of flexibility you may encounter problems if you breach these limits.

Timing and revision   Check on deadlines. Most people cannot get their writing right first time. It is only when you have a draft in front of you that inaccuracies or inadequate argument leap from the page. You may need two or three drafts. And revision is most effective when it is based on reflection, when you re-approach your draft with a fresh eye. *Re-evaluation requires time*: the earlier you start drafting, the better. Try to write up each chapter or section as the material comes to hand. Once you start writing do it regularly and for reasonable spells. The student who leaves writing up until everything else is done is heading for last minute panic and potential disaster.

Style

Comments made earlier on style will be relevant. In *The Modern Researcher* Barzun and Graff (1977) suggest you write as if you were addressing the whole educated community: 'Can another trained mind not expert in my subject understand what I am saying?' (p. 27). Wright Mills (1976), quoting Lionel Trilling, suggests 'you take up your pen assuming you are going to give a lecture on your subject to an audience of teachers and students from all departments of your college supplemented by a variety of interested members of the local community' (p. 243).

They are trying to get across the need for straightforward expression accessible to those with minimal induction into the mysteries of the subject. An added advantage of writing with precision and simplicity for a wider audience is that you are compelled to ensure that your own understanding is clear. We are able to express for others most cogently and vividly what we completely understand ourselves. You should be excited by the results of your project work. Try to bring it alive for others. Think a little about methods of presentation: the use of headlines, indents, figures, graphs, tables.

The format of your report

Read carefully guidance on presentation. What follows is a conventional model which may be varied to strengthen presentation.

1 Title page   State your final title, any explanatory subtitle, your name and your course.

2 Acknowledgements   Thank your supervisor, other tutors, technicians, typists and those who have helped with your research.

3 Contents page   List with page numbers the titles of all main sections/chapters as well as appendices, references and the bibliography.

4 List of tables and figures   This is relevant if you have used illustrations frequently. If there are only a handful of tables or figures, don't bother.

5 Abstract   A brief – say, 250-word – summary of the report. It may go under the title, after the title page, or before the introduction to the main report.

6 Introduction   State briefly the research problem, your objectives, methods and results. Revise your introduction in relation to your conclusion to avoid repetition.

7 Literature review   Analyse the relevant literature stating how your project develops it (see p. 343). You may well write this up first deciding which system of referencing you will use and how you are going to employ headings. Don't overload your review in relation to the report of what *you* discovered.

8 Restatement of research problem   Having set your research, *briefly* reformulate the problem and the dimensions of your study.

9 Procedure and methods   Explain how you went about your investigation – the methods employed, brief details of experiment construction, size of sample and measurement techniques if relevant.

10 Reporting and discussing the findings This constitutes the main body of your report and should be divided up into chapters or sections. Always *link your findings to the review of the literature*. The set of guidelines quoted earlier state, 'You will typically want three to five main chapters; more than six chapters may make for a disjointed or "bitty" result.' An alternative method is to deal first with the outline of the findings and then in separate sections with their analysis. Use headings and subheadings to break up the material and, if relevant, tables and graphs.

11 Conclusion Briefly summarise. State what you have achieved.

12 List of references List alphabetically by author the full details of works cited or referred to in the text.

13 Bibliography List the full details of works referred to in the text and other books and articles you have used. Generally you need only a bibliography – not a list of references as well. Only include items not cited which have been important to your report. Don't pad the list with extras.

14 Appendices Include a copy of a questionnaire you used, a model of an experiment, a transcript of a crucial interview. We are talking about appendices to a report, not the file on your work. So do not include 50 questionnaires.

Submission

The ability to use a word processor becomes invaluable because of the opportunities the computer provides for easy revision and swift reorganisation. If you cannot word process yourself then it is best to have the report produced on disk rather than typed as changes are much easier to make. Get somebody else to read and comment and help you with proofreading. Scrutinise the accuracy of references, quotations and calculations. Check on how many copies you have to submit. Meet your supervisor to get feedback on the final product.

Key points

1 Think about your project early. Establish formal requirements and regulations; the role it plays in course assessment; the time scale for completion.
2 Develop a number of topics – try to refine them into guesses, problem–propositions, hypotheses which you can test in your research. Have a preliminary look at existing studies; think a little about research methods.
3 Produce more precise proposals with working hypotheses to discuss with your supervisor. Start a thorough search of the literature.
4 Write up a synopsis of your proposal; continue with your literature review.
5 Make sure you and your supervisor agree on the proposal. Ensure there is a clear work schedule and that joint arrangements are made for its development.
6 Keep records of all references; a log of tasks; important meetings and deadlines; a personal journal to reflect on progress; and carefully filed notes on all aspects of the work.
7 Agree with your supervisor which research methods will provide the best tools. Talk to computer staff, typists and others about your timetable.
8 Start writing your literature review to consolidate your grasp of the area, place your problem in its setting and further sharpen its focus.
9 Firm up arrangements for practical research; begin work. Consult manuals on research methods in your subject but also first-hand accounts of research.
10 Cultivate key research virtues: be organised, sensitive, accurate and balanced. Keep an eye on deadlines. Stay in contact with your supervisor.

11 Write and read at all stages of the project so that materials for your final report are gradually generated.
12 Begin writing your final report as soon as the groundwork is completed.

Things to do

1 Think about why research is important in higher education. Why is it important in your subject?
2 Do a literature search to see if you can find a book(s) which gives first-hand accounts of how research is done in your subject.
3 Select two topics you would be interested in doing a project on. Formulate a hypothesis for each. Compare notes with other students.
4 Take one of the topics and write up a synopsis for a research project.
5 Do a literature search on the lines outlined in this chapter to generate material for your proposal.
6 Explain in detail how you would go about doing a project on access courses in your town or city.
7 Brainstorm what makes a good researcher.

Further reading

The Double Helix, by James D. Watson (Penguin, 1968), is an exciting first-hand account of how scientific discovery occurs, whilst Sir Peter Medawar's seminal article which questioned the basis on which much research in science was allegedly conducted, 'Is the scientific paper a fraud?', was republished in *Experiment*, a book edited by David Edge (BBC Publications, 1964). Valuable first-hand accounts of doing research are contained in *Doing Sociological Research*, edited by Colin Bell and Howard Newby (Allen and Unwin, 1977); *Doing Feminist Research*, edited by Helen Roberts (Routledge, 1987); and *Doing Educational Research*, edited by Geoffrey Walford (Routledge, 1990). Bruno Latour and Steve Woolger's *Laboratory Life: The Social Construction of Scientific Facts* (Sage, 1979) is another fascinating read. There are similar books in other subjects.

John Scott's *A Matter of Record* (Polity Press, 1990) deals with documentary research whilst *Research Methods* by Pat McNeil (Routledge, 1990) is a valuable up-to-date general primer. Two classic works are *The Modern Researcher*, by Jacques Barzun and Henry Graff (Harcourt Brace Jovanovich, 1977), which is of relevance to a wide range of disciplines, and *The Sociological Imagination*, by C. Wright Mills (Penguin, 1970), which contains a brilliant discussion of research methodology.

Judith Bell's *Doing Your Research Project: A Guide for First-time Researchers in Education and Social Science* (Open University Press, 1987) is packed with valuable guidance. Also of practical value are George Watson's *Writing a Thesis* (Longmans, 1987) and Sarah Gash's *Effective Literature Searching for Students* (Gower, 1989).

12

Passing your exams

I rose at 6 am, drank a great deal of coffee, worked until 8, went into college for breakfast, took my seat in the library by 8.45, worked until 7, returned to the Iffley Road, worked until 9, prepared for myself a Vesta Beef Curry or a Vesta Chicken Supreme or – best – a Vesta Paella (not a single item of genuine nutriment, I can safely boast, passed down my throat) returned to my desk and worked until 1 am. I rose at 6 am ...

Martin Amis, *My Oxford*

12.1   **Introduction**

In assessing learning there has often been an inflexible adherence to the 'unseen', largely written, test. Exams have often been addressed as an afterthought, rather than an essential ingredient in course design. They have sometimes been seen as half-external to teaching, not meant to be user-friendly. Students have seen exams as an obstacle course and initiation rite. You suddenly become a *candidate* rather than a student and find yourself in purdah, if not purgatory, staving off anxiety in a last mad rush before judgement day. Exams stay with many for the rest of their lives in nightmares, rather than recalled learning. They raise doubts about the relationship of the assessment ordeal to the liberal ideals of higher education and the long-term educational growth of the individual.

In recent years there have been signs that the log jam is breaking. Systems of continuous assessment take account of course work, give students more feedback and the chance to improve and spread evaluation through the course. Project work has become an assessed part of more courses. There is a greater understanding of the fallibility of assessment and the need to make it more diagnostic and student centred. However, the formal unseen exam still plays a central role in higher education. The purpose of this chapter is to locate it in its context and to discuss practical approaches which will enable you to maximise your performance. As in other areas of study, a strategic approach can help you to acquit yourself well in an area which can affect your future.

- Section 12.2 begins by talking about assessing student learning and some of the means that have been developed to do this.
- Section 12.3 deals with information on how exams are set and graded.
- Section 12.4 looks at how you can come to terms with problems such as anxiety.
- Section 12.5 emphasises the importance of the study of previous exam papers so you are able to familiarise yourself with layout, instructions, and the content and form of questions.
- Section 12.6 moves on to look at the importance of revision, how to organise it and how to make it *active*.
- Section 12.7 then discusses some of the basic but important aspects of exam technique.

12.2   Assessment at university

Most people would accept that some form of assessment of students is necessary. Assessment, it is argued, is essential to

- *motivate* you to learn. The challenge or threat of assessment, it is claimed, stimulates you to apply yourself to your studies.
- *diagnose* how well you are learning. Your performance when assessed, it is argued, provides you and your teachers with vital feedback. This provides an essential basis for improving learning.

N

- *evaluate* the quality of teaching and course design. Feedback from assessment can provide your tutors with evidence of their own strengths and weaknesses and show them where they can improve.
- *select* those students who will continue in higher education. Assessment is essential to provide the basis for deciding which first-degree students are capable of going on to study for Master's degrees and Doctorates.
- provide *credentials* for particular occupations. Assessment, it is urged, is necessary to pick out those students who possess the ability and understanding to pursue a particular profession or study for further vocational qualifications.
- *maintain standards*. Through testing and the improved learning which flows from it, higher education, it is claimed, is able to protect high standards. It is also able to assure employers that in hiring graduates they are taking on individuals who have demonstrated *under test conditions* that they are a skilled, adaptable resource.

You might question some of the above arguments. For example, first-year formal exams at university have often been the occasion of little feedback to students and finals have often been a closed book. Some teachers who mark scripts ask where *they*, rather than the students, have gone wrong. Some do not. The extent to which exam performance is a good predictor of future occupational performance is obviously questionable – look at the differing educational attainments of top politicians, civil servants, judges, industrialists and entrepreneurs. And, of course, the extent to which the anxiety induced by assessment is creative, rather than debilitating, provides grist for perennial controversy.

Methods of assessment

The commonest form of exam has been the three-hour paper based on writing essays and reports or solving problems or simulated case studies. Some exams have also been based on objective tests where students have to select the right answer from a number of alternatives.

The traditional unseen exam has been justified by its supporters as effectively meeting the requirements of assessment listed above – or meeting them better than other methods. They have argued the following.

- It is more *objective* and *fairer* than a report on students' course work. It excludes, to a greater extent, personal bias. Look at the subjective factors involved in assessing a student's class performance. Everybody knows what is expected and has an equal chance to prepare. There is equality of ignorance as to the questions to be asked.
- Anxiety occurs with *all* forms of assessment. Most students overcome it; the formal traditional exam is a good training ground in which *students learn to handle stress* – as they will have to in their future lives. The unseen exam is *flexible* and can be improved by, for example, providing a greater choice of questions.
- Whether we like it or not, *competition* is part of life. Reasonable competition can help improve performance.
- The traditional exam is helpful in corralling problems, such as the need for intensive focused effort and the stress it can induce, into *one clearly defined exam season*. With other forms of assessment tensions continue throughout the course.
- Students need a challenge and, yes, sometimes a threat in order to *motivate* them to learn. Some are self-motivated. Others need an external stimulus.
- Employers appreciate this clear-cut form of assessment. Formal exams can act as a useful climax to the course, a device for helping students to bring together and *crystallise* what they have learned.

In contrast, critics of the exam have argued the following.

- It is sometimes unclear *just what exams are attempting to assess*. Objectives are rarely explicit. It is difficult to see how the abnormal task of writing answers under intense pressure in 40 minutes is the best way to test achievement. This artificial exercise does not test the ability to write well. It shows only how well you can *write fast and answer exam questions*. Ability to select and understand evidence would be better assessed where students have access to books and adequate time.

- Traditional exams *often fail to properly assess your educational development*, as distinct from manual motor skills and the efficiency with which you stuff your mind full of facts and arguments – which you retain only temporarily. Exams test skills in question spotting and regurgitation. They do not test originality, the ability to work in a normal situation, the qualities required by the future teacher, social worker or investment analyst.

- Exams are far from *objective*. Success or failure may say more about your background or how you handle anxiety than your level of educational development.

- There are thus clear problems of *validity*. Moreover, marking schemes are fuzzy. Markers are not reliable assessors. They may have different views as to what meets the requirements of a good answer, and what constitutes clear structure, intelligent argument, careful deployment of evidence. Different markers will appreciate different qualities in answers, motivated by their own values and pre-conceptions. There will always be 'hard' markers and 'easy' markers.

- Exams often inhibit rather than stimulate creativity and intellectual development. They are dysfunctional to the avowed goals of higher education. *They can detract from the course as a learning experience* by focusing far too much attention on a three-hour obstacle course rather than continuing learning. In a civilised education system there should be better ways of motivating students than fear.

Research over many years certainly supports some of these criticisms. The extent to which the exam essay successfully assesses intellectual qualities is open to question (Rowntree, 1977; Henderson, 1980). Some students, for example, think deeply and effectively: they do not think *fast*. Numerous studies demonstrate that different markers gave different marks to the same answers and that individual examiners also give different marks to scripts they have originally marked when, after an interval, they are asked to mark them again. Recent studies demonstrate disturbingly that 'the quality of handwriting, the length of the essay, the effects of marker fatigue and the position of the script in a series e.g. after a run of good answers or after a run of poor ones, can all affect the mark given' (Beard and Hartley, 1984, p. 279). Variations are particularly crucial in higher education where the difference between 'a fail' and a first class can be as little as 37 marks and a small variation affects your class of degree.

So-called objective tests have been criticised in similar fashion. Their development has been restricted by the view that they are essentially more limited than the written examination, testing little more than the ability of factual recall. Moreover, their design presents difficulties and can be time consuming although they are now being linked to computer-assisted education. Studies of practical tests have also demonstrated a similar range of difficulties particularly with variability of marking.

On the other hand, the problems with traditional exams are not necessarily insuperable and there have been attempts to limit deficiencies. Three ways of doing this include restricting the scope of questions, introducing double and triple marking and improving marking schemes. But difficulties remain. Studies of the relationship between exam grades and adult achievement conclude that how well you do in exams bears little relationship to how well you will do in later life. Undoubtedly some would identify with the feelings expressed by one of Becker's students about exams: 'you can learn what's necessary to get the grade and when you come out you don't know anything at all. You haven't learned a damn thing' (Becker, Geer and Hughes, 1968, p. 59).

Such dissatisfaction has led to greater emphasis on continuous assessment. Marks are awarded for essays and projects which test skills under normal conditions although written exams still usually play a role. Continuous assessment is more properly termed *periodic assessment*, as in most cases only samples of course work count. In some cases only the student's best work counts. In others there is the chance to revise submissions after tutorial comment. Continuous assessment is defended on the grounds that the assessed work is completed under more real conditions and assessment is based on work over the course, rather than 15 or 20 hours in the exam room. It gives students a fairer crack of the whip, reduces tension, and provides a more credible yardstick of performance in the real world. However, students will still experience anxiety and assessed areas of work can become the strong focus for student attention. Moreover, the problem of variability of marking is still there. It seems that most students like continuous assessment but some still prefer exams (Beard and Hartley, 1984, p. 273).

Criticism of traditional approaches has also produced greater interest in the open-book exam, where students can use books and articles for all or a number of answers. This brings the examination room closer to reality. In life the skills of selection, organisation, integration and evaluation that exam questions are supposed to test are deployed in relation to materials you have in front of you. Other changes in recent years include 'seen' papers where students are given the questions in advance of the examination. But again this method does not completely dissolve difficulties. Some studies show no difference in stress or performance compared with the unseen exam whilst others show that stress is reduced but differences in performance are minor (Jehu, Picton and Futcher, 1970).

When all is said and done the traditional exam with its very real deficiencies continues to be important. There are a variety of reasons for this, from administrative neatness through academic conservatism and convenience to genuine difficulty with alternatives and the view – perhaps that of the majority of tutors – that as no one assessment technique gives completely satisfactory results *a mix is to be preferred*. It is likely that you will have to live with its problems and make the best job you can of the examination game.

12.3 Thinking about exams

So think about exams . . . think about them early on in your course. The more you view exams as something you will *have to* deal with, the more you will find yourself coming to terms with them and positioning yourself to combat natural feelings of tension and anxiety that may appear as your tests get closer. You will recall the work of Miller and Parlett (1974) which suggested that if you adopt a strategic approach you can improve your performance (see p. 186). Working at exam technique is an important ingredient in exam success (Entwistle *et al.*, 1971). When considering exams, here are some points to note.

1 Whatever their deficiencies, your examiners are not trying to catch you out. Quite the contrary. With a much greater emphasis on teaching performance and appraisal, most lecturers will be more worried by high failure rates on their courses; 'most examiners take examining very seriously, try to be open-minded, fair and diligent in their setting, marking and decision-making' (Miller and Parlett, 1974, p. 6).
2 Unlike with A levels, your interrogators will now be the lecturers who are teaching you. Their approach, their syllabus, the assignments they set should all help you in your exams. The exam paper will represent the culmination of

your learning and the culmination of *their* teaching. The courses you are taking will have been developed by course teams from your own department; they will write the exam paper. It will then go before a meeting of the whole department. Lecturers will comment, criticise and revise the paper to ensure that it reflects course work. They will take pains to ensure that the questions are pitched at the right level and don't require too much but are demandingly phrased. Each paper will be marked by at least two lecturers, who will have intimate knowledge of coursework. They can thus be expected to be critically sympathetic. Furthermore, external examiners from other universities are appointed for each course and annually review syllabus, exam papers and samples of student scripts.

3 If you work well throughout the course, keeping your exams in view, you will be preparing yourself well for the coming challenge. By attending your lectures and classes, working hard on your essays and projects and keeping up with your reading, you will be learning what you will be tested on in the examination room. But your daily work should also be punctuated by periods of revision. We often think of revision as dominating the six to eight weeks prior to the exams beginning, say, with the start of the Easter vacation. This final revision is essential. But you will get the most out of it if you have given yourself time for brief periods of *routine* revision throughout the course. This requires you to look back over, say, the last month's work, making a few brief notes on key points, thinking about key problems, examining what you have learned and what you have not.

Too much can be made of routine revision. Work during term time is intensive; the demands of looking forward to new work militate against looking back on the old. Do what you can. It is important that you do not lose hold of what has gone before and can see the overall pattern and structure of your learning. If you are struggling with new material, revision or *re-seeing* of previous learning can yield crucial insights. And the greater the degree to which you are in command of your year's work when you reach the Easter before your exams, the more productive will be your final revision. It will start at a higher level.

4 Finally, it is useful to find out as early as possible how exams are organised and set, how marks are awarded and how degrees are graded. The overall pattern of degree results is set out in Table 12.1. Until recently the examination process in universities was the subject of some secrecy. Giving students breakdowns of their marks – more extended comments on how they had performed – was sometimes forbidden. Most students had a hazy idea of what was involved and in some cases this is still true today. *There is no reason why you should not know how your papers are set, marked and graded*; it is important for an efficient approach that you *do know* these things.

Table 12.1   Class of first degree obtained at traditional universities, 1989–90

	Men (%)	Women (%)	TOTAL (%)
First class honours	4,555 (10.52)	2,171 (6.41)	6,726 (8.72)
Upper second	16,052 (37.07)	14,840 (43.82)	30,892 (40.03)
Lower second	13,260 (30.62)	11,180 (33.01)	24,440 (31.67)
Undivided second	189 (0.44)	56 (0.17)	245 (0.32)
Third, fourth and Aegrotat	4,096 (9.46)	1,857 (5.48)	5,953 (7.71)
Enhanced first degree	177 (0.41)	20 (0.06)	197 (0.26)
Pass and ordinary	4,873 (11.25)	3,697 (10.92	8,570 (11.11)
Not known	100 (0.23)	48 (0.14)	148 (0.19)
TOTAL	43,302	33,869	77,171

Source: UFC/CVCP

You should be asking a number of questions. How many marks for formal written examinations? Do exams before finals count? How many marks for essays, reports and other assignments through continuous assessment? How many marks for a research project?

A typical degree classification breaks down like this:

First class	70% or over
Upper second	60–69%
Lower second	50–59%
Third class	40–49%
Pass	34–40%
Fail	Below 34%

But there are often variations. Some grades are slightly different and some classifications stop at third class. If your mark is less than 40% you fail. How you get your final mark can be complicated. Different departments will have different rules of thumb for aggregating the marks on a number of papers into an overall degree mark.

In some departments these degree conventions are relatively straightforward. In one common case you sit eight final exams and you are awarded the mark and degree class of your five best papers or the mark you achieved in your four best papers as long as your next two marks fall only one grade lower.

But take another department. Here six marks are taken into account in awarding the final degree. Of these, four are the marks from written exams in the third, (final) year, one is the aggregate of marks from written exams taken in the second year and one is the mark from a research project. If four out of six of the marks reach a certain class you get that overall mark, provided no other mark is more than one class below it. You can also 'trade up' marks, with an upper second (or 2(i) – 'a two-one') and a lower second (a 2(ii)) equalling a first. Where the distribution of marks fails to produce a clear result, for example if you get three 2(i)s and three 2(ii)s, then an average of the six marks is taken, but *on a new scale*. First class now equals 68% upwards; upper second, 58–67.9%;

lower second, 48–57.9%; third class, 38–47.9%.

As you can see, things can get very complicated although matters may be simplified with the introduction of modularisation. None the less, try to get some idea of how examination conventions work. Your department may have a handout or booklet for students describing how the exam process works.

Table 12.2   Percentage of first-class degrees: The top ten universities

	1989–90	*1984–85*	*1979*
Cambridge	21.4	18.5	17.8
Oxford	14.2	12.2	12.0
Bath	13.4	10.0	7.0
Aston	12.2	4.7	4.0
Loughborough	11.3	8.2	5.6
Salford	11.3	4.1	3.5
Strathclyde	9.8	5.2	4.2
London	9.6	8.0	7.8
UMIST	9.5	7.5	7.3
Bristol	9.2	6.6	6.1
TOTAL	8.3	6.4	6.0

Source: UFC/CVCP

12.4   Anxiety and stress

Examinations induce different feelings in different people. Some profess to feel only minor butterflies as exams approach but most of us feel more stress. Some feel anxious, worried and depressed; but some are overcome by panic which a small minority are unable to overcome. One recent book is titled *How to Pass Exams – Without Anxiety*. Many students would fervently chorus you *can't* pass exams without anxiety!

Or at least *some* anxiety. The level is all important. For most of us, some degree of tension and nervousness is to be expected.

It is natural when facing any test: if it focuses our attention, motivates us to work and revs us up so we concentrate intensely and work speedily in the exam itself, it is useful and creative. Pre-exam anxiety can, however, reach levels where it becomes destructive: it paralyses rather than enhances motivation and performance. Thinking about exams early on as a built-in part of your course and finding out how they work does, as we have suggested, help some students. Fear of the unknown can wreak havoc with feelings. *Knowing* what is expected of you, *knowing* that the person setting and marking papers is only Tom the tutor, not Torquemada, can set fear at rest.

So, of course, can efficient intensive preparation. Last minute panic is often expressed in terms of fears that students have not done enough revision, that the exam questions will be 'above' them, that they can think of nothing but the work they have *not* done. If you organise your revision well you should at least bring your problems down to controllable dimensions. There is the danger of going to the other extreme. Some students make themselves sick through overwork. Try to find the right balance and remember the need to stay fit and healthy. Remember: for many of us some nerves and tension are required to get the adrenalin flowing. If we don't feel some anxiety we can get complacent rather than motivated.

So *think positively*: if you have worked through your course and followed the right revision regime you should acquit yourself well. Practice makes perfect and familiarity can breed confidence: so look at what we have to say about *practising* exams. Get your tension over early, outside the exam room, by confronting exam papers in your revision. Luck in the exam itself often boils down to hard work in the previous weeks.

Have a look again at what we said about overcoming stress and relaxation exercises (see Chapter 5). If things do get too much for you consult your doctor or the student health service as soon as you can and keep your tutor informed. Your teachers will be sympathetic and understanding. They accept pre-examination stress is a reality, not an excuse of last resort for malingerers.

12.5 Learning from the exam paper

Box 12.1 Passing your exams

1 **Find out how the system works**
  - *Assessment marks, grades*
2 **Study past exam papers**
  - *Layout, requirements, questions, time*
3 **Review your course work**
  - *Interrogate key books, articles, notes, assignments in relation to exams*
4 **Develop a revision timetable**
  - *Review study schedule.*
  - *Start early.*
  - *Plan methodically.*
  - *Set targets.*
  - *Monitor achievement*
5 **Make revision active**
  - *Practise decoding questions and writing answers.*
  - *Talk to tutors and colleagues*
6 **Deploy exam technique**
  - *Take a strategic approach to answering your paper*
7 **Review the experience**
  - *Ask for feedback from tutors*

Looking at recent exam papers will familiarise you with what is required; make the exam seem less of a distant external threat; help in dissipating anxiety; help develop your strategy for success. Look at last year's paper – and be aware of any changes in regulations or syllabus since then. But look further back over, say, the last five years' papers. A broader sweep enables you to see patterns of questions and approach.

The form of the exam

Ask yourself some key questions:

- How many papers do I have to sit?
- How long is each exam?
- How many options are there on each paper?
- How many questions do I have to answer?
- Is the paper divided into sections? Do I have to answer questions from a number of sections?
- Are there any compulsory questions?

Marks and time

Find out *how the marks are divided up*: firstly, between papers and, secondly, in relation to the questions on each paper. This will give you some indication of the amount of time you should spend on each question. For example, if you are faced with a three-hour exam paper containing five questions, with marks equally divided between them, you will want to allocate roughly equal time to each question. If you spend an hour on your last question and get 95% the last 25% of marks are expensive, 70% being enough to land a first class. If this means you don't have time to produce anything on your fifth question, then the big '0' you register there will pull down your overall mark and the standard of your degree. Take an example. Desmond spends so much time on his first question he gets 80% marks. He then brings home 60% on his next three questions but has no time to answer the fifth. He therefore gets an average mark of 52% – a lower second. Siobhan has prepared in a similar way. She, in contrast, gets 70% for her first and best question, 60% for the next three and 40% for the last one, having made time for it and taken a courageous stab at it. Siobhan thus gets an average of 60% and an upper second.

A good rule of thumb is: in an equal marks situation, *always answer all questions*. Given the way marking schemes work, it is relatively easy to get *some* marks on any question you attempt. The examiners gave Siobhan 40%, a bare third class, for demonstrating a very basic grasp of the last question. It's fairly easy to get 40%. The further up the scale you go the harder it gets. Desmond was killing himself to get the ten marks between 70 and 80. Like Siobhan, he could much more easily have piled up 40 on the last question and got a better degree. Of course, if some questions carry more marks than others your strategy will be different. In that case you will want to spend proportionally more time, both in your preparation and in the exam room, on those areas which attract the most marks. If in a two-section, four-question paper, the two questions in the first section offer 60% of the marks compared with 40% for the second section, take this into account. But again do not concentrate *all* your efforts on the first section so you do very poorly on the second: 50% added to 30% is better than 60% added to 10%.

Content of the exam

Look at the subject matter of the questions.

- Are there certain areas of the course you may be able to largely discount, such as foundation or comparison sections which do not appear to come up in the examination? Beware of the neglected area which has to come up some time.
- Do the papers religiously and sequentially cover the whole terrain you have traversed in your studies?
- To what degree do the papers allow you to select in your answers and thus your revision?

You will have greater room for selection if you have to answer five out of twelve questions, than if you have to answer five out of eight questions. Your room for manoeuvre will be more restricted if certain questions or sections are compulsory or carry more marks than others. Do certain questions recur or, more likely, do questions on *certain subjects* recur, phrased and angled in a different way? A key question is whether you can cover *all* the material in your course up to the standard of the degree you want, or whether you need to and can *select*.

Selection of topics

In most cases some selection is necessary – and permissable within the structure of the exam paper. If you only have to write answers in five out of twenty areas then intensive revising of all twenty may be counterproductive. But certain safeguards are useful.

- **Know your way around *all* your course**   Even though you are going to concentrate on certain topics, you should know *something* about other areas. Remember the utility of being able to get 40 marks on your final question.
- **Spot topics, not questions**   If questions on certain subjects come up frequently revise the subject from all angles, not just the angle of the question. Examiners like to ring the changes and they are trying to test your understanding of the area, not your ability to prepare a rote answer. Topics may recur. Questions usually do not.
- **Hedge your bets**   Intensive revision of too many areas may mean you spread yourself too thin. Conversely, if you concentrate on too few topics and Lady Luck deserts you, disaster looms. Insure against her fickleness by *revising twice as many topics as you feel you will need*. For example, if you have had weekly lectures and classes which can be broken down as covering 15 subject areas and you have to answer five questions, then revising intensively ten of the topics should do the trick. But a fall-back is essential. Look over the remaining areas just in case.

Standard and type of answer

Different questions require different lengths of answer.

Quality counts, not quantity. The key thing is deciphering what the question demands, what *level* of knowledge is required. You should be able to do this to do some extent on the basis of your essays. But under exam conditions the good essay often requires some stripping down. You may not be able to reproduce the dense, detailed argument and elegant structure in 40 minutes. You may have to limit introductory scene setting, examples, or illustrative quotes. *Talk to your tutors about the appropriate level of knowledge and detail expected.* Get them to go through one or two model answers in revision classes. Your understanding of level and approach will be developed further through practising answers in your revision.

The form of the questions

During your course you will have progressed from 'Write all you know about . . .' to 'Critically evaluate' to more opaque and disguised questions (see Chapter 10). Often examiners place a strong emphasis on the skill of decoding. Students are often happy with the 'discuss' and 'analyse' formulations. They can be taken aback by the pre-shrunk question, the lean and abrupt statement: ' "There's always room at the top." Is there?' or ' "Between 1933 and 1939 National Socialism represented economic chaos for Germany." Is that so?' You are being asked to expand concise statements, locate them in relation to the topics covered and perhaps approach them from a new angle. With exams it is particularly important to get used to interrogating apparently simple concise statements. Develop the technique of ballooning them up, seeing them as they really are, translating them into language you understand, relating them to your course work.

There is no one interpretation of a question and no one model answer. The *kind of answer* which is to be expected will be discussed but there can be slightly different interpretations of what is demanded between examiners. So different approaches are to be expected amongst students. Different examiners will have their own views of what is required but will agree, in compromise: 'You could it this way . . . or you could do it *that* way . . . both would constitute good responses to the question.' You are not trying to produce some model answers but *to get within the range of reasonable interpretations of the question.*

Talk about it

Finally, talk about the exam papers with your fellow students and tutors. Remember the work on the 'hidden curriculum' by Becker, Geer and Hughes (1968) and Snyder (1971) as well as Miller and Parlett's (1974) research on *The Exam Game* (see Chapter 6).

- Have your tutors laid particular emphasis on different areas of the course? Have particular topics come up in revision classes?
- Have there been new developments in a particular area – is it controversial just now?
- Are you getting any cues?

Clarify with your tutors any outstanding points on how your examination works and how your answers are marked. *Do this as early as you can.*

12.6   Organising your revision

Now draw up a revision schedule and finalise the subject areas you are going to revise. In your selection you may take into account: the frequency with which questions based on particular areas come up; the amount of work you have put in on particular topics; the degree to which certain areas motivate you and the extent to which you find certain areas difficult. Before making your selection review *all* your study materials. Skim read, noting any gaps, materials missing, books you need access to. Look over the *whole* of the course on which you will be examined.

Revision timetable

Don't start revising too late. Make sure you have adequate time to revise successfully. Be clear as to dates and the periods between different exams. You want a good first exam. But it is only the first hurdle in a long race. So don't concentrate too much on the first paper compared with others. Set targets for each revision period, each day and each week. Make time to monitor progress.

Are you the kind of person who likes to spend a whole day revising for one paper? Or do you prefer revising for one paper in the morning and a different one in the afternoon? Are you going to revise your best topics first to establish confidence and a good routine? Or tackle the toughest to give you more time to solve its conundrums? Resist the temptation to spend too much time working on the papers and subjects you like. Keep a balance between work on the different papers and the different topics within each paper. Some problems and issues will interest you more than others; you can pursue them at your leisure *after* the exam. Will you now work more at home, less on campus, as you have all the materials you need and you wish to avoid social temptations? Or do you need a period in the library? Will you vary where you study? It is time, certainly, to knock off that part-time job. Whilst you may wish to cut down outside commitments, some social life helps you relax and work better when you return to your desk. Pace yourself. Don't overdo it at the start so you run out of steam.

Working with others

Discuss problems with partners, family and friends. You are now going to have to spend a fair amount of time working hard in isolation, but do not cut yourself off completely. *Special revision classes* can often be useful in clearing up difficulties or reinforcing important points. So can talking through points with fellow students. Interaction with others makes you think. You may already be part of an informal student learning group and now wish to turn it into a revision group with regular meetings. Or you may wish to meet *ad hoc*. If *revision* means 're-seeing', you may benefit from how others see things. The usual rider applies: everybody must pull their weight!

Revise actively

You should not be taking on new work of any significance, such as reading big books for the first time. Moreover, it is vital that you revise *actively*: sitting reading or making new detailed notes on a text requires less effort, but is less effective, than active preparation which confronts the actuality of the exam. Start by pondering the questions on the exam paper and then, in the framework of answering them, working on your books, notes and essays before returning to the questions with your material now organised into answers. An active approach involves continuing interaction between your materials and the exam paper. The question–answer approach prepares your mind for the exam and the essential technique of reorganising your knowledge to meet the requirements of new, slightly different questions.

1 Break your notes and essays down into areas covered by exam questions
2 The second stage involves reading and note making, working over your material in one area with pen in hand and with the kind of questions that come up in mind. You have to rearrange your material, relating it to questions to re-see it and to learn it anew. You are not seeking to expand your material by making copious notes. You are seeking to boil it down to its essentials to discern the bone structure. Your

notes should now move towards the skeletal outline, rather than the packed page. Summarise, get to the main points, reach towards the principles. Many students find it useful to use diagrams which show contours and connections with detail sheared off. You may develop brief one-point, one-sentence notes or re-jig important areas using a card index for summaries, lists, statements of key issues. Always approach your study materials afresh, critically, from where you are *now*. Relate what you did *then* to new insights and connections so that what is involved is an active re-making and re-learning of the material.

3 Having worked over your material, look in detail at a couple of exam questions on the topic. Which areas of understanding is the question asking you to deploy? Do you need to brainstorm? How are you going to organise your answer? Think up *slightly different questions* on each subject and answer them. The more you get used to re-arranging and re-organising your knowledge in different combinations, the more you will be practising successful exam technique.

4 Try to work out a brief *outline* without using your books, notes and essays. Then go back to your materials and compare your outline answer. Does your outline flow; have you selected correctly; do your conclusions stand up? Work through points and areas you have missed. Then try again to construct an outline without them. You are now directly relating your revision to your specific target, the exam. You are reading, writing, thinking to achieve a specific task. Some students find it useful to talk through an answer, others to tape answers and play them back.

Practising complete answers

Following the same technique, you can move on to the *note answer*, where you jot down under each outline point two or three amplifying sentences. This assures you that you can expand, explain and give examples to illustrate your points.

Write fuller notes on key definitions, arguments or debates you find difficult: clarify by writing. Now put some flesh on the skeleton. Try to write out a *complete answer* without using your books, essays and notes. You are now getting closer to the reality of the exam: that is why this is the best training. Next, try to complete the answer *in the time you will have available in the exam.* Return once more to your books and notes and go over your timed answer, amending it. Then go to the other extreme: note down the briefest of outlines using only key words and phrases that will bring the whole answer back into your mind.

Study groups and mock exams

Interaction works best when you have already done the spadework in developing your own understanding of a particular problem. When you have worked over your material it is useful to get together with fellow students to compare experiences. How are your peers progressing? Are *you* doing too much or too little? This often helps morale if the isolation and hard work are starting to get to you. You can also talk through stubborn problems, compare your answers to exam questions and clear up any queries about strategy. You can hold buzz sessions where you analyse and brainstorm questions together.

The small group provides the best setting for moving beyond the complete answer to the timed complete answer. You can mark each other's answers, and then 'teach' each other answers. This gives you practice in doing what you will have to do in the exam itself: analysing, assessing, constructing, and writing *fast* – practice under pressure. Don't worry if your answers look messy, shorter, less well articulated than your essays. Timing should bring home to you the need for condensation and blitzkrieg. Get into the real meat of your answer, displaying quickly the top-notch knowledge the examiner wants. Long introductions and explanations of peripheral points will have to go. You will not be able to reproduce the patient build-up of your essays. In football terms, when taking exams you have to switch a little more to the long ball game: get the ball into the crucial goal mouth area where you can use your heavy artillery as quickly as possible.

Some students find it useful to organise realistic mock exams like you had at school; others find this a little over-elaborate and prefer to stick to answering one or two questions at regular intervals under exam conditions.

12.7 Taking the exam

The day before

Some students prefer to take it relatively easy, do some skimming revision during the early part of the day and then take the evening off. Others like to keep the creative tension going and do a full day's work. Two good rules of thumb are: don't kill yourself if you do work; have a quiet evening and an early night.

But do not put the exam out of your mind. It is important to check over the arrangements and make sure there are no last minute hitches. Make a final check to ensure that you know

- where the exam is being held, how to get to the room itself and when it starts
- how you are getting there and how long it will take you
- any checking-in procedures
- the form of the exam, its length and the examination instructions and that
- you have everything just so – the car is in working order; you have your rail or bus fare; you have any examination cards; your watch is not going bust.

Examination day

The last thing you want on the first morning are last minute problems which will disturb your concentration. If you need an alarm call, book one so that you are up and about a little earlier than usual, just in case. Arrive a little early – early enough to overcome any problems such as finding the right room, not so early that you have to stand around with exam nerves rising to the surface. Some people find conversation just before the exam disturbs concentration or increases anxiety. If this describes you, avoid your colleagues and go straight into the exam room.

If you are unlucky enough to be taken ill or have an accident, then follow the procedure for letting your examiners know. Resist the temptation to put this off until later.

Passing your exams

Some students dig straight in; they race through a question they think they can answer. Others will find that the question is more difficult, or deals with more than they bargained for. Still others find that having rushed through a good answer, they lose momentum: they spend too long on selecting a second question. There is no optimal method that suits us all. But it is worth at least considering a more measured, systematic approach.

1 Preliminaries Deal with preliminaries such as filling in registration slips and writing details on answer books. Note any technical requirements, such as using different answer books for different questions or writing on only one side of the paper. In the event of any difficulties, consult the invigilator.

2 Read the paper Read the whole paper slowly and carefully. *Check the instructions.* Make sure they are as expected.

Then *read through the questions carefully a second time*. Dwell on them rather than rushing around reading half of each. If you can get yourself into a calm and methodical frame of mind now, you should be able to work in this manner throughout the exam.

3 Pick possibles and probables Focus on those questions from which you are going to select. Look at your 'possibles' and 'probables' closely. Underline key instruction words. Look for the double directives which ask you to do two things: 'Describe *and* analyse', 'Evaluate, *illustrating from* . . .' Circle or box other important words: names, dates, theories which situate and circumscribe the response required. What are the major ideas or concepts you are required to deal with? If the question is epigrammatic or opaque, write it out in your own words. Be realistic and address the questions on the paper not the questions you *wish* were on the paper.

4 Select your questions Divide possible questions into those which should be eliminated, those you can attempt with difficulty, which should be held in reserve or ranked last, and those about which you feel knowledgeable – which you will answer. Now rank the questions in the order you are going to answer them. Some people like to tackle the questions they think will be toughest first. But for most of us the way to get our brains working well, build up confidence and start as we mean to go on is *to do our best questions first*.

5 Time your answers You may already have spent a worthwhile five to ten minutes on preparation and selection. It is also useful to budget for five or ten minutes at the end to check over your answers and ensure no major mishaps have occurred. If marks are allocated equally to all questions then remember the marginal rule: *ten minutes on a new last question will produce more marks than spending an extra ten minutes on a question you have already answered reasonably well.* Having knocked off your 'start' and your 'finish' quota, divide your time more or less equally between the questions. Keep an eye on the clock: if you need to, jot down finishing times for answers.

6 Plan your answers   If it works for you, sketch an outline plan. A clear structure to follow is even more important in an exam than when you are writing an essay at home: you have less time to re-orient if you take a wrong turning. Most students find it more efficient to write each answer once it is planned, rather than making four or five plans and then starting writing. Once you have one or two complete answers in the bank, confidence soars. On the other hand, some students, particularly with the first and second – their best – questions are able to write a good answer straight off making a few jottings along the way. Because of effective revision they can hold the structure in their mind.

You cannot spend too much time on planning or let it become a barrier to beginning writing. With a 40-minute answer we are talking about five to ten minutes' thinking and planning, around 25 minutes' writing and around five minutes for going back over the question, a process which many find suggests new points and improves your answer.

Once again, recall the points made in Chapters 9 and 10. Translate the examiners' question, don't twist it. Accept its contours and complexity, get the command words right, don't waffle or over-elaborate. Cover all aspects of multipart questions. Emphasise conclusions – de-emphasise introductions.

Box 12.2 Keep your answers relevant

Frank: Rita, how the hell can you write an essay on E. M. Forster with almost total reference to Harold Robbins?

Rita: Well you said bring in other authors.

Frank: Tch.

Rita: Don't go on at me, you said: y'said, 'Reference to other authors will impress the examiners'.

Frank: I said refer to other works but I don't think the examiner, God bless him, will have read (*he consults the paper*) *A Stone For Danny Fisher*.

Rita: Well, that's his hard luck isn't it?

Frank: It'll be your hard luck when he fails your paper.

Rita: Oh that's prime, isn't it? That's justice for y'. I get failed just cos I'm more well read than the friggin examiner!

Willy Russell, *Educating Rita*

---

7 **Write as fast as you can.** But make sure the examiner can read it. Separate your planning and jotting from your answer. Translate the structure of your plan into a composite answer by using your broad headings as main sections and your subpoints as paragraphs. Decide how much, if any, definition of key ideas and terms is required. Keep checking for relevance. Show the examiner your powers of analysis and evaluation and that you are able to organise your knowledge in a relevant way. Demonstrate that you are able to develop judgements and conclusions backed by supportive evidence rather than assertion. Keep an eye on spelling. Stop when you have used your budgeted time. The law of diminishing returns dictates you must get on to that last question. If time is running out then do your last answer in note form, getting straight into the core of the question. Use your last five minutes or so to check over your paper.

8 If you hit rough water   During the exam you may run into a number of difficulties.

- **Nerves**   If you feel nervous tension rising, take a few minutes to relax. Most moments of panic can be overcome by switching our minds off momentarily. Let your muscles go limp and breathe in deeply, holding your breath for five seconds. Then release your breath also taking five seconds. Repeat the exercise five times and you should be in a position to continue. Look at another problem before returning to the one that got you going – perhaps you can approach it from a different angle later.

- **Writers' cramp**   This can be a problem if you are not used to writing thousands of words in a few hours. The fact that this occurs constitutes a good reason for practising answers under timed conditions. In most cases, a brief pause will ease the problem, or you can crash the pain barrier: by keeping going you make it go away. However if you are completely immobilised call the invigilator.

- **Memory blocks**   The idea is down there somewhere but just will not surface. Don't panic and don't give up. Think back to when and where you worked on the problem, the essay in which you wrote about it, the class in which you argued it through. Jot down points that do come through or which are related; suddenly the problem point may jump back into your mind. But if it does not, then move on; you must keep to your time budget. Sometimes switching onto something else helps. While working on the next question the important issue in its predecessor may come swimming into view.

- **Illness**   Try and overcome feelings of nausea or fatigue by concentrating on what you are doing. Try the relaxation technique or call the invigilator so you can go out for a breath of fresh air. If it is insuperable let the invigilator know: better to postpone your examination than fail when it is not your fault.

After the exam

There is always a temptation to relax after your first exam. There may well be a case for a period of relaxation but it is best to keep celebrations until you have completed *all* your exams. If you go out on a spree you may feel under the weather the following day when you should be preparing for your next exam. If you feel you have not done as well as you should, a 'good night out' may leave you feeling more depressed when you should be concentrating on getting yourself back 'up' for your next exam. Exams are more like marathons than sprints. You need stamina and energy conservation. Too much relaxation after each exam can mean you are inadequately prepared for the next one. Take a brief break then start preparing for your next challenge.

There is not a great deal of point in an immediate post-mortem after each exam. But you definitely need a post-mortem when all your exams have been completed. After all, exams are supposed to constitute a learning experience and the extensive revision you have carried out should provide a basis for the next stage in your studies or career. When all your exams are completed talk to your tutor: you need to know where you went wrong to set it right.

Resits Discussion with your tutor is vital. There is no need to lose heart. Exams are a lottery and there are many factors outside the control of the individual. Numerous students have failed exams and gone on to complete them successfully the second time around. Be a good loser: take it on the chin. We all suffer defeats in life. Be a bad loser: determine to get even with the examiner next time.

Aegrotats If illness has precluded your participation in exams, your case will be discussed by your department. The term 'aegrotat' – the Latin *aegrotare* means 'to be sick' – is sometimes used. Your tutor will put your case to the other examiners, so make sure he or she is well briefed on all the details.

Appeals procedure

Hopefully you will not need to resort to this but your college will have a formal procedure so that students who are aggrieved at the outcome of their exams can take their case further. Once again this requires detailed discussion with your tutor (see Box 12.3).

If exams do relate inadequately to course work, if there is too great a gap between teaching and testing, if students are thrown back upon regurgitation, then there is cause for concern . . . and for action. The exam system in each department should be the subject of keen scrutiny and detailed comment by student representatives on course committees.

Box 12.3   When things go wrong . . .

In the late 1980s Francis Foecke, a Bristol University student of Maths and Computing, mounted an ultimately unsuccessful, four-year, £100,000 legal battle over his exam results. He argued against the examiners' decision to downgrade his finals marks on the grounds that the nature of his answers suggested cheating. The Foecke case drew attention to a new scrutiny being applied to assessment. Students are increasingly having to pay their way, more pay full fees, more are older and experienced, there is a greater inclination by politicians and administrators to characterise them as 'clients' or 'customers'. Perhaps in the new climate students are less ready than they were in the past to accept assessments they consider dubious, particularly when they affect future career prospects.

● Universities usually have an appeals procedure which enables resort first to the faculty board and then to a special appeals committee.

- The former polytechnics had a standardised procedure through the CNAA though internal arrangements differed.

There have been complaints that procedures are unclear, inadequately publicised to those who might need them, and lacking an external appeals stage, so that the academics within a college act as prosecutor, judge and jury. The number of appeals has remained small – although this could reflect inadequate machinery. The government's Student Charter promises stronger individual rights of appeal whilst the National Union of Students wants more collective involvement in assessment procedures. The shake-up in higher education will undoubtedly produce a new examination of how assessment systems work and who, when things go wrong, assesses the assessors.

Key points

1 Assessment is justified on the grounds of motivation, diagnosis, selection and credentialling of students and evaluation of courses.
2 The traditional exam still plays a key role. Criticisms of it range from the view that it rewards speed writing and memory more than intellectual development, to variability of marking.
3 The traditional exam has been supplemented by continuous assessment and 'open book'. Current orthodoxy favours a mix of methods.
4 Know the system in your department: how many marks each form of assessment carries, how marks are divided between papers, who sets exams and who marks them. Find out how your degree is graded.
5 Sustained work throughout your course with periodic, limited revision is essential preparation. Start your pre-exam revision in good time. Study past exam papers. Consult tutors and attend revision classes.
6 Divide your efforts between papers in proportion to the potential marks attached to each. Within each paper answer all questions required. If marks are equally divided between questions remember the marginal rule: ten minutes on a new question yields more

marks than ten minutes on an already reasonable answer.

7 Pre-exam revision should be *active* revision, pitched at answering exam-style questions.

8 Decide which areas you will concentrate on, but ensure you know something about the whole course.

9 Practise writing outline answers, note answers, full answers and timed full answers. Experiment with different questions to sharpen your flexibility. Remember the advice on de-coding essay questions (Chapter 10). The exam essay should be concentrated and start at a higher level.

10 Work with fellow students, in practising answers. Remember the need for relaxation. Check last minute arrangements.

11 Spend some time on selection of questions. Plan your answers. Always attempt the last question. Leave time for checking.

12 Keep up the momentum for your further exams. At the end of the exam schedule talk things over with your tutor.

Things to do

1 Think about what your feelings are about exams. Why do exams make students anxious and worried? How can these feelings be overcome?

2 'Traditional written examinations do not stimulate learning, they arrest educational development.' Discuss whether this is true.

3 Consider the pros and cons of continuous assessment and open book examinations.

4 Have a look at three recent exam papers in your subject. How do the questions relate to your syllabus? Do they concentrate on certain areas and not on others? Do they fairly represent the whole range of subjects you have dealt with on your course?

5 Discuss with a fellow student the form that questions take on the same examination papers. Why are they drafted in this way?

6 Working in pairs, prepare two outline answers to questions on one of the exam papers. Then swop with a friend who has prepared answers for two different questions. Discuss the different approaches you have taken.

7 Working in pairs, prepare a complete answer to one of the questions within the time you would have in the exam. Swop answers, read and mark your friend's answer and then compare notes.

8 Find out all you can about how papers are marked in your exam. Which qualities in answers attract most marks?

Further reading

A good all-round account of many of the problems in this area is *Assessment in Higher Education* by John Heywood (John Wiley, 1987). Derek Rowntree's *Assessing Students: How Shall We Know Them?* (Harper and Row, 1977) is a stimulating book with interesting proposals for change. Research on how exams work and how they are marked can be found in *Teaching and Learning in Higher Education* by Ruth Beard and James Hartley (Paul Chapman Publishing, 1984). Tom Fawthrop's 'Education or examination?' in *Student Power* (ed. Alexander Cockburn and Robin Blackburn, Penguin, 1969) is a strong plea for an end to the traditional exam. *Up to the Mark: A Study of the Examination Game* by Carolyn Miller and Malcolm Parlett (Society for Research in Higher Education, 1974) has interesting material on how students see exams and play the system. There is more information on examination technique in *How to Pass Exams* by David Acres (Northcote House, 1987).

13

After your degree

We receive three educations, one from our parents, one from our schoolmasters and one from the World. The third contradicts all that the first two teach us.

Montesquieu

13.1 Introduction

Once you are the proud possessor of a Bachelor's degree, you face two main choices: stay on to take some further course of study or training, or enter the world of work. If you have not yet entered university it might seem premature to be considering this, but it's never too soon to consider seriously what you want to do for a career. It is worth thinking about early and often. Few sixth-formers in practice choose their A levels without *any* thought of what they might do when their education is completed. (See Chapter 3). But many students either enter university with no clearly defined career plans or change whatever ideas they have as a result of their study experiences. This chapter is written mainly with this latter group in mind.

- Section 13.2 examines postgraduate courses at the certificate, diploma, Master's and Ph.D. levels.
- Section 13.3 discusses transferable skills: how skills you have learnt at university will be useful to you in your career.
- Section 13.4 concludes with advice on searching for and obtaining a job.

13.2　Postgraduate courses

Why study for a postgraduate qualification?

The most obvious answer to this question is, interest. If your intellectual curiosity has been aroused by your degree studies, postgraduate work offers the opportunity to pursue areas of study or specific topics to a greater and more satisfying depth. But there will almost certainly be additional reinforcing reasons. In some cases you will need to pursue an extra course in order to achieve the professional qualification you need to fulfil your career ambitions: a teaching certificate, for example, or a certificate in social work. Other degree holders will seek to strengthen their position in the increasingly competitive employment market by acquiring supporting qualifications – the assumption here is that someone with a Master's degree will seem more attractive to an employer than someone with a mere B.A. In recent years there is firm evidence that a proportion of graduates have remained in study chiefly because the graduate job market has been so adversely affected by economic recession.

What kinds of postgraduate courses are there?

The number of postgraduate courses has proliferated in recent years – of 5,669 degrees awarded at the University of Manchester in 1991, 1,778 (32%) were postgraduate. The available choice is potentially baffling. This is partially explained by the growth of professional courses but also by the development of postgraduate schools specialising in new kinds of course work and aimed at boosting research output. Three major kinds of postgraduate course are identifiable.

Certificates and diplomas

There is no real agreement between universities as to which qualification – certificates or diplomas – is the higher. The academic level is often similar and both qualifications are usually acquired after one year's full-time study. Part-time courses and distance learning versions are also available but inevitably they will take longer. Some certificates/diplomas are wholly 'liberal' in their orientation. Continuing education departments, for example, offer a range of part-time certificates and diplomas mostly aimed at adult learners. Courses are available in subjects as diverse as Egyptology, Anglo-Saxon history and European studies. The majority of certificate/diploma courses, however, are 'vocational' and are linked to particular professions giving total or partial exemption from required professional qualifications. Teaching (the Post Graduate Certificate in Education – PGCE) and social work (the Certificate for Qualified Social Workers) have already been mentioned but hundreds of other opportunities exist for people wishing for example, to achieve qualifications recognised by professional bodies (such as a diploma in accountancy) or achieve training in special skills (such as a diploma in tourism or journalism). When you are choosing which course to study you will need to accept fully any vocational implications of the choice made: it's no good studying for a PGCE if you have not made a career decision to become a teacher. However, many vocational courses are not so closely locked in to particular professions but still open up other career opportunities. For example, you might be a history graduate but choose to study for a diploma in computer science.

Master's level degrees

Master's courses (see Chapter 2) typically comprise three or four examined courses topped off by a short dissertation. In some cases diplomas are awarded on the basis of nine months' course work and the three-month dissertation moves you up to the Master's level. The courses will entail specialised work in specific areas of a subject and although the dissertation might involve some original research, these are not 'research' degrees in any real sense of the word. Such courses often have a professional training orientation – like a Master of Business Administration (MBA) – and may constitute exemption from the requirements of a profession. In other cases they will provide a higher level training in a particular discipline and can prove attractive to people who wish to broaden their intellectual repertoire. Someone who has studied social history, therefore, might choose to do a Master of Sociology course; a biologist, a Master of Embryology.

It is often believed that Master's courses are much more difficult than undergraduate courses. In practice, the difference is not that great but the level of achievement in examinations is, and ought to be, somewhat higher. It is still possible to acquire a Master's through thesis alone but these days such degrees are frequently designated M.Phil.s: practice varies at different universities.

Doctorates

The Ph.D. is the highest available postgraduate qualification and is the one which has changed least over the years (see Chapter 2). In Britain a certain amount of course work has been introduced in some subjects but typically a doctorate is acquired through the submission of a thesis alone. A doctorate usually takes three years to complete and can take much longer. Many universities now have strict time limits – typically, seven years – which if exceeded require a candidate to re-apply and re-register.

Doctorates make original contributions to research literature whilst providing a valuable intellectual training experience. Research topics are often very specialised and critics are right to question whether dedicating several years to such an endeavour is a cost-effective use of an intelligent person's time. The rationale, however, is that whilst the perspective of a Ph.D. topic might be narrow, it penetrates – providing it is well chosen – to the heart of the discipline. To understand its context, wide background reading in the discipline is needed, together with the ability to contribute to academic debates at the highest level. Someone who has negotiated the lonely path from first degree through to a doctorate should, so the argument runs, have achieved intellectual maturity: the learning and confidence to stand up and argue with the best in the discipline. The production of a book-long thesis, moreover, involves the management of vast amounts of information according to the most rigorous intellectual standards. To achieve this, it is argued, a special kind of self-discipline and motivation is required. All this is true in the majority of cases, but the American practice of insisting on wide-ranging course work probably makes their doctorates a more worthwhile developmental experience for the emergent intellect.

Having a Ph.D. is usually regarded as holding a key to academic life but this is by no means always the case. You can find Ph.D.s in business, in the civil service, even in Parliament; at the same time, a fair percentage of academics do not feel it worthwhile to acquire the title of 'Doctor'.

If you are seriously considering doctoral studies it is important that you observe the following points.

1 Select a topic which you will be happy exploring for at least two to three years. If it is a scientific topic, you need to be especially sure your research has a good chance of producing worthwhile results. One case known to us involved a mathematician working for two years on an equation which he subsequently found had been copied down wrongly from the original source! Scientific research often takes place in teams and in these cases guidance on suitable topics is freely available. Indeed, in some instances graduates are asked to apply for doctoral studies in designated research areas. In any case, your topic will be closely scrutinised by the academic authorities and will require formal approval.

2 Choose the right department in which to study. It is easy to discover those departments with a high academic rating

either through word of mouth or through checking the Higher Education Funding Council research ratings. Leading departments have ratings of 4 and 5 but you also need to find out how research students are treated: Do they have their own rooms? Is there a series of research seminars? Do they have opportunities for teaching?

3 Choose a good supervisor. This decision might also determine your choice of department, of course. Not all leading researchers make good supervisors. If they are really eminent they will, after all, be travelling abroad to conferences and not available to give you the guidance you will most certainly need. Word-of-mouth recommendations are probably the most reliable.

4 Appreciate that you will need to achieve a good degree – a first or an upper second – to be accepted for Ph.D. study. In certain areas (such as British Academy Postgraduate Awards) competition is so strong that many applicants with first-class degrees fail to gain acceptance.

5 Realise you will have very little money. Typically, maintenance grants from the Science and Engineering Research Council work out at £5,190 if you are living in London; £4,125 if you are living outside London; or £3,059 if you are living at home (1991 figures). Additional funds might be available from undergraduate teaching but this cannot always be guaranteed. Many postgraduate students are forced to eke out their existence with part-time jobs. (See also Chapter 4.)

6 Realise that the life of a postgraduate student may prove to be alienating and lonely. This clearly is less likely to be the case if you are part of a lively research team but often Ph.D. students undertake individual topics and face endless solitary hours in libraries poring over obscure sources. After the camaraderie of degree studies with all those lectures and seminars and noisy coffee breaks, this can be quite a culture shock and a tough challenge to your motivation and commitment. To an undergraduate, academic research can seem

like an exciting intellectual adventure at the highest level: in practice much of it is tedious, routine researching and checking.

7 Come to terms with the fact that you have taken on a formidable task. Most successful Ph.D. students will tell you that there were times when they felt they were never going to finish and that giving up was the only way out. You do not need to be intellectually brilliant to acquire a Ph.D. – though of course it helps – much more important is 'stickability', the determination and stamina of a marathon runner.

8 Recognise that you will need to pass an oral exam or 'viva'. As you approach the end of your studies, an external examiner will be appointed. After he or she has read your thesis, you will have an oral exam in which you will be required to stand up to critical questioning from one of the leading authorities in your discipline. This could prove a mere formality but it all depends upon the quality of your thesis and the character of your external examiner. If your thesis is not up to scratch you may be asked to re-write parts of it; if it is thought to be below the necessary standard, you may be awarded the lower qualification of M.Phil. or M.A. If the worst happens you could fail altogether, but a heavy responsibility rests on your supervisor to ensure that your thesis is up to the required standard before submission takes place.

The above is not meant to appear negative but to help you make an informed and realistic decision about whether postgraduate research is for you. Conversations with research students and academic tutors will almost certainly endorse the warnings we have given but will also confirm that such a period in your life can be intensely stimulating and satisfying. Endless deserts of routine are dramatically interrupted by rich oases of discovery. After years of course work which culminate in hastily written examination scripts, postgraduate research produces something tangible. Few things can exceed the pleasure you experience when your hands first hold your neatly typed and professionally bound thesis.

Applications

It would be prudent to find out about opportunities for postgraduate studies during the summer term break before your final year but applications in the following autumn term are still acceptable. If you leave your enquiries any later you may find that all the places have gone or, just as bad, all the available funding has been taken up. Therefore you need to apply in the autumn term, ensuring that you give a good account of yourself on paper. Some departments will ask you to fill in an application form but others will ask for a letter of application with a curriculum vitae. You may be called for interview either late in the autumn term or more usually, in the Lent term. Quite often you will be given a place on a postgraduate course conditional on the achievement of a particular degree grade – usually, but by no means always, an upper second or a first.

Finance

You may well find that getting a grant is much more difficult than being accepted on a course. You may be one of the many postgraduate students who are able to fund their own study through savings, parental contributions, bank loans and so forth. If this is the case then being accepted by a department will constitute your chief hurdle. Departments may be particularly interested in self-financing students, but do check carefully whether you will have to pay course fees (which can be anything from £500 to £2000 for a year's study and more for overseas students) as well as your living or maintenance expenses. If you are seeking public finance, you will need to check the many and varied opportunities carefully. The research councils (see Chapter 4) give quota awards to certain departments: when you apply to a department, therefore, you may well be seeking finance which is within its gift. In other cases, you will have to make your own application for funding. The main sources are shown in Table 13.1.

Table 13.1 Sources of research funding

Source	Topics funded
The Agriculture and Food Research Council (AFRC)	Food related research
British Academy (BA)	Mostly arts and humanities subjects
Economic and Social Research Council (ESRC)	Social sciences and related subjects
Science and Engineering Research Council (SERC)	Physical sciences and engineering
The Natural Environment Research Council (NERC)	Life and geological sciences
Medical Research Council (MRC)	Biomedical subjects
Ministry of Agriculture, Fisheries and Food (MAFF)	Agricultural, science and economics
Department for Education	Nominated taught courses of a professional or vocational nature
Local education authorities (LEA)	Mandatory awards for PGCE but all other awards discretionary

Each source of finance will have its own timescales and procedures and eligibility rules – for example, some research councils will not offer you any funding until you have been accepted for study by a university department. You will need to get hold of the specialised leaflets relating to each source of finance but you cannot do better than begin with the excellent booklet by Janet Widdows, Monica Jalloq and Lesley Knaggs: **Postgraduate Study and Research**, published by the Association of Graduate Careers Advisory Services. This booklet contains much useful advice and all the addresses and further reading you will require if you are interested in postgraduate studies.

13.3 **Transferable skills**

An idea that seems irresistible to certain undergraduates is that universities exist solely to provide them with a carefree, hedonistic interlude between school and work. Reading this book should have disabused you of this enticing and widespread illusion. At several points we have stopped to point out that what goes on at university does have great relevance to your career. On the face of it the idealised purpose of universities – the reflective pursuit of truth through learning – does not have much direct relevance to, say, chartered accountancy. However, even where the ideal is pursued in its purest form, all kinds of useful life skills are developed along the way. In this section we explain some of them.

The content of your subject

Naturally, the *knowledge* acquired at university is likely to be of value to you in your career and in many other aspects of your life. This is particularly true if you are studying a vocational subject like architecture, law, medicine, nursing or accountancy: the knowledge absorbed will be directly applicable to your professional activities. You will also absorb the central concepts of your professional discipline, the intellectual frameworks developed for the analysis of data, problems and so forth. The same is true to a lesser extent if you join a profession which has a strong link with your degree specification; for example, if, having studied sociology, you do social work, or with a degree in political science you go into the civil service. Some words of qualification are necessary here, however.

It is often said that you need to 'unlearn' what you have learnt at GCSE when studying for your A levels or to do the same with your A-level studies when you get to university. To some extent this happens when you begin your professional career. Absorbing information and ideas for a coursework essay which affects no one but yourself is qualitatively different from learning the facts of a case of a client you are representing, say, as a solicitor. When you have a professional obligation to fulfil, what you study really matters and you find that you absorb it in a different way. The difference is akin to that between a rehearsal and a proper performance.

On the other hand you might very well end up in a career which has virtually no connection with your degree subject; for example, someone who has studied literature might choose to work in local government or business management. If the link between the content of academic study and employment is so often tenuous or non-existent, why, you may ask, do potential employers place such a high value on university education? The answer is that they are looking for skills and personality qualities which the university experience develops. When caught up in the maelstrom of your studies it is difficult to appreciate that important transferable skills are being developed. But they are, as the rest of this section makes clear.

Lectures

These teach you important concentration and listening skills as well as the ability to make accurate summaries of what you have heard. These skills will prove invaluable in any profession you choose to join.

Seminars and tutorials

As a seminar presenter you need to be well prepared, calm, articulate and persuasive. You must defend your views but be able to take criticism in your stride as a natural part of the exercise. As a member of such a discussion group you can help in a number of ways. You can:

- *contribute* more information and ideas;
- *summarise* the discussion so far;

- *lead* the group back to the point when discussion strays;
- *indicate* where further work needs to be done;
- *offer imaginative solutions* to problems;
- *suggest tentative solutions* and ideas for further activity;
- ensure that the group's *tasks are completed*.

Alternatively, you can contribute constructively towards the group dynamics by smoothing down tensions between group members, relaxing everyone with an injection of humour, and ensuring that the task of the group is completed.

The parallels with committee meetings in the world of work are obvious here. Whether working in business, the civil service, local government, the media, teaching or just about any profession you can think of, you will need to be effective in committees. Virtually all the skills mentioned above are highly relevant but there are important differences.

1 Committees, which involve gatherings of several people drawn from a wide area, are expensive to organise. Consequently there is pressure on time: contributions need to be brief and extremely clear.

2 A presentation could be the culmination of a considerable period of preparation and be crucial to your future progress. The form of your presentation may need to be much more disciplined than in an academic seminar and audio visual aids may be much more important. Your purpose will be to win support so you will need to be more authoritative and more persuasive than in a seminar: you will need to *sell* your line of argument rather than merely present it.

3 Committee members are not fellow students but may be competitors for promotion. This can create a tense atmosphere and make it more important that you prepare and defend yourself well.

4 Constructive contributions will be expected of you as a committee member; it will not be possible to sit silently as students often do in seminars. Especially encouraged will be authoritative contributions of information, problem-

solving suggestions, and ideas for further action. Being good in seminars won't necessarily make you a good business manager or civil servant but it could provide you with some of the vital prerequisites.

Written assignments

As indicated earlier, written skills are eminently trans- ferable. Good essays need to be founded on a solid base of preparatory research. The same will be true of projects you will be asked to prepare by your employer: your ability to absorb vast amounts of information rapidly and make sense of it will be put to good use. All the relevant elements in a problem need to be identified and properly addressed in an essay: so it is with problems you will encounter in your career. Just like a good essay, committee papers need to be well organised and clearly structured. Essays are often written late at night or early in the morning: employers will welcome someone used to working and thinking outside office hours. Finally, a good literary style, which ensures your essays are easily understood and enjoyed, will help your committee papers (shorn perhaps of literary flourishes) persuade your colleagues that your ideas are worth supporting. All these skills constitute criteria by which your professionalism will be judged.

A critical enquiring mind

Within higher education intellectual curiosity is encouraged. You are taught not to accept any argument at face value but to look for evidence and possibly illogical reasoning. You become aware of connections between information and ideas and are encouraged to come up with original creative analyses. Once ensconced in your profession you will find that your employers are not especially interested in your philo- sophical and ethical reflections but they will greatly appreciate an eager, enquiring and athletic intellect, fecund with new ideas and problem-solving suggestions.

Examinations

Those who urge the complete abolition of examinations (see Chapter 12) overlook their valuable training function. Many aspects of professional life resemble examinations. Whatever your occupation, you will be required at times to function under great pressure yet still think clearly and produce high level work. Examinations provide valuable practice in working to deadlines and learning how to handle the accompanying nervous tension. A civil servant may have to write a top level paper for his minister within half a day or less. A barrister may have to brief himself on a client's case and stand up in court to speak to it within an hour or even minutes. A television producer may have to work through the night to prepare a programme for national transmission. If you are good at examinations or have the potential to be good then you will soon come to cope with the demands of professional life.

Extra-curricular activities

University life is a complete experience which potential employers appreciate can be enriching and character forming in all kinds of ways. Your extra-curricular activities therefore will be of interest in job interviews; particular attention will be paid to whether these activities have fostered the special skills which the employing company is after.

Despite some of the stereotypes which abound of student life – the best known are probably found in the comedy series *The Young Ones* – a university education i
developmental experience. Typically, 18-y
leave home and fend for themselves in a r
They have to make major decisions about w
where and how they live. To survive they ne
finances adequately and manage their time

lectures and seminars are attended and work handed in (more or less) on time. Being a successful student means being independent and used to using your own initiative. For a variety of reasons, usually very understandable, a small percentage don't make it but most students survive and prosper: employers are still very interested in the product of this special form of education.

Involvement in university sports, for example, shows a number of qualities: the ability to get involved, be part of a team, or – if you are captain or vice-captain – exercise leadership. Being an Oxford or Cambridge 'Blue' is widely recognised as an achievement which will count with employers but representative honours at other universities also carry weight. The same goes for any involvement in university societies and clubs like drama, debating or political societies. One note of caution, however: a background of radical dissent might give the wrong signals to certain kinds of employers. Employers might be interested in the energy you have shown in organising holiday jobs or even holidays themselves: a month's hitchhiking holiday in Outer Mongolia could be interpreted as evidence of an imaginative and enterprising personality.

You can also improve your personal marketability by adding to your skills. Especially important these days is fluency in one or more European languages. Keyboard, computing and numeracy skills will also give you an important edge.

Box 13.1   Qualities employers look for

We spoke to Malcolm Carter, a Technical Manager for British Steel, and asked him what qualities he looks for in potential recruits. Many of his points reinforce those we have already made.

> Our industry, like any other, has a number of special requirements. It goes without saying that we are looking for someone with high intellectual capabilities and good academic results but, once again like most companies, we are seeking to fill a variety of very

different positions: for research jobs we are particularly interested in good academic grades but for trainees for *all positions* we place *high* emphasis on personal qualities.

I suppose the first thing I look for is some kind of presence or bearing, charisma if you like. In our industry it is necessary to have a certain force of character. For this reason I am less interested in the predictable line 'I like meeting people' than I am in hearing the message 'I like influencing people.'

Secondly, I look for leadership qualities. I look at the applicant's university career, whether they have taken an active part in sports or societies. However, I am not looking exclusively for leaders because for every one of those you need to have maybe a dozen 'followers'. I am also looking for people who can work well in teams, who are good mixers and who will fit in successfully.

Thirdly, I want to see if applicants are flexible: can they accept the inevitability of change? Will they be able to adapt easily within a fast-changing business environment?

Fourthly, I lay great emphasis on the ability to communicate, at all levels. Can they express themselves fluently, clearly and persuasively? Do they have the ability to project their personality in front of other people?

Finally, I ask myself whether applicants are honest: are they spinning me a line, trying to impress me, or are they genuine?

Could universities prepare students more effectively for their professional lives? Almost certainly they could and there is some evidence that they are trying to. Many employers praise sandwich courses and it is now possible to study as a sponsored student (see Chapter 4). If you want to gain a flying start to your career then this could be the way for you. The Government has encouraged universities to prepare students for working life and has funded a specially targeted scheme entitled Enterprise in Higher Education which is designed to permeate certain professional skills throughout the whole of the student body. It comprises training in communication and presentation skills and can also involve management skills teaching as well.

13.4   Searching for a job

This chapter is entitled 'After your degree' but if you are
not taking a postgraduate course or taking a year out, the
search for a job should begin well before your final exams. This
is not always easy. University life can seem captivatingly
carefree and self-contained. It is often hard to believe that the
party must come to an end and that mundane worldly matters
like employment have to be addressed. Others cannot focus
beyond their exams and reflect on a subject which is really of
considerable importance: what they are going to do with the
rest of their lives. Just like the application process for university, there is a beginning and an end to the job search cycle and
it is important to key into it at the beginning of your final year.

Each spring for the past two decades, the polling agency
MORI has been quizzing 1500 final-year students from 18
universities about their employment plans. In 1983, 24% had
decided on their career field before going to university but by
1990 this figure had fallen to 16% – perhaps reflecting
uncertainty in the job market. A similar decline took place in
the number of students who had plumped for a specific career
by their final year: 69% in 1985 down to 58% in 1990. The
1990 survey also reveals that 53% looked for 'sufficient intellectual challenge' in their jobs; 36%, the opportunity to be
'creative and original'; 34%, the opportunity to 'work with
people rather than things'; 32%, 'responsibility'; 31%, the
opportunity for foreign travel; and, perhaps surprisingly, only
20% made a priority of a high starting salary. (The average
expectation of a starting salary in 1990, incidentally, was
£11,250.)

But is studying at university worth all the trouble? Are
employers still as interested in graduates, and are there enough
jobs to go around? In the late 1980s the answer to both
questions would have been emphatically in the affirmative. In
1989, graduate unemployment hit a record low: only 4.7% of
that year's graduates were still out of a job by December of that

year. The Institute of Manpower Studies predicted that 30% more graduates would be needed within the next ten years to meet the demands of the economy. Demographers weighed in with a prediction that the number of 18- to 24-year-olds would decrease by 15% by 1996, reinforcing expectations that graduates would be in a sellers' market by the early 1990s. This has proved not to be the case.

The most important reason was the down-swing in the economy causing a 20% decrease in graduate vacancies in 1991 and pushing up graduate unemployment to well over 10% in 1992 (the highest since 1982, when it reached 12.5%). The Association of Graduate Recruiters (AGR), reported in 1991 that one third of employers perceived an over-supply of graduates. The recession also encouraged employers to re-examine graduate recruitment policies. Helen Perkins, Chair of the AGR, thought that after the recession employers would not return to the practices of the eighties: 'Most employers are concentrating on quality rather than quantity and apply rather more stringent selection criteria.' Malcolm Carter from British Steel bears this out:

> We are changing at British Steel. A few years ago we took 80–120 graduate recruits but now we take a maximum of 20 each year. But we have calculated that it costs £100,000 a year to train a graduate once all the attendant expenses are taken into account and it is arguably more cost effective to put our resources into training existing staff.

The same story is provided by many other firms:

- Marks and Spencer recruited 150 graduates in 1990 but only 20 in 1991;
- ICI recruited 314 graduates in 1990, 120 in 1991 and 100 in 1992;
- Ford recruited 270 in 1990, 110 in 1991 and 120 in 1992;
- Digital recruited 60–80 during the eighties yet only 20 in 1992.

These figures reveal just how devastating the economic

recession can be for previously buoyant industries such as computing. The financial services sector – into which so many graduates flocked in the eighties – has also said farewell to the boom years. Employers who used to queue up to exhibit at careers fairs lost interest: the 1990 Summer Fair at Reading University attracted 130 employers in 1990 but in 1992 only 47 turned up; Manchester drew 174 in 1990 yet only 78 in 1992. Employers soon realised they were in a buyers' market and 'treated students in a cavalier way', according to Margaret Wallis, Deputy Chairman of the Association of Graduate Careers Advisory Services in 1992. 'There has been a lack of politeness. Some have not acknowledged applications or let students know about the progress of applications.' Yet she urged students to 'spread their nets widely and persevere'.

In an economic upturn more jobs should become available but the steady increase in the proportion of young people going to university – predicted to be one third by the year 2000 – is likely to counteract the mid-decade demographic decline. But thousands of jobs will still come up every year and companies still need talented new staff: 'We cannot afford to stop recruiting even in a recession', commented a TSB spokesperson in 1992; a Digital spokesperson commented, 'We cannot afford to go on without new blood.' Even when graduate unemployment is high, 90% of applicants are successful in their searches. With careful planning and commitment, there is every chance that you will find the job that suits you.

So how should you start to plan? Our suggestion is that you should begin by thinking not about your employer but yourself. Take a long hard look at your own personality, your likes and dislikes, your strengths and weaknesses. You can do this by personal reflection and discussions with friends and family, but you might find it useful to get hold of a book by Jim Barrett and Geoff Williams entitled **Test Your Own Aptitude** (Kogan Page, 1990, second edition). This contains a number of self-applied tests, including the FLAG personality test, which helps you to identify the positions you occupy on a number of continua: Are you factual or sensitive? Calm or lively? Aggressive or passive? A team player or an independent? Once you have taken the test you can see which of the 16 major personality types you are closest to, such as the manager, the teacher, the campaigner, the provider, the artist. Together with the motivation questionnaire, this test will help you to narrow down the kind of occupations with which you are likely to be compatible. There are other similar books on the market: Sander Meredeen's **Career Choice Job Search** (Harcourt Brace Jovanovich, 1990) explains the Holland Model of personality types and the Myers-Brigges Type Indicator. For mature students there is Godfrey Polzen and Philip Plumbley's **Changing Your Job after Thirty-Five** (Kogan Page, 1985).

Another useful self-discovery exercise is to use the computer-based Gradscope. This computer program interprets the answers you give to 50 questions and then offers you a list of 20 occupations which seem to offer the best match with your particular qualities and proclivities. More advanced is Prospect (HE) which asks probing questions during a three-hour 'consultation' and helps you clarify your mind on your skills, values and interests. How can you gain access to these programs? The answer to this, as to so many other career-related questions, is your university careers information service (CIS).

This service, provided by every university in the country, is invaluable, and if you are sensible you will make contact at the beginning of the first term of your final year and start to monitor all the relevant information and activities. Many career services produce regular bulletins giving you information about vacancies, employer presentations and so forth. You may think you are better off reading advertisements in the press but this is not the case: most employers find it cheaper to publicise vacancies for new graduates via careers information offices. The CIS will also give you useful information and advice on a whole host of career related topics.

Counselling CIS staff are very experienced, always friendly and are paid to help. They will be very happy to talk to you about your career plans or, if you haven't any, to help you to formulate them. Be sure to make the most of this excellent free service.

Directories Your CIS will have access to directories giving you information regarding all the main employers in the United Kingdom. The computer-based 'roget' scan can be accessed via most CIS offices: this responds instantly to a range of possible enquiries including type of occupation and location.

Video tapes There are 2–300 corporate videos available made by employers which you can view via your CIS. These give you a better idea of what is on offer as well as briefing you for any interview you might eventually fix up.

Employer presentations A regular flow of employers will pass through your university, usually in the autumn term, giving lunch time or evening presentations. Your CIS will have all the details.

Vacation work Several organisations welcome the energy and enthusiasm of university students willing to work during the vacation. Reference books are available and your CIS will often publish bulletins giving regular details.

Vacation courses Several employers run short courses of up to a week during the vacations which offer an enjoyable 'hands on' experience of what working for them would be like.

Placements with employers This is an excellent way of combining study – usually in your third year – with work experience. The disadvantage is that you will possibly lose touch with many of your fellow students with whom you began your studies.

A year out after graduating After three years of study this is an attractive option which could provide you with a valuable character-forming experience. Opportunities include travel, overseas study and working for charitable organisations. Your CIS will have all the relevant reference books.

Job fairs These, already referred to, are occasions when employers set up stalls in an exhibition area and encourage final-year students to consider careers with them. Usually there are two or three fairs every year; in Manchester the largest takes place in the autumn term. Some universities also hold 'Alternative Fairs', giving an opportunity for less well publicised careers, like those in alternative medicine, consumer protection and environmental conservation, to make a pitch for the graduate market.

The 'milk round' This is the name given to the regular series of interviews which employers undertake every spring in British universities. From your point of view this is an ideal arrangement because you are saved any travel costs and any substantial inroads into your precious final-year time. You can find details of milk round visits, sometimes called the 'visiting interviewer's programme', from your CIS. Details of spring visits are usually available in November but note that chartered accountancy and solicitors' firms begin their interviewing during the autumn term so you will need to find out about this at an earlier time. Interviews are not automatic: you have to apply in writing and be considered suitable. The quality of your application is of key importance – of which see more below. The number of employers regularly using the milk round has fallen in recent years but this is still a very effective way of making initial contact with your potential future employer. If you do well in your first interview you will normally be called for a second. This is usually held on the employer's premises so travel will be involved, although you can usually expect to have your expenses reimbursed. To fit in with your studies, second interviews are usually organised during the Christmas and Easter vacations.

Procedures vary considerably: you may face a half-hour interview only, or you may be involved in a two- to three-day series of interviews and tests. The National Freight Company, for example, requires you to attend for two to three days in a hotel with other applicants. During this time you undertake a series of observed management exercises culminating in a short presentation and a final interview.

What you have learnt so far in this necessarily brief section is not the whole story by any means.

- *Many employers have their own procedures.* The civil service, for example, gives regular presentations at universities – sometimes involving very senior officials like Sir Robin Butler, the Cabinet Secretary – but does not join the milk round. To join the prestigious Administrative Grade as a trainee you have to take quite a stiff examination; if you are successful you are summoned to an intensive two days of interviews, exercises and tests. After this you will need to survive a final selection interview before the Civil Service Commissioners before you are allowed to enter the corridors of power.

- *Some employers advertise mainly via the press.* Academic jobs, for example, appear in the *Times Higher Education Supplement* and the Tuesday Education Supplement of the *Guardian*.

- *Personal contacts* A number of graduates find jobs every year on the basis of their own contacts made through family, friends and other acquaintances. This is not unduly self-serving or careerist but merely sensible use of available social networks.

- *Self-employment* You may have your own plans to set up your own business (but here again remember your CIS can give you valuable counselling and advice).

Applications

Finally, a few words on applying for jobs. Many employers have their own application forms but others use the Standard Application Form. This asks you to list your educational history, work experience, activities and interests, career choice and many other things about yourself. You also need to give the names of two referees, one of whom should be an academic. It is very important to fill out this form carefully and intelligently. Remember that your application will convey *all* that your potential employer will initially know about you. It is no good having an excellent academic record, being laden with prizes, having a quiver full of additional talents and a winning personality to boot if none of this comes over in your application documents.

You may be required to submit a 'letter of application' in which case you will need to draw up a curriculum vitae (CV) detailing your sterling qualities. Your CV should not be more than two to three sides long and should be clearly laid out with your key achievements and skills highlighted. You will need to tailor your application for each job you apply for, giving prominence to those aspects of your personal profile which suit the post in question. Having your CV on a word processor facilitates this kind of adaptation as well as vastly improving presentation. A covering letter can give further emphasis and convey something of your own personality and commitment. For further information, see **Applications and Interviews** by David King *et al.* (AGCAS). See also the useful booklet by the University of London Careers Advisory Service, **How to Write a Curriculum Vitae.**

Most careers information services will give you advice on making out your applications and some will provide special training, utilising video recordings, in interview technique.

Box 13.2   Applying for a job: advice from an employer

We asked Colin Jakeway, Operation Manager of NFL plc, what advice he would give to an aspirant employee in his/her final year at university.

The first obvious requirement is that you should be sure that you genuinely want to work for us. This will require quite a bit of research and thinking on your part but if you have merely applied on a whim the chances are you will be wasting your time and ours.

1 Your written application is very important. It needs to be as comprehensive as possible and should be clearly presented. Getting it typed is a good idea but I never mind handwritten applications as long as they are clearly legible. It is very important that your application form is filled in grammatically and without any spelling mistakes! This is bound to create a bad impression and your interviewer may form opinions which he or she will subconsciously reinforce during the interview.

2 It is a real advantage if you have done a little homework about the company before you turn up to the interview. I will have spent half an hour reading through your application so I'm going to be favourably impressed if you have returned the compliment. Very few applicants fully realise this.

3 Try to have some clear ideas about your objectives within the company should you be selected. These need not be hard and fast but it helps to show that you have thought a few stages beyond merely getting in.

4 Opinions vary on what clothes you should wear for interviews. I personally am not put off by casual clothes and indeed they often look better than the crumpled 'interview suits' which some final year students exhume from their sixth-form days. However, too casual an appearance will give the wrong impression so it's best to play safe.

5 During the interview try to be relaxed and fluent. This is easier said than done but practice certainly helps. Someone who is nervous tends to talk too fast, exhausting themselves and their interviewer. Try to slow down, think about what you are saying: the pauses in your conversation won't seem anywhere near as long to the interviewer as they do to you. Don't be frightened of

your interviewer; a tip I was given always helped me: 'Imagine your inteviewer in his underwear and he doesn't seem anywhere near as formidable'. Avoid fidgetting and slumping in your chair. Look your interviewer directly in the eye.

6 If you feel enthusiastic over something, show it! You gain no points for being too laid-back.

7 Be honest, don't spin us a line or try to be somebody you are not. Be yourself.

Key points

1 The main postgraduate qualifications available are certificates and diplomas, master's degrees and doctorates. Careful thought and planning are required if you intend to study beyond your degree. It can be tough but the intellectual and career rewards can be considerable.

2 Even though you may not be aware of it, your degree studies are preparing you for your employment. Lectures, essays and seminars all develop skills which will help you excel in your future profession.

3 The extra-curricular aspects of university life – sports, intellectual societies and so forth – can also be of great interest to your future employer.

4 You should start thinking about your career as soon as possible and not later than the autumn term of your final year.

5 You should begin your career search by analysing your own strengths and weaknesses before making full use of your careers information service, a university facility designed specifically to provide you with free advice, support and counselling.

Things to do

1 Think about which aspects of the subjects you are currently studying might interest you for postgraduate specialisation. Would an interdisciplinary topic appeal?

2 Discuss with friends or, better still, someone who has studied at the postgraduate level, the advantages and disadvantages of such study. Ask yourself whether you would be more interested in the

status such awards bestow, in their career value, or in the intrinsic interest of study at this level.

3 Try to observe the dynamics of informal discussions with friends. What roles ('summarisers', 'completers') do the various participants perform, especially you? In some discussions, make a conscious effort to play a variety of roles.

4 Imagine you are a senior personnel manager for a big company. Plan how you would make a presentation to your board of directors, advocating paid educational leave for employees.

5 Imagine you are a Home Office civil servant tasked with writing a paper (two to three sides) for your minister arguing that clocks should no longer be turned forward in the winter.

6 With friends and family identify (in rank order) the five careers you would most like to pursue.

7 Ask yourself the following questions. How important is your career to you? Are you more interested in making a lot of money than in a career which fulfils and interests? Do you have any ethical worries about possible careers – for example, would you happily work in the City or for a tobacco company?

Box 13.3   Speaking in public

Your formal university education won't usually involve any public speaking though your extra-curricular activities may provide many opportunities. Being able to make an effective presentation in public is a very useful life skill and accordingly we provide some advice from Edith Newman, a life-long teacher of drama and public speaking.

Employers today are looking for articulate people skilled in the art of presenting themselves clearly and effectively with enough authority in the voice to hold an audience whether it be colleagues or customers. The most able people often quail at the thought of facing an audience but take heart – it is a learnable skill! Try and follow these rules:

1 *Preparation.* Prepare your talk carefully and thoroughly, making sure it follows a clear, logical plan. Have a good strong opening and conclusion. Write out your talk *in toto* using short conversational sentences and transfer it onto cards for the talk

itself. Rehearse so that you internalise but don't learn by heart as this will take away your spontaneity.

2 *Appearance*. You are judged from the moment you stand up so be well-groomed. Avoid new, tight-fitting or garish, attention-diverting clothes.

3 *Relaxation*. Tenseness suggests hostility: make sure your shoulders are relaxed and lowered. Taking two or three quiet short breaths before starting helps to alleviate tension as does humping and dropping the shoulders a few times.

4 *Posture* is very important for correct breathing and for how you are perceived. Don't slouch but stand tall, feet slightly apart, back straight, weight well distributed: erect but not rigid.

5 *Body language*. Use hand gestures to stress your points but don't be too extravagant. Smiling will relax you and your audience. If using visual aids move slowly and smoothly to and from them.

6 *Eye contact* breaks down barriers. Engage all parts of your audience. If you prefer, look slightly above eye level, aiming at their hair lines.

7 *Vocal technique*. Vary your pace, speeding up for anything exciting or material of lesser importance. *Lift* up the voice at the beginning of fresh ideas and use pauses to let them sink in. Go slowly at the beginning and end of the talk. *Don't* drop the voice at the end of sentences – this is a common fault. *Don't* be frightened of using the voice – have courage!

8 *Attitude to audience*. Be careful not to talk down to your audience: show warmth and be sincere.

9 *Answering questions*. Listen to the whole question before answering and answer with civility, patience and good humour. If you do not know the answer, admit it.

10 *Vitality and enthusiasm*. There is no substitute. If you are enthusiastic about your subject the audience will be too – it is infectious!

Further reading

How to Get a Ph.D. (Open University Press, 1992) by Estelle Phillips and D. S. Pugh is a useful starting point if you are contemplating taking this particular plunge. A number of annual publications will also be useful including: the *British Universities Guide to Graduate Study* issued by the Committee of Vice-Chancellors and Principals and published by the Association of Commonwealth Universities. If you wish to study in a European country, get hold of *Higher Education in the European Community: A Directory of Courses and Institutions in 12 Countries* (5th edition, HMSO, 1988).

For transferable skills see Chapter 7 of Patrick Dunleavy's *Studying for a Degree in the Humanities and Social Sciences* (Macmillan, 1986).

The Association of Graduate Careers Advisory Services issues an excellent series of booklets which you will find in your careers information office (see Chapter 3).

In addition to those books on careers search mentioned in the text take a look at: David Cleaton, *Making a Choice from 21 Onwards* (Charles Letts, 1991); Roger Jones, *How to Get the Job You Really Want* (Alborough Press, 1990); Chris Phillips, *Coping with Job Hunting* (New Point, 1987); and Celia Roberts, *The Interview Game and How It Is Played* (BBC, 1985). Mature students are referred to Derek and Fred Kerrup's *Mid Career Action Guide* (Kogan Page, 1981).

Punctuation exercise from 'Things to do' Chapter 9.

Labour's defeat in 1992 can be attributed to a number of factors: the failure of Neil Kinnock, a very competent politician, to win the respect and sympathy of a broad swathe of the populous; the enduring distrust which remained within the electorate over Labour's economic competence; and a last-minute realisation by a crucial minority that even though they had flirted with the idea, they did not want a Labour government.

Bibliography

Books and articles about higher education and learning

M. Abercrombie, 1979, *Aims and Techniques of Group Teaching*, Society for Research into Higher Education.

P. Abrami, L. Leventhal and R. Perry, 1982, 'Educational seduction', *Review of Educational Research*, 52, 446–64.

D. Acres, 1987, *How to Pass Exams*, Northcote House.

K. Adderly, *et al.*, 1975, *Project Methods in Higher Education*, Society for Research in Higher Education.

M. Allen, 1988, *The Goals of Universities*, Open University Press/Society for Research into Higher Education.

M. Argyle, 1983, *The Psychology of Interpersonal Behaviour*, Penguin.

R. Barnett, 1990, *The Idea of Higher Education*, Open University Press/Society for Research into Higher Education.

R. Beard and J. Hartley, 1984, *Teaching and Learning in Higher Education*, Paul Chapman Publishing.

H. Becker, B. Geer and E. Hughes, 1968, *Making the Grade: The Academic Side of College Life*, John Wiley.

D. Bligh, 1971, *What's the Use of Lectures?*, Penguin.

A. Bloom, 1988, *The Closing of the American Mind*, Penguin.

J. Brennan and P. McGeevor, 1988, *Graduates at Work, Degree Courses and the Labour Market*, Jessica Kingsley.

G. Brown and M. Atkins, 1988, *Effective Teaching in Higher Education*, Methuen.

T. Buzan, 1979a, *How to Study: Brainpower*, Encyclopedia Britannica.

T. Buzan, 1979b, *Speed Reading*, David and Charles.

R. Calfee and P. Drum, 1986, 'Research on teaching reading', in Wittrock, ed., 1986.

A. Cockburn and R. Blackburn, 1969, *Student Power*, Penguin.

S. Cormier and J. Hagman, eds, 1987, *Transfer of Learning: Contemporary Research and Application*, Academic Press.

DES, 1987, *Higher Education: Meeting the Challenge*, White Paper, HMSO.

P. Dunleavy, 1986, 'Much to do about knowing', *Times Higher Education Supplement*.

N. Entwistle, J. Nisbet, D. Entwistle and M. Cowell, 1971, 'The academic performance of students', *British Journal of Educational Psychology*, 41, 3.

N. Entwistle and J. Wilson, 1977, *Degrees of Excellence: The Academic Achievement Game*, Hodder and Stoughton.

N. Entwistle and P. Ramsden, 1983, *Understanding Student Learning*, Croom Helm.

N. Entwistle and H. Tait, 1989, 'Approaches to learning, evaluations of teaching and preferences for contrasting academic environments', *Higher Education*, 18, 1–24.

T. Fawthrop, 1969, 'Education or examination?' in A. Cockburn and R. Blackburn, *Student Power*, Penguin, pp. 99–103.

A. Fransson, 1977, 'On qualitative differences in learning', *British Journal of Educational Psychology*, 47, 3, 244–57.

G. Gibbs, 1981, *Teaching Students to Learn*, Open University Press.

S. Griffiths, 1991, 'His and not her story', *Times Higher Educaiton Supplement*, 7 June.

H. Gull, 1933, *Projects in the Education of Young Children*, McDougall.

R. Hayman, ed., 1977, *My Cambridge*, Robson Books.

S. Hari-Augstein, M. Smith and L. Thomas, 1982, *Reading to Learn*, Methuen.

E. Henderson, 1980, 'The essay in continuous assessment', *Studies in Higher Education*, 5, 2, 197–204.

J. Heywood, 1987, *Assessment in Higher Education*, John Wiley.

Higher Education Information Services Trust, 1991, *Higher Education: The Student Experience*.

D. Jaques, 1984, *Learning in Groups*, Croom Helm.

K. Jaspers, 1965, *The Idea of the University*, Peter Owen.

D. Jehu, C. Picton and S. Futcher, 1970, 'The use of notes in examinations', *British Journal of Educational Psychology*, 4, 3, 335–7.

C. Kerr, 1973, *The Uses of the University*, Harvard University Press.

P. Mann, 1974, *Students and Books*, Routledge and Kegan Paul.

E. Martin and P. Ramsden, 1987, 'Learning skills or skill in learning?' in J. Richardson, M. Eysenck and D. Warren Piper, eds, *Student*

Learning: Research in Education and Cognitive Psychology, Society for Research into Higher Education.

F. Marton, D. Hounsell and N. Entwistle, eds, 1984, *The Experience of Learning*, Scottish Academic Press.

F. Marton and R. Saljo, 1976, 'On qualitative differences in learning', *British Journal of Education Psychology*, 46, 1, 4–11.

C. Miller and M. Parlett, 1974, *Up to the Mark: A Study of the Examination Game*, Society for Research into Higher Education.

National Union of Students, 1987, *The Future of Our Universities*, NUS.

J. H. Newman, 1976, *The Idea of a University*, Oxford University Press.

R. Palmer and C. Pope, 1984, *Brain Train*, Spon Publishing.

G. Pask, 1976, 'Style and strategies of learning', *British Journal of Educational Psychology*, 46, 2, 128–48.

W. Perry, 1970, *Forms of Intellectual and Ethical Development in the College Years*, Holt, Rinehart and Winston.

J. Powell, 1985, 'The residues of learning: autobiographical accounts by graduates of the impact of higher education', *Higher Education*, 14, 2, 127–47.

K. Raaheim, J. Wankowski and J. Radford, 1991, *Helping Students to Learn*, Society for Research into Higher Education/Open University Press.

J. Richardson, M. Eysenck and D. Warren Piper, eds, 1987, *Student Learning: Research in Education and Cognitive Psychology*, Society for Research into Higher Education.

Lord Robbins, 1963, *Higher Education: Report of the Committee*, Cmnd 2154, Her Majesty's Stationery Office.

D. Rowntree, 1977, *Assessing Students: How Shall We Know Them?*, Harper and Row.

J. Rudduck, 1978, *Learning through Small Group Discussion: A Study of Seminar Work in Higher Education*, Society for Research into Higher Education.

M. Sanderson, 1987, *Educational Opportunity and Social Change in England*, Faber and Faber.

P. Scott, 1984, *The Crisis of the University*, Croom Helm.

B. Simon, 1991, *Education and the Social Order, 1940-1990*, Lawrence and Wishart.

A. Smithers and A. Griffin, 1986, *The Progress of Mature Students*,

Joint Matriculation Board.

B. Snyder, 1971, *The Hidden Curriculum*, Knopf.

A. Thwaite, ed., 1977, *My Oxford*, Robson Books.

V. Tinto, 1975, 'Drop-out from higher education: a theoretical synthesis of recent research', *Review of Educational Research*, 45, 1, 89–125

T. Tysome, 1991, 'One in five buys no books', *Times Higher Education Supplement*, 10 May.

T. Tysome and H. Richards, 1991, 'Union advises students to sign on for part-time bonuses', *Times Higher Education Supplement*, 18 October.

M. Warnock, 1989, *A Common Policy for Education*, Oxford University Press.

J. Widdows, M. Jalloq and L. Knaggs, *Postgraduate Study and Research*, Association of Graduate Careers Advisory Services.

M. Wiener, 1985, *English Culture and the Decline of the Industrial Spirit, 1850–1980*, Penguin.

J. Wilson, 1981, *Student Learning in Higher Education*, Croom Helm.

M. Wittrock, ed., 1986, *Handbook of Research on Teaching*, Collier Macmillan.

A. Woodley, 1985, 'Taking account of mature students' in D. Jaques and J. Richardson, eds, *The Future of Higher Education*, Society for Research into Higher Education/NFER-Nelson.

J. Wyatt, 1990, *Commitment to Higher Education: Seven West European Thinkers on the Essence of the University*, Society for Research into Higher Education/Oxford University Press.

Practical guides

Many of these are annual and others are regularly updated. So make sure you are reading the latest edition.

J. Adair, 1988, *Effective Time Management*, Pan Books.

Advisory Service for Squatters, *The Squatters' Handbook*.

A. Arden, *Manual of Housing Law*, Sweet and Maxwell.

A. Arden, 1989, *The Private Tenant's Handbook*, Sphere.

Association of Commonwealth Universities, *Financial Aid for First Degree Study at Commonwealth Universities*.

Association of Commonwealth Universities, *Higher Education in the UK: A Handbook for Students and Their Advisers*, Longmans.

Association of Graduate Careers Advisory Services, Signpost series.

R. Barass, 1978, *Scientists Must Write: A Guide to Better Writing for Scientists, Engineers and Students*, Chapman Hall.

J. Barker, 1985, *The Student's Cookbook*, Faber and Faber.

J. Barrett and G. Williams, 1990, *Test Your Own Aptitude*, Kogan Page.

J. Bell, 1987, *Doing Your Research Project: A Guide for First-Time Researchers in Education and Social Science*, Open University Press.

K. Boehm and J. Lees-Spalding, *The Careers Book*, Macmillan.

K. Boehm and J. Lees-Spalding, *The Student Book*, Macmillan.

M. Brewer and G. Wallace-Hadrill, *Sandwich Courses: A Guide to All Courses in Universities, Polytechnics and Colleges*, Careers Research and Advisory Council.

British Council, *How to Live in Britain*, Evans Brothers.

Cambridge Admissions Prospectus.

Cambridge University Handbook.

Careers Research and Advisory Centre, *Student's Eye*.

D. Cleaton, 1991, *Making a Choice from 21 Onwards*, Charles Letts.

Charities Aid Foundation, *Directory of Grant-Making Trusts*.

Committee of Vice-Chancellors and Principals, *British Universities' Guide to Graduate Study*, Association of Commonwealth Universities.

Committee of Vice-Chancellors and Principals, *University Entrance: The Official Guide*.

Committee of Vice-Chancellors and Principals/Universities Central Council on Admissions, *Mature Students and Universities*.

C. Cooper, R. Cooper and L. Eaker, 1988, *Living with Stress*, Penguin.

Department of Employment Careers and Occupational Information Centre, *Sponsorships Offered to Students by Employers and Professional Bodies for First Degrees*.

Department for Education, *Grants to Students: A Brief Guide*.

Department for Education, *Guide to Grants: Designated Courses*, DFE.

Department for Education, *Student Grants and Loans*, DFE Publications.

Design Council, *Design Courses in Britain*.

A. Dickson, 1987, *A Woman in Your Own Right*, Quartet Books.

P. Dunleavy, 1986, *Studying for a Degree in the Humanities and Social Sciences*, Macmillan.

Family Welfare Association, *Money to Study*.

D. Forbes, 1989, *Racial Harassment*, Legal Action Group.

H. W. Fowler, 1983, *Modern English Usage*, Oxford University Press.

S. Gash, 1989, *Effective Literature Searching for Students*, Gower.

The Grants Register, Macmillan.

M. Haynes, 1987, *Making Every Minute Count*, Kogan Page.

B. Heap, annual, *The Complete Degree Course Offers*, Trotman Publishing.

M. Higham, 1989, *Coping with Interviews*, New Opportunity Press.

P. Holford, 1988, *The Family Nutrition Workbook*, Thorsons Publishing.

P. Holford, 1988, *The Whole Health Manual*, Thorsons Publishing.

A. Jamieson, *The Which? Guide to Sponsorship in Higher Education*, Consumers Association/Hodder and Stoughton.

R. Johnson, 1991, *Studying Fiction*, Manchester University Press.

R. Johnson, 1991, *Writing Essays*, Clifton Press, PO Box 100, Manchester 20.

Joint Matriculation Board, *21 Returning to Learning*.

B. Jones and R. Johnson, 1990, *Making the Grade* (2 volumes), Manchester University Press.

R. Jones, 1990, *How to Get the Job You Really Want*, Alborough.

D. Kerrup and F. Kerrup, 1981, *Mid Career Action Guide*, Kogan Page.

D. King *et al.*, *Applications and Interviews*, AGCAS.

M. Korving, *The Mature Students Handbook*, Kogan Page.

R. Lovelace, 1990, *Stress Master*, John Wiley.

S. Meredeen, 1990, *Career Choice Job Search*, Harcourt Brace Jovanovich.

National Bureau for Handicapped Students, *Applying to Higher Education: Notes for Disabled Students Their Parents and Advisers*.

National Society for Education in Art, Craft and Design, *Guide to Courses and Careers*.

National Union of Students, *Welfare Manual*.

Oxford University, *Undergraduate Prospectus*.

E. Partridge, 1991, *Usage and Abusage*, Penguin.

C. Phillips, 1987, *Coping with Job Hunting*, New Point.

E. M. Phillips and D. S. Pugh, 1987, *How to Get a Ph.D.*, Open University Press.

Polytechnic Central Admissions System, *Guide for Applicants*.

G. Polzen and Philip Prumbtey, 1985, *Changing Your Job after Thirty-five*, Kogan Page.

G. Randall, 1991, *Housing Rights Guide*, SHAC.

C. Roberts, 1985, *The Interview Game and How It Is Played*, BBC.

The Royal Society, *General Notes on the Preparation of Scientific Papers*.

Scottish Education Department, *Guide to Student Allowances*.

Scottish Universities Council on Entrance, *Scottish Universities Entrance Guide*.

A. Segal, 1989, *Careers Encyclopedia*, Cassells.

D. Smith, 1987, *One Is Fun*, Coronet.

Standing Conference of Principals, *Guide to Colleges and Institutes of Higher Education*.

J. Stockdale, 1986, *Sexual Harassment in a University Setting*, mimeo., City University.

M. Temple, 1990, *The Pocket Guide to Written English*, Michael Joseph.

M. Tight, *Part-Time Degrees, Diplomas and Certificates: A Guide to Part-Time Higher Education Courses*, Careers Research Advisory Centre.

A. Trinci *et al.*, 1991, *How to Write a Thesis*, School of Biological Sciences, University of Manchester.

Universities Central Council on Admissions, *How to Apply for Admission to University*.

Universities Central Council on Admissions, *Industrial Sponsorship and the Universities*.

University of London Careers Advisory Service, *How to Write a Curriculum Vitae*.

G. Watson, 1987, *Writing a Thesis*, Longman.

Which?, 1991, *Buying and Selling a Flat*, Hodder and Stoughton.

Which Degree?, Newpoint Publishing.

K. Whitehorn, 1986, *Cooking in a Bedsitter*, Penguin.

Other works cited

J. Barzun and H. Graff, 1977, *The Modern Researcher*, Harcourt Brace Jovanovich.

C. Bell and H. Newby, eds, 1977, *Doing Sociological Research*, Allen and Unwin.

L. Canfora, 1991, *The Vanished Library*, Vintage.

T. Eagleton, 1983, *Literary Theory: An Introduction*, Blackwell.

D. Edge, ed., 1964, *Experiment*, BBC Publications.

A. Giddens, 1989, *Sociology*, Polity Press.

T. R. Henn, 1960, *Science in Writing*, Harrap.

B. Latour and S. Woolgar, 1979, *Laboratory Life: The Social Construction of Scientific Facts*, Sage.

P. Medawar, 1963, 'Is the scientific paper a fraud?' in D. Edge, 1984.

A. Orenstein and W. Phillips, 1984, *Understanding Social Research*, Allyn and Bacon.

H. Roberts, 1981, *Feminist Research*, Routledge.

J. Scott, 1990, *A Matter of Record*, Polity Press.

C. Tomalin, 1990, *The Invisible Woman: The Story of Nelly Ternan and Charles Dickens*, Viking.

G. Walford, 1991, *Doing Educational Research*, Routledge.

J. D. Watson, 1968, *The Double Helix*, Penguin.

W. J. West, 1991, *The Strange Rise of Semi-literacy in England*, Duckworth.

C. Wright Mills, 1970, *The Sociological Imagination*, Penguin.

Addresses

Advisory Service for Squatters,
2 St Paul's Road,
London N1.

Art and Design Admissions
Registry,
Penn House,
9 Broad Street,
Hereford HR4 9AP.

Association of Commonwealth
Universities,
John Foster House,
36 Gordon Square,
London WC1H 0PF.

Association of Graduate Careers
Advisory Services,
c/o Central Services Unit,
Crawford House,
Precinct Centre,
Manchester M13 9PL.

British Council,
10 Spring Gardens,
London SW1A 2BN.

Cambridge Inter-Collegiate
Applications Office,
Kellet Lodge,
Tennis Court Road,
Cambridge CB2 1QJ.

Careers Research and Advisory
Centre,
Hobsons Publishing,
Bateman Street,
Cambridge CB2 1LZ.

Central Council for Education
and Training in Social Work,
Derbyshire House,
St Chad Street,
London WC1H 8AD.

Chartered Society of
Physiotherapy,
14 Bedford Row,
London WC1R 4ED.

College of Occupational
Therapists,
6–8 Marshalsea Road,
Bayswater,
London SE1 1HL.

Committee of Directors of
Polytechnics,
Kirkman House,
12–14 Whitfield Street,
London W1P 6AX.

Committee of Vice-Chancellors
and Principals,
29 Tavistock Square,
London WC1H 9E2.

Council for National Academic
Awards,
344–5 Gray's Inn Road,
London WC1X 8BR.

Department for Education,
Elisabeth House,
York Road,
London SE1.

DFE Publications,
Despatch Centre,
Honeypot Lane,
Cannons Park,
Stanmore,
Middlesex HA7 1A2.

Department of Employment
Sponsorship Information,
The Paddock,
Frizinghall,
Bradford BD9 4HD.

ECCTIS,
PO Box 88,
Sherwood House,
Bletchley MK3 6DL.

Endsleigh Insurance Services,
20 The Promenade,
Cheltenham GL50 3NR.

Erasmus Student Grants
Council,
The University,
Canterbury,
Kent CT2 7PD.

The European Commission,
8 Storey's Gate,
London SW1P 3AT.

Family Welfare Association,
501–5 Kingsland Road,
London E8 4AU.

National Bureau for
Handicapped Students,
336 Brixton Road,
London SW9 7AA.

National Union of Students,
461 Holloway Road,
London N7 6LJ.

Scotland
12 Dublin Street,
Edinburgh EH1 3PP.

Wales
107 Walter Road,
Swansea SA1 5AA.

Open University,
Walton Hall,
Milton Keynes,
MK7 6AA.

University of Oxford,
Information Office,
Wellington Square,
Oxford OX1 2JD.

Scottish Central Institutions,
Room 54,
Moray House College,
Holyrood Road,
Edinburgh EH8 8AD.

Scottish Education Department,
Haymarket House,
Clifton Terrace,
Edinburgh EH2 5DR.

Scottish Education Department,
Awards Branch,
Gyleview House,
Redheugh's Brigg,
South Gyle,
Edinburgh EH12 9HH.

Scottish Universities Council on
Entrance,
12 The Links,
St Andrews,
Fife KY16 9JB.

Standing Conference of
Principals,
c/o Administrative Office,
SCP,
Edge Hill College of Higher
Education,
Ormskirk,
Lancs L39 4QP.

Student Loans Company,
100 Bothwell Street,
Glasgow G2 7JD.

United Kingdom Council for
Overseas Student Affairs,
60 Westbourne Grove,
London W2 5FG.

Universities and Colleges
Admissions Service,
PO Box 28, (Inquiries)
PO Box 67, (Applications)
Cheltenham,
Gloucestershire GL50 3FT.

Universities Information Unit,
29 Tavistock Square,
London WC1H 9E2.

Examining Boards

England and Wales

Associated Examining Board,
Wellington House,
Aldershot,
Hants GU11 1BQ.
Tel: (0252) 25551

Joint Matriculation Board,
Manchester M15 2EU.
Tel: 061–273 2565

Oxford and Cambridge Schools
Examination Board,
Brook House,
10 Trumpington Street,
Cambridge CB2 1QB.
Tel: (0223) 64326
and Elsfield Way
Oxford OX2 8EP.
Tel: (0865) 54421

Oxford Delegacy of Local
Examinations,
Ewert Place,
Summertown,
Oxford OX2 7BZ.
Tel: (0865) 54291

Southern Universities Joint
Board for School Examinations,
Coatham Road,
Bristol BS6 6DD.
Tel: (0272) 36042

Universities Entrance and School
Examinations Council,
University of London,
66–72 Gower Street,
London WC1E 6EE.
Tel: 071–636 8000

University of Cambridge Local
Examinations Syndicate,
Syndicate Buildings,
17 Harvey Road,
Cambridge CB1 2EU.
Tel: (0223) 61111

Welsh Joint Education
Committee,
245 Western Avenue,
Cardiff CF5 2YX.
Tel: (02220) 561231

Index